SO WHAT!

THE GOOD, THE MAD, AND THE UGLY

Edited by Steffan Chirazi

Broadway Books New York

PRINTED IN THE UNITED STATES OF AMERICA

BROADWAY BOOKS and its logo, a letter B bisected on the diagonal,
are trademarks of Random House, Inc.

Visit our web site at www.broadwaybooks.com

First Edition published 2004.
Library of Congress Cataloging-in-Publication Data
Metallica (Musical group)
So What! : the good, the mad, and the ugly : the official chronicle / Metallica;
edited by Steffan Chirazi — 1st ed. p. cm.
1. Metallica — Entertainment. 2. Metallica — Heavy Metal (Music) — Pictorial works.
I. Chirazi, Steffan. II. Title.

ML421.M48m5 2004   782166'092'2—dc22   2004045839

Creative Director: Steffan Chirazi
Designed by Zen Jam Graphic Design, San Francisco, CA Art director: Mark Abramson
Design: Mark Abramson, Rose de Heer, Aleksandra Jelic, Lesley Crawford
Production: Aleksandra Jelic, Lesley Crawford, Miriam Lewis

ISBN 0-7679-1881-9

1 3 5 7 9 10 8 6 4 2

Printed in the United States of America

BROADWAY

CONTENTS

CONTENTS

METALLICA FLOWS THROUGH OUR VEINS!!
AS CORNY AS THAT SOUNDS, IT TRUELY DOES.

IT **FUELS** US. IT TAKES US TO PLACES WE WOULDNT &
COULDNT GO ON OUR OWN. PLACES MUSICALLY, PHYSICALLY,
SPIRITUALLY & EMOTIONALLY.

IT **SWALLOWS** US. THERE ARE TIMES WE FORGET THERE IS LIFE
OUTSIDE OF METALLICA. OUR WIVES AND FAMILIES CAN VOUCH
FOR THAT.

IT **SCARES** US. WE SEE, HEAR AND EXPERIENCE THINGZ ON
AN ACCELERATED AND EXTREME LEVEL. AND ARE EXPECTED
TO REMAIN NORMAL.

IT **TESTS** US. WE ARE CONSTANTLY CHALLANGED WITH TRAGEDIES
AND TRIUMPHS. DEATHS, BREAKDOWNS, FIGHTS AND FAME. STATING
OUR BOUNDRIES YET REMAINING HUMBLE AND ACCESIBLE... AND
MOST OF ALL IT **SATISFIES** US. IT IS A GOD GIVEN GIFT
THAT WE HAVE MET EACH OTHER AND HAVE COMBINED OUR PASSIONS &
ENERGIES INTO A STRONG AND ENDURING UNIT.

THIS BOOK IS A DIARY OF SORTS. A COLLECTION OF
ARTICLES FROM OUR FAN CLUB MAGAZINE "SO WHAT" FROM ITS
INSEPTION IN LATE 1993 UP TO SUMMER 2004. THE IDEA BEING TO
BREAK THE MYTH THAT A FAN CLUB CANT BE MORE THAN
SOMETHING THAT DEMANDS $25 FROM FANS AND THEY GET SENT A
MERCHANDISING FLYER ONCE A YEAR. WE WANT
SOMETHING THAT GOES BEYOND JUST INFORMATION. A DEEP
AND HONEST LOOK INTO US AS HUMANS AND THE FUN PAIN WE
GO THROUGH. THIS BOOK (IN OUR BEST ATTEMPT) SHOWS OUR
WARTS AND ALL INSIDE AND OUT. REMINDING OURSELVES THAT
WE ARE "WORKS IN PROGRESS".

'04

OK. INTRO TIME. IT'S GOING
TO BE SHORT AND SWEET.
CHECK OUT HOW MUCH WE'VE
CHANGED, GROWN, AND PRESENTED
OURSELVES OVER THE COURSE
OF THIS MAGAZINE'S TENURE.
PRETTY COOL HUH?? IT'S
A WINDOW INTO OUR PAST,
AND, IN A WEIRD WAY
SLIGHTLY PROPHETIC
OF OUR FUTURE (IN SOME INSTANCES!)
I HOPE YOU GUYS ENJOY THIS
AS MUCH AS I HAVE, BECAUSE
I DECIDED IN THE VERY BEGINNING
TO JUST HAVE AS MUCH FUN
W/ THE MAG AS I FELT LIKE,
AND I HOPE THAT TRANSLATES
TO YOU READERS OUT THERE — AND
I'M NOT ABOUT TO APOLOGIZE FOR
ANY OF THE BAD HAIRCUTS,
BAD FASHION, OFF THE CUFF
COMMENTS, WHATEVER!! I
GUESS IT'S ALL A MEANS TO
AN END — BUT THIS ISN'T
REALLY THE END, IS IT??
THANX ANYWAY FOR
BEARING WITH US AND
ENJOY THIS FOR WHAT IT
IS — WHATEVER IT IS!!!

3/04

SO WHAT!?!

STRANGE, INSANE, GENIUS
WHAT A CLEVER WAY TO
BOND & UNITE WITH OUR
FRIENDS THE FANS...

Sometimes
    being
      in
    THIS BAND
      is
    LIKE
    BEING IN
    College
I NEVER THOUGHT I'D
  BE WRITING A BOOK
      INTRO
(It's 3:53 am and I)
    LUV IT!

THIS IS AN INTRODUCTION! I DON'T REALLY HAVE A
PARTICULAR AGENDA, ANYTHING SPECIAL I WANT TO SAY,
BUT SINCE WE ALL AGREED TO WRITE INTROS, HERE IS
MY DRIVEL! THIS IS AN INTRODUCTION! I DON'T REALLY....
OH, STOP!!! WELCOME TO THE BOOK! WELCOME
TO THE 'TALLICA BOOK! WELCOME TO THE FIRST
OFFICIAL 'TALLICA BOOK! THAT CAN'T BE TRUE!?
THE FIRST OFFICIAL 'TALLICA BOOK (IT SEZ HERE...).
WOW! WHAT THE FUCK TOOK YOU SO LONG!??
23 FUCKEN YEARS???? WELL, WHAT DO YOU WANT??
WE'VE BEEN BUSY!! A COUPLE A RECORDS, A FEW GIGS,
A BEVERAGE OR TWO, YOU KNOW? WELL, HERE IT IS!!!
AND YOU KNOW WHAT, I'M PROUD OF THIS FUCKER!
'COZ THIS IS US, OUR SHIT, OUR STUFF, OUR PERSONAL
ESCAPADES, OUR PERSONAL THOUGHTS, OUR EXPRESSIONS,
OUR EFFUSIONS, OUR HEARTS, OUR SOULS, OUR US....
RIGHT ON YOUR COFFEE TABLE!

WHAT YOU'RE HOLDING OR LOOKING AT IS THE BEST
BITS OF US FROM THE LAST 10 YEARS! THE BEST BITS
OF OUR DIRECT CONTACT/CONNECTION TO/WITH
OUR FANS! THE MOST DEDICATED ONES, THE ONES
THAT BELONGED TO (AND HOPEFULLY STILL DO!!) OUR
LITTLE CLUB-HOUSE, OUR CLOSEST FRIENDS/FAMILY!
IT HAS FELT GOOD TO HAVE THAT DIRECT LINK TO
OUR MOST DEDICATED (I ALREADY USED THAT WORD!
I'M RUNNING OUT OF ADJECTIVES!) PASSIONATE
(THERE IS A NEW ONE!) PALS, AND NOW IT FEELS
EQUALLY GOOD TO SHARE SOME OF THOSE
EXPERIENCES WITH ALL Y'ALL!! WITH PRIDE WE
HAVE USED THE 'SO WHAT' MAGAZINE AS OUR
PLATFORM FOR COMMUNICATION, FOR NEWS, FOR
EXCLUSIVES AND FOR CONTACT AND NOW WE
HAVE HAD FUN REVISITING THE OLD ISSUES AND
MAKING OUR 'BEST OF'! AN INTERESTING AND
A SOMETIMES CHALLENGING WALK DOWN MEMORY
LANE, IT FEELS VERY COOL TO FINALLY HAVE
SOME OF THIS IN BOOK FORM, EVEN THOUGH
THE (BAD) HAIRSTYLES ARE SURPRISING,
DIFFICULT TO ACCEPT/DEAL WITH!! THERE IS
A LOT HERE, SO TAKE YOUR TIME AND HAVE
FUN WITH IT! I HOPE YOU ENJOY THE BITS
THAT HAVE BEEN CHOSEN, IF NOT MAYBE
THERE WILL BE A SECOND BOOK SOMETIME (!?)
AND VERY SPECIAL THANK TO STEFFAN FOR
OVERSEEING, SELECTING, SORTING, EDITING, WHIP-
CRACKING AND PATIENCE TESTING!!!!

DIVE IN!!!   LOVE x
                  C-YA IN A BIT,

1

If people like us we welcome them;
if they don't, fuck 'em.

METALLICA '84 REVISITED

The following was the first article written by Steffan Chirazi about Metallica way back in October 1984. It was published in a now sadly defunct English music paper called "Sounds."

As we trundle through Paris at 12:35 a.m., precariously perched in the METALLICA tour bus, the forehead of bassist Cliff Burton suddenly makes a close but rhythmic acquaintance with the front dashboard. The explanation for this over-zealous behavior is the tape of the Anti Nowhere League which blares out; Cliff is simply showing his appreciation in the strongest possible way.

WITH METALLICA, WHETHER ON THE ROAD OR THE STAGE, THERE ARE NO PRETENSES. No demonstrations of cool rock star behavior, no flash tailored garments. Nope, this lot are as basic as you or I, none of this false, haughty 'we're famous now' attitude, more a 'hello' 'ow ya doin' down-to-earth approach. Indeed it is worth noting the next time you catch a glimpse of Metallica, that Cliff is the owner of the biggest, oldest and scruffiest Levi flares currently in existence.

But enough of this – I'll serve you up with the basic and important Metallica logistical data first of all. Formed in early '82 by Lars Ulrich and James Hetfield (drummer and rhythm guitar/vocals), Metallica were completed by lead guitarist David Mustaine and bassist Ron McGovney. McGovney was soon replaced by Cliff Burton, who was good enough to convince the band to uproot to San Francisco from L.A., and the band's following started to take off in a big way.

It was at this time that it became evident that Mustaine, alcohol, pressure and therefore Metallica didn't mix, so Mustaine was replaced by Kirk Hammett, another club circuit discovery. Out came "Kill 'Em All" in '83 and presto, Metallica have been growing bigger, better and stronger all the time.

So back to the present day, and among the chaos, confusion and plain goddamn fun that surrounds a foreign festival, I managed to collar lead guitarist Kirk Hammett and Lars Ulrich in the already mentioned 'headbangin' heaven' bus. I always did find it strange how such a fast, heavy and powerful band should suddenly rear its ugly head from amongst the Journeys, Survivors and Kisses of the humdrum, stagnating U.S. rock scene of the time.

"Yeah, well, we got sick of seeing every band in the States trying out this kind of AC/DC, Kiss, Journey approach, and we just wanted to go out and play our way. At first we had to play a few covers because we immediately went for doing gigs, but the important thing was that we were out there playing and playing them our way."

One gets the feeling from this that there was a conscious rebellion against the American rock scene, although Lars stressed that nothing Metallica does is consciously planned.

"I think that there is some truth behind the rebellion bit, but it certainly wasn't a conscious feeling. Everything Metallica does is spontaneous, I think if we lose our spontaneity we will be in one hell of a lot of trouble."

Everything Metallica does may well be spontaneous, but the change from the out and out thrash metal on "Kill 'Em All" to the more melodious, mid-paced thrash of "Ride the Lightning" is surely a planned progression.

"No way. As far as I'm concerned, Metallica really changed with the arrival of Kirk and Cliff. Incidentally, I'd like to say that Metallica bears no grudges against Dave Mustaine and that we thank him and acknowledge his contribution to early Metallica.

"Anyway, as I was saying, it was just before "Kill 'Em All" that we really changed, y'know, and between the two albums there has been a progression, but through what we've learnt and seen, not sitting down and really planning as such.

"I mean, we did 'Fade to Black,' a ballad right? We didn't think 'hey man, let's construct a heavy ballad, yeah,' we just all felt it was right and so we did it. Metallica are a feeling not a preplanned package, we don't deliberate on things for weeks and weeks. Oh yeah, I hate the f**kin' phrase 'thrash metal,'" says Lars complete with upturned nose and very loud 'eeuuurgghh' to match his disgusted expression. I must say I don't understand his apparent vehemence – after all, Metallica are the best thrash metal band around.

"The phrase 'thrash' suggests lack of music ability and that's one thing we do not suffer from. I don't know exactly what I'd call us but I hate the phrase thrash, ugghh!

"It's all down to personal taste, I can see your view but I can also see Lars' point of view. I guess it's a reasonably accurate description if used properly," pipes up Kirk.

I feel that "Ride the Lightning" is ample justification of both arguments, on the one hand providing some good ol' heads-down thrash and on the other, copious displays of musical ability within it all. On that point I embarked upon the band's live show. Is that also spontaneous?

"I think it is, yes. We go out there and do it as we feel it. If Cliff wants to headbang whilst he's playing 'Whiplash' then he will, if he doesn't he won't. (Wow — Ed). It's not a pre-rehearsed venture. The only thing we play before we go onstage, is that we're gonna try and kick as much f**kin' ass as we can. We do play for ourselves though to a large extent. If people like us we welcome them; if they don't f**k 'em."

"We have a certain reputation," continues Lars, "inasmuch as we are expected to go out there and whack out with energy and 500mph speed and we satisfy this demand; now although that's real nice, we'd like to think that the same feeling and goodness can also transfer to vinyl. Some bands can only do it live – they fell flat on record, whereas I think we really pull it off!"

Certainly, Metallica's vinyl energy is there in all its glory, but it is their live show which is guaranteed to produce flying hair and air-guitar players and to boost the post show aspirin sales. This live show really does kill, dammit – even lensman Tony 'Wayne' Mottram, a person with fussy tastes, is raving the Metallica live cause.

Britain will get to see Metallica during October/November. Initially, the band were going to hit the road for a full European tour, this little affair starting in France starting the whole onslaught. However, the inescapable hassles of business have intervened.

"Yeah, well we're currently involved in a legal dispute with Johnny Z and Megaforce Records back in the U.S. We're not under either anymore. Although certain complications have grown, we expect the legal situation to be cleared up very soon. Johnny Z did a great job for us but we felt that we'd outgrown each other."

This all means that Britain will see Metallica headline four to six dates including the Birmingham Odeon and London Lyceum.

"We also want to release a single for the European tour which could be 'Ride the Lightning' but once the legal shit is fully sorted out we're gonna make things happen."

Metallica have been making things happen for quite a while in Europe, as is apparent by the amount of patches I saw adorning the jackets of European metallurgists, and by their extremely high record sales across the channel and yonder. Everybody loves Metallica, as was evident at their performance yesterday, where headbanging was a literal affair and not just a few polite nods.

The band will certainly blitz Britain, believe me, the British metal banger having had only one fleeting chance to catch them before, in the hellhole of Soho, the Marquee Club. And let me personally assure you lads 'n' lasses, we're talking bloody big blitzes of pure metal here. However Lars has still left me with a niggling point, that of his refusal to accept the term 'thrash' in conjunction with Metallica. The stubborn bugger still refuses to totally accept the phrase, saying "If you were to call us the original, the first thrash metal band, then maybe you'd have some justification, but even then I find it difficult to justify as an adjective for Metallica."

Well, one point at a time eh? Primarily, it is patently obvious to all the acts such as Exciter, Anthrax and Slayer are simply by-products of a style of music created and perpetrated by Metallica. These bands are the offspring of the thrash metal Metallica invented. Secondly, justification of the term 'thrash' can be found in "Kill 'Em All" and the latest 'n' greatest "Ride the Lightning" and owners of these two platters will undoubtedly offer their own mutual support.

But really, what the hell! At least we have Metallica, and whatever way you want to classify them, these San Franciscan stormers continue to pick their audiences up by the scruff of the neck, violently shake them for 90 or so minutes and deposit them gleefully back into their seats, watching the infatuated faces beg for more. Everyone wants more of Metallica, which makes a statement Lars made – "y'know, we're gonna wake a few people up," profoundly punctual in its delivery. People are waking up all the time to this particular metal beat... do the sensible thing and wake up with them. ●

BAND COMMENTS

AAAH YOUTH.. "THESE YOUNG PUNKS THINK THEY
KNOW EVERYTHING!!

          3/04

SEEMS SOOOO LONG AGO -
EVERYTHING WAS FRESH + NEW
WE WERE SO PUMPED UP +
READY TO TAKE ON ANYTHING +
EVERYTHING - AND WE DID!! IT
ALMOST FEELS LIKE WE WERE
TRYING TO DENY OUR PLACE
IN HISTORY AS IT WAS HAPPENING
- TRYING TO DENY WE WERE A
THRASH BAND UNLESS, OR ACKNOWLEDGE
THAT WE INVENTED IT! HOW'S
THAT FOR A BUNCH OF SNOBBY
YOUNG PUPS!!

                   3/04

Oi!
THAT PIC IS FROM '85!
THATS STEFFAN IN THE MIDDLE!

YOUNG, DRUNK, FULL OF SPUNK!

WOW!

5

WHEN I FIRST MOVED TO SAN FRANCISCO from London in 1986, Cliff Burton was the man who introduced me to friends, chaperoned me around the city's 'hot-spots' (a rock club called The Stone and a burrito hole which drowned said food in 'the green sauce') and generally made me feel welcome. Cliff was, you see, a Bay Area man through and through.

I would traditionally meet him in the city on Broadway. Often, I'd be standing around waiting for him to arrive before a VW station wagon would lurch onto the sidewalk, Misfits blaring from open windows and a flood of reddish brown hair flying around the driver's seat as Cliff's fingers beat the middle of his steering wheel (that emblem was cracked, fractured and beaten from the Burton finger-drumming).

He wasn't a flash man in any way, neither was he interested in posing. Cliff was just a good guy, dedicated to music, smart, funny and friendly. Thus when I got word from Sweden on Sept 27th 1986 that there had been a bus accident and that Cliff had died, I was both sad and confused.

He was unique.

He will always be missed, but equally he is always remembered.

Editor — February, 2004

CLIFF

"He was a good student, very focused. He knew what he wanted. He was the kind of student who always came in with the lesson prepared, which is not all that common. We did a number of different rhythm studies. I can hear some of the odd metered rhythms we studied in his playing." He went on to describe Cliff as a quiet and serious student. "I had many serious students, but Cliff had that rare inner drive to get out and do something about his music. I can't take credit for that; it was already there even when I taught him."

Steve Doherty, bass teacher

"...we'd go out in the hills (Maxwell Ranch) and fire up the generator. Me and him and another fella named Dave. We were the only guys around for miles. We'd play this really weird shit and record it. His mom heard some of the tapes and she goes, 'You guys sound like fucked up weirdos!'"

Jim Martin, guitarist, friend, collaborator

BURTON

"From 1980 until he died, the three of us were inseparable. Literally inseparable. We were never bored. But we never really 'did' things. We went to places and hung out. We laughed, and laughed. I think the best way to describe our relationship, was that it was just so spontaneous. It was like it was in a make-believe world. There was always something going on, but nothing planned. We fed off each other quite a bit."

Dave Donato – friend, drummer and jamming collaborator

"Jim, Cliff, Dave and Rick... came up in my truck... made volume 4, Maxwell tapes... tried to play D&D but for the most part were unable to... Jim's character (Ktulu) went to the 7th level... Cliff brought up a lot of recreational tools... recorded volumes 5 and 6... a marathon trip... PS... you can never bring too much beer... ears took a beating due to loud music, guns and Dave's mouth... Jim has sick wild hair."

Maxwell Ranch log book entry, 6/30/85

"We had a couple other offshoot bands that we did... we had this one band called Agents of Misfortune. We got together some of those tapes that we made in the hills. We just took sections out of 'em and figured out how to play it. And we strung 'em together. They give you 12 minutes. So most people do 3–4 songs in 12 minutes, we just did one huge one."

Jim Martin

Rich 'Bang that head that doesn't bang' Burch with Cliff and James.

7

"Jim and Cliff were so alike in being late. I remember the first time Metallica ever played at the Oakland Coliseum, for the Day on the Green Festival. Me and Cliff are fuckin' around and he says 'Fuck! What time is it?' I saw 'It's 1:00.' He says 'No way?! No way?!' he says 'I got a soundcheck at 2:00! We gotta go now!' So Cliff grabbed his guitar, and his other shit and we left. So we get on the freeway, we're driving along and all of a sudden it's bumper to bumper traffic. Cliff is really worked up at this point, as the traffic is edging along."

"We were almost at our exit when all of a sudden we get rear-ended. Cliff goes 'Ah fuck!' He jumps out of the car. He's got his black Misfits shirt on, with the skull on the front of it. He walks over to the car that hit us, and all these kids are wearing Metallica shirts! They don't even know who he is. They were saying things like 'Oh fuck! Ah man I'm sorry!' Cliff looks at his car and says 'Fuck it! It was a piece of shit anyway! SEE YA!' He gets back in the car, he whips over out of the right lane, and starts driving on the shoulder of the freeway! He was driving right through the ice plant, the car is on a slight angle, and he's cutting off all these people! They're all screaming at him and he's like 'Fuck you!' We drove like that for about half a mile. Cliff was laughing about it."

Dave Donato

CLIFF BURTON

"I don't think I ever saw music move Cliff the way The Misfits did. When Cliff drove to the pier, he would play The Misfits. He would headbang and drum on his steering wheel, to the point of breaking the steering wheel. There was pieces of it to drive with. He had it all duct taped together. Whenever Cliff played his Misfits tapes, he just went wild. Just like fuckin' yelling, screaming, spitting and headbanging. The Misfits were a great moment in his life. I think he enjoyed The Misfits more than anything else, period."

Dave Donato

"Cliff used to have this green Volkswagen station wagon. It was called the 'grasshopper.' That thing was a piece of junk. It might stall somewhere, and you'd have to climb underneath it, and hook the fuel line back up to the fuel pump...he (also) used to have this weird, it was like a hillbilly hat, more like a cowboy hat. It had like green mold growing on it. It was called "The hat that lives."

Jim Martin

"He was pretty much an inspiration for me as well. He showed me that it could be done. **(Martin went onto to star in Faith No More — ED)** Cuz lots of people around me were telling me, "How many guys do you think are gonna make a mark being a musician? Forget about it, just do it for fun. Get a trade goin' or something like that." He just went ahead and did it. Y'know? Despite the attitude most people have. So it was like, shit, I guess it really can be done."

Jim Martin

8

" I SURE MISS CLIFF."

JH 3/04

I WISH I COULD SPEND TIME WITH CLIFF IN MY CURRENT STATE OF MIND!

Cliff.

THE MAN, THE WARLORD, HIS SPIRIT IS WITH US ALL THE TIME

I'm at Mike Bordin's (GUEST ROOM)
It's 2 OR 3 AM] I'm WORKING,
PREPARING FOR MY AUDITION W/ THE BOYS
(SLASH, GENE, DAMAGE, FLIGHT #3;)
AND HE'S WATCHING
CLIFF'S
CHECKING
ME
OUT
(OK HIS PHOTO)
I ACTUALLY LOOKED AT
THE PHOTO AND SAID
" I WON'T LET YOU
DOWN."
WHAT A TRIP

RJ DX 04

ONE RECOLLECTION —

ONE TIME CLIFF WAS STAYING AT MY HOUSE, AND I TOLD HIM I JUST GOT REAR-ENDED ON THE BAY BRIDGE. I TOLD HIM I WAS ALRIGHT AND SET OUT TO DO WHATEVER WE WERE DOING THEN. THE NEXT DAY I WOKE UP AND COULDN'T TURN MY HEAD — I HAD WHIPLASH! IT HURT TO STAND UP STRAIGHT, TO WALK, TO TALK, TO LAUGH — YOU GET THE POINT. WELL, CUZ I COULDN'T DRIVE, I ASKED CLIFF TO DRIVE ME TO THE HOSPITAL, AND I TELL YOU, THAT WAS THE MOST PAINFUL, EXCRUCIATING RIDE I HAD AT THAT POINT. CLIFF DROVE LIKE A MADMAN, SWERVING ALL OVER THE PLACE, SCREAMING MISFIT SONGS AT THE TOP OF HIS LUNGS, BANGING ON HIS STEERING WHEEL THAT WAS BROKEN IN FOUR PLACES, AND ME HOWLING IN PAIN CUZ I COULDN'T KEEP MY NECK STILL. AT ONE POINT I SAID " CAN'T YOU DRIVE A LITTLE MORE CAREFUL ?? MY NECK IS KILLING ME!

AT THAT POINT HE JUST LOOKED AT ME AND SHOUTED

POOOS!!
(SHORT FOR FEMALE GENITALIA)

AFTER THAT I TRIED NOT TO RIDE WITH HIM TOO MUCH, ONLY WHEN I HAD TO.

3/04

9

Metallica Museum

FIRST REVIEW EVER!
"Saxon could also use a fast, hot guitar played of the Eddie Van Halen ilk. Opening quartet Metallica had one, but little else. The local group needs considerable development to overcome a pervasive awkwardness."
—TERRY ATKINSON
LA Times, March 29, 1982

James had $'s, I was broke.
Bonus question: Which fast food chain was our neighbors?
February 1983, El Cerrito, CA

James Personal Loan:

MON 2/14	BURGER KING	$3.-
TUE 2/15	LOAN (AT BK)	20.-
THUR 2/17	BK (2 P.M)	2.-
THUR 2/17	GAS	3.75
THUR 2/17	Liquor (7.50 : 2)	
THUR 2/17	Liquor (5.50 : 2)	
THUR 2/17	BK	2.-
FRI 2/18	DENNYS	3.50
FRI 2/18	TICKET STONE	6.-
SAT 2/19	SPAGHETTI DINNER	3.-
SUN 2/20	LIQUOR BEFORE MRB	2.50
SUN 2/20	BURGER KING	2.-
MON 2/21	Groceries (37 : 2)	18.50
TUE 2/22	MIKSER	
FRI 2/25	Groceries + Liquor (18 : 2)	9.-
SAT 2/26	Liquor: (4:9)	$4.50

YO, SO HOW ARE THINGS BACK THERE! JUST FINISHED NEW ALBUM YESTERDAY AND ITS NICE FINALLY TO BE THRU' WITH THAT AND GET IT OUT AND PLAY LIVE AGAIN. APART FROM THE VENOM TOUR WE ONLY DONE THE MARQUEE TWICE SO THE MINI TOUR WE ARE ABOUT TO DO WILL BE FUCKING GREAT. AROUND 6 DATES WITH T. SISTER (WHO?) + THE BIG FESTIVAL IN BELGIUM W/ M.H. SISTER MANOWAR, FATE ETC. EUROPE WILL BE DESTROYED PART 2. AAARRRGGHH! HANGIN OUT W/ FATE ALOT. GREAT FUCKIN' GUYS!! THEY ARE DOIN' THEIR NEW ALBUM RITE NOW TOO. BY THE WAY, THANX ALOT FOR THE TAPES I GOT SHIT BACK IN FEB. SEE YOU SOON. LARS. DRINK x DESTROY.

BRIAN LEW
438 JOSHUA WAY
SUNNYVALE
CALIF.
94086.
USA

LUFTPOST
PAR AVION

SMART ASS NOTES

Lars' early list of possible band names, 1981

Deathwish
Deaththreat
Deathchamber
Deathray
Flying Tigers
Blitzen
Helldriver
Snake Widow   NIXON
Bad Musicians Nist
Bigmouth and Friends.
Empty Barrel EMPTY.
DUMB FUCK.

What's that brown shit on my upper lip?? London, March 84

"Gold" for 100,000 copies of "Creeping Death" sold in Europe, Lyceum, London, December 20, 1984

CRISTIAN MICHAEL, INC.

CARRIER AGREEMENT
HOME DELIVERY

Agreement dated __10-6-82__, to become effective on __10-6-__ hereinafter called between Cristian Michael, Inc., a California corporation, hereinafter called "the Company" and __Lars Ulrich__, the "Carrier".

The Company is engaged in the business of assembling and delivering Los Angeles Times, a newspaper published seven days a week. The Company desires to retain the services of the Carrier as an independent contractor to deliver the Los Angeles Times to those Los Angeles Times subscribers identified by a route list and the Carrier desires to render such services to the Company, in accordance with the provisions of this agreement.

1. The Carrier agrees as follows:

(a) To deliver the Los Angeles Times to the home delivery subscribers of the Los Angeles Times who shall be designated to the Carrier by the Company from time to time in the form of a route list containing the adress of each home delivery subscriber in the delivery area and designating the type of service which each home delivery subscriber is to receive. The Company will supply the Carrier regularly with additions to, deletions from, or other changes in the subscriber delivery list so as to keep the list current.

(b) To deliver a complete copy of the Los Angeles Times, including special sections, in a convenient and proper place in a dry condition to each home delivery subscriber in the delivery area by not later than, under normal conditions, 6:00 a.m. on weekdays and 7:00 a.m. on Saturdays and Sundays.

(c) Not to stamp upon, insert in or attach to copies of the Los Angeles Times any advertising or other matter which is not furnished to the Carrier by the Company, except with prior consent of the Company.

(d) Not to impose any charge upon the home delivery subscriber for delivery or other services rendered pursuant to this agreement.

2. The Company agrees to pay to the Carrier the following fees:

(a) $ __400.—__ for each calendar month, to be paid in equal increments on the 20th of each month and on the 5th of the following month.

(b) The Carrier shall be paid a fulls day's fee for each day in training unless the Carrier leaves the Company within 30 days of hire, in which case the Carrier will be paid only for the papers he delivered as partial route fee.

My first band Obsession, 1979, telling one fan to come the fuck on.

MILITIA ALERT

METALLICA's equipment was stolen in Boston on January 19th. With the exception of two guitars, virtually everything was taken and has yet to be recovered. Due to these circumstances, the band has been forced to rent equipment while in Europe, and the financial loss suffered by this experience will not easily be overcome. Jon Zazula and myself urge all metallists to help the band by setting up a series of benefit concerts throughout America, with the aim of buying the band new equipment. Bands, club owners and anyone else interested in putting together such a benefit are urged to please contact the METAL MILITIA or Jon Zazula, 60 York Street, Old Bridge, New Jersey 09957 (20...

Kirk, James, & Fred, proud drunks; 1986 Spastik Children

Early gig flyer.
(Still watching / waiting for EP on High Velocity Records!!)

Yet another list of Lars' hot band name options. Early '82

THE MANIACS RETURN!!!

METALLICA
METAL UP YOUR ASS
OLD WALDORF
MON. NOV. 29
SPECIAL GUESTS: VICIOUS RUMOURS & EXODUS

LITES
MECHANIX — James
PHANTOM
JUMP
MOTOR
REMORSE — James
SEEK
WHIPLASH — James
EVIL?
METAL — James
ENCORE
PRINCE

Coude you please help me, I want a (Don't know the name in English)
→ that one = JEANS JACKET

I hope you understand me If you'll send me that stuff tell me how much you want and I'll send you the money as possible I can.
★ I Love Metallica they're my absolutly favoritband their tracks Phantomlord, Hit the lights and metal Militia is great! Please tell me their story, all their songs and when & they'll mode an album. That's all for this time, write back soon!

HEAVY METAL Thunder!
#4 Sept.

METALLICA—By Sheila Gray

METALLICA is one of the best new HM bands to come from America in a long time. Formed by Lars Ulrich and James Hatfeild in Nov. '81. The current line up started in Feb. '82, with Lars on drums, James on vocals and guitar, Dave Mustaine on the screamin' B.C. Rich guitar, and on McGovney on bass.

The band is heavily influenced by Motorhead, Diamond Head, and Sweet Savace. They are a very foursome, playing some of the best metal in the L.A. area. They opened for Saxon last time Saxon played L.A.

They have a demo tape out called "No Life Til Leather", which proves how great this band can play, with songs like, "Hit The Lights, featured on the Metal Massacre compilation. Also on the demo are songs like "Motorbreath", "The Mechanix" "Metal Militia", a real smoker, and others.

They have been playing the L.A. club scene but that hasn't been to helpful. The clubs say that METALLICA is too loud, too heavy, and that they draw very drunk and disorderly crowds, which is beyond me, why they would let punk bands play with their crazy antics, and not let some fine metal band like METALLICA. The other set back is other local bands won't let them play with them saving they're not good, when in reality it's because METALLICA is blowing them away.

METALLICA have what it takes to be one of the best NWOHM bands in America. They are all excellent musicians, and all very serious of what they do. If your interested in the band, and would like to get the tape, write to Lars Ulrich, 2600 Park Newport, Newport Beach, CA. 92660 U.S.A.

Early press. This was like the cover of Rolling Stone to us. Summer '82.

SWEET SILENCE STUDIOS

4.
FADE TO BLACK
(HETFIELD, ULRICH, BURTON, HAMME...)

1) ★ LIFE IT SEEMS, WILL FADE AWAY,
DRIFTING FURTHER EVERY DAY.
GETTING LOST WITHIN MYSELF,
NOTHING MATTERS, NO ONE ELSE.
I HAVE LOST THE WILL TO LIVE,
SIMPLY NOTHING MORE TO GIVE.
THERE IS NOTHING MORE FOR ME,
NEED THE END TO SET ME FREE.

2) THINGS NOT WHAT THEY USED TO BE,
MISSING ONE INSIDE OF ME.
DEATHLY LOST, THIS CAN'T BE REAL,
CANNOT STAND THIS HELL I FEEL.
EMPTINESS IS FILLING ME,
TO THE POINT OF AGONY.
GROWING DARKNESS TAKING DAWN,
I WAS ME, BUT NOW HE'S GONE.

Please send ANYTHING pertaining to METALLICA- who are our FAVORITE new band at the moment!! It's a miracle that the US have created such a monster band, and you're the chosen metal mercenaries picked to lead the stateside metal militia out into the HM minefield to SEEK and DESTROY the opposing top-40 wimps and their radio-dominated garbage!!

Also, I've just been informed that KUSF radio station in San Francisco would be interested in giving your music extensive airplay (I sent the DJ a tape of your demo) and they would like to run the interview I get with you also! Everyone I've sent your demo to has totally SHIT!!! They've all gone apecrazy over METALLICA's brute ferocity and power! Your tape has already reached the UK and Europe extensively (according to my other penpals) and is being received well.

My ex-old lady said to me that she wasn't going to Priest (tonight!!) because after seeing Metallica, anything else made me sick. She says the only bands she'll see are Metallica, Mercyful Fate, and Venom. She's a good head.

NO ONE BUT ME CAN SAVE MYSELF, BUT ITS TOO LATE,
NOW I CANT THINK, THINK WHY I SHOULD EVEN TRY.
YESTERDAY SEEMS AS THOUGH IT NEVER EXISTED,
DEATH GREETS ME WARM, NOW I WILL JUST SAY GOODBYE.

Handwritten lyrics for "Ride The Lightning" album.
These were the ones that the inner sleeve was typeset from.

Early fan mail. Summer '82.

GUEST STAR
THRAX
CTUBRE 21,30 HORAS
NICIPAL DEPORTES
en los puntos habituales

11

W.A.S.P.
Special Guest
Armored Saint
SATURDAY, FEB. 9, 1985 7:30 PM
ARAGON BALLROOM
ROCK RADIO IS DEAD
Phone the JAM Concert Line
666-6667
FOR COMPLETE CONCERT INFORMATION

Miller High Life Concerts

Cliff at Breaking Sound Festival,
Paris, France, August 30, 1984

THE STONE — S.F.
YKS74
412 BROADWAY
18&OVER/2 DRINK MINIMUM
METALLICA / CULPRIT
Sat MAR 19 1983 9:00 PM GEN ADM

GUNS N' ROSES/METALLICA
Rain or Shine
FRI JUL 17 1992 5:30PM

THE EXPLOSIVE POWER
OF METALLICA
INVADES THE
STADTHALLE KOLN
DECEMBER 5TH 1984
ALSO WATCH FOR METALLICA EP.
APPEARING ON THE COMPILATION ALBUM
METAL MASSACRE ON METAL BLADE RECORDS

20 August 1982:
"Woodstock", Anaheim, Ca.
Set:
Hit the lights
Seek & Destroy
The Prince
The Mechanix
Jump in the fire
Phantom Lord
Motorbreath
No Remorse
Metal Militia
Crowd: 150
Pay: $4.25
Remarks: Played first.
Place is a chicken dump.
Treated like shit. Just
an average gig. Went
down pretty well though.

27 August 1982:
"Whisky", Hollywood, Ca.
Set:
Hit the lights
Seek & Destroy
The Prince
The Mechanix
Phantom Lord
Jump in the fire
Motorbreath
No Remorse
Metal Militia
Crowd: 15 → 50
Pay: $25
Remarks: SHIT!! Ron
broke a bass-string on
PL and the rest of
it was just awful. Star-
ted at 9:15 with no one
around.

Metallica meets Ktulu,
July 1984

IDIOT'S GUIDE TO THE METALLIPSYCH...
e questions you should never ask...
What's it like being at the fore...
movement?
Making a record with Bob Rock is...
3) How can you play heavy metal, se...
4) Read any good books lately?
5) What's it all about?

Five questions you should always as...
1) What's it like being at the fo...
movement?
2) Do Metallica feel happy with t...
neo-minimalism?
3) Well?
4) Do Metallica play as loud as...
society collapsing?
5) What is it all about?

12

THE HEAVIEST NIGHT OF YOUR LIFE
SAXON
WITH
METALLICA
THE YOUNG METAL ATTACK

Whisky a Go Go MARCH 27

2 SHOWS   9:00PM / 11:30PM

KEYSTONE PALOALTO
PRESENTS
SAXON
AND
MÖTLEY CRÜE
PLUS SPECIAL APPEARANCE BY
TRAUMA

TUES. MAR 30ᵀᴴ 8:00
$5 ADV/$6 AT

This is rare, rare, rare! Cliff's old band Trauma's handmade flyer for when they opened for Saxon, 3/30/82. Motley Crue cancelled.

METALLICA
Night of the Rivvit-Heads

the thrash metal

selling out, right?

it's so sexist?

lica:

of the thrash metal

ve from crypto-nihilism to

to block out the noise of

THEY SAID IT WOULD NEVER HAPPEN
GUNS N' ROSES
METALLICA
WITH SPECIAL GUEST
FAITH NO MORE

SATURDAY, SEPT. 5
TEXAS STADIUM 3:30 P.M.

RESERVED SEAT TICKETS GO ON SALE
TOMORROW 7 A.M. AT ALL RAINBOW TICKETMASTER
LOCATIONS INCLUDING STARS, SOUND WAREHOUSE

Ad from L.A. Times 1982

Whisky a Go Go
NO AGE LIMIT 652-4202 DINNER

AUG. 27	SARGE · STORMER METALLICA GREG LEON INVASION
AUG. 28	SEAGULL LITTLE TOKYO CANDY · THIEVES
AUG. 29	FORMER DRUMMER FOR THE RUNAWAYS SANDY WEST DIETRICH · DANTE FOX · JOEY
AUG. 31	THE UNKNOWNS SHADOW MINSTRELS · TOYMUZIC
SEPT. 1	ARE YOU READY FOR THE SEX TOUR GLEAMING SPIRES CARL STEWART · THE PRESS
SEPT. 2	THE BLASTERS JAMES INVELO · ROCKIN' REBEL RED DEVILS
SEPT. 3	THE BEAT FEATURING PAUL COLLINS THE SIGHTS · KID TWIST
SEPT. 4	White Sister

TICKETS AT TICKETRON
OR CALL CHARGE LINE (213) 387-1329

METALLICA

THE BAND

James Hetfield	Vocals, guita:
Lars Ulrich	Drums
Kirk Hammett	Guitar
Jason Newsted	Bass

THE REASON

Metallica's fifth long-playing recording, entitled "METALLICA". "Here it is. "Metallica". Black sleeve. Black logo. Fuck you."

THE MOTHER OF ALL ALBUMS

"Metallica" was produced by Bob Rock, (known for his work with The Cult, Bon Jovi and Motley Crue) with James Hetfield and Lars Ulrich. Hungry for hot news - or, failing that, lukewarm rumour - the rock community has been behaving as if this was the single most important and telling factor of Metallica's decade-long career. It isn't.

"He opened our minds to a few things, that's all" says James Hetfield. "There's no hurt in letting someone do their stuff, you can always say no. In the long run it was pretty much us anyway. No rules but Metallica rules."

"You say Bob Rock, and you say shorter, simpler songs, and people will paint a negative picture instead of a positive picture" says Lars Ulrich. "Human nature is strange. There's been this mass hysteria over nothing. It's been fun to sit and watch it happen, though."

"Metallica" is the antithesis of "...And Justice For All", Metallica's previous album. "Justice" was technique. "Metallica" is instinct, pure and organic.

"'Justice' was cool at the time, it was a challenge," states James. "This time Lars is just pounding, Jason keeps it pumping and we let

Cont/...

Article in Playboy, August 1985

Gimme an F!

These guys don't look too weird. They're called METALLICA. They live in the Bay Area and disturb the peace. They hang out with Ednas (their word for groupies). They play heavy metal. Loud. They're currently writing songs for a new opus. The old one, *Ride the Lightning*, was on the charts for a long time. You can see that success has given them a new appreciation for art. They're keeping it simple. And they're smiling.

Band, Scott Ian, and Jon Zazula in London, March 1984

13

THE BAND ANSWERS FAN QUESTIONS

To the "FOUR DRUNKMAN:" Which is your favorite Mexican beer and what do you think about tequila?
Federico P., Mexico

JH: My favorite Mexican beer is Pacifico, though my favorite Mexican beer was called Tequila (no wonder I got so fukt up).
LU: Corona – love it, tequila – love to hate it.
KH: I love all Mexican beer, and when I drink a lot of tequila I just stop thinking altogether.

I was wondering if Metallica is planning to record another album. Because some of my friends said that they were. If this is true, what is the name of this album going to be?
James G., Carrollton, KY

JH: Do you believe everything your friends say? It's safe to say a new album is in the future for us. Where? When? What's it called? What will I have for dinner? Who knowz?
KH: The album is going to be called "Let's Bomb Carrollton..."

What is the song that is used to open your shows before you come on stage?
Blythe M., Australia

JN: 'Ecstasy of Gold' by Ennio Morricone from "The Good, The Bad and The Ugly" – Clint Eastwood.

This question is for Kirk in reference to the in-studio portion of the video "A Year And A Half In The Life." During the laying down of Kirk's guitar track for 'Nothing Else Matters,' Bob Rock and Kirk had a disagreement on how the solo should be played. It was kind of funny listening to their different perspectives on how it should be done. How was the solo played, Bob's way or Kirk's way?
Tim O., Tarpon Springs, FL

JH: Jaymz's way. Kirk never played a note on 'Nothing Else Matters' on the album.

Did you borrow part of the song 'America' from 'West Side Story' for 'Don't Tread On Me'? (Big argument between a friend and I.) Were the words for 'So What' and/or 'Am I Evil?' ever printed on any of your releases? What is your musical background? Formal, private, or just taught yourself training?
Cassi S., Lancaster, TX

JH: Yes, '...Tread' has part of 'America' in the intro (your friend owes you a beer). The lyrics to 'So What' and 'Am I Evil?' were printed on the Japanese CDs (Sony) so if you can read Japanese you're OK. Maybe we should translate them in the magazine so you can sing along too. I was self taught (no one would admit to teaching me after hearing me now).
JN: I was self taught, mostly from watching and jamming with other people – about three formal lessons total.
KH: My musical background is partly formal, partly private, and partly teaching myself.

I have a habit of looking at jewelry people wear and wondering what it symbolizes. I noticed Lars wears a necklace that looks like a St. Christopher medal. Is he Catholic?
Gina F., Whitestone, NY

LU: The St. Christopher medal was a gift from my ex-wife. I wear it for good luck while I'm travelling.

I recently got the "$5.98 EP Garage Days Re-Revisited...and more." No one in my family can identify the design on the CD itself, so I was wondering if you could tell me? Do letters addressed to Metallica care of Elektra Records (New York office) get forwarded to the band?
Amanda W., Waynesville, OH

JH: There is no '...and more' in the title of the discontinued/rare $5.98 EP. The official EP contains six cover songs and has a picture of the four of us in black on the cover. I'm not sure what design yer talkin about.
JN: Yes, we get our letters. We're trying to catch up now that the club is in operation. Please correspond through the club, it's better that way now.

I recently bought a live Metallica CD entitled "Open Graves." It was recorded in Genova, Italy under the label of Moving Sound, and was released in Italy. The sound quality in many places is pretty bad, and there are numerous misspellings of song titles and band member names. I bought this CD for $25 at my local music store. I was wondering, is this album a bootleg, and how rare is it? Can you tell me anything else about this album or the concert it contains?a
Brendan M., West Sayville, NY

JH: Definitely a bootleg!! Ask before you buy it. Be careful when buying that shit. A lot of bootlegs are older ones or ones you might already have, but with different covers. As for the spelling or the sound quality, they are put out by people who don't give a fuck about the band or know the songs. They are out to rip you off (most of them). Before you buy any music, make the record store play it for you (most will!).

Where the hell was Flemming Rasmussen on the new album? I (we) would hate to think Metallica was turning to money and not their fans (true Metallica fans).
David S., South Bend, IN

JH: We felt it was time to taste some new blood. Bob was a fresh victim. No doubt our friends understand needing to move on, and believe me, Bob was slightly more expensive.

Was Cliff buried in San Francisco or were his ashes spread over a ranch somewhere in the west?
Brian S., Seymour, TN

JH: His ashes are spread in a few of his favorite spots around the Bay Area including a secluded ranch.

Jaymz, how do you usually go about the process of writing lyrics? Your lyrics are so vastly different from everyone else's. (Not to mention vastly superior!)
Michael B., Crosslake, MN

JH: Usually it starts with a subject, or a title, or a beverage. Then the chorus comes together which usually sums up the meaning. Then depending on how much I want to give away, fill in the verses.

Just curious–what are each of your individual favorite Metallica songs, and do you have a collective favorite song that you like to perform?
Jenna D., Staten Island, NY

LU: There are too many to mention, but certain songs indicate turning points: 'Whiplash,' 'For Whom the Bell Tolls,' 'Fade to Black,' 'Orion,' 'Enter Sandman,' and 'Nothing Else Matters.' My favorite songs to perform are 'Sanitarium' and 'For Whom the Bell Tolls.'
KH: I fuckin love 'Sad' and 'Sandman!' Also 'Thingy,' 'Sanitarium,' 'Harvester,' 'Creep,' 'Bellz,' and 'Motorbreath' cuz they kick ass!
JH: 'The Thing That Should Not Be.'

I wanted to know where James got his wolf pendant. If someone made it for him or if he bought it somewhere.
Aaron H., Cedar Falls, ID

JH: The Great Frog – London (Lemmy shops there, woooow).

What's that weird Egyptian dance that Jaymz sometimes does during 'Am I Evil?' about?
Dave S., Wichita, KS

JH: It's a signal to my roadie for 1) a cold beer; 2) turn me up; 3) my zipper broke; 4) all of the above.

In "Binge and Purge" what is the riff that James plays before 'Unforgiven?'
Anonymous

JH: 1) just a little somethin' to get you in the mood; 2) my attempt at classical guitar; 3) nothing in particular; 4) all of the above.'

James, who in their right mind in the whole of the USA would give you a gun license? And what the hell were they thinking of?
Debbie M., Sydney, Australia

JH: Officer Charles Manson.

I read in SO WHAT! that Ron McGovney was in the release of 'Hit The Lights' in the "Metal Massacre 1" compilation, but in my magazine by Movie Mirror (Aug. '93) it says that only Lars, James and Lloyd Grant performed on this. Which one is correct?
Donald M., Flint, MI

LU: There were two different versions of 'Hit The Lights' recorded for "Metal Massacre." The first one was James, Lloyd and myself released on Brian Slayer–Metal Blade. It has skulls on the cover. Later on another label picked it up and re-recorded a different version. It has a plain grey cover.

Jaymz, where did you learn to hunt? Metallica, where do you see yourselves ten years from now?
Vicente T., San Marcos, TX

JH: 1. Outside (it's more challenging than inside). 2. Still in the studio working on drum sounds.

How do you guys manage to stay in such great shape considering the fact that your lives are so hectic with being on tour for sometimes up to three years?
Michele C., Elmwood Park, IL

JH: We load and unload our own equipment to keep our muscles worked out (just kidding). Touring itself!! I think sweating for three hours five times a week might have something to do with it.
KH: I am preserved from drinking way too much in my younger years – just kidding! I ride my bike when I'm off tour and being on stage is a workout.

This question goes to James and Jason: why did you guys come up with the idea of James starting a song and then Jason finishing it in like 'Creeping Death,' 'Whiplash,' and 'Seek and Destroy?'
Christopher A., Fort Polk, LA

JN: By mistake, fatigue and sore throats. We just stumbled upon it and stuck with it.
JH: Choose your favorite answer: 1) I forgot the words; 2) I like singing backup vox; 3) Gives me a chance to run around; 4) Those are the only songs Jason can sing and play at the same time; 5) Give my voice a rest.

What the fuck does "Mommy, where's Fluffy?" mean at the end of 'Breadfan?'
Aaron L., Duluth, MN

JN: Fluffy is a toenail-less rodent covered with poo.

A friend of mine said that 'Enter Sandman' was first sung by some guy about 4–5 years ago. I say it was written by Metallica. So who's right?
Darren G., Arlington, TX

LU: According to my calculations, you're right. WE wrote it summer 1990."
JN: '…Sandman' was definitely written by Metallica.

Did Jaymz' girlfriend get murdered and was she going to have a baby? Did y'all lose anything in the '89 earthquake?
Cynthia S., Prairieville, LA

JH: My friend Vinnie said it was an accident.
KH: I think you're confusing this with a woman named Sharon Tate.
JN: I lost my balance in the quake.

Kirk, is your custom M2 with Fuck You at the twelfth fret gonna be on your custom line by ESP? Have you ever played a Hamer guitar? If you did, did you like it?
Mark D., Toledo OR

A KH: That guitar is a custom instrument. It is a one-of-a-kind. I've played Hamer guitars, but never got around to buying one.

James, I noticed the skull ring on your left finger. Did it belong to Cliff? In "Cliff 'Em All" I noticed Cliff wearing the exact same ring.
Anthony F., Dallas, OR

JH: Yes, it was a ring Cliff wore.

Lars, I read an article in Metal Edge that said that the guy from Winger was pissed at you for throwing darts at his picture in the "Nothing Else Matters" video. Is this true?
Paul T., Fort Myers, FL

LU: As far as I know, it's true. I read an article somewhere that said I was single-handedly responsible for fucking up his career by throwing darts, and he was gonna kick my ass. I'm scared!
JH: Why? It's the most publicity he's ever had.

Me and my friends have been wondering and arguing for a long time about the song 'Leper Messiah.' Whose voice is it that counts at the beginning of the song?
Anthony G., Huntington Park, CA

LU: Yours truly!! ●

Bi-De-Le-Dew, Bi-De-Le-Dew

the TRUTH, the WHOLE TRUTH...

by LARS ULRICH

Scattered thru' out this here fine magazine, are various takes, reports and supposed first person accounts on those wonderful coupla weeks in the late summer of '95, when we packed our bags, fucked the studio off and went in search of adventure and a much needed change of scenery!!!! However, all those stories are probably wildly exaggerated, full of inflated information, near and mostly half-truths and are only written by these wannabes to use their "near" Metallica experiences to see their own name in print, and get going on their allotted 15 minutes... probably!! However, there is one person you, the loyal and well respected SO WHAT! reader can trust to give you the truth, the whole (gin-soaked) truth, and no inflated or self-congratulatory bollocks... namely, your humble and modest drummer and part-time scribe... me!!!!! (surprise!!)

——————————————"WHAT HAPPENED????" WE ALL LOOK AT EACH OTHER, WONDERING, "WHAT THE FUCK??" WE HAVE ONCE AGAIN STOPPED HALF-WAY THRU' A SONG, NEATLY IN THE PROCESS OF BUTCHERING SOMETHING WE HAVE PLAYED LIVE 712 TIMES. I THINK WE HAVE (FINALLY!) LOST IT!! IT'S MID-WEEK, MID AUGUST. IN 10 DAYS WE LEAVE TO HEADLINE ONE OF THE BIGGEST GIGS OF OUR LIVES AND THE IDEA OF CALLING THE METALLICA COVER BAND, "BATTERY," TO SECRETLY REPLACE US COMES UP IN CONVERSATION. "AT LEAST THEY PLAY OUR SHIT GOOD. WHAT WE'RE DOING HERE SOUNDS LIKE A BAD METALLICA COVER BAND!!" MUCH DESPAIR AND MISERY!!! ——————————————

I guess this is what happens when you're foolish enough to think you can pull off playing gigs in the middle of having every waking moment of your life deep in the bowels of "new record hell"! I mean, fucken 'Creepin' Death'! We should be able to play that while we are on the toilet! After a few rounds of, "Wait a minute. We're Metallica (we do actually say that to each other sometimes!!), we can fucken get it together!!", Jason leads us

into warface mode and off we go again and it's actually cruisin' downhill from there on!!... Wow!!

The next few days are spent fuckin' around with the set, tryin' to make it different from last time we played in England and figuring out what, if any, new shit to play!! We agree that '2x4' and 'Devil Dance' are a good introduction to where our heads are at right now with the new shit and the only question is whether to play the whole songs or let them "fall to shit" after a couple of verses. We decide to go for it! What rock & roll rebels we are!!

"Maybe we should go down the street and play a small intimate gig at this joint New George's, instead of all this fucken rehearsal??" I throw this out, 'cuz I have realized that for us, rehearsing to four white walls and a coupla bored roadies, doesn't do much for our vibe!! Within a few minutes, in open forum, the idea comes up of inviting some of our local "Met Club" friends down to our turf, instead of schlepping all the crap out to a club. This seems like a twisted and unknown enough of a situation to be inviting. Playing to 30 fans in our rehearsal dump?? Let's fucken do it!!! Cue, three days later, and there we are, face to face with a bunch of "Metalliclubbers," warfaces, eye contacts, slight tingling in stomachs, and full fucken' roar!!! I like it!!! After a few uncomfortable minutes, it settles down and... Now, we get to a new one... I start the drum roll for '2x4' and here comes the riff... And... Wow, nobody leaves the room in disgust. Good sign!!! Two hours later and four pounds lighter, we all hang around and bullshit with our new friends / critics / vibe-inducers(??) and all come to the conclusion, that this is definitely the way to fucken rehearse. Don't be surprised next time somebody calls and asks you to come to San Rafael!! And sorry to about a dozen of you, who didn't answer your phones the previous night!!!

LONDON — CLUB GIG

"Those shoes are pimp!!??" Kirk's enthusiasm for this particular set of footwear is huge. We are somewhere in London, it's Monday, August 21, and me, Kirk and Randy, after arriving from the west coast a few hours earlier, are fightin' the urge to sleep, with gin & tonics and half-assed attempts at shopping!! Kirk buys these shoes(??!!) and is once again, one step closer to becoming some character from a "Superfly" movie from the early '70s!! Early Tuesday, me, James and T. Smith jump daringly into a helicopter and flip up to the site at Donington to check out the scene!! It's strange being at a gig four days before the event and there is a quietness about the whole thing that seems kinda awkward (how poetic!!). The stage, rig and everything is already up and everything is lookin' fuckin' massive!! I think back to what I said in a few interviews "a couple ago" about how we were just goin' to go for it and pretty much down scale everything. Nice try!! Twice as fucken huge as before!! How '90s!! I talk to the promoter, Maurice, about the possibility of maybe taking some sort of vehicle (preferably a fast one!!) around the track (for those who don't know, Donington is a race track!!), which is met with raised eyebrows by James and a look of horror by Tony, and we decide that on Friday, when we do sound-check, he will have something lined up. Later that night, back in London, we head over to the "L.A.2" for a sound check. This is the joint we have decided to do our warm-up show at and upon closer look, feels, sizewise and vibewise, like the perfect place to do this sort of thing. There are a bunch of banners left hanging around from the previous night's festivities, which we leave up and even use one as a backdrop while we are jammin'. The idea of leaving them up for the show tomorrow is met with mixed reaction, so we decide we will see what happens!! Oh, yeah, all of them said "Welcome to gay night!"... After sound check and much sulking from Jason, 'cuz we had him turn his bass down (the ceiling was looking dodgy!!), we decide to all head out for a nice little quaint late night dinner somewhere. "Tony, sort it out!!" It's 10 o'clock in one of the largest metropolises on the planet and it's looking grim!! Tony suggests we all pile into a couple of vehicles and go for a drive. We end up in the only area of London which has anything open(!!??) and... eh... how do I say this??... Due to the geographical origin of most (all!!) of the customers... and in the spirit of not starting trouble... we decide to give this a miss. "Tony!! What the fuck??" Andy Battye has an idea. What the fuck turns into ending up at the crew hotel, sittin' in the lobby in front of the elevators, ordering from the room service menu, eating mainly french fries and gettin' strange looks from the flow of business men and their escor... I mean, dates, who flow thru' the lobby, lookin' at these 12 or so misfits, chowing down in the middle of the night!!!!! Don't tell me we have lost it yet!!

The minute you wake up it's there!! That feeling in your stomach!! Everytime we haven't played live for a long time it's just there. I wish I knew what the fuck for. Nerves? Actually, it's more like anxiety. Like, it's noon and you just wanna go on stage and get going, but you got nine hours of sweaty palms ahead of you. So in case you just crawled out from under a rock, tonight we are doing a special Donington warm-up gig just for members of the Met Club, meaning you (motherfucker!!), and it's the first time since Miami at the end of the "Summer Shit '94" that we have jammed live, so... aaarrrrggghhh!!! Once the day gets going, the anxiety slowly turns into confidence and for some reason I feel really fucken strong about the gig and generally everything about Metallica at the moment.

A LOT OF TIMES WHEN I'M IN ENGLAND I GET REALLY WOUND UP AND FREAK!! MAYBE IT'S THE PRESS, THE GHOST OF "NWOBHM," OR THE LACK OF CRUSTS ON THE BREAD, BUT I USUALLY GET VERY INTIMIDATED AND FEEL LIKE I'M THREE FEET TALL!! BUT THIS TIME EVERYTHING FEELS VERY "IN THE POCKET" AND CERTAINLY A MILLION MILES AWAY FROM REHEARSAL TWO WEEKS EARLIER. AMAZING WHAT A QUICK ROUND OF WARFACES CAN DO!!! ANYWAY, I HOOK UP WITH MY FRIEND, NEIL (YOU CAN READ HIS "LIES" ELSEWHERE), FOR A CARBO OVERLOADED DINNER AND STRANGELY ENOUGH I HAVE NEVER FELT THIS GOOD ABOUT A GIG IN ENGLAND!! THREE HOURS LATER I'M ON STAGE, STILL FEELING GOOD ABOUT THE GIG, BUT WONDERING IF I'LL PASS OUT FROM HEAT-EXHAUSTION AND DEHYDRATION!! I SURVIVE!! THE GIG GOES REAL FUCKEN WELL AND I ACTUALLY GET ONE OR TWO COMPLIMENTS FROM THE OTHER GUYS ON KEEPING THE TEMPOS WHERE THEY SHOULD BE. AND BELIEVE YOU ME, COMPLIMENTS ARE THROWN AROUND BETWEEN THE FOUR OF US, ABOUT AS OFTEN AS THE OLYMPICS ROLL AROUND!! SLIGHTLY HOT, BUT NONE THE LESS, FUCKEN RIGHT ON ALL AROUND. EVERYBODY FEELS GOOD AND ONCE AGAIN THE NEW SONGS WERE VERY WELL RECEIVED. I THINK WE BETTER HAVE A BEVERAGE!!

One of the great things about record companies is that they usually pick up the tab if anything like food or booze is involved, so we mask gettin' all our friends, including C.O.C, the guys from Therapy, Almighty, Brian from Diamond Head, and various liggers from the press, etc. together, as a small "party", and end up around the corner in a restaurant and the double g&t's, among other things, start flowing!! For some unexplainable reason, we get thrown out at four a.m. and decide to head back to the hotel with a couple of C.O.C's in tow and after gettin' refused entry to Kirk's private gathering (don't ask!), me, James and the rest, end up in my room, with my most valued acquisition of the evening, the new AC/DC album, ready to be explored!! Somebody once told me, that if you don't have anything good to say, don't say anything at all, so let's just say we had a few "bevies" and... here comes daylight... must be time to go to bed!!!!!!!!!!

Twenty four hours later I'm still on the verge of passing out from heat-exhaustion, but this time I'm in the crowd. We are at "The Borderline," Warrior Soul are playin' their warm-up gig and full on rockin' and it just

so happens to be about 400 degrees in here!! I guess double hard booze drinks don't help much, but you know, day off and all that shit!! Events from this evening are slightly hazy, but I remember Warrior Soul were fucken great, something about piggy-backing on Jaymz, chargin' into innocent bystanders on Oxford St., going over to the Columbia Hotel, where both W.S and C.O.C were staying, and having wonderful, deep insightful conversations with various people that were stupid enough to stand within shouting distance from me. Great fucken hotel!! They keep the bar open 'til the last people leave and the barman is about 112 years old, probably has never gone home!! A very hard hotel to get thrown out of!!

The next morning we have to helicopter up to Donington again, this time all of us, for sound check. There are one or two unnamed casualties!! Evian!!! Over the next 45 minutes, the words "shit" and "thermal" get plenty of airtime!!! The 'check goes good, we jam on some other new songs, and do a 20 minute blues deal, where Jaymz improvises some great lyrics about gin and the after effects!! Did somebody fucken record that!!?? An interesting sight out on the field, are these fucken huge piles of earth sittin' everywhere. Are these for the mandatory mud slingin?? Isn't it stupid to supply the tools for this?? We press the issue, but are met with the answer, that it's so the kids don't slide down the hill!? Yeah, okay and the album is coming out next week!!! Also, my drive around the track mysteriously fails to happen!?? While we are sound checking, there are cars flippin' around out there having fun, but the minute we stop and I hit up the promóter rep for my turn, they give me some song and dance about a curfew and the track is being closed!!! Very convenient, eh!??! Tony??? Mensch??? We go thru' everything else for tomorrow, like the pyro-cues, and deal with the fact that the Snakepit is so huge, Jaymz is in a different time zone than I am, when he is out at the tip, and how that affects us playing the same song at the same time, but thru' the miracle of monitors and time delays, the shit is dealt with!! Let's do a fucken gig!! Man, I'm pumped!!

——————————— I KNOW YOU WON'T BELIEVE THIS, BUT I HAVE THIS SUPERSTITION, THAT THE NIGHT BEFORE REALLY, REALLY BIG GIGS, I DON'T

DRINK!! SO ONCE WE ARE BACK IN LONDON, I DECIDE TO LAY LOW. I GRAB ADAM AND VINNIE (SEE THE CREDITS OF THE LONG FOUR HOUR VIDEO!!) AND DECIDE THAT A GREAT LOW-KEY PLACE TO HANG IS "THE BOMBAY BRASSERIE" FOR SOME GOOD SNACKS AND A HEALTHY HELPING OF "PERRIER." WE GET OURSELVES SITUATED, ORDER AND... OOOHHHHH NOOOOO, HERE COMES A BUNCH OF LONGHAIRS... IT'S FUCKEN SLASH AND HIS BAND!!!!! MY IDEA OF A QUIET MEAL JUST WENT HAYWIRE!!! AFTER 10 MINUTES OF HELLOS, HUGS AND TAP-DANCING, I FINALLY CONVINCE THEM THAT, "THANKS, BUT NO THANKS!!" I'M GONNA BE LOW KEY TONIGHT, WHICH IS BASICALLY THE FIRST TIME EVER FOR ME, THAT HAS HAPPENED AROUND SLASH. THEY ARE QUITE PERSISTENT OVER THE NEXT HOUR, BUT I RISE ABOVE EASY TEMPTATION AND GO THE FUCK HOME, SOBER AS A BABY IN A NUN'S WOMB!!!!... FOR YOU!!!! (YOU CAN GO PUKE NOW)!!! —————————

DONINGTON — SOUND CHECK

23

DONINGTON – GIG

    IT'S FUCKEN D-DAY!!!!!! We are headlinin' Donington!!! After workin' our way up the bill for 10 years, we finally get to close, play in the dark, be the last band on before the fireworks, etc... Yah fucken hoo!! For some reason, I feel a lot calmer than I usually do in these situations and something inside me sez it's gonna be a "top" day!! When we last played here in '91 with AC/DC, I was really petrified and hid in the dressing room the whole afternoon and was basically a miserable cunt, which everybody picked up on. But right now, that's about 12,000 beers ago and I'm a happier guy all around and it's the new happy "Metallica" and I should just get the fuck on with it, instead of giving you all this psychological bullshit... So it was a great day, everybody was in a good mood, the other bands kicked ass, we played great and it was a huge fucken success!! Good-bye!!

―――――――――――――――― ACTUALLY... IT WAS PRETTY WEIRD TO WAKE UP AT NOON IN LONDON AND KNOW THE 2ND BAND WAS ALREADY ON STAGE. WHAT IF WE HAD OVERSLEPT?? BACK ON THE 'COPTER AGAIN (I CAN FLY THE FUCKEN THING MYSELF SOON!!), AND-BOOM- TOUCHDOWN IN THE WARZONE AROUND 4 P.M. ALL THE BANDS WERE HANGIN' AROUND IN THE DRESSING ROOM AREA AND EVERYBODY SEEMED TO BE PRETTY UP, EVEN THE GUYS IN SLAYER SEEMED TO BE IN A JOLLY MOOD. WHAT'S UP WITH THIS!! DID SOMEBODY PUT HAPPY PILLS IN THE FUCKEN WATER OR SOMETHING!!?? I KNOW, AS YOU ARE READING THIS, THE WORDS "HAPPY" AND "GOOD MOOD" KEEP APPEARING, BUT WHEN I SIT HERE A FEW DAYS LATER AND THINK BACK ON IT, THE OVERALL VIBE WUZ JUST REALLY COOL AND EVEN WHEN TALKIN' TO OTHERS ABOUT THE DAY, THESE SAME ADVERBS KEEP COMING UP. SORRY!! I GOT A CHANCE TO CATCH A FEW SONGS BY SLAYER (STRANGE TO SEE THEM IN FULL DAYLIGHT!) AND SKID ROW (A LOT RAWER THAN LAST TIME I SEEN 'EM!), IN BETWEEN THE USUAL "YOU GOTTA GO TALK TO MTV," "JUST SAY HI TO THE GUY FROM THE ITALIAN RECORD COMPANY," "CAN WE GET A PIC OF YOU AND SNAKE TOGETHER??" BUT IT WAS GREAT SEEIN' A LOT OF PEOPLE WHO I HADN'T SEEN FOR A WHILE. I THINK HOW GREAT IT WOULD BE TO HANG OUT HERE AS A GUEST, HAVE A FEW BEERS, AND... "LARS, 15 MINUTES 'TIL WE ARE ON!!" OH, WELL, NICE THOUGHT!!! ――――――――――――――

    "Due to the death of heavy metal, Metallica have been cancelled. Please exit in an orderly fashion." I think a few fuckers actually believed our attempt at a humorous intro... They wish!! "Fuck you... Bread-faaaaannnnn!!!!" Jaymz subtly announces and off we fucken go!!!!

    About halfway thru' the set I realize I haven't really fucked up yet. Usually I can't say that halfway thru' the first song. Wow!! Big gigs like these are a total blur, cuz you are just so focused on what you are doin', but when I come up for air, it feels fucken great. We are crushing!! Without sounding too corny, it's really cool bein' back in a situation or an environment you are totally familiar and comfortable with and you kinda realize this is why you do this shit in the first place!! Moments later, we are in my favorite

part of the set, the (new'ish') jam at the ass end of 'Seek,' which is the part of the set where we really get a chance to loosen up (remember!!! New songs!!! Loose!!!) and all of a sudden… 'So Fucken What!!' hovers… "Goodnight, we will see ya next year with a new album and tour"… Time flies when you're havin' fun!!! Then it's time for the fireworks from hell (accompanied by the very fitting "Heavy Metal Rules") and there you go!!! Back in the dressing room, we realize we couldn't have scripted a better gig and we kinda wonder why these two gigs this week are among the best we've ever played!!?? No answer, and anyway, the blue bottle of death looms in the corner. Hello!! There is an after show party in Birmingham for all the bands and assorted liggers and after a few, this seems more & more inviting!! We do a caravan vibe with four "vehicles" for the hour long drive there and are very lucky we don't get shot (we would've in the States!!!), when all the cars pull over on a residential street and about 10 of us get out and piss on this guy's white fence, literally 10 feet from his house!! The next six hours are spent trying to rid the Birmingham area of booze, and since everybody from the gig is there, this comes very close to happening. But I'm sure you don't want to hear boring stories from this session, so around 6 a.m. I head back to London or wherever the fuck I ended up!! Good morning and good night!!!!

————————————————— THE ONLY PLACE IN EUROPE THEY HAVE A TACO BELL IS IN LONDON AND AROUND 5 P.M., WHEN I WAKE UP, SOME MAGNETIC FORCE DRAWS ME TO LEICESTER SQUARE FOR THE BEST HANGOVER REMEDY YOU CAN GET FOR UNDER $10. AS I SIT IN THE TAXI, STILL RUBBING SLEEP FROM MY EYES, I THINK BACK TO YESTERDAY AND HOW "PERFECT" EVERYTHING WENT (EVEN JEFF HANNEMAN SAID HELLO TO ME, SO WE CAN'T BE OVER YET!!)… OH SHIT THERE WAS ONE SEMI DARK CLOUD!! WHEN I FINALLY WENT INTO THE AREA THAT WAS RESERVED FOR ALL YOU CLUBBERS AND US TO HANG IN AND BULLSHIT AND SO ON, ALL OF YOU GUYS HAD LEFT!! NOT ONE FUCKEN PERSON!! WHEN WE TALKED ABOUT THIS SETUP LATER, WE REALIZED THAT THIS WAS DEFINITELY NOT THE WAY TO DO THIS KIND OF "MEET & GREET" THING, AND BELIEVE ME, THIS WILL BE WORKED OUT FOR THE NEXT GIGS!! WE HAVE ONLY HAD THIS CLUB GOING FOR 18 MONTHS AND OBVIOUSLY WE FIX THE FUCKED UP SHIT AS WE GO ALONG!! SORRY ABOUT THAT ONE!! (CUE THE MUSIC FOR THE TAP-DANCING!!!)

I GET DROPPED OFF, AND WALK TO WHERE THE TACO BELL IS, OR AS IT TURNS OUT, WAS, CUZ NOW THE JOINT IS A FUCKEN SHOE STORE, WITH NOT A TACO SHELL IN FUCKEN SIGHT!! I SHOULDA STAYED IN BED!!! TIME TO GET THE FUCK OUT OF ENGLAND, THANK YOU VERY MUCH!!! —————————————————

"If you look out the window now, you can see where the tree line ends!!" Thanks Captain!! In other words, we are approaching tundra and we are really fucken far north. I guess the polar bears are next!! It's five days later, we have been flying for five hours and we are on our way into another unknown!! Tuktauukksomethingtuk, here we come!! A few months ago this seemed like a good way to break from the recordings, then came the gigs in England, but now this is finally reality. "Courtney missed her plane in Seattle, a little while ago and now we have to stop over and pick her up!!" Tony is walking down the aisle in the plane, trying to wind us up for a few seconds. Kirk has a look of horror on his face, but I assure him this is only a windup, not really calming myself down in the process!! But since my dad lives in Seattle, I soon recognize the city from a comfortable 37,000 feet, and tell Kirk he's ok. This can end up being a long 36 hours!! After a stop-over in Inuvik(?), we change to a small "plane" (??) and the word "W.A.S.P" is uttered a few times around the cabin (long fucken story!). We stay at a comfortable 2,000 feet(??) and a few minutes later Gaktibumfuck is in sight. Okay!! This place is tiny!! The tent where the gig is takes up about half the town. As we do a fly over, we are fed a few details by our friendly Molson rep, main one being that the town is in total darkness for six months of the year and that it is a "dry" town (no alcohol), which seems like an odd place for a beer party. Don't ask!!!

We go straight to the tent for a 'check, and quickly realize, we have played far smaller and worse set up gigs than this, and not even that long ago!! The mood is very loose and somebody decides to get some gin martinis going, so we jam for about 90 minutes, while things get sillier & sillier from drinking freezing martinis in 25 degree weather (that's very cold for our non-fahrenheit friends)!!!!! Kirk starts his newfound cigar vibe, which is a sure sign that things will get out of hand and we grab our photog, Mark, to do a few snaps before shit gets too ugly. There is a rumor of a party in the local hockey rink, with the guys (and girls!) from the other bands, but upon closer inspection, everybody seems to be doing their own thing, in various different mental states, so we decide to keep drinking and doing photos. It's 11 p.m. and still light!! Time for another one, "Yeah, good, hold that position!!" Good thing I got my shades on!! I'm seeing three photographers!! Time to retire soon!!!

Everybody is staying in the only two hotels around (basically this event has taken the town over!!) and all the band and managerial people are in this one. I think I'm the first one up!!! Linda & me head down to the kitchen and soon a few others, including Peter Mensch, show up and we decide to do our own breakfast in the kitchen, since the chef is obviously still zonked out!! Eggs, bacon, juice, "Let's start the grill, to do the bacon..." "It must be this knob," sez Mensch and... eh... five minutes later the bacon is black, the kitchen is filled with smoke and... "Get the fuck out of my kitchen!!!!" And

a good morning to you too!! The owner/chef is awake and not real happy!! "Thirty seconds more and all the fire-alarms would have gone off!!!!" It turns out, it was that knob, but somebody(???) had turned it on to full power, 700 degrees, and now we hear stories about 2–3 hour clean-up jobs, just to scrape the shit off!! I think it's time to go for a walk!!!!

WE HAVE NEVER BEFORE PLAYED A SHOW WHERE WE MET EACH INDIVIDUAL BEFORE THE GIG, SO THIS IS A FIRST. WE ARE IN THE SCHOOL AUDITORIUM AND WHAT HAD ORIGINALLY BEEN A "Q & A" SESSION ENDED UP AS A "SHAKE HANDS WITH EVERYBODY IN TOWN" VIBE. COOL. DIFFERENT. A LOT OF SHAKIN' HANDS, BUT EVERYBODY IS VERY HAPPY (THERE IS THAT WORD AGAIN!!) THAT WE ARE THERE, AND IT'S INTERESTING TO HEAR FEEDBACK FROM THE PEOPLE WHOSE TOWN MOLSON HAS BASICALLY INVADED. EVEN THE MAYOR AND THE TRIBAL ELDERS COME OVER AND WE PAY OUR MUTUAL RESPECTS!! VERY CIVILIZED!! THEN IT'S TIME FOR THE 300 OR SO CONTEST WINNERS TO COME ROARING THRU', AND FOR THIS THE OTHER THREE BANDS (HOLE, VERUCA SALT & MOIST) JOIN US. THREE HOURS, 300 AUTOGRAPHS (AND ONE MARRIAGE PROPOSAL!!) LATER, WE HEAD OVER TO THE GIG (300 FEET AWAY) FAIRLY EXHAUSTED, BUT THEN AGAIN, THIS IS A SPECIAL VIBE, SO WHO GIVES A FUCK!!!!

We are sittin' in the dressing "room" and I bounce the idea off Jaymz, to maybe do a slightly shorter set than the last couple, due to the fact that there is no alcohol served, and everybody is over 21... We re-arrange the set list slightly (is anybody really gonna miss 'Breadfan' in Fucktishittuk??) and off we go once more!! This turns out to be by far the most fun gig of the three, the songs are sittin' really good now and the tent vibe is actually pretty fun. Cuz of the cold, I play in jeans, probably for the first time ever, and after a few songs I know why. I soon realize it's, probably, also the last!!!! When we go back up for the encore, Flemming hands me a martini, and when I look around, everybody else has got one, so bottoms up... 'So Fucken What' once again... Goodnight and Bob's your uncle!!

AFTERWARDS, WE SIT AROUND AND TRY AND ANSWER THE QUESTION OF WHY THESE THREE GIGS TURNED OUT TO BE AMONG THE VERY BEST WE HAVE EVER PLAYED!!!! "CUZ IT WAS ONLY THREE, WITH A LOT OF DAYS OFF IN BETWEEN!!," "CUZ WE ARE A LOT BETTER PLAYERS, AFTER BEING IN THE STUDIO, THAN WE USED TO BE!!," "CUZ MAYBE WE HAVE LEARNED TO RELAX MORE AND ACTUALLY (SHOCK, HORROR!!) HAVE FUN ON STAGE!!!," "CUZ THIS AND THAT!!" WHATEVER, WHO GIVES A FUCK, BLUE BOTTLE COME HOME TO DADDY... WE SAY OUR GOODBYES, HEAD TO THE AIRPORT, JUST AS IT STARTS SNOWING, AND REVERSE OUR TRAVELS FROM 36 HOURS EARLIER, THIS TIME GUIDED BY SOME INCREDIBLE NORTHERN LIGHTS AT CRUISING ALTITUDE... SIX HOURS LATER, THE BEAUTIFUL CITY OF OAKLAND HOVERS ON THE HORIZON AND WITH THE PRECEDING WEEK AND A HALF SAFELY BEHIND US, WE NOW GO STRAIGHT TO THE STUDIO FROM THE AIRPORT (AT 6 A.M.) TO CONTINUE ON THIS FUCKEN RECORD, SO WE CAN GET IT TO YOU AS SOON AS POSSIBLE, CUZ WE CARE.......... BOB!?!?.....................

WOW, WHAT A MOUTHFUL!!

LOVE, LARS

27

Metallica Scrapbook

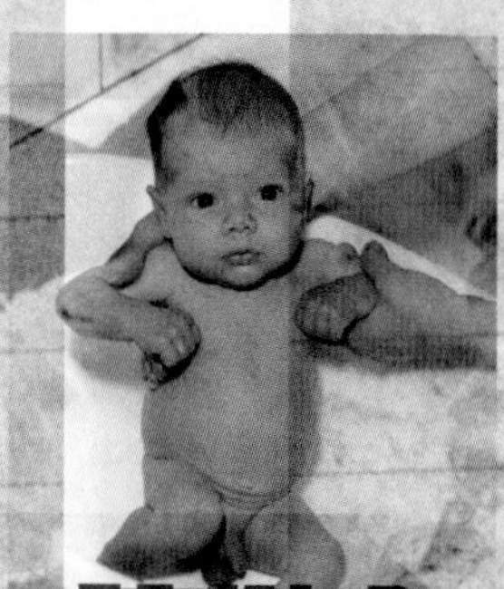

Wow! I was better hung at 6 weeks than I am now!

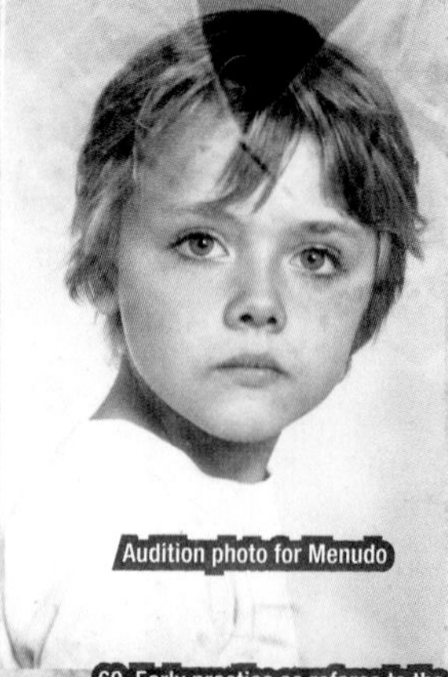

Audition photo for Menudo

66, Lost in London zoo. Where is the tour bus?

Morocco 75, Early posing.

69, Early practice as referee to the Jaymz/Dave Mustaine quarrels.

Me, Pop and the French Alps

64, My half a year birthday.

Wimbledon 1966

Feeding time at the zoo! Mom and Dad feeding the chimp.

Helping dad

71, Slow news week in the Danish press.

Dreaming wishfully of being the next Bjorn Borg

68, Me with only one ball... but a really large racquet.

76, Jamming with Deep Purple live (in my dreams!)

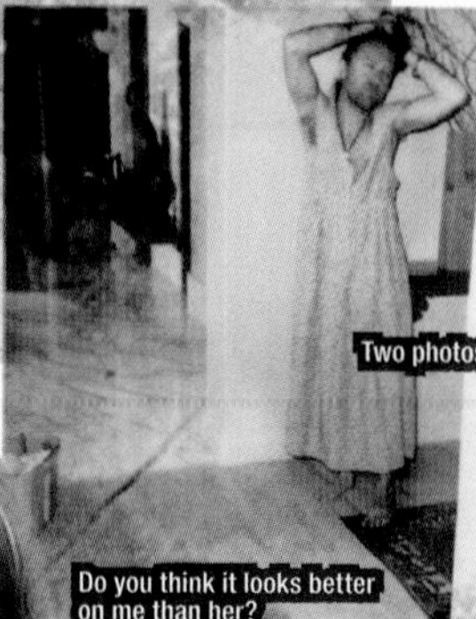

Lars Ulrich

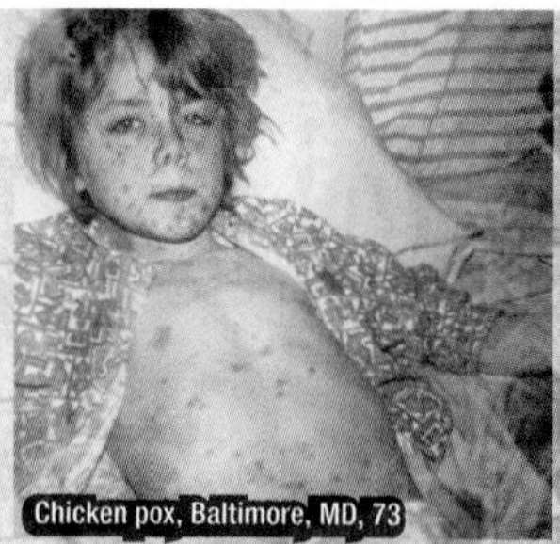

Chicken pox, Baltimore, MD, 73

1966, Dad! I've got sand under my foreskin!

1991, My Sebastian Bach impersonation.

Two photos you shouldn't see!!!

Do you think it looks better on me than her?

Winger audition photo

Palau 1994... enjoying a tropical water dive.

GRADUATE #50 from Back Bay High School

LARS ULRICH   June 16, 1982

High school graduation. 1982

Halloween 93, Dressed as a Danish 'Roligan' football supporter.

Proof that my parents really are my parents.

Quarteao du Pinga + 1 on
a bit of the 'ol hop & grain

63, 1st Christmas with brother Greg
in background

Jason at one year of age

One of my bass heroes, Mike Dean
of COC and me at Donington '95

Christmas 67, Michigan

May 77, 1st band "Diamond"

Christmas 1981
Phoenix, Arizona

his greeted me on my 1st Metallichristmas
at home in Michigan

Christmas 83,
just a few months pre-Flotsam

68, 1st grade Niles, Michigan

Devilock at the 100 Club

Cuttin' loose at the Chophouse

'95, Grandpa and Grandma Newsted
with Elizabeth and myself.

Christmas in Brazil with Sepultura

1983, Scottsdale, Arizona. 3rd line-up of Dogz L-R:
Kelly Smith, Jason Newsted, Eric A.K., Donny Crist, Mark Vasquez

Jason Newsted

31

James Hetfield

A few Christmas photos from the early 70's.

Peace off, man!

I am saying fucking cheese!

My rookie year!

Where's the pot dude?!

Are you sure this will work, Lars?

Sushi anyone?

Whaddya mean I gotta give it back?!!

Yo ho ho and a bottle of rum milk.

Hey mine's bigger than yours!

Hopefully the death of leisure suits.

Beware the real Ktulu has risen!

I wonder what Mom meant by trolling for sharks???

OK Dad you can dig us up now... Dad... Dad?!

First haircut!

Catholic schoolboy thinking of Satan!

Excuse me, sunglasses, PARTYING and attitude started very early for me!

The original Gerber Baby!

Kirk Hammett

Another early Exodus shot, probably in someone's garage.

Sunglasses and attitude started very early for me!

An early Exodus gig.

you think a pocket protector uld look good with this?

Oh, yeah, wanna buy a shirt?

33

A DAY IN THE LIFE

So it's "morning," and I stumble out to check today's FedEx fodder and... aaarrgghhh!!!... it's here!! Once again, it's that time!! The xeroxed rough outline of the next SO WHAT!, ready to be "edited" and glanced over by its four senior editors and as usual the magazine is all done, apart from two blank pages with the words "Lars' Article," which means it's once again high noon and time for me to write my promised piece, which I usually get around to within... eh... let's just say as soon as I can (cough!!).

Anyways, with this issue there were two more blank pages than usual. Quite strange!!! Surely nobody within the Metallica organization lags more behind time-wise than I do, but what have we here...??? Two blank pages with the words "Bob Rock's Article" written all over them!!

Wow!!!! Upon close investigation, it turns out, probably in a (brief) moment of temporary Metallica overload, Bob promised our beloved whipcracker, Tony Smith, founding editor, a piece for this here issue about what really goes on in the studio, you know, **"A Day In The Life Of Bob Rock And How Metallica Slowly Torture And Drive Me To An Early Retirement And Legal Insanity!!"** You know, one of those jobs!! So over the last few days, I have had the self-imposed task (and quite enjoying it, thank you!!) of basically reminding Bob, roughly every 90 seconds or whenever Kirk's fingers stop surfing his fretboard, that he needs to cough up his article!! This is usually followed by a quick change of topics: discussing the weather, details from obscure Loverboy album from 1956 he worked on, or how he looks forward to his next cooking class that him and R_ _ _ _ take every Wednesday!!!! But I nail him and nail him and fuckin' nail him, and you know why?? Because I finished my shit for this issue (fairly) quickly and can go to the studio with a clear conscience, that for once (actually, for the first time!!) I am not the one preventing this wonderful piece of journalistic nonsense from arriving on your doorstep!!!!

"Bi-de-le-dew, bi-de-le-dew." Me and Bob are still working with Kirk ("The Hammer," "Mr. Elite '94," "The Pimp," "The Best Guitar Player In The World... And I Love It"... etc. ... (very inside stuff!)), and of course the torture continues. The excuses become better and better (or worse, depending on how you look at it!)... "I don't know how to write," "What would I actually write about?," "Are you sure I promised this to Tony?," "Why would the kids care about what I have to say?" and the cream of them all... ready??? "I don't have the time!!" Aaaaarrggghhhh!!! Coming from a man who spends a few hours on a midweek morning preparing sophisticated French cream sauces for a school project, who scares the residents of the small idyllic northern Californian town, where he is currently holed up, with his early morning jogs and Tai-chi somethin' or other workouts, and gets the old cran-tini vibe going at random moments with no official warnings!!! "I don't have time!!??" (Yawn, sigh, cough... I didn't get a hhrruummpphh out of that guy!!??). Anyway, after painting scenes of teary-eyed Metallica fans sittin' around wondering whether we have abandoned them forever, and being on the brink of total mind collapse, sending life-threatening hate mail to Tony Smith, wondering where the fuck their next SO WHAT! is, Bob finally utters the phrase that will haunt him for quite some time... **"Lars, I just can't fuckin' do it. Will you help me?? Will you write it for me??!!"** As me and Kirk fall on our ("leatherpant") asses in disbelief, the end has obviously been reached for Mr. Rock!! Of all 5 billion people plus on this planet, he wants me to write his story!!

Isn't there somebody he would trust maybe slightly more??? Oh, well, I guess it's all taken a bigger toll on him than I had thought!! Bob, your wish is my command!!! Here goes...

# of BOB ROCK

by Bob Rock

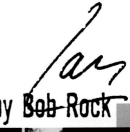

"A DAY IN THE LIFE OF BOB ROCK" BY SOMEONE WHO KNOWS…

I get up in the morning usually around eight. For some reason, no matter when I go to bed, I always wake up at eight. I understand it has something to do with advancing in age. My first thoughts always go to the project. I usually smile as I think of how lucky I am to work with such talented musicians and wonderful human beings as Lars, James, Kirk and Jason. Their new songs and approach for their current record is absolutely fantastic and I consider myself privileged to be involved. Next I call my wife and tell her and the kids what a great time I am having in the studio and how much easier it is to work with them this time around and how much they have matured since the "Black"

album. Then I go for my morning jog, sweat all over town, and nearly cause traffic accidents. Before I go to the studio, I listen to the new Oasis album, so I can answer Lars when he sits there and asks me why they are so good and why Noel is the best song writer around today (next to James of course – Lars). I arrive at the studio and as usual, the guys are all there before me preparing their parts, eating, warming up and generally being ready, so

that when I arrive, we can always start right away. The sessions then get going and I am always pleased with how carefully they listen to my ideas, and how the creative vibe at any given time is somewhere between stunning and euphoric!! I am also really happy with how knowledgeable the guys are about what they want and how to get it and, like I said before, the progress they have made as songwriters and musicians still amazes me! We usually break for dinner around seven, and I often order tofu burgers, because it's… well, healthy, of course!! It's amazing how much they taste like real burgers sometimes! The recording then continues uninterrupted for the rest of the evening, 'til around midnight when the guys usually burn out. I always want to keep going, but the guys, from concentrating so much on their parts all day, are really tired. The last thing we do is talk about the scheduling the next couple of days and even though they always want to keep going and work weekends and holidays, I feel it's good to have a few days off!! Actually, the funny thing about those Shark hockey games they go to, is that the home games always seem to fall on days off, which is great, but I know the guys would be here at the studio anyway, if the games were on work days. The guys always leave right away, the minute the sessions are done, but I always stay for a couple of extra hours, do rough mixes with Randy, and focus on new ideas and what I can add to the project the next few days. Then it's home again, with a satisfied smile on my face that we pushed ourselves as far as we could that day, and the boundaries of hard rock were once again moved a step further away from the expected. As I put my head on the pillow, the last thing flashing through my mind is the same as the first thought of the day, **"I love Metallica and my life,"** and with that, I roll over, smile and go off to never-never land!!!! ●

WHIPLASH

THE BAND ANSWERS FAN QUESTIONS

I wanted to know if any members of Metallica smoke and if so, which members?
Donna S., Canada

JH: Only when I'm on fire.
LU: Fuck no!

When and why did you decide to make music your career?
Emilie D., Albany, NY

JH: After the "Black" album.
KH: When my career as a nun failed me.
JN: About 1980 at age 17, I wanted to do something that really meant a lot to me, at least try it before I went the college / occupation route.
LU: Fuck knows! At that point in time it seemed like the right thing to do.

Kirk, you seem to be the quiet one. Do you like to party hard, or just sit back and relax?
Angela C., Middletown, ID

KH: You obviously don't know me! I just don't let on that I'm actually a raving lunatic when I get drunk or whatever!!! I am a bit moody, and so I just don't feel like communicating to people some of the time, that's all.

Larz, if I sent you $50 could you make me a copy of 'No Life 'Til Leather' like you did for others in the early dayz? I know $50 might not mean anything to you guys (except for Jason), but maybe you could put it towards the fan club.
Jim H., Minneapolis, MN

LU: Don't forget to send a return address also.
JN: $50 is $50 whether you have $100 or a squillion $.
JH: I'll do it for $45.

Kirk, why do you play with your middle finger sticking out, is it habit or image?
Jaime C., Plano, TX

KH: I like flipping off everyone and getting away with it! I never really noticed that my finger stuck out 'til I started seeing pix of myself playing live, and I thought that it was pretty funny, actually!

Do you guys wear earplugs or anything to protect your hearing? James, are your arms and hands insured?
Aida N., Bronx, NY

JH: What? What about the rest, Mrs. Bobbitt?
LU: Yeah, all four of us. Not only protects hearing but makes on stage sound more definable.
JN: We all wear earplugs on stage – it's the smart thing to do.

I was very disappointed when I was looking through the 'Leper Messiah' lyrics. I always knew that the song wasn't one of the nicest Metallica songs, but I didn't think it was so negative. Is it a song that you would rethink if you guys were going to do it again?
Gary K., Wayne, NJ

JH: A negative Metallica song? Sorry, Reverend Gary.
LU: Since everything we do is 100% instinctive, I never question things we've done.
JN: Hell no – it is excellent the way that it is. What bothers you about it so much? Jaymz is just speaking truth!
KH: Are you considering a job in the Television Evangelist field?

What was the most embarrassing thing that ever happened on stage? You all are really good looking, has anybody ever thought about getting into movies?
Nikki Y., Edison, NJ

KH: I once fell down on stage and Lars started laughing at me, I was really embarassed, so I tried to look cool and tackled him for laughing at me!!!
JN: I fell down on stage in one of my first U.S. 'Tallica shows and last tour I fucked up my neck bad and couldn't play for a few minutes. That sucked. Lars wants to be in pictures, he practices constantly.
JH: Button popped and zipper broke (I was excited.) I sneak into movies once a week.
LU: Yes – I want to follow the great paths of rockstars turned movie stars such as Vince Neil, Brett Michaels and Janie Lane!! As for embar-

rassing, pick one: Houston '89, something hits me on the forehead while we are playing. I stop in the middle of a song and ask James to announce that if anyone throws anything else, we will leave the stage. We finish the show without incident. After the show my drum tech informs me that I had actually hit myself with a drumstick!... or Madison, WI '91. During 'Four Horsemen,' the drumkit I am playing on begins to be lowered under the stage, instead of the other kit on the other side of the stage. Try playing whilst you are under a stage that the other guys are on top of!!

Kirk, my girlfriend and I have been going out for the past four years and we are getting married in the fall. Can you give me/us any advice?
Eric T., West Lafayette, ID

KH: What do I look like, Ann Landers??? O.K., if you really want to know, I advise mass quantities of anti-depressants be available at all times during this, and everything will be just fine.

How do you choose the songs you play in concert?
Eric G., Canada

LU: The ones we can play, ha-ha! Seriously, I'm the one that basically gets stuck with writing the set list. I try to balance it out as much as possible with all the different sides of Metallica. When you have a new album, obviously, we want to throw in a bunch of new stuff and still try and create a good dynamic balance. Old/new, faster/slower, harder/mellower... and of course we try and play different songs when returning to a city for the second or third time on one tour.

Has Metallica ever been asked to record a song for a movie soundtrack?
Lisa H., Fairfax, VA

JN: Yes, we've been approached a few different times to do movie stuff, but no dice.
JH: The sequel to the children's movie 'Bambi' – 'Bambi II: The Bloodletting.'
LU: Yes – many times. Generally we turn the things down, but when/if the movie with the right overall vibe comes along we might jump on it.

Why isn't '...Thingy' played live more often?
Brandon B., Spring, TX

JH: Too heavy, it hurts Lars' ears.
LU: Too heavy, it hurts James' bowels.

What do you all consider as your best album?
Brian R., Gallatin, TN

JH: "Ride..." and the "Black" album.
LU: "(What's The Story) Morning Glory?"
JN: The new album is the best one, another is "Master of Puppets."

Lars, why do you tape up your fingers to play? I noticed in one of your videos you guys were putting something on (maybe oil). What is it and what purpose does it serve? Jaymz when and why did you switch from the Gibson to the ESP Explorer? Do you guys have an extensive collection of bootlegs (or shows you wanted recorded) from your shows? Are there any shows you wish you had?
Dan W., Rochester, NY

JH: I like the Explorer shape but some things I didn't like. ESP can custom make them with different woods, fret boards, inlays, etc. the way I want them. Lars oils up to slip into his spandex. I wish I had some more Misfits footage.
LU: I don't do that anymore because of the Easton sticks I am using now. But I used to, 'cuz of the green gauze tape I used to wrap my sticks in was very rough and gave me blisters. I have a fairly big collection, certainly not everything out there. Cool fans/friends keep me up to date with what is out there. There are certainly other bands' bootlegs I'd like to have!!

Jaymz, what do you think about the Raiderz getting their asses back in Oakland?
Rob M., West Palm Beach, FL

JH: Fuckin' great! Other body parts should follow soon.

How long does it take for an album to be released once recording is done?
Andra E., Hayward, CA

JN: Once the tapes are delivered to the record company it can take approximately one to three months.
LU: It depends on what kind of hurry you're in. Minimum is three weeks, average is six to eight weeks.

What would you guys say to someone who said that your lyrics are rude and that your music is the reason why kids are shooting and robbing people?
Elizabeth K., Memphis, TN

LU: Oh God – another letter from Tennessee!
JN: I would say that they're wrong.
JH: Bullshit! Now gimme your wallet before I shoot you!!

Jason, in SO WHAT! vol.2, issue 2 on page 35, the picture of you in the studio you sorta look like Jules (Samuel Jackson) from "Pulp Fiction." What's up with the fuckin' hair?
Dan L., St. Pete Beach, FL

JN: The hair does whatever it wants to, dig it Dan.

Was the song 'Of Wolf And Man' inspired by "The Wolf's Hour" by Robert M. McCammon or any other book?
Warren V., Felton, PA

JH: It was inspired by the movie 'Wolfen.'

Kirk, how do you come up with your guitar solos? I try to, but hell it doesn't work for me.
Ken W., Walnut Creek, CA

KH: Coming up with guitar solos is something that takes a lot of time to learn how to do. It all begins with improvisation, when you come up with a part that you've improvised and you like it, you keep it and go to the next part, etc., until you have a solo. Then you have to kind of arrange it, come up with an intro, an outro, little melodies and whatever. My newest thing is to take melodies from songs I have heard on the radio that I think are particularly catchy and bring them into the songs. There really isn't one way to do it though, and this is just one approach to doing this.
JH: What's wrong with playing rhythm guitar... huh?

Of all your songs which is the most difficult (technical or otherwise) for each of you to play?
Kevin D., Springfield, MO

KH: '...And Justice For All' was a bit much for me to play live because I couldn't bear watching the people up front start to yawn at about the eighth or ninth minute of the song.

With so many people who worship the ground Metallica walks on, how does it affect you? Do you sometimes find yourselves becoming arrogant?
Alex L., Tulsa, OK

JN: It affects me in weird ways, sometimes it's just unavoidable – human is human. I feel that I have a good handle on my 'low-keyness' now.

JH: No, and how DARE you bother The Mighty Hetfield with that meaningless little comment, you peon.

Kirk, I recently saw you play at Donington in England and it appears that you have got rid of your dreadlocks. Many people, including myself, thought they were cool, so why did you get rid of them so soon after getting them done? Also, at Donington, what the hell was the song attached to the end of 'Harvester of Sorrow?'
Scott B., Scotland

KH: I got rid of the dreads because people were confusing me with Lenny whatsit...! The thing at the end of 'Harvester...' was just some little ditty I came up with so as to make time for a guitar change.

Kirk, while running across the stage during a concert have you ever tripped and fell?
Joe N., Medford, NJ

KH: I have fallen numerous times and I always have to take a minute to laugh cuz I think it is so damn funny!! One time in Switzerland I fell completely off stage and landed on a road case.

Are you still able to walk around the town you live in and do your errands peacefully? Or do people pester you a little more after the success you had with the last album?
Helena J., Bar Mills, ME

JN: I can go anywhere, anytime with no problems. People are usually very cool.
KH: I live in San Francisco, and people really don't give a shit. ●

3

There is only love in this room

metallica, the interview

not so long ago,

I realized that one of the few things Metallica had never done was allow themselves to be sat down and interviewed together for a couple of hours. There may have been the odd fortuitous situation where a journalist came across them all in a room, but one would always sneak away. I put this to Lars Ulrich and he agreed that yes, it hadn't ever been done properly before. I asked him what he thought would happen if it was done now, and he said he could see it ending up as a wise-ass session. I disagreed. He thought some more about it. Put it to the others in the band. And here we are. What follows is undoubtedly the most unique Metallica interview in many years. Unique because it happened. Because topics were discussed which, quite frankly, no one has ever got the band members to discuss individually let alone together.

The evening took place at The Plant Studios in Sausalito, California where Metallica have fortressed themselves, on Friday, February 2, 1996.

Our meeting was the sole item on everyone's agenda. The band came in together, relaxed, cheerful but perhaps with a hint of apprehension. Lars, James, Jason and Kirk all sat within a few feet of each other around the dining room table, myself at the head of it directing the order of conversation. Until Lars had some wine about fifteen minutes before fatigue set in, no-one was drinking anything other than water. Kirk and James lit up two enormous Cuban cigars and proceeded to puff them down to stubs. And photographer Mark Leialoha paced quietly around taking photos as things happened. So as you can enjoy the conversation exactly as it ran, what follows is a totally unedited transcript. A closing thought before you start: so shocked were the band at their own candor, they came to view the whole evening as therapy and to myself as "Doctor C."

We'll start with a light topic! Just how long has it taken for you to be comfortable with each other? Are you all comfortable in the same room doing things like this?

LARS ULRICH (LU): Yeah.
KIRK HAMMETT (KH): We always have been comfortable with each other.

Hmmm... it just seems that sometimes you spend a lot of time separate to each other especially in recording situations.

LU: I think we've spent more time together on this album than we have on any other before. It used to be me and James doing a lot of stuff just the two of us, and we started opening up a lot more to the group thing with Bob (Rock) the last time. He thought what was missing on the "...Justice" thing was a group sound, a group vibe that we had live. So he started talking to us about trying to capture that in the studio. We started on it with the last record and we've really honed in on it with this one. This is the most time we've ever spent together on a record.

JASON NEWSTED (JN): When we all played together this time to record Lars' drum tracks, it was leaps and bounds more comfortable and more fun and productive than it was on the last record. The last record was kinda weird doing that with his drums, being in L.A. and everything, but this time when we did it with him it worked out to be good for everybody and especially best for him, the vibe of everybody being there knowing what was at stake, being more serious. Taking care of business really, much better.

KH: And tons of vibe. You could feel it tracking off the floor when we were tracking certain songs, and it felt so great!

LU: There's actually stuff of what you heard where there's the whole band off the floor. I mean off the floor! If you'd said that to us six months ago or five years ago that would've been unheard of. Bob has pushed and pushed for that group Metallica thing to come across, and I think we're finally 101% comfortable with it. One can say, 'why did it take so long,' and whatever, but it's just a natural evolvement process and it works!

JN: The studio thing has definitely gotten more comfortable and I think since everybody has their own life, separate life really strong in its own way with their own set of friends, I think we're really comfortable when we do get together and do things like this. Like the big 'cool' photo shoot we did two weeks ago, or going to dinner, when we do get focused and it's always comfortable.

You've lead me into dealing with the differences in each other. It seemed to me when you were in the middle of doing the last record in L.A. that it was nearly impossible for you all to be in the same room at the same time. Right or wrong, was that the toughest time? Talk about looking at each other as individuals and saying, 'all right, I can deal with him,' when did that start to happen more?

JN: When we grew up, being able to have patience with each other.
JAMES HETFIELD (JH): Getting away from each other helped us grow not apart but in our own ways, and then when we got back together we learned new ways of growing together. And I think that has happened in the studio as well. Lars was always, 'I have to record my drums this way,' I was, 'I have to record my vocals this way,' guitar and bass even, we were always kinda really stuck in one way. And we've kinda seen from each other how each person records their own way as well, and it's loosened up a lot.

LH: I think what happened in the year that we took off, is we got a chance to hang out in our own world more, so as you're not always living in the shadow or presence of the other guy. It was always, 'well how am I dressed? What's James going to think? What's Kirk going to think?' Do you know what I mean? You're always playing off each other so when you spend a year off from each other and suddenly come back like we did for the summer '94 tour after a year off, everybody was a lot more comfortable and confident with their own selves. And that brought a lot to the table.

JN: Since I joined the band that was the first time anybody got to go away and enjoy the fruits of the labor and all that kind of thing, that was the first time anybody got to go and be themselves and truly enjoy doing it. Whether it was gun stuff or scuba stuff or whatever stuff.

KH: I think we came to a point where our confidence grew both personally and with each other. We got more independent but within the context of our relationship together things got stronger.

The peripheral view would be that the Guns N'Roses tour was the pinnacle of everything. Obviously it was the biggest this, that and the other, but do you also think it might have been a time where you all looked and thought, 'fuck me we're either going to become like them or we're going to remember that it doesn't have to end there'...

LU: The Guns tour was the low point in terms of social. It started off high and it went down a little bit that summer of '92 and when I look back it was a bit of a low point.
KH: Definitely.
LU: We were all into our own scenes...

But was that the breaking point where you thought, 'well fuck it we're either going to become like those bastards or...'

KH: I don't think there was ever any danger of that.
JN: The thing was for bands like that, especially if you're looking at that band, we usually learn from it going, 'OK we're doing the right thing, they're doing the wrong thing,' so it made us more confident that we were doing the right thing.

Who's the first one out of all of you if there are communication problems that are building, who sits down and says, 'right, this is out of order, we need to talk about this shit,' etc, etc. Does it move like that?

LU: No it doesn't...

JN: It seems like everything just comes to a head and everybody just kinda realizes it.

LU: We deal with a lot of stuff, as you know, through sarcasm. And there comes a point where (you can talk about truth through sarcasm) when somebody says something sarcastic for the sixth time in a row, then maybe it's time...

KH: It's just our type of communication.

JN: When a guy goes home, when he's thinking about it later on, thinks about what his friends were saying to him, then the message starts to get home a little bit.

LU: We've never had many of those type of discussions, and I think maybe in the last six months we're starting to get a little more comfortable heading in that direction. I've had a couple of talks more in that direction with James, and it's not like we're in a bar drunk at four in the morning and can really say what's on our mind. This is more like you get together and it's actually daylight outside and there's no alcohol involved, and you say, 'this is maybe not so right.' That's starting to come now because, as we said ten minutes ago, everybody's more confident and comfortable in themselves. Certain things that have come up in the past couple of years, I couldn't have pictured five, eight, ten years ago those things coming up in conversation.

JN: Also we know when to take things seriously, even though we ride on lots of fun and pokin' at each other, sarcasm, we've always known when to get serious. No matter how much we disagree on things it always seems to come right in the end.

Alright, dwell on it for a moment. If each of you can, pick a point when you've been absolutely frustrated to a point where you've just thought, 'fuck this I'm gonna chin someone!' Each of you must have a moment, and if you wouldn't mind sharing it...

JN: From which month? *(much laughter)*

KH: I always seem to be late... that pisses everyone off!

JN: Are we calling it from that side or what side?

Any side... all right. I'll give you a quick lead-in...

LU: What about 'The Day I Left The Studio' by Jason 'Miserable Fuckin' Newsted?! *(more laughter)*

KH: No, hey but my angle was the best 'cause you were looking at me and I saw Jason walk in behind you right as you said that!

JH: Yeah, we saw him comin' and let you fire away.

JN: Usually when there's three guys out of the four, they always end up talkin' about the other cat that ain't there. Usually it's kept within our happy family, close company, but it always does happen. So Lars was goin' off about, who knows if it was silly shit or whatever, he was just being (adopts miserable dumb tone) 'James fuckin' this, Jason 'Miserable Fuck' Newsted, Kirk fuckin' whatever...'

JH: Hmm, it wasn't like that! *(much laughter)*

JN: This is how I think it should've been, this is how I really want it to be because if it was not like that, I'm going to cry!

LU: What was really funny about it, was that we were sitting in this very room, the three of us and a couple of other people. And you've gotta admit *(looking at Jason)* you were going through a period for a while at the very beginning of the record where you hadn't clicked in yet in terms of wavelength and vibe and stuff like that. You were maybe a little bit askew of where everyone was in terms of moods and stuff like that. I was sitting in here, we were talking about Jason being a little moody recently. So I'm sitting right on this ledge right here with the door open, and all the guys...

KH: You were talking to me and I was sitting right there in that seat *(points to mine)*.

LU: Right. So I used the phrase Jason 'Miserable Fuck' Newsted. Unbeknownst to me, Jason had walked into the room at that time and was standing right behind me.

JN: He turns, ooooo, this red.

LU: And what do you do when you get caught with your dick in your hand? You try and pretend nothing happened. He storms out of the studio, into Bob or something saying, 'I'm not going to record today.' We're sitting in here and five minutes later we hear Jason's truck pull away...

Understandably it must be said, I'd be pretty annoyed.

JH: At least you didn't hear your Porsche start up! *(much laughter)*

LU: Yeah, but me and Jason have our moments probably more than anyone else. A couple of times in a few dressing rooms we've had some cat-fights, come to blows and then we kiss and make up five minutes later. But if you're looking at the four of us, it's probably me and Jason who get through most of that stuff.

But you two (Lars and James) were butting heads pretty regularly five years before that sorted itself out, right?

JH: Between Lars and I, we've both lightened up in our own stubbornness and our own ways. We're not butting heads as much. I'm a little more open-minded to some other stuff and I don't think he's taking so much control of stuff. So both levels have come down to where it's a reasonable friendship. I think there's times when each one of us is really boiling inside and doesn't want to cause a scene or want to be the ass of everything...

Getting away from each other helped us grow not apart but in our own ways

LU: Definitely, he's right...

JH: ...On tour. Fuck, I know a lot of personal shit gets involved in it, but at one point it's like, 'fuck I am not touring anymore, this is insane.' This is after 15 months out and 'let's do two more months dude'...

Which asks the brief question, who's the first for those extra tour dates and who follows behind them?

KH: That would be Lars and I.

JH: The guys who don't sing! So anyway, you kinda boil inside, you wanna be reasonable about it, you don't wanna start yelling, 'FUCK YOU, FUCK THIS SHIT I'M OUTTA HERE!' But still, if you don't put your two cents in then, you're stepped on. You've gotta say something without being a total ass, because otherwise everyone rides you harder, 'haha, we've got him!'

JN: You have to have will, you have to be professional...

But it seems to me that this would've been a major turning point. Would that not have helped this record go more easily?

LU: What happens with arguments is that when you get to a boiling point, we're all wise enough to sit down. Literally within 15 minutes of Jason leaving the studio, he came back and we had a two hour talk about things in the studio. I told him about what I thought of what he brought to the party and he told me how he felt about coming to the party. Talking is the best, you sit down, talk the shit through and we're better at that than we've ever been before. We're a lot further along than we were a year ago. There are some things on this record that, even say three months ago, I've been able to talk to James at a level about, for instance, his lyrics which I've never been comfortable doing before.

JH: My what?!!! *(chuckles)*

LU: There are just new levels of comfort that have come about, it gets better and better. I dunno, you can sit down and analyze it, is it because we're older, wiser, more independent, more confident? Who knows but it keeps pointing in the right direction.

KH: I know for me, the stuff between James and I as far as guitar stuff is concerned, they're a lot more open to my ideas now than ever before and that inspires me.

JH: I think before we were strangling these two *(points to Jason and Kirk)* guys.

You're walking into my questions, which is good. For many years, probably right up to the "Black" album, it seemed to be this iron-clad 'it must be seen as the four, if it isn't seen as the four it's fucking... errum, out the door!' When was it decided to come out and be open about how it is, that there's basically the main nucleus of Lars and James with Jason and Kirk coming in with ideas. How easy was it for you, Kirk and Jason to acknowledge that? Was it easy?

KH: It's never easy for me just because it's... never easy. A lot of the time these guys had such a strong vision that it was hard for them to stray a little bit this way or that way. But nowadays, like I said, they're much more open-minded and it makes a really big difference in the old 'vibe' sense. It's better this way because we feed off each other a lot more having the same vibe.

Has it been easier, not saying that it was pretense before, but not having to keep up this 'iron-clad-four-as-one' image?

JH: That's just confidence within each other and within ourselves.

LU: We're a lot more open about whatever goes on with us. Me and him had a very narrow vision, the fact that we're more open and trying new things and moves musically and attitude-wise. And there's so many things not

just within but around us that has changed. Look around.

You're talking about success.

LU: No no, more about the musical climate and people's attitudes, how to deal with it. There was very much a time maybe five years ago where it was 'Metallica, this is what Metallica is and this is what Metallica should be' and I think it keeps sort of expanding. I think we're a lot less locked into what Metallica should be. If anything to me Metallica is about blossoming, growing...

JH: Evolving even more.

JN: To return to the question you asked. The bass thing, opening up... November of '94 when I first went in to learn some of the initial songs for this record, compared to my tracking in January of this year, it's night and day.

LU: We'd sit there and tell him exactly what to play, we didn't even give him a fucking chance!

JN: I just took my notes, wrote down what James played, the chords, and tried to do my own thing with my own feel to it, and I'd still get it into E1 as the main notes behind the guitar parts and try to work around it. And these guys have opened up to that kind of thing.

JH: But that's right along the line of, there's the song-writing part where we know what the bass should do here and still adding your own style to it and us not freaking out about it.

JN: That's the whole thing about opening up. And the thing with our thing, when Lars and I got into it, it was a lot more 'closed' then and everything. When I went into the dungeon room at his house to learn things it was so uptight. And as we jammed more here, jammed with Lars, noodled around here, had more fun and started to discover how much fun it was to jam with each other again. It was a whole new world.

LU: There was a period of, say, nine months where me and James were getting the main song-writing done. We really didn't see Jason much, and there was this situation with this 'demo-tape' the 'IR8 thing'... there were a couple of things that put some distance between us for a while. We really didn't see each other for a while. What Jason said about what we've done in hanging out these past six, eight, nine months has done a lot for the unity, hanging out, bringing us together. And it's brought a lot of the respect back. The respect level is so much better I'm sure on a mutual level.

So what stops the three of you a year ago looking at each other and saying, 'this ain't working out... see ya'?

JN: Because I had to...

Or even from your perspective, 'I'm off to do something else?'

JN: Well I always try to keep myself busy, but when we had 'the talk'... it needed to happen. Maybe the reason that brought it about shouldn't have happened, maybe the talk we three had should've happened sooner.

LU: I think we should give some background...

JN: The demo-tape. Somebody copied it and gave it to somebody, Peter Mensch (manager with Cliff Burnstein) heard it and freaked out.

LU: I was out in New York finalizing the Elektra lawsuit thing. Me and James had been writing for a couple of months. I was up at the office one day and Peter Mensch came in with a tape in his hand and he said, 'What's this?' I said, 'I dunno, what is it?'

And he said, 'It's a demo thing that's circulating of Jason and some side-band.' I didn't know what the fuck he was talking about! And having our manager look me in the eye asking, 'What is this?!' So that was kinda how it came about. I came home, saw James and said, 'Check this out, blah blah blah.' The first thing we did, was we called Jason and that evening we sat around the kitchen table at my house and we had a really long talk. We all said our pieces, he said his piece...

JN: The heaviest talk I've ever had with anyone in my life other than maybe with my Dad once.

LU: That was the beginning. There was a lot of tension in the few months after that because there were a lot of things talked about but it never really felt like it was 100% resolved.

JN: I was, like he said, distance man. I stepped out of line totally, I realized how ugly it could be, right? It caused a lot of tension between us, but once we got it off our chests, and like he said it took a little while for that to filter. I started playing songs with 'em and it was still a little bit 'uh-uh', I was just trying to pay attention to what I was trying to do.

LU: The first time we played a couple of songs there was definitely a mood in the room.

So what makes you hang in?

LU: You have to rise above it.

JN: Because I've known that those guys write the songs, they come up with the stuff. That's how it's always been and that's kinda how it is. I don't know if they learned as much as I did from that meeting, but they learned something too, I think, in the way of opening up, giving people more space and everything. For me it chiseled off a lot of shit, almost everything.

LU: It was definitely the beginning of the turning point. We always had this thing in this band of 'the tight little fuckin nucleus' that nobody strays out of. I've done the Mercyful Fate thing, but it's almost like going in front of the Pope or the Godfather, go in front of the rest of the guys in the band, you get down on your knees and say, 'It really would mean a lot to me to do this side project.' And Jason did the side project without us knowing about it, and all of a sudden I'm at Q Prime and Peter Mensch has it, it's on the radio and KNAC are playing it. James went nuclear and it was not a pretty couple of days! *(much laughter)*

JH: A minor nuclear explosion at my house!

And we have a live caller to KNAC, it's James from Metallica... (laughter)

LU: So if you wanna go back you could probably say that was the beginning of us opening our minds, seeing that he had some musical things to deal with because we were so locked up in our stuff.

KH: And I think a lot of it has to do with Bob Rock. His attitude at the beginning of the record. He came up to me and said, 'Y'know you and Jason are going to have a lot more to do on this album than before,' and I think in a very subtle way he opened that up and planted the seed with those two.

LU: The seed was planted on the last record but it just took five years to get fully comfortable with it.

JH: This whole word of 'looseness' on the record. It didn't really come into play I think until a bit later when we were all kinda sittin' and jammin' together. One thing for me was that I went on this hunting trip for a couple

of weeks and, hahaha, soon as I come back there was this tape. And it was like, 'all riiiight, we did a few things,' and there's this tap-dancing in the background, 'a few things we experimented with.' Yeah? OK, what is it? 'Weeell... Lars was joking around doing some singing...' Oh yeah, funny ha ha. 'There's this other thing... Kirk played rhythm guitar.' WHAAAAAT!!!!!! So I listened to the stuff, and it was pretty fuckin' cool. We got two guitar players so use two guitar players.

LU: This happened about a week later! *(laughter)*

JH: Well, yeah, it took a little time. It's all about conditioning, you're conditioned to doing something one way for 15 years and then all of a sudden it changes 'wooooaaaaa hold it! Troubling!'

LU: Especially when it changes in a place where he's three days from the nearest phone. He comes back, and to this day he thinks we had it planned...

KH: I was afraid he was going to hit me, ha ha ha.

LU: But it's a perfect example of adapting and Bob trying to make it more of a band.

JH: Deep down I always had this feeling of 'Kirk's the amazing lead guitar player and I'm the rhythm guitar player.' But him experimenting with new sounds in the studio, different stuff while we're tracking, WOW is that how bands record? We've discovered a whole new way of recording.

LU: *(to me)* You're looking very stiff right now.

Because I don't want this tape to run out and miss a pearl of your wisdom!

LU: One of the most interesting things is, that in terms of basic guitar riff and basic guitar ideas, this is probably the most Kirk has ever contributed to a Metallica album.

KH: Even in the song writing thing, I've contributed.

It seems to me, we talked about the tiff just then, but you (Kirk) seem to glide through things without butting heads with anyone.

KH: Well...

JH: Look how smooth he is!

KH: It all makes sense to me in the end. A lot of their decisions make sense to me initially. I'm thinking the same thing, it's just that many times Lars has beaten me to the punch.

JN: And I have to argue with everything he (Lars) says! Just to make sure he's right. See, he thinks I argue with him just because it's him...

LU: And I will think that until the day I die! *(laughter)*

JN: Now a percentage of that, perhaps, is true...

LU: Like 'high 90's!'

JN: But a lot of the time I argue so as to stir shit up, so as we can make sure that we know and have checked on the shit. Usually he has it covered anyway.

46

Now in no way suggesting you're still a new member Jason, but do you think it's easier for you to do that because relative to these three you're still four years newer.

LU: Na, Jason's always the one that keeps me in check when I stray.

JN: He doesn't like it, he reeeaally doesn't like it.

LU: But he knows that I know that when I'm straying a little and getting wobbly, Jason's always the first to politely tap me on the shoulder and say, 'Oi! Calm down.' I will never to my dying day give him credit for that, but between me, you and the four walls…

He wants this for his answering machine (laughter). If you can, analyze each other and name a quality that's indispensable to the band. For example you've (Lars) just said that Jason keeps you in check, so give me a musical quality. And then both for the rest of you.

LU: Definitely I think Jason's the most stable of the four of us.

KH: I'll agree with that.

JH: (looking weirdly at Lars, grinning slightly) What? Just because I write fucked-up lyrics?! Poor old twisted me.

LU: I think he (Jason) is the most grounded and stable, which is good in some situations and not in others. I think musically he's always open to try out different shit, and maybe because more than the three of us he's got his own thing going out where he lives musically and with the kind of interactions he has. He has much more interaction with other musicians than me, James or Kirk. I think it brings a quality to the party, just that knowledge, seeing different things, playing with different people and I value that a lot. Just when I ask him 'tell me about this or that band', we're sitting there putting Lollapalooza together and he knows a lot about music stuff that I don't fucking know anything about.

OK, so now Jason to Lars and then you two can play this game.

JH: Wow… Dr. C.!

LU: It's like fuckin' therapy isn't it? We should do this once a week!

KH: It's good.

It's going to get even better so carry on!

JN: OK, on the human-personal thing… it's his vigor. How he goes at everything 25 hours a day, when he puts his mind to something he really goes for it. It kinda ties in with the same thing musically because of the way he looks out for everybody in the band, the way he works on the arrangements and oversees everything. He puts in a lot of time listening to the shit, at home, in the car, he listens to it all the time. He puts all his time into talking with other people and thinking about stuff…

You mean like the time he went to New York to deal with the Elektra lawsuit, that 'right I'll go and deal with this' attitude.

JN: Yes that's one point, but then people also respect him when he gets there. They'll listen to his words.

And now (to Kirk and James) whichever one of you wants to lead off on the other.

JH: I'd like to talk about myself!

LU: He does that already in his lyrics!

KH: James has an amazing way of playing guitar that is so miraculously simple. It blows me away how simple it is…

JH: Either that or I can't play!

KH: … but at the same time it's very complex. He just always knows the simplest, easiest way to get something across. Whereas I, I fucking have to jack off for 15 minutes before I come to some sort of conclusion!
(much laughter)

And as a personality?

KH: He's very stern, knows very much what he wants and what he needs. I respect that.

JH: I think with Kirk, he's got this quality of not giving a fuck that I really like. He's kinda 'fuck it man,' not caring what people think in terms of many aspects. Dressing, hanging out, doing stuff, he's just really very comfortable with things. He never gets uptight, he's just really smooth. I really respect that. His playing? Some of the rhythm stuff he played, some of the nuance stuff that Bob helped draw out of him… well. I mean, I was always afraid everything had to be tighter than a gnat's ass, but just little things here and there (he's doing) are adding so much dimension to this project, and live is going to be pretty interesting. He's adding lots of cool new shit without losing strength.

KH: It's gonna be a lot more spontaneous.

JN: That was nice…

OK then, how easy is it for you all to sit here and evaluate each other's 'worth' like that?

JN: It was great because we've never done anything like that no matter how much we've wanted to.

LU: We would never have done this five years ago…

Honestly, would you have done this five weeks ago?

KH: I think so.

JH: At the beginning of the project, no.

LU: But what we were talking about at the beginning of the interview, the reason we're doing this now is because things have come around full circle. Really.

JH: There's huge new strength in all of this. You share feelings with each other, you feel more of a family vibe, more of a camaraderie. People will back you up even more instead of battle you. And that's even more forward momentum for us as individuals and a band.

LU: I've gotta tell you that there really is a spirit in this band right now.

JH: Gin!

LU: I'm not getting into too many details right now, but there really is a vibe of 'experiment' and the unit standing together and trying different things musically and attitude-wise. We did some photo stuff a couple of weeks ago, and without getting more into it we did some stuff that we'd never have tried before. And I walked away from that session feeling we were a stronger unit because we went for it at the same time. Musically, the hardest thing is going to be to curb all the experimenting because we have to finish this record in a couple of months. Instead of five years ago when it was 'oh well let's try this' now it's a case of not getting so out of hand, of containing the desire to experiment. That spirit in the ranks has really brought us closer together than ever before.

KH: I think we're at our fullest potential now than ever before. The sky's the fucking limit.

LU: All pre-conceived pre-existing ideas of who we are and what we've done are at a point right now where we're standing at a massive potential point of rebirth.

Interesting you should see it that way when so many people who get to that position see themselves as standing at the edge of a precipice waiting to fall off and die.

JH: Yeah, 'it's the end.'

LU: Every other time we made a record I always knew the end point before we started.

Even for the "Black" album?

LU: I knew the 12 songs we were going to record before we started. I knew what the record would look like, I knew what the record would more or less sound like. When we started this record last summer, there was still no cap on. We were still writing new songs in November, there's two songs on the album me and James wrote in fucking November, that's two months ago! Now you can see the end of it, but when we started it we had all these songs, all these ideas, we knew there might be more songs and more ideas so we kept an open mind and tried shit. This is the first time I've been able to see the end of this record.

JN: When we first started we were looking at a mass of 25–30 songs, 'who knows if it's going to be three albums' how could you see the end of that?! Finally the stages we went through, the personal things, the seeing together, meeting with management resulted in that many songs? You're going to do that many songs and take that many months you'll have strangled each other. So what's it going to be?

LU: After we started writing we got to 24–25 songs and we said, 'This is crazy, we can carry on writing songs until the year 2007. Let's go in the studio and start recording.' The ideas for songs were still lying there, we had to curb ourselves and put a lid on it because we could still be in there writing now. That's how many ideas kept surfacing, so it really became an exercise in sitting down and figuring out what you wanted to do. But looking back I think the last year has been great. The fact that we went and did those gigs did so much for us in terms of making the record, so many things have happened in the last year that have brought us to the moment we're at now. I don't think we would feel so good about what we're doing right now if it hadn't evolved like it has.

Let me ask you this. In everyday life there's pressure to follow-up things you may have done well at work in the past. So to most people looking in, the pressure to succeed 15 million sales of the last album must be enormous. And it's inconceivable that you wouldn't have each sat down, perhaps by yourself, in the past year and thought, 'fuck me this is too much, I can't handle that! How are we going to top it?' Was doing something like Donington a way of proving to yourselves that people still care and that you haven't lost touch?

LU: People will never believe this, but I've gotta tell you I've never felt any pressure to follow-up that record. Y'know why? Because deep in my heart I know we'll never top it numbers wise. We can top it creatively, we can top it from a personal satisfaction point of view, but when you ask about it that way you're only asking about numbers. And I know we can never top that record again. And going into that with that understanding means I didn't feel any pressure.

JN: I don't like cutting and drying it like that. You never know, a certain couple of singles could suddenly go from 180 to number five in a couple of weeks…

See, you do dwell on it from time to time then.

JN: Yeah. But the anticipation of it and the excitement and as it starts to get bigger and bigger to the stage where the record is starting to sound like something… all of that outweighs just about everything. There's the expectations people have about it, the expectations we're meant to have about it. And the songs are good, it's the most musical album Metallica's ever made. They're listenable as far as melodies and toe-tapping. And a lot of people enjoying the songs.

JH: Especially us. Numbers have never meant 'good.' 'This album's good because it sold blah!' We've never looked at things like that.

LU: The type of pressure he's talking about is that 'you've got to top the last record now' attitude.

Yeah yeah, I keep on using Guns N'Roses as an example not for anything other than they fit every stereotype you can find for the classic situation of relevance and being relevant. There's a guy (Axl Rose) who wakes up every morning wondering if anyone still cares, but wouldn't anyone in that situation? Isn't it comforting for you to know that you can relax and enjoy this process because people are waiting for you, you don't have to chase them? Didn't Donington and its success give you a little more comfort, a little more space, the feeling of knowing how nice it is they still want you?

JH: Oh yeah there's some of that. It is nice to know that people like you, sure. But there's also an energy you feed off when people don't like you, that you have something to prove.

KH: I've always felt that the main thing, and I don't want to sound trite, that the main thing is being satisfied artistically and creatively and that numbers are just numbers. Numbers have no emotions.

We've done the 'praise' thing, now let's look the other way. What are some of the things you see in each other that you don't like, or that could get out-of-hand without intervention?

JH: Are you tryin' to start a fight?! (laughing)

LU: There is only love in this room.

JH: 'On the couch with Dr. C.' is taking an EVIL TURN!

JN: On the nail-bed with Dr. C.

LU: How about instead of that, why don't we answer it as what we do that we know annoys everybody else?

JN: That's cool.

LU: OK, here's what I do musically that really annoys James. Sometimes I like to not accent the 'one' and it sometimes gets James really annoyed.

JH: And? (much laughter)

LU: That's the only thing!

KH: James really hates it when I play out of key.

JH: I'm starting to like it. Why's it all me, am I the 'hate' guy? Do I get to enjoy all the hate?

we're standing at a massive potential point of rebirth

Funny, no one has leveled a criticism at James yet which I find intriguing.

JH: No, I'm meant to say what I know they hate about me.

Oh that's right, sorry, well come on then.

JH: Lars hates it when I'm totally complacent and he can't get an answer out of me. I get poker-faced sometimes.

KH: I really hate it when they call one of my riffs 'the circus riff.'

(much laughter)

LU: Kirk hates it when we make fun of where he's ripped people off from.

KH: Yeah, like you've never ripped the odd-one off yourself.

LU: Yeah, but I cop to it, though.

Jason has remained silent during this segment.

LU: There's too much metal in his right hand sometimes.

JN: I like to play fast, heavy rock and heavy metal music. And sometimes I like to play it during mellow, acoustic songs.

LU: Yeah, the guy who says he listens to more blues than anyone hardly ever plays it.

JN: I'm always on top of the beat because I'm so happy about jamming.

LU: He's so happy being with his friends, and when he's with his friends he misses being with the three of us!

JH: So he plays faster so as he can be with them.

It's interesting. Because it seems like it's a very difficult thing to talk like this. I suppose I'd find it difficult to look at him (photographer Leialoha) and say I hate something he does. But it is difficult to look and keep each other in checks and balances. Is that why it takes so long to get through an album for example, because maybe you watch them for a couple of weeks or so wanting to say something and never quite getting it out.

JH: Oh, I see where the Doctor's going!

LU: I think it's coming quicker than before. I'm tracking drums and he'll (James) tell me... maybe not the minute he wants to, but certainly sooner than he did in the past. And likewise, I'm more comfortable with bringing something up sooner than I have in the past. I remember way back on "...Justice," for two or three months he'd sing 'Harvester of SorrowS' and it drove me up the wall!

(much laughter from everyone, especially James).

LU: And then finally, right when we were about to go and start mixing, I said, 'How about making it singular? 'Harvester of Sorrow'.'

JH: That's why it sold so much. The 'S' was missing. (laughs)

KH: Hey, I just remembered something! That was my title!

LU: What, 'Harvester of SorrowS?'

KH: No, 'Harvester of Sorrow.'

JH: But guess what's going to happen on this next tour?!

LU: For three months it bugged the shit out of me, and every time I saw him for three months I wanted to bring it up but I always pussied out.

JH: Oh God! 'Sssssso, howsssssss thingssssssssss...'

LU: But do you know what I mean? That long and finally I said something and he re-sang it and... (deflates a little in the face of increasing laughter) the point I'm trying to make is those things come up a lot quicker.

So, looking at each other once again...

KH: JEEEESUS!

But that's why you're all here together. Interesting, the charm of this little session's starting to wear thin I see. But seriously, things you might have shown each other... Oasis for example. I know you (Jason) were turned onto Oasis by him (guess who), so maybe some things you would've each looked at three years ago and thought 'oh fuck you' whereas now you're open.

JN: In the first six months Hetfield turned me onto some stuff that has turned out to be...

JH: CRAP.

JN: ... some of my top ten bands of all time.

Such as?

JN: Los Lobos and Tom Waits. In my all-time top ten. And other cool shit, like Hüsker Dü, stuff I hadn't really given a chance before I was turned onto it by that guy.

Indeed, he turned me onto Ministry back in 1988.

JN: All that weird British stuff like Trespass too. And from him...

LU: He won't say Oasis.

JN: I really like Oasis.

Which Lars turned you on to. (much laughter)

JN: LARSSSS ULRICH, OASSSSISSSS. Then there's Kirk who turned me onto Godflesh, Fear Factory, KMFDM, Kirk's listening stuff. And it continues.

KH: Cliff turned me onto The Misfits.

JN: Most of the time you won't be given the time of day unless you have the music actually playing.

KH: Lars turned me onto Black Grape.

LU: A fine band. Kirk has opened my eyes to a lot of the more new-fangled stuff. I really like Nine Inch Nails a lot, Kirk tells me about certain things and usually it takes me quite a while and he laughs at me when I come around. But he knows that from the first time he tells me something to when I get around to listening to it to when I start vibing can be three months. It takes a while. For example PJ Harvey. He told me about her a year ago...

I told you about Black Grape not that long after. Sorry, just had to get that one in.

LU: I'll edit that out! Anyway, PJ Harvey for instance, I'm really into her latest record and Kirk told me about that six, eight, nine months ago. I think I've

turned him onto a lot of the English stuff I've been into, Black Grape for example. And some of the stuff we've explored together, some we like, some we hate. We checked some of the Blur stuff and the Britpop stuff, and some of it we really like, some of it we really hate. James… James…

JH: I turned you onto Thin Lizzy! *(laughs)*

LU: A bit of a stretch. James… James…

JH: 'James hates music!'

KH: James who?

LU: James… and I don't think this is out of line. When I'm really into something I tell everyone, I discover Oasis I tell him, him, everyone. James is maybe a little less…

Obsessive? (James laughs very loudly)

LU: No. James is maybe a little less outgoing. If there's something he's vibing on he doesn't necessarily call me and say, 'Hey you gotta check this out.' Me and Kirk and, to a lesser extent, Jason are a little more sharing. James is a little harder, I don't think he necessarily throws as much at us. Is that a fair thing to say?

JN: There are some things, some bands, that we like to hold dear and say, 'I knew about them first,' and you don't want the other guys to know…

Such as…

JN: Him with Oasis or something. I wasn't really going to let him know that he turned me onto something that was big, that he was right. You don't want to give him the satisfaction that he was right.

LU: I'm trying to think of something you were playing that I really liked that I wasn't going to let you know I liked… what was it? And sometimes we're really guarded because if there is something we're really vibing on, we don't want the other guy who we really respect to, if we say 'check this out it's fucking great', say 'urrrrggghh.' I purposely kept Oasis from him (James) for quite a while because I knew it wasn't his vibe.

JH: It doesn't matter though. I think everyone blows it all out of proportion. You like different types of music, it doesn't mean that's suddenly how you're gonna start writing.

Have any of you managed to pitch any of your outside influences into this project do you think?

JN: Like when Lars was talking about the experimenting thing, yeah I think so. Definitely with the experimenting thing. Definitely with this guy *(points to Hetfield)* and the western flavors, the 'B' benders, the peddlesteel type of things.

LU: Definitely. And also, once again, as opposed to five years ago we're a lot more comfortable talking about it and acknowledging it. Without sounding like that broken record we are more respectful of each other's vibe.

Getting back to recording. Recording live off the floor, how has it helped and not helped your relationship musically?

LU: I'll give you an example. There's a song on the new record which was written basically when we hit on a jam while recording and Bob was in the control room saying 'wait a minute…' and us going 'OK.' We've recorded 70-80-90 songs over the last 15 years. There's never anything that's come from a jam, on the new record there is. So yes, things are evolving. And the interesting thing is that basically it's the last song we wrote so that might signal an openness to that kind of approach.

The material seems once again, from what little I've heard, simple enough. You always think that amount of time spent must equal complexity of material, but the songs seem very loose.

LU: You've gotta remember what we're talking about. We've recorded almost 30 songs. That's not a secret. This time we recorded maybe 29-30 drum tracks, 30 floor takes, 30 songs, breaking up the recording by touring, by rehearsing, by continuous writing, by fan club winners' visits, by putting Fan Cans together. There've been a lot of fires burning in the last couple of months, added to being at home. There are more distractions at home, both good and bad. But it's nice to be home, it's nice to be with your loved ones, in your own abode and world. But it's definitely slowing things down. When we go away we're definitely much more focused because there is nothing else. Being at home definitely slowed us down, and I don't mean that necessarily in a bad way, just physically it's taking longer to record. But it's been very comfortable.

JH: I think recording off the floor kinda stuff? I think we were all a little afraid in our own ways to totally let loose, or maybe show our own personal limits? Like, 'here's what I can sing and that's it.' But we'd try without being afraid to fail in front of everyone, so just letting loose a little more in the studio. When we're all on that level it's easy to do that, but it's really hard to just fucking walk in and do something. Everyone's always been frightened to say when something's not so good, but now you try and if you know inside it ain't so good then fuck it, at least you tried!

LU: I think before there was a thing of being afraid to fail in front of the other people.

JH: Right.

LU: What if I fuck up in front of everyone doing my drum tracks.

JH: But not so much even to fuck up the part you're doing, but 'I'm gonna try something I would never do but I wanna fuckin' do it. So fuck it if I fail.'

KH: It all comes down to that loose vibe of being confident again. Just being comfortable with each other and confident enough to be able to try things that might not necessarily work, but might just.

Do you (Kirk) think six months of the last year has been spent getting to that 'comfort' point? Before it started getting really productive?

KH: Yeah, absolutely. But just having 30 songs kinda like gives you a little more space. You have 30 tracks to do, so if something fucks up here it's OK, because we have 29 other songs…

LU: And you can fuck up the other songs!

51

LU: I think the one thing that going to New York will do is put us in what we call 'crunch time.' That's basically seven days a week, 16 hours a day, no distractions, you wake up, go to work, nothing else. And I think we all felt that vibe would be best accomplished somewhere else, away from home and away from whatever potential distractions there might be at home. I think Bob was also instrumental in bringing forth the idea of a change of scenery, saying, 'Let's get to a point instead of here where when we're finished with the sessions, we all go home and hang out, a place that's isolated. Where after the sessions we'll go out, have a beer and talk about the day's mix, or the album cover. It will be what we call 'crunch-time.' Then Mensch and Burnstein were pretty instrumental in saying if we went to New York, as opposed to some of the places we were talking about like Minneapolis or Atlanta, we would be right there in terms of everything. The artwork, the interviews, everything in terms of decision-making would be so centralized.

JN: OK'ing an art thing, for example, Fed-Exing it from there to here and then from here back to New York, you're using three work days to ship things back and forth. A few weeks pass by, that's a lotta time.

LU: Also, New York is the central point between Europe and the West Coast. Mensch had a lot of reasons why New York made sense. And I think there's an energy in New York, a mood, that might actually – we've never worked in New York so I don't know...

LU: *(exasperated)* We've never worked in New York City. We've never done any recording stuff in New York City. And I think there's an energy and kind of a vibrancy that might actually be pretty cool if we were to tap into it for the last couple of weeks.

KH: Frrrrraaaaantic!

LU: In some weird way, yeah.

JH: Well it's also just getting the fuck outta here. We've been here a long time.

KH: Change of atmosphere's going to do us a lot of good.

JN: And New York made sense once we'd discussed it.

JH: We're not there to enjoy the city, we're there to work.

KH: Eat, sleep and shit Metallica.

LU: We're delivering the record to the record company on May 3rd...

RANDY STAUB (engineer, passing by): 'We're delivering it when I'm good and ready!' *(much laughter from James)*

LU: *(continuing through cross-talking with stubborn determination)* That's the date we've put...

JH: Randy Staub has spoken, old Rand-has-spoken!

LU: ... we're mastering the record May 1st and 2nd. You've got to remember something. It was only six weeks ago we even decided which 14 songs were going on the first record. We cut almost 30...

LU: Yes, first record. We had a long-term idea. It's not 30 songs, picking the best 14 and 'binning' the others. So about six weeks ago, Peter and Cliff came out and we sat down to discuss what we were going to do... (at this point James yawns loudly, Kirk looks sleepy and Jason fidgety. Lars shows no sign of fatigue, uncorking some wine and settling in for the long haul)...

and the plan, the way it sits out, is this: 14 songs will be on the first record. A lot of those songs that won't be on the first record have had a lot of work done on them, some of them are done basically. So instead of making a record every five years, we're gonna do a record now, finish the other songs and put out another album in a year, year-and-a-half from now.

LU: That's just how focused I am! *(much laughter)*

A few more to go so hang in. I know you all like to go to bed
early and we're past your bedtimes. Political interests, side
interests, the bigger you get the more they get amplified.
You (James) for example have been turned by some into 'guns/
hunting' you (Kirk) 'socialist/liberal.' Are there ever times
you look and think, 'fuck that, our band is being represented
like that?' Do you ever have words with each other and say,
'hey, could you try and keep that down a bit?'

KH: It's all crap. And I mean it.

JH: Politics is crap. Maybe with the Metallica Club magazine a lot more personal things have come out. You get to know guys, for example, the hunting pictures. And that's what the magazine's for, to get to know the people. More personal shit. Everyone seems to think they know us through the music, and actually knowing the person aside from the music? Does that fuckin' matter? I don't fuckin' know, I don't care. I don't really care what Joe Blow does in some other band really. It shouldn't get in the way of the music.

JH: Lottatheloozers.

JN: The Re-Metallization Of The Nation's Soul.

LU: Well the way it was presented to us was that we would not necessarily have...

JN: Trying to get the message to YOU!

LU: ... *(a little frustrated by interruption)* we would not necessarily have a final say. They would certainly listen, respect and appreciate suggestions we would bring forth. What they've talked about are more stages than ever before with more bands than ever before...

JN: More love, more skin, more drugs...

LU: ... stuff we've seen on paper in terms of potential bands being thrown around...

JN: We're trying to put on the alternative to alternative music.

LU: ...We haven't talked about anything specific right now, we're just trying to lock in ourselves, Soundgarden and a couple of the other major bands. Then we get to have fun and have all our friends on the other stages.

KH: The Reverend Al Green.

Alright then, we'll finish off with a nice inflammatory
question which will probably start a fight where you'll all
try and beat me up.

JN: Cool let's do it.

I thought you'd like that. Never let it be said that I'm not
good at perhaps closing in on the fact that the focus is waning
somewhat. I've managed to catch that one.

JH: Sorry, what?!

LU: I was disappointed that everyone pussied out on the political thing. Really lame.

KH: There's no real solution. Well there's one, that's annihilation!

LU: You asked such a loaded question, and I was surprised that no-one went for it. But I think there's nobody that gets out of hand with it...

53

JH: SHAD UP! *(laughs)*

LU: You kind of know where everybody stands on stuff and that's OK, but nobody ever gets to the point of being so pushy that it pushes Metallica in one way or another.

KH: What is your final question?

It's a question which I think interests many people. It's about publishing and money and what it might mean to each other at any time. Has there ever been a moment where you two (Jason, Kirk) have thought, 'fuck me, they get more publishing than I do and it pisses me off.' (At this point James looks thoroughly disgusted at me for asking the question). I remember hearing about when Kurt Cobain went back to other two members of Nirvana and said, 'By the way, I'd like some of my publishing back...'

COLLECTIVE: Huh?

You never heard about that? OK then, has money every caused problems?

JN: My opinion and voice? You get what you work for, these guys (Lars and James) work the hardest, they get the most. He (Kirk) works the next hardest, then he gets the next...

And live it's all equal right?

JN: Whenever it comes to any of the performing part of it, we're all as one.

KH: None of us are particularly greedy.

LU: Money has never been an issue.

I know, James, that it might seem a question you think is stupid, but ego we touched on earlier, money, these are all things that to 99% of the world cause massive problems. And here you are in a huge band with huge money rolling around, and many people might think it would cause some problems. That's why the question was asked.

LU: It's never been a problem.

JN: You can't dig up anymore dirt? Shit to sling? *(everyone laughs)*

JH: *(To Jason)* No, he just brought up live. Ha ha, I mean, do other bands do it any differently, 'I play more than the other guys up here so...'

I've no idea. That's why I asked.

KH: It would definitely be an issue if there was a 'hired hand' situation, but Metallica's always been a band.

Well, there is a final dirt-digging question. When it comes to watching how each other shags, who has the best...

TAPE IS TURNED OFF. PEOPLE SIGH, RELAX, START TO GET READY TO LEAVE. LARS WANTS TO CARRY ON.

How hard has it been to sit and listen to some of these questions and have to look each other in the eye and answer?

JN: It's the best damn interview we've ever done.

LU: From now on we will only do interviews like this with you.

I know you (James) are very private, so is it hard to talk about money or music or whatever?

JH: Well, when you get things out in the open there's less fuel for people to burn or dig for. The more you've got out there, the more cut-and-dried it is, it's like we're not afraid to hide it. But there are just some things that ain't people's fuckin' business, that's all! These days people aren't satisfied with that, they wanna know how many times you wipe your ass a day.

Well, it's funny you should say that...

KH: I don't wipe my ass.

LU: I think people would also be very surprised at just how little dirt there really is. You're asking questions that nobody's ever asked before. And certain other bands in certain other situations would have so many more conflicts between them on some of those things. And part of the reason we're sitting here as such a strong unit is because those things aren't a big issue. We don't sit there and say, 'he's in the studio more, he's writing more, he's at home, he's riding his bike, he's counting his money...'

JH: HEY! *(laughs)* I love to do that too.

KH: I pay someone to count mine.

LU: But that's why we can answer those questions so calmly. We split everything we do except for the publishing. And we *(points at James)* take care of most of the songwriting, so we get most of that money. Wow.

JH: And who gives two shits? If we don't, why should anyone else? They're good tunes, so who cares about the fuckin' money?!

But you know the reality of it is that the goldfish bowl gets bigger, people want to know more and it isn't going to get any easier.

LU: I mean, the only reason that question has never been answered is because it's never been asked. There's a lot less dirt when you start digging, and you almost feel people might like it more if there was more. If you sat down with Axl, Slash, Matt and Duff, for example, there would be so much stuff you couldn't really talk about.

(CONVERSATION FADES, PEOPLE START SAYING THEIR THANKS AND LEAVING.)

THE END (for now)

55

BAND COMMENTS

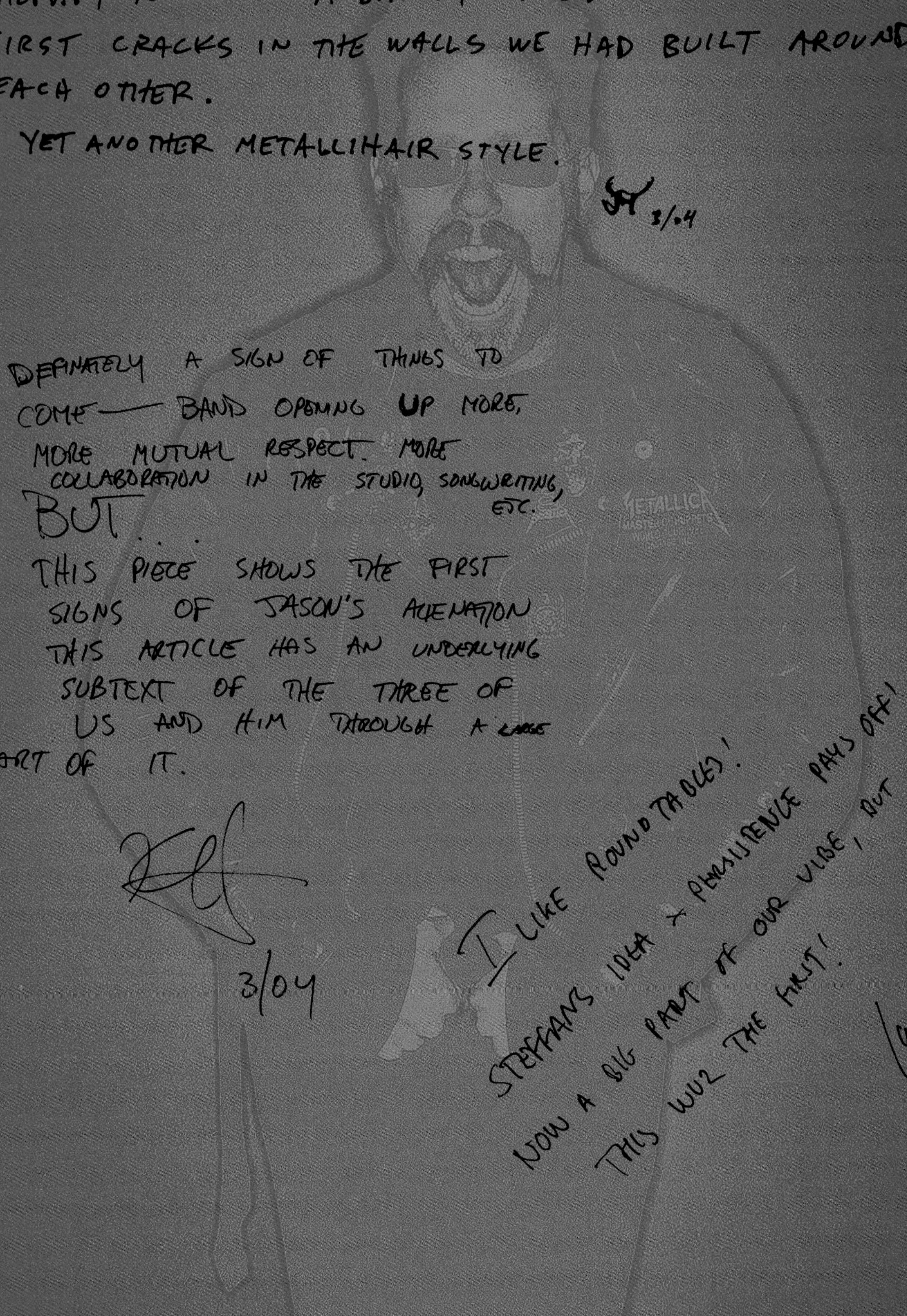

STEFFANS IDEA OF A ROUND TABLE INTERVIEW MIMICKED THERAPY TO COME. A BALLSY MOVE. I FEEL IT PUT THE FIRST CRACKS IN THE WALLS WE HAD BUILT AROUND EACH OTHER.

YET ANOTHER METALLIHAIR STYLE.

3/04

DEFINATELY A SIGN OF THINGS TO COME — BAND OPENING UP MORE, MORE MUTUAL RESPECT. MORE COLLABORATION IN THE STUDIO, SONGWRITING, ETC.

BUT . . .

THIS PIECE SHOWS THE FIRST SIGNS OF JASON'S ALIENATION THIS ARTICLE HAS AN UNDERLYING SUBTEXT OF THE THREE OF US AND HIM THROUGH A LARGE PART OF IT.

3/04

I LIKE ROUNDTABLES! STEFFANS IDEA + PERSISTENCE PAYS OFF! NOW A BIG PART OF OUR VIBE, BUT THIS WUZ THE FIRST!

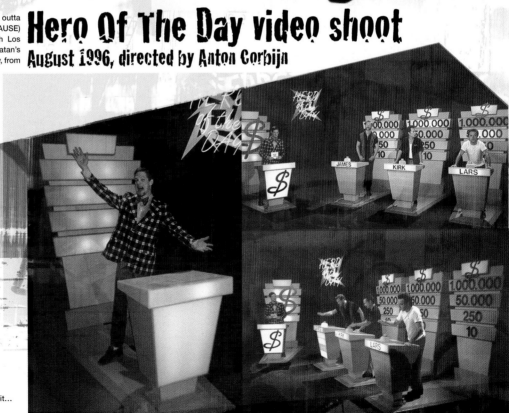

JASON: Hullo Ladees and Gents, straight outta Hoboken New Jersey, James Hetfield. (APPLAUSE) Next, a lead guitarist from somewhere South Los Angeles, a brain surgeon for the band Satan's Children, Kirk Hammett. (APPLAUSE) And finally, from Copenhagen Denmark, Lars Ulrich.

Who plays lead guitar in Yngwie's band?
JH: Bon Jovi.

How far is Wyoming from you now?
KH: Crack cocaine!

What kind of sandwich is your favorite?
LU: Bacon sandwich.
Good, good enough, close.

What is your favorite color?
JH: Georgia on my mind.

How many chicks can you get into your room at once?
LU: As many as I want.

What is the bass player's name in Sepultura?
JH: Jim Martin.
What is your Mom's middle name?
KH: Me.

What country do you want to go to?
JH: Dog shaving.

When was your first sexual experience?
JH: With you in the back of the bus.

JN: How many creatures have you killed in your lifetime?
JH: FUCK YOU!
Amazing, that is so correct, yes, I can't believe it…

Hero Of The Day video shoot
August 1996, directed by Anton Corbijn

A LOAD O' LOLLA AND BEYOND

With the "Load" album done and an interesting Lollapalooza U.S. festival tour completed, the band headed to Europe and broke open their enormous, elaborate and entertaining "Load" tour set. Filled with all sorts of bells, whistles and general caper, this was the most ambitious stage set Metallica had ever put together, easily eclipsing the 'snake pit' from the "Black" album marathon. This was also the time Metallica shed their stylistic inhibitions, cutting their hair, wearing some designer togs and even slapping a bit of eye-liner on from time to time! Furthermore, there was a new era of 'gloves off' discussion and opinions, both about their pasts and each other. Spicy! Thus James and Jason each took tape time at the end of the Lollapalooza run, whilst Lars and Kirk sat down a month or so later at the start of the European "Load" tour to discuss all the above. And reading back, I have to say some of this is pretty damn funny! Editor – February 2004

LARS ULRICH

Band relationships

"I think they're somewhere between the same as it's always been and a little better. Between me and James there's a higher level of tolerance than there was on the last tour, so it's a little better. Realizing that a lot of the tour friction between James and me was rooted in the fact that we were pulling in two different directions was important. We were in different directions on things from length of tours, in terms of number of gigs and songs, set-lists and so on. What has happened on this tour, and in my current frame of mind, instead of pulling things away from him and trying to make the sets and tours longer, I'm kinda more interested in shorter tours and shorter sets. We see a lot more eye to eye on those things, and that makes for a lot less friction. So we were in Milan about two weeks ago, and he came up to me about fifteen minutes before we went onstage... very timid, pretty funny. And he said 'I'd really like to cut a song or two' and I just said 'yeah, fine, cool.' And he almost fell over. He told me afterwards that he thought my response to that was very surprising. I think because I'm changed in terms of not breathing down everybody's neck about stuff and trying to be less stressed out, those things aren't worth the friction to me anymore. I'd rather get on good with him and two songs isn't gonna make that big a difference in a set of two hours and twenty minutes...

"I think with Kirk and Jason the relationships are not very much different. I don't socialize with Jason, I never have socialized with Jason. Me and him have a very... friendly, respectful, almost cordial relationship, we're together around the music and that's it. With Kirk it's probably socially stronger than it's been for a while because a couple of years ago I think he went through a period where he was distancing himself from the band because of certain relationships he was in and stuff like that. He was a little lost for a while, so socially he's a lot more involved again."

Different approaches to the music

"I've gotta tell you, I've never been one who's particularly interested in endless 'sit smoking pot for six hours and just jam with whoever's in the room.' I have no interest in that whatsoever. I've always been into the band format, in writing songs and I explore the mindless jamming thing once in a while but it really isn't for me. So I think where we (Jason and Lars) have different philosophies is that he's always the one who thinks we should practice more and be more rehearsed and I think we should practice less and be less rehearsed. He thinks more from the angle of 'the mighty Metallica machine, the unit' and an almost militaristic approach to the whole thing about 'it can't stray away from what is the tightest and the strongest.'

"I think music is much more interesting if you add the human elements to it. To me those are that you don't play the same every night, you have nights where you're really cooking, you have points where you're 110% or 95%, but there have to be human elements in it. You have to leave room for magic to come and also for certain things to happen, like trying certain things and so on. The loosest person in those terms right now, is James. I've had James' guitar in my monitors for so many years, and in the last three months he's loosening up so much in terms of basic rhythm playing. The nuances in the riffs are different, and sometimes he totally throws me off now because he's trying something. And that's the beauty of what we do, you can take the riff from 'The Four Horsemen' and then one night, out of the blue, he plays it totally different...

"What I'm afraid of right now, and I'm gonna start changing the set-list around because of it, is that the last two weeks are probably some of the best gigs we've ever played and some of the tightest shows we've ever played. And I'm afraid it's a little too mechanical. It's in danger still, right now, of turning into the big Metallica machine rolling through the land. We definitely had that on the 'Black' album tour last time out and I'd really like to try and avoid that this time."

A happier Lars

"Hmmm, yeah. It's a very good soundbite 'he's happier than he was before and the reason he was so stressed and driven before is that he wasn't happy.' But there's a lot more to it than that. I don't sit down and analyze my life that much, but I do realize that obviously things are different and I am obviously happier. I do sit and look at someone like James and see that they did have much more of a life outside Metallica than I did. But the one thing that prevents me from agreeing 100% and saying that I've finally joined the ranks of the other three with a life outside Metallica, is that if I have that life at that same level then there's no-one really taking control of it (the band) like I have. When I was the one taking control of it always, it was license for the other guys to go and do their things because they knew I would take care of everything... I would, in the past, literally sit and check ticket counts, merchandising numbers. Every day. I would get reports everyday on those things and spend 30 minutes a day thinking about them. I would figure out where and when we needed to do more promotion to help certain places go to 100% capacity. I just don't do those things anymore, it doesn't exist in my life."

Getting more personal

"Maybe I was hiding a lot of that stuff behind band stuff, yeah, sure. It's not like I had any of these answers clear yet, I hadn't reached any conclusion because it's an ongoing process. Definitely in the early days there was an unwritten rule that personal stuff was very much in the background, and that band interviews were speaking on behalf of the band even if they were individual. They were always band oriented, it was never an interview with Lars Ulrich, it was an interview with Metallica represented here by Lars Ulrich. It's very important to realize that 95% of the interviews I've done have been about Metallica and not about me. So there's a lot of those things that have been kept supressed because they were never

really talked about. And if the interview was straying that way, there was always the thing about 'the sum of our parts' and the solid fist thing in the background.

"Now we're more comfortable with disagreeing in public, copping to the fact that we're four completely different people. So when you say I've never gone into a lot of the things that have gone on in the corridors, it's because I've never really been in a position for that. I look at the Axl Roses, Eddie Vedders and I guess I prided myself on the group unit thing Metallica had that those people didn't. I feel more comfortable talking about myself now, talking about the differences between us in the band. I feel less inclined to go into interview mode where all of a sudden the tape recorder's on and you cannot stray into an area there because of how it would look. I'm more comfortable going into areas I've never been in, more personal, less guarded, getting away from the 'oh I can't talk shit about so and so' or 'I can't say what's really on my mind about so and so.'"

Drugs

"...I'm sick of covering things up, sick of hiding things, sick of playing down any major 'issues' like money or drugs or whatever. The main thing, and I think the reason I feel OK about talking about it in the press, is that those things are being talked about, not because they're worse than ever, just because it's being talked about for the first time. So it's pretty much the same as it's always been, the only difference is that we don't go out of our way to pretend that side doesn't exist. So for people who are only just getting exposed to it I can see it would be a shock, but from our end partying at whatever level it's been, is really not a big deal...

"I think at the time James wrote the lyrics to the song 'Master Of Puppets' 75% of the rest of the members of Metallica all dabbled in cocaine use at a very social level. Social. That song is written about people who have very addictive personalities and who aren't in control of their lives. And people have to understand that it's the same as when someone goes out drinking for a couple of nights a week, or smokes a little pot or takes medication or does a little bit of cocaine without being addicted to it. It is possible. Thanks to people like Dave Mustaine, Nikki Sixx, Steven Tyler people think that rock'n'roll is either all or nothing. Nobody in this band has an addictive personality, and that goes for everything. Nobody sits here eating 12 pepperoni pizzas a day and turns into Meatloaf. The only one who doesn't drink or do any drugs whatsoever is James Hetfield. But it's not that big of a deal, and it is possible that you can dabble with these things at a recreational level."

JAMES HETFIELD

Lollapalooza?

"Haha, well, it worked for some people. We've definitely had some fun, the first shows left me with the impression that it was a lot better than I expected. A lot less green and purple hair and uppitiness than I expected, less of that snobby shit than I thought there'd be. We definitely got some new people to 'bang, but it's hard to gauge who's really new to us and who isn't because when you ask how many people have seen you before everyone raises their hand because they don't wanna look like an ass. We pride our fans on knowing the lyrics, and there have been times when I've stopped to let them sing and there' been a lotta open mouths or just 'bleeuurggghh.' At least they're yelling though. But there are some hardcore motherfucking fans out there helping out, whipping people into shape...

"I was expecting more anti-Metallica stuff, I'm a little disappointed. And all the goddam reviews I've read go on about what color the kid's hair was and how many piercings they had 'some kid had purple hair and his butt cheeks pierced together'... makes no goddam sense. Oh yeah and there was music too. And when they do talk about the bands it's usually not us because they've gotta hit deadlines or whatever, so usually it's Rancid...

"There's a little animosity there, we're definitely backing down a lot (production-wise – ED). But we have backline people for ten years who know what the fuck they're doing, how they do it, how to get it. But we've got to back off some always 'OK OK it's not our show' and leave a lot of stuff for Lollapalooza even though that might not be the best thing to happen."

What Metallica stands for

"I know that 'gang mentality' has been a part of Metallica for a long time, partly because parents hated it and nobody knew who we were. Radio wouldn't touch us. It was total underground, this 'gang' thing, a big giant gang that never really liked being part of organizations. I've always preferred to be my own thinker, some people need to feel part of a family, and there Is a family feel to Metallica. People will always want you to be what they want you to be, and we've always done whatever the fuck we wanted to do. Some fans like that attitude so long as it's something they like, and it doesn't make much sense.

"Everyone likes Metallica for a different reason, and you can't be all of them, you can't be every man's Jack. We can't please every fucker. There's bands that try it and they stumble and fail. I've had fans come up to me just saying, 'dude you're in Metallica I used to listen to you in high school.'

And it's like 'yeah what happened?!' Now you're out of high school does that mean you don't listen to music anymore, or you don't like the new shit? I think high school is kind of a time in your life when you have to be a part of something or you're not anybody, it's all peer pressure until you get out of there and start being yourself."

Perception of James versus reality

"You see in some of the pictures people have drawn of me for the fan club what they think. Half-wolf half-man, which is fucking cool, yeah without a doubt, but there's other times when I go out to dinner with my stepmum and it's like 'uh? no you cannot do that!' But that's just youth, and youth is great. Everyone else is the enemy and they know who you are and what you are, and it's cool as long as you don't ruin it for them. 'I saw James feeding the cat instead of killing it ARRGGHH!'

"I think before I was limiting myself a lot, not really wanting to talk to people or giving a shit about what they thought. I guess now I'm getting better at coming into a situation and taking control with actually saying something, speaking words instead of giving looks. On stage it's a totally different thing, the buddy thing and the cussing thing. I've had a lot of people ask me why I cuss a lot onstage, and I tell them that onstage 'fuck' is such a great word and 'motherfucker' is even better. Especially delivered at high volume, so communicating up there is a little different. You cannot pretend you're the same guy up there that you are off stage. Something happens to you up there, and if it doesn't then you're a boring fuck."

Short hair, drugs and beyond

"It's the media's job to make a big deal of little things. I was reading that *Details* magazine, and it bugs the shit out of me when they get onto something that's not what I think is a big deal... Kirk and Lars tonguing or whatever the fuck they do. I don't care, they can fuck each other in the ass so long as it doesn't affect their performance, so if they drag the name Metallica in there then it bugs me. 'Metallica is not drug free,' uh, what is that? Why not say 'hello, my name's Lars and I snort cocaine, thank you, goodnight.' That's fine, that's fucking fine but to say Metallica... that word 'Metallica' means a lot to a lot of people, and when someone says Metallica is not drug free 'we get up to things you don't know about' quoted to Lars or Kirk, that bugs me a little bit. 'Metallica wear make-up now.' Kirk puts the shit on on stage, Lars really exaggerated on the video and I don't like wearing make-up. We're four grown men most of the time, and we're old enough to know what we wanna do but, of course, the name follows 'it' whatever 'it' is."

Personal partying habits

"I've definitely partied though not like the Jaeger days of 'Monsters Of Rock,' when I'd run into people who hated me, 'hey what did you do, you tackled my Mom on the lawn and jumped on some guy's car telling him to go to work, you peed on my bed' and whatever happened that really happened. It's not that bad. The other two indulge in other things, and sometimes it's a bit cliquey... that's all drugs are anyway, trying to find a 'club' or some little clique or buddy."

Making mistakes

"I know there are some nights where Lars is playing fucking crap because he's done, whatever, a few bumps the night before and he's not playing as well as he could. As long as it doesn't make the band look bad. Because in interviews you can say 'I do this blah blah blah' but if you fuck up big live, it ain't just you its the fucking band! I mean, if I fuck up the lyrics, the song goes on, the crowd sings, if I fuck up a guitar part I go 'oh fuck' and have a laugh and get back on it continuing on. If Lars fucks up a drum part everything crumbles. If the beat's off, everyone's like 'wow.' Most of the time one of us can fix it, the vocals get everyone on the beat. But I mean, when you fuck up, you've gotta laugh about it, not let it drag you down. Just let the shit happen and learn from it. But if it's a repeating thing over and over... you've got to get your shit together!"

James' father dying

"When my dad passed away, there was a lot of stuff to take care of. My sister helped out immensely, and suddenly it was a case of 'you're the man.' You have to deal with shit, people are crying and freaking and someone's got to have their head together. But then there are times when (I realize) I haven't got to grieve about it all, or more reflect on what it really means. There are little things here and there, some things will make you break down. You look at a picture of us together and think 'fuck, cool, that was a great time' but then I'll look at a receipt for a guitar he bought and then it really hits me. Weird things, you'll just hear a song and BOOM, he liked that song..."

"(In the last two years) we had a lot of good talks. The religious thing was always an ugly thing between us. And he understood why I felt the way I did, and I now understand why he believed in it. You've gotta believe in something, and that worked for him. I never really communicated with family too much. My sister, who lived with my dad a lot more than I did, was telling me some of the things that happened and how amazing the guy was. Towards the end we got to talk about heavier things that never came up before, a lot of 'guy' chit-chat, trucks, fishing, shot a badger on the property, all that stuff which was really good. And we got into some heavy talks too. Having Waylon (Jennings – country music legend) I just fucking wished my dad was there to see it.

"I mean, I get mad. Why did he have to go that way, why ask why, shit happens, it happens for a reason. I feel him inside me, I feel him helping me along sometimes. But the Waylon shows... my dad turned me onto Waylon and I turned him onto other stuff. So it was like 'we're playing together. Why can't he be here? But I flew my stepmom out, and she talked with Waylon about the phone chats he'd had with my dad which had cheered him up. They had a few things in common. Waylon was saying, 'I talked to your dad and he never complained at all, ever.' "

Calmer as a result

"I don't let shit wind me up like it does Jason now. I've learned to laugh at it. I can't, and won't, battle it because it puts me in a shitty mood and they'll just laugh it off and do it anyway. I just laugh it off, 'who cares man, be fools, have fun.' They're grown men, they do their thing, I do my thing. Jason as well, but he gets wound up. I wind him up a bit and it's not even fun anymore. I know where he's at right now, which is why I don't wind him up anymore because you just get shittier and shittier. It's so selfish to do that. The stage is where it all happens. All is forgiven, all is done because on stage is where it clicks and you have fun. It's not about attitudes, winding up and all that bullshit, it's about playing music. That's gotta be it."

JASON NEWSTED

Traveling solo during Lollapalooza

"The whole thing started out when Tony Levin, the bass player of Peter Gabriel and King Crimson fame, created this thing where he went around dealing with various people and recording with them. Sometimes it was in a studio but mostly it was in various hotel rooms with DAT players and such. It became a personal journal for him, so that was where I got the idea. I wanted to take out the bus for that, and also so as I could have some control over my hours, because my lifestyle's a bit different to the other guys in the band right now and I wanted to do my own thing out there and maybe hook up with these bands.

"It seemed like there'd be plenty of opportunity out there with 18 bands and people changing, and it seemed like I could get together with people and get some cool shit on tape like I always do at home anyway. I wanted to bring it out on a portable basis, and I knew that there would be guys like the Rancid guys who are really into ska, and I know what it's like but not what it's like to play ska. And that was the kind of thing, I thought, would be cool to mish-mash with my 'rock' whatever that I always make at home when all sorts of people show up. Like Jim (Martin – ex Faith No More guitarist), a freaky jazz drummer, a weird horn player and myself just make sick cacophonies which are very interesting. That was my intention.

"Aside from recording, there was also the bikes. I was able to call my shots, get to places where I wanted to and go ride the bike. I added up on paper how much time we were playing... 32 hours in 45 days. OK? The rest of the time what are you gonna do, be a drunk? You need to do some other shit, forward moving, productive positive shit. And taking the bike out was a step in that direction rather than getting rotted."

Recording solo material on Lollapalooza

"The tour bus had all my recording equipment, instruments, bongos and shit because I wanted to get the vibe I have at home when Jim Martin and (Jim's brother) Lou get together with us and we have drum circles, where people bang and sing stupid shit, complete wankery, but it feels really good. Some people choose a toxin, or not, whatever, and just have a good time. But it's all about doing whatever you have to do. I had different levels of recording gear too: a simple DAT player, a four-track cassette thing and a full-on digital recording and mixing thing. So we had each step. So when it came to playing with, for example one of the cats in Rage Against The Machine, then we were able to find a room where we wanted full-on-digital clean as hell stuff. Voivod was the same thing, for a couple

65

of days we were together with clean digital sound in a hotel room. I had 20 tapes and I barely got 3.5 filled, because of the way things crossed paths, people coming and going, itineraries never sticking to what they say. The coolest full-on thing was with the Rancid guys in a Ramada Inn in Vermont in the middle of nowhere. We had a room about this size (small) with a keyboard, three guitar players, horn player, electronic drums, these background singers, kids packed into the hall. We did some stuff on the regular porta-studio and we got it all on tape. It was really clean plus they showed me some ska stuff I didn't know about. I had told Tim Armstrong that I was tracking him for a while."

Enjoying Lollapalooza

"I didn't know whether it was going to be egos flying everywhere or people who were down to earth like us, real folks. So I was glad to see the Rancid guys were cool, the horn players were cool, partying in the sun when their set was done. It was great to see some bands I'd never had a chance to see before that kicked my ass. The Beth Hart Band kicked ass, the chick was fucking amazing, a turbo Janice Joplin! It's better because of the bus. I was able to get there on my own time. I was able to wake up in the town where I was playing the show, whereas to these guys that isn't such a big deal but to me it's a very big deal. I don't like to travel right before a show more than an hour. I've been getting to Lollapalooza to watch Rancid, watch Melvins, then hang out with people, bullshit, jam, whatever, then go and ride my bike around the place checking stuff out, ride in with the kids with my helmet on and shit. I got inspired by Rancid, they were fucking great, and I'd say about half the shows I went out and checked out the whole thing for myself.

"I've been making my own meals, doing a lot of my own stuff and it's been great. You become like very spoiled brats y'know, everything is catered to us. People are paid big fucking money to do what we say, to make sure everything's 'kosher.' When you're on tour there is a reason for that, you are there to be an artist and do the best job possible for that two hours and everyone is paid to make sure you can do that. So it was weird to do everything for yourself, but it was great."

Growing self confidence

"When the (Jason's own – ED) studio got completed in August '92, our first jam in there, everything started to change for me. I was able to jam with other people, and other respected people who from other areas of music who couldn't separate Metallica from Cream. They'd see the records on the wall and they were like 'great man' without saying what they'd done. I'd find out later that this guy had seven albums and so on. And you'd find out afterwards some amazing achievements. Real musicians, real people. They'd show me things I'd show them things, we'd work together to make this cool, ugly soup. It was cool because it was pure, it wasn't having to match up to something or try to be something or be a sequel to something. It's like 'here's what happened in this 38 minutes on that day. This is what happened.' It wasn't about doctoring and band-aiding and taping and gluing. Once I started to see this mutual respect happening from these guys, it made me feel very good about myself and wanting to play more with them. It just gets better too, all the time. Some day it'll show up somewhere, but not now, this is not the time.

"No matter how much I play with other people, it's great to be able to have so much fun playing onstage with Metallica, to just get up there and crush it and not hurt. Not hurt in my head, my hands or anywhere, just know that when I get up there it's going to be 'ccrruunnch! I learned from these jazz cats how to speak the music I wanted to play, I learned that way

of communication. Another major turning point. Before I used to do a lot of 'chattering' (soloing, etc) onstage, give a little speech before one of my bass solos and all that shit: it was meant well, but now I wouldn't subject people to that shit. As my confidence built with those other cats, I found the confidence to stand up to these guys."

Current relationships within Metallica

"All the fun-poking, the fun that's still poked, is usually for building. No-one's comfortable with being outright mean 'you're a fucking asshole do it this way!' so there are seeds planted. It had to come to a head, there are different intensities to bring it there. We're very well able to withstand partnership work, business and so on. What struck hard about the time we had major discussions over that tape (there were major, and somewhat heated, discussions within Metallica about a tape of Jason's solo projects – ED), was that there were serious emotions behind it. It was me, it's what I do and it all just got a little out of hand. It was me doing what I do, and now I make a very conscious effort to just keep low key. Sometimes I'm even too low key, I should pay a little more general attention to different things that take place. I'm not getting too uptight about things, I'm just letting things be more than ever.

"I suppose it must be weird to look in from the outside. I get asked a lot of questions about 'have I thought about leaving the band' because they see the separation, they see us doing different thing from each other. Even small things get people asking, like at one Lollapalooza show those guys took a golf cart to the stage and I walked. I was asked 'why do you hate each other, is that it?' And it was, of course, 'errrr no, I don't like eating dust off the back of that cart so I thought I'd walk.' Some people do not get that."

The attitude and antics of others

"Some folks are really good at that, getting out there carousing and partying and God bless 'em. I'm not preaching against it, I'm not concerned about amounts of consumption or what it is they're doing because the bottom line is to have a good time... I still have a good time every so often. Being out there and being the social butterfly is something they're really good at. Which is all good. But some of the things, some of the pretentious shit that I see, I don't want to be associated with that. Who's got the longest car and the nicest clothes and the nicest looking chick, who'll let you in past hours, different things like that. That scene, I mean come on. I don't want to look down on people, that to me is like saying 'you're better than this person.' I don't wanna be that. So all I'm doing now is being myself. I still love hanging out with these guys, laughing and joking but now everybody is their own person.

"Our individual personalities are very important to the balance of the band. These past 30 days I've not been on the plane have seen the balance screw up everywhere, because everybody's so different in their personalities. Those guys have been doing their thing with security guards and the fancy plane and whatever, I've been doing my little thing on the bus, but the main thing is this soup needs a little dash of each. It needs a pinch of each to keep its freshness. If I was a fucking maniac, if I was partying all the time, if we were all that way then I don't know if this thing would've been able to last this long and in as good condition as it is now. The influences we have on each other are big.

"Sometimes we don't even have to plant seeds, you can just see by example. When I got my bike, Lars saw that and he's always run and worked out but he now runs every day. He's gonna run every day just to make sure that he's not doing less than me. One thing I want to say here. Do you remember on the "Year And A Half..." video, kids made the biggest deal about this, when I was making sandwiches at the gig to take away? People were going on about 'the motherfucker's got millions of dollars the cheapskate.' That became a bigger deal than anything to everyone because I was taking food out instead of buying room service. And I'd tell people, I have plans for those millions and it ain't spending it on sandwiches! It was 1991 when that happened. Less than a year later EVERYONE was taking home their own cooler with their own specific stuff from the rider on it. So I'm just saying, with this huge fat example, that this sort of stuff takes place. I mean it's a totally practical thing to do, we've paid for the food already, why not? But no-one's ever going to come up and say 'you were right' you'll just see it happen in front of your own eyes. Sometime it takes a while to develop, but it happens."

'The Kiss" and beyond

"It's been misconstrued (Jason's vitriolic reaction to Lars and Kirk exchanging a kiss in public — ED), it was just concern like you'd show over your sister or brother. I wasn't trying to swing the cross or preach, it was concern about the musicianship and practice ethic. Nobody wanted to rehearse, nobody. I rented this rehearsal place for the time we were in New York, a 24 hour rehearsal place. I went there every night. I've got 12 full tapes of various projects, and through the five weeks I'd ask those guys in different manners, in different moods and at different times of the day 'dude let's go and jam, do come and jam. There's gear there, show up if you want to. Lars came a couple of times, for 15 minutes at a time and he was loopy, he was with his new girlfriend which is great. Have a good time, party, cool. But it just wasn't good. You could tell he hadn't played drums for a long long time, people would look at me like 'what?' When he didn't come in and just lock it in, that made me feel weak. I want to look, as a fan of Metallica, at the drummer of Metallica and go 'fuck me, FUCK ME!' That's what I want. I wasn't trying to be mean, I just wanted him to come and fucking jam more, it didn't have to be Metallica and I don't care if he'd had ten beers, just come and rock out.

"Somehow it all found its place, we did two days of full rehearsal and everything clicked. There are some good vibes happening out there, but some of the sounds... it could be anything, typing, drawing, brain surgery. It needs practice. If you're going to do whatever you're going to do in front of people you have to practice, you have to focus on what you do. You play and you practice."

Learning from the other band members

"It may seem silly, but from James a stretching regiment. His girlfriend Francesca knows all the proper shit. I didn't go up and ask him how to do it, I just watched him do it and picked it up like that. Eighteen months down the tour I was doing the stretches, so you just take from each other over and over. From Kirk I learned one of the most important things ever, which are my eating habits. Getting away from meat, to really get together with myself on what I put into my body. When I first joined the band I'd go to IHOP and I'd order bacon, extra bacon. He'd look at me and just say 'dude!' And as I watched him just stay a 15 year old, ten years have passed and he's still a 15 year old, I said 'OK you're right.' I don't eat double bacon anymore, grains and whatever now, but it's from his initial example. There's a lot from Ulrich... a lot...

"We have a really serious 'brotherly' thing way way down that transcends all other shit. He was the one that basically chose me for this band, he was the one who fought for me. Big enough reason right there, a lot

of things, but that's the main one. There are a lot of business things I've learned from him, he gets 113 faxes a day, deciphers it all down and spits out the lot in five minutes. The way he's put himself as the middle man of the band, the manager within the band, he didn't have to do that. I mean, every spare minute of his time is taken up with other business and band related shit, so no wonder he doesn't have as much time to practice drums as I'd like him to. He has so much shit on his plate. To be able to do that and still get there and rock out 'Whiplash' it may not be 100% but at least he's there."

Kirk Hammett

Making personal changes

"During the "Black" album tour the seeds of change started to sprout. People had been drawing a lot of attention to the difference in political views between me and James. I mean, we're very similar in a lot of ways and didn't see eye to eye in a lot of ways. Since then he's come more left-of-center and I've gone more towards the center. And that was the whole beginning of having differences and standing behind them. I think after we all took time off from the "Black" album tour, with time away from each other, we had the time to explore life away from the band.

"I've always been very open-minded and curious about everything. When I got off tour ("Black" album tour — ED) I went to school at San Francisco State, and I took Asian Studies class because I am part Filipino and I wanted to find out more about my own indigenous culture. I took a film studies class because I'm very interested in film, and I really felt that school made me become anonymous again. One of the masses. And it felt

really great. Plus I was trying to stimulate myself in a non-musical way. I'm always trying to make myself a better musician but this way I was trying to be a better person all around. For the last month or so I've decided that I want to learn to make films, I don't want to act, I want to make them. I took a jazz class too, which was very stimulating because up until then I had thought jazz was boring. Then one day I realized I'd been listening to the wrong stuff."

...and changing image

"I didn't feel that I had to follow the strict band guidelines, so with everything else changing I didn't see why I couldn't change my relationship within the band, my attitude, perception and approach. So I started wearing other things than a motorcycle jacket or a t-shirt with the sleeves cut off. I started wearing pants that weren't skin tight. That was gradual over the course of the "Black" album. In San Francisco I have a lot of friends who are in the vintage clothing business, and I started hanging out at a bar that played nothing but jazz and swing music, where the people dressed in nothing but vintage gear. Hats, ties, spats, everything. My friends were hanging out there, and they'd have these swing shows where everybody was dressed like that. I started going and dressing up like that, and somehow or another it mutated into this Cuban-gangsta-pimp thing. I dunno how it happened, maybe because I smoke Cuban cigars but also because I grew up in the Mission in San Francisco. I had Latin roots and I was going back to them, plus the wing club, plus my friends in the vintage clothing business, suddenly I found myself dressing like that. It felt sooo different and it felt soooo good.

"I think also moving back into the city of San Francisco from the East Bay made a big difference. I started hanging with some great people, lot of musicians, artists, gay people who were artists and musicians, people who were heavily into tattoos and piercings, people who were very open minded...

"Gay people are people just like anyone else, they just have a different sexual preference. Some are a little more overboard than others, but there's no difference between seeing an overly campy gay man and an overly macho guy.

"The reason I wear eye-liner isn't for any feminine or glamorous reasons, but because I think it looks fucking evil. It accentuates my eyes, people can see my eyes and other direction of my stare from a lot further. The Misfits were an influence of that, the way that Syd Barrett (ex-Pink Floyd) used to wear eye-liner made him look crazy, Ozzy's done it for many years, Iggy Pop, lots of people have done it. Let's get down to bare bones here. We have a very macho image, we're a heavy metal band, we put out an image that seems very testosterone driven, very macho, very strong, very

solid, very manly. And y'know, I don't doubt that for one minute because the music's that way. But the mental image they had of us was sentimentalized. Seeing us was probably relatable to points in their lives just like certain albums might've meant certain things. And they want to be able to look at us and still see the same image that correlates to all the same emotions they've attached to them. They want consistency. And change is very difficult for a lot of heavy metal fans to deal with if you're not open-minded. But if you can deal with change on an intellectual level, then it's fine. In time, none of it will matter."

The drug issue

"Again, not only was our image very 'metal' it was also very puritanical. We were openly drunk all the time, never on stage, always afterwards. But the drugs thing? Let's be honest, it's always been there. Of course James never did, I exclude James from all this stuff. It was something we didn't necessarily want attention drawn to, and let's face it, we felt at the time we didn't wanna talk about it because it could be misconstrued. Our drug use is very, very small, no-one's got a drug problem and we've acknowledged the fact that yes we have done drugs here and there. It's never been every night, it's never affected our performance in the studio or on stage. That's the story. We've always been into the 'be what you wanna be' thing where you're honest and open about things. Plato once said that 'a life left unexplored is a life not worth living.' And y'know, right now at this particular point, that resonates so heavily. I want our fans to be that way too. Be yourself and do what you wanna do. We all have that attitude within this band."

The infamous Lars/Kirk kiss shocker

"Well, it was about flirting with taboos in public. It's like playing with fire if you're a pyromaniac. As a little kid I used to love playing with fire, not that I was a pyromaniac, I just loved playing with it because it was a bad thing to do. For those same reasons is why Lars and I were doing that. We're not homosexuals, we're not lovers... ask all my girlfriends... but going back to that thing before, we're just pushing buttons with a sense of humor. And if people cannot see it with a sense of humor, then y'know? We're not losing any sleep from it, James isn't losing any sleep from it, Lars isn't losing any sleep, it's no skin off our backs. If Jason can't see it for the humor that it is and it gets him all riled up, then... I dunno, at least he'll go out and play an extra good show 'cause he'll have all this aggro. I'm sorry if he's not comfortable with it... I don't think any different of him, he doesn't think any different of me, it's just all about pushing buttons really."

Enjoying self-expression

"I wanted to express and show who I am, and we are all different personalities and we should express it. Because at the end of the day, it's a lot more interesting, the freedom to express yourself is a lot more healthy and people would relate to us as different people. Now the mix is stronger, if the ingredients are all stronger and more interesting by themselves then it's going to make a much better stew... It's all about challenging people, in any way, making them think about their own lives as well as just getting on with the changes and rolling with them. I'm not the only one who feels this way, everyone's into expressing themselves in a way that's truer to themselves. Don't get me wrong though, at the end of the day it is all in good fun. You have to see it with a sense of humor at the end of the day, I'm not here to push certain philosophical views or certain fundamental ideals, I'm not! I'm just trying to make it interesting and have a big laugh!" ●

BAND COMMENTS

Wow! A BIT OF A DIFFERENT HEADSPACE THAT AT ONE MOMENT! PART OF THE RIDE, BABY!

DON'T REALLY REMEMBER MUCH FROM THIS PERIOD — NOT REALLY SURPRISING IS IT? I REMEMBER ONE THING — BY THE END OF LOLLAPALOOZA THE COPS WERE AFTER ME! CAN'T REALLY REMEMBER WHY!

3/04

GOD BLESS FREEDOM OF SPEECH. A GREAT MIRROR TO REFLECT WHERE YOU WERE THEN AND WHERE YOU ARE NOW.

3/04

70

UNTIL IT LEAPS

NOTES FROM ALLEYS OF

META METALLURGY

by Torben Ulrich

**Lars thought that it might make a nice change
to hear from another Ulrich. So at Lars' special request, his father (Torben)
wrote the following thought-provoking article
exclusively for So What!**

From the alleys, it says. Alley as something that goes between, an in-between. More concretely, going quickly: Which alleys, what in-between?

Between so what and so what, between issues, deadlines, words, the in-between where writing always seems to linger, out of breath, and close to the garbage cans.

But also, more concretely, the space between Slim's and Apple, we're talking June 1996, warm nights in San Francisco, a smoking alley, a massive noise. Which Slim, what Apple?

As for Slim's, it's easy to go back to a previous issue (Volume 3, Issue 3), where Steven Wiig's careful coverage took us through the details, of Metallica playing a warm-up gig, a club setting, compact walls, Metallica Club members filling space, sweat and song blending, things

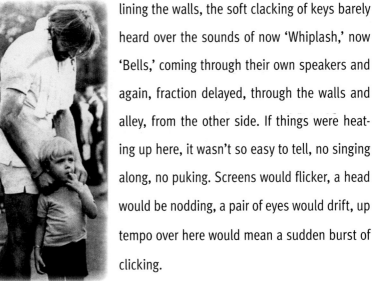

heating up, beer flying, slightly calmer air to be reached through the back door, a stumble into the alley.

As for Apple, it's also easy to say, yes we're talking computer people, now they are across the alley from Slim's, filling large rooms in a rented studio-type place, setting up shop to broadcast, yes webcast, Metallica. Rows of computers are lining the walls, the soft clacking of keys barely heard over the sounds of now 'Whiplash,' now 'Bells,' coming through their own speakers and again, fraction delayed, through the walls and alley, from the other side. If things were heating up here, it wasn't so easy to tell, no singing along, no puking. Screens would flicker, a head would be nodding, a pair of eyes would drift, up tempo over here would mean a sudden burst of clicking.

A strange place then, the alley, this in between, still early in the evening. From one side you'd see pale and blackened warriors crawling out, through the alley door, faces weathered, from years of arena air, bodies armed with metal knowledge, their stride somewhat cautious, eyes half closed, half alert, what: Could those four fuckers in there still play music?

Into the alley, from the other side, would enter another cast, no less alert, eyes targeting, stances upright, their pace quickened by a certain zeal, a hurry, like time wasn't on their side. They were men and women briskly at work, their bodies maybe not quite resonating with the questions brought inside to Slim's that evening. Rather, as we would learn, their concern was how to get this stuff moving on to a computer screen. How to get four musicians moving, not in spastic struts, eleven times a minute. But move, flowingly, in so-called real time. Not just today, tonight. Maybe more particularly, tomorrow.

The alley thus a passage, an opening, where different orientations would meet for a moment, in a crossing, a smoke, a brief interplay between eyes set on different horizons. Those that had come to hear, at Slim's, came heavy with knowledge of the past, of metallic lore and the music's more minute history. Their attention, early that evening, seemed pointed in a particular, for them crucial direction: Were those four guys still their guys? Or had something gone radically wrong?

Those that came to work, over at Apple, were obviously not looking at the same set of questions, comparing past and present. Obviously their energies were cast into the situation at hand, early June '96, yet maybe even more so into the larger setting, of years to come, coming soon, where a whole other set of rules might govern how we would travel, along with this music, on the Internet. In other words, they were working also, this very evening, to shape the binary questions of tomorrow: the ways we listen and see.

A little more specifically: What were they doing? They were, as I understand it, making a digitized video version of the music at Slim's, making it come alive, more or less, on the Internet. More or less would here mean according to their ability, but even more so maybe according to your ability, in terms of what your receiving equipment would be capable of. Again, sitting at home, you might have a fairly live audio version, but a pretty jerky visual version, because your computer would not be able to handle, transform quickly enough, the full stream of incoming signals. Or, say, if traffic were way up a particular evening you might not even have access to a signal, or a fully streaming signal. Again, more pertinent perhaps in years ahead, how long would a streaming version remain accessible, or would a fully streaming signal, for copyright reasons, be accessible at all? In other words, all of a sudden it would not be a question of capabilities, yours or theirs, but what kind of version they would want to see released.

The last line reminds me of something James H. is quoted as having said, in November of '92: "We didn't know anything about producing or any of that crap, so the whole thing was kind of innocent. A kind of innocence that you can never recapture after your first time in the studio. I remember they wouldn't let us in for any of the

> So I'm Lars' father. And I'm writing to you as the first common member of his fan club. His mother was president, and I the one assigned to rinse the fan-can.

mixes or anything like that. I remember hearing the album and going, 'Oh my God, that sucks!'" (M. Putterford: "Metallica: In Their Own Words." Omnibus Press 1994.)

 kind of innocence. What I'm trying to portray then, let's say still from the viewpoint of the alley, was the kind of excitement that flowed out of the Apple rooms, the charge, a kind of riding the waves of the unknown, maybe a naive clicking away, perhaps an innocence, when we get to look back on these things, years from now. Compared with the seasoned situation in the rooms across, over at Slim's, where fans would sing along, the well-known energies pumping, the bell that tolls, the fading to black.

A kind of innocence. At Slim's three video cameras were operating, two on tripods, one on the move. The signals, as pictures would be seen across the street on a video control unit, about the size of a man. At various times through the evening I was fortunate to be right next to this unit, thus being able to see three clear pictures of the band playing. Three pictures simultaneously. Whereas three were not to be broadcast, webcast. Only one. Which means a reduction took place, a choosing, a kind of mix, an interpretation, to be made or taken quickly. Two gentlemen were standing next to me, they were in charge of pictures, of selecting one rather than the other. If they were familiar with Metallica music, the specific songs that were being played, I could not detect it, not from their words, not from their choices. This is not to criticize, it was really very interesting, I thought, to be there, to be let in. But I thought of James' words. And I could see how you might want to put constraints on the signal, to refrain from giving a full stream version.

While I try to recall these summer moments at Apple, sitting in Seattle, early November, the phone rings, and it's Lars' mother. She wants to ask something about vitamins. She asks what I'm doing, and I say that I'm trying to write some of that stuff that I promised Lars for the next issue of So What!. She says, do you remember the time when he had spread all the lids, from the kitchen pots and pans, all over the floor? I said, of course I remember, but maybe it's not so much those things that I was going to get into.

But maybe it is. In some sense, this whole thing is about Lars spreading the lids all over the place. And us picking up the pieces, when it's getting close to dinner.

This of course goes back to a time when he was small, small. In Denmark. Later we would sit, at night in Southern California, and wonder if he and the boys would make it back, safely, from band practice, the hour-long drive on the road. His mother would worry.

So I'm Lars' father. And I'm writing to you as the first common member of his fan club. His mother was president, and I the one assigned to rinse the FanCan.

In some sense, it's still like that. In Danish, when you write the father, it's written faren. If you take the re out and put it in front, you get re-fan. Like re-writing, return, repeat, recall, you go back, reflect, you do it again, you continue.

But when you read it, in Danish, just like it is, faren, it also means the danger. And we know from Greek mythology and onward, how the father can be the danger, Oedipus, and so on, into Freud, Reich, Jung, etc.

However, it can also be understood, I think, as being aware of the danger. And thus the father being one to protect from danger. And of course the mother, too. Parents as those who continue that way, are obliged that way, to care, to cover.

But sometimes there's nothing you can do about it, you try to protect, but it happens. And as parents, in some sense, you know that situation, even if it hasn't happened to you, directly.

But it happened to Cliff Burton's mother. And I remember being there, in a small studio in the Bay Area, the first nights when the band was practicing again, Jason's first live songs as a member, and Cliff Burton's mother was there. And we had a moment together, I had my arms around her, and we always knew there was that danger, and now it had happened. And we had that moment together. Afterwards, at the end of rehearsal, Cliff's mother went over to Jason, and they embraced, sealing as it were: the continuation.

I'm thinking of her loss, now years later, and I'm sharing it with you also to try to reconnect with you: where we were, in the alley, early June. At that time, but maybe more so in the weeks and months before, there had been a constant concern, a worry. And we had seen it, particularly on the computers, on the Internet. A small barrage of daily letters, e-mails and dispatches, wondering what it all meant. Was "Load" still metal music, was "Load" still the right music, were these guys right out of their minds, cutting their hair, cutting their balls, cutting their tempos, painting their fingernails, selling the whole load to the highest bidder? Was Metallica losing it?

Being in the alley those nights, then, was to experience not only the differences of the two outlooks, fans and apples, but to see how strongly they also intersected, interconnected, sharing modes and modems, how the fans were changing, transforming, with the times, communicating and expressing themselves in new ways. Yet wanting the band to remain the same, stay where you are, where you were, fuck "Load," fuck you, we the undersigned, sincerely on the Internet.

Still, what seemed to take place, even within the hour, within the tight locality, the walls at Slim's too close for the usual arena feedbacks and delays, the proximity of band and listeners, what seemed to take hold was a kind of coherence, that cut across lines and discursive limits and made the room open up to the band's energy irrespective of album titles, date of songs, name of tune. In other words once the band got going, and the people in the room started to let go of whatever they were carrying in with them, things were not that different, the texture pretty even. By that I mean it would be pretty silly for someone to divide these hours up into segments of: this year, that year, second album, sixth album, here they are still rockin', here they are selling out. I thought Steven Wiig wrote some pertinent observations in the last issue, like: "'Sad But True' is without a doubt, the heaviest it's ever been. With the tempo held back just a bit, the weight of the song triples." By the time they got to Aberdeen, on that truck trip, was it not even a

Being in the alley those nights, then, was to experience ... two outlooks...to see how strongly they also intersected, ... how the fans were changing, transforming

tad slower? That's the best I ever heard it, tempo-wise, the kind of grease in there. Back to Steven's point later.

Did Mack come to Slim's? In the *Village Voice* of June 16th Donna Gaines has an essay called "The Metallipalooza Moment," where towards the end she writes: "Although he likes the hypnotic 'Until It Sleeps,' 21st-century metal man Mack, like older fans, feels betrayed by Metallica's "Load." 'When a band changes like that, it's like a friend dying,' he says." Donna Gaines adds she's "waiting for "Load" to grow on me the way "...Justice" did. James Hetfield's Cowardly Lion can really sing, and in my dreams, the looser, more bluesy guitar work enters Danzigland. But my friends complain the album is boring."

Donna Gaines herself says she looks foward to hearing the band live, adding: "While some fans blame Nirvana for the death of metal, others argue that the fall from grace came with Metallica's eponymous "Black" album, which moved away from thrash, back towards hard rock."

What does that mean "back," towards hard rock? It couldn't mean where they came from. Could it mean back like on a timeline, like hard rock would be prior to thrash (and should stay there)? Could it mean from one fold into another, like into the hard rock fold, that kind of fall? Like hard rock being somehow a fixture in space, a certified landscape (back to the USSR)?

Are we getting so hooked on boundaries, so carried away by our verbal designs, that we begin to take them seriously? Metal, the name metal, the category, lead, didn't all that start as irony, a self-deprecating joke, and didn't it lead to led, without an 'a', so that later even the Americans would get it? Or did I get that wrong, maybe that's not the right story, the right story being grimmer, more correct, official. Anyway, here's a version picked up from the Led Zeppelin FAQ on the Internet: "Jimmy Page joins The Yardbirds in June of 1966, first playing bass, then dual lead guitar with Jeff Beck, then replacing Beck in November of the same year. In December, John Paul Jones does string arrangements for the Yardbirds' album "Little Games." In 1997, Robert Plant and John Bonham come together in The Band Of Joy. In March of the same year, Jeff Beck releases a solo single entitled 'Hi Ho Silver Lining,' which is backed with a Page composition entitled 'Beck's Bolero.' This song is recorded by Page, Beck, Nicky Hopkins, John Paul Jones, and Keith Moon. At this session Moon and John Entwistle, who are tired of The Who's infighting, discuss forming a band with Page and Beck. It is here that Moon announces that they should call the group Lead Zeppelin, because, '... it'll go over like a ***in' lead balloon!' (The 'a' was later removed from 'Lead' so that Americans would pronounce it correctly.)"

End of quote. They call this one the Moon version, since Entwistle claims that he was the one that made it up and also was responsible for the idea of having "an LP cover with like the Hindenburg going down in flames." (Same FAQ page.)

But if you stay with that cover for a moment, isn't it so that the Hindenburg was this proud

German ship that had already crossed the Atlantic, in other words been up, now going down in flames. Whereas in the Moon version the joke is maybe in the metaphor itself: Will it ever get up, being fuckin lead, being heavy metal?

So for all of us, in Europe, in Britain, certainly in Denmark, since the days of Sidney Bechet and Louis Armstrong's first visits, the problem was how to get it lighter, how to "swing that music." Certainly for the horn players, but even more so for the rhythm guys. Certainly we had our problems in Denmark, but we used to feel when we visited in London, in the Fifties and Sixties, that they had even more problems than we did: that their rhythm work sounded even more, well, non-arising, and in the medium and faster tempos often metallic, a pounding, hammering away.

In other words, although we could easily hear and perhaps respect the degree to which a Page, a Clapton, a Peter Green could emulate the music of the Black masters of the blues and related fields, it was also very obvious, sometimes painfully so, what was missing. And of course we knew why men like Muddy Waters (born in Rolling Forks, Mississippi, 1915), when they'd come over, would look somewhat bemused, if also not uninterested. To them we were kids, in more ways than one.

To be a kid, then, at that time, and to struggle with the qualities of being a drummer, laying down a beat that had to be really solid and tensely light, ongoingly vibrant, heavy and at the same time not heavy at all, to be working in that field could be wonderful but also exasperating. And maybe it wasn't that different in this country.

White kids, then, not getting it up. Sounding like fuckin' lead balloons? Well phrased, Keith Moon. Lead guitars, lead drums, lead like the heaviest of metals, trying to transform this state of play, see if it could be lightened up, purified of its stiffness, distilled, maybe refined, redefined, working on what was still lacking, barely there.

A process, then, of transmuting the coarser metals into lighter veins, of alchemy if you will, towards silver, quicksilver, etc. And still not take leave of what's there, of who you are.

In saying well said, Keith Moon, I have of course no way of knowing if his words above have anything remotely to do with what I've tried to express here, the turning towards Black ways of phrasing fifty, forty, thirty years ago, and the obstacles that come up with such an approach. What I would like to try now would be to connect some of those thoughts, of alchemy and rhythm, to the situation in June '96, the alley.

White kids...not getting it up. Sounding like fuckin' lead balloons? Well phrased, Keith Moon. Lead guitars, lead drums, lead like the heaviest of metals, trying to transform this state of play, see if it could be lightened up, purified of its stiffness, distilled, maybe refined, redefined, working on what was still lacking, barely there.

Still in there, at Slim's, the band's warming up, for its summer tour, next door the Apple people are doing their stuff, and all over the country reviews are beginning to appear, the field of critics taking their shots at "Load," the album released in the stores just the week before. Some quotes from the review by Ann Powers in the *Village Voice* are selected for several reasons. Using past tense, Ann Powers first gives a background, laying out a larger view of the albums gone before: "... Metallica created a music of separation, based on time signatures too fast or too slow for the average ear, and guitar and vocal harmonies that echoed medieval modes and European art rock instead of the blues. Within this sound Metallica embedded a mythology..."

These observations I think are well taken. In this context perhaps the one about the blues is particularly worth noting. "Instead of the blues", as Ann Powers says. If there's a key point in the things I've tried to express in these pages it would be the following: That Lars & Co., but in any case Lars, was inspired primarily by musicians that were not directly turned towards Black music. You might say that Metallica, if its ears were turned towards (early) NWOBHM as a major inspiration, the band was at least twice removed from Black rhythms. And it seemed that already the people they were listening to (in terms of being really influenced by them) did not have Black ways of playing as a fundamental problem, an obstacle or a concern. Maybe they (NWOBHM) didn't even hear it that way, as something worth a concern, because it wasn't even an aspiration or an ideal. Black musicians were not their heroes. At least it didn't sound that way. Whereas it did for the generation before, Stones, Cream, Page, Green, maybe Blackmore, etc.

To return to Ann Powers and her review of "Load," in her second long paragraph she is still looking back, I think: "... Metallica's mythos wasn't psychological or personal at all. Instead it distilled the essences of comic books and horror movies and the fantastic literature of metal itself, until it touched a Platonic ideal of alienation and rage. Unquestionably white and male, favoring emotional violence, it did nothing to change the surface of rock. But on the more mysterious level where rock jumps identity to become a soul-transforming tool, it pushed further, opening up new ways to contemplate the extreme."

In these lines you might say that Ann Powers comes close to using a language that reflects also the alchemical approach and process I was referring to above. Continuing in this way (archetypes, death, fear, boiling, lead, etc.), via U2 she now goes into "Load" itself, but unlike so many other writers she makes, I think, a pertinent stop: at the photograph on the cover: "… while the Irish bombardiers invoked "Exile On Main Street"'s introspection with "Achtung Baby" (released the same year Metallica, the band's last disc, achieved world domination by boiling those old archetypes of death and fear in lead), the thrash kings adorn "Load" with Andres Serrano's blood-and-cum splash photographs. It's an excellent choice: Serrano's manipulation of fleshy substances (piss, semen, gore) within images both tactile and abstract exactly parallels the primordial quality of Metallica's music. They may flaunt their downtown duds in far too many Anton Corbijn photographs inside the CD booklet, but Serrano's coagulating stain still represents Metallica's enduring strength."

Ann Powers continues her review from there, stating a moment later that "… it can't be denied: there are moments on this record that will make you shake your hips instead of bang your head." We will not continue, although it can't be denied that I feel her entire review is really well written. The idea at this point would be to see if we could link up the themes of alchemy and rhythm, the transformational processes of alchemy, of the coarser metals, and the energies of rhythm, the boiling in lead, to see if we could link up these themes with the subject of the cover, the cover itself. The Metallica cover, as such, the six albums as a series of statements, over the years, pointing both to the music inside, as protective cover, and to the process of play, from album to album, as something also to be tried, dis-covered. Maybe.

In any case, since we don't have a larger footnote apparatus set up, I would like to put in place, as further background, as a kind of foundation, another couple of quotes. The first is from Lars, it relates to and expands on the reference I made above on the letters NWOBHM, puts it in a more embodied framework: "What we got from Motörhead back in '80/'81 was the aggression and the energy and the speed that Motörhead had back then, around the "Overkill"/"Ace of Spades" albums… That's why the band sounds so European. When I moved to L.A. in 1980, we wanted to get a band together that had a European-sounding background, and since I came from over there I had a lot of the influences with me, like Motörhead and other bands like Diamond Head and some of the other early New Wave of British Heavy Metal bands."

I have taken this quote from Chris Crocker's book *Metallica: The Frayed Ends of Metal,* (St.

Martin's Press) page 24. In the same work, on page six, it says: "The term heavy metal is said to have first appeared in William Burroughs' 1959 landmark avant-garde novel *Naked Lunch.* It doesn't. His 1962 follow-up, *The Ticket That Exploded,* does contain a number of references to 'heavy metal.' While having nothing to do with rock'n'roll, they somehow convey the right atmosphere.

"When Steppenwolf sang about 'heavy metal thunder' in their 1968 hit 'Born to Be Wild,' it may have put a bug in the ears of those fans or rock critics who put the term to use."

To this may be added a few lines from a verse, estimated to be from the neighborhood of the '70s, maybe by Thomas Norton, of Bristol in England, a student of the master George Ripley: "Then depart them by destilling/ and thow shallt see an Earth appearing/ heavy as Metall should yt be/ in the which is hyd great privitie." (From E.J. Holmyard: *Alchemy,* Dover Publ., p. 198).

In Mark Heffner's *Dictionary of Alchemy* (Aquarian), under Georgius Agricola, the metallurgist, we learn about "De re metallica" from 1556, "in 12 books, dedicated to Duke Maurice of Saxony. This posthumously-published work was Agricola's crowning achievement, laying firm foundations for the rapidly growing science of metallurgy."

And in *Alchemy: The Secret Art,* by Stanislas Klossowski de Rola (Thames and Hudson) there are these words associated with Dom Pernety (p. 13): "True alchemy consists in perfecting metals, and in the maintenance of health."

We move now to the subject of the album cover for "Load." There is a book called *Andres Serrano: Body And Soul* (Takarajima Books) that shows the photographs of Serrano from his different periods of work and also contains the photograph on the cover of "Load," with its full title: "Semen and Blood III, 1990." On the inside of the cover of the book itself, the first lines are a quotation from Senator Jesse Helms. It reads: "I do not know Mr. Andres Serrano. And I hope I never meet him. Because he is not an artist. He is a jerk."

The inside cover lines then continue: "Andres Serrano's name became a household word on May 18, 1989, when Sen. Alphonse D'Amato tore up a picture of the artist's "Piss Christ" on the floor of the U.S. Senate. The act launched the so-called Culture Wars, a national debate over free expression and federal funding of the arts. But, while Serrano's "Piss Christ" became widely known, the rest of his photographic work received scant attention."

In an essay early in this book called *The Radiance of Red: Bloodwork,* the American writer bell hooks (her name spelled like

The term heavy metal is said to have first appeared in William Burroughs' 1959 landmark avant-garde novel Naked Lunch. It doesn't. His 1962 follow-up, The Ticket That Exploded, does contain a number of references to 'heavy metal.' While having nothing to do with rock'n'roll, they somehow convey the right atmosphere.

that) talks about Serrano's work. At a certain point she uses the phrase "defamiliarize by provocation," which seems relevant also to our situation here (photographer and band). She dares to bring together the sacred and profane, to defamiliarize by provocation. In the introduction to *Arresting Images: Impolitic Art and Uncivil Actions,* Steven Dubin describes his own visceral response to the Serrano photograph "Milk, Blood (1986):" 'As the grandson of a kosher butcher, my immediate reaction was 'You don't do this; you don't mix milk and blood. It just isn't done!' Once again this reaction startled me, for although I do not observe kosher laws, this image struck me as a violation of a very basic sort. Categories which I long rejected intellectually, I suddenly desired to uphold emotionally; they seemed natural and inviolable. But not only had they been juxtaposed, they seemed to bleed into one another down the middle of the photo. Unthinkable, and yet here was the record of this transgression.'"

So let's situate ourselves once again, where are we? In the in-between, between deadline and past it, between covers, this one and the next, in other words between "Load" and "Load." In the December issue of *Metal Edge,* Lars is quoted as saying: "The main thing right now is to do the tour and live up to the promise we made to ourselves to go in and finish these other songs and get them out sometime at the end of next year. I want people to understand that although it's a new Metallica record it's really part two of "Load." All the songs were written and recorded at the same time and in terms of feel and sound and style they're a part of this whole thing, so it's important we get it out as soon as possible. I was listening to the stuff a few weeks ago and it all sounds really strong but I want to get it out there before it starts sounding dated."

I asked Lars if he thought that Serrano would be involved in the cover of the second "Load," and he said he definitely thought so.

Where are we? We are at the risky point where we will try to give a reading (a reading in terms of the dynamics of rhythms and alchemy) of the albums, on the basis of their covers. The six albums, on the way to the seventh, from that perspective, that kind of hindsight, not to be taken seriously.

The cover as metaphor. I always thought it was incredible that an album with a phonograph record in it could not be called "Metal Up Your Ass," could not, but could be changed and apparently quite easily be called "Kill 'Em All." Pretty good picture of our society, our cultural ways. In Mark Putterford's book Lars is quoted as saying, in August of 1983: "I really like the cover... The idea of a sledgehammer lying in a pool of blood may sound kinda simple, but it looks real neat..."

So here we have the idea of a sledgehammer, iron fist, heavy metal, or maybe led as found in s(led)gehammer. Metal in a pool of blood, already that chemical marriage, the energies of being human coming together, the thrust of force as a hammer, etc.

If you take the six albums and divide them in three, you might call them, so far, the early, the middle, and the late. The two early albums would then be about energy, the riding of the energies, the lightning, the onslaught of force, its coming to a halt, the pool, the chair, etc. And inside the cover the music itself shoots up, rides the pulse, singing death, surviving death, fuck death, up yours, here we go.

But is there in this pulse a kind of sledgehammer approach, the fast rhythms perhaps having a kind of metronomic feel, going to the leaden side rather than to the blood? Above we talked about this hammering away, the British way, here we have a newer breed, faster attack, erupting speeds, killing, killing, maybe even the tempos.

Met(all)ica. As there is led in sledgehammer, what kind of all is there in early Metallica? Metal up your ass seems to be a friendly gesture, a committed insistence, inclusive at least to the degree that you yourself are seen as part of the procedure. Take Putterford's book, page 9, where Lars

is quoted as saying, in August of 1992: "Remember, you're talking to the guy who brown-nosed his way through England in 1981 with Lemmy, Diamond Head and Iron Maiden! That side of me has been there! That's one of the reasons Metallica exists, because I'd sit there and learn from the Motörheads, Diamond Heads and Iron Maidens, because I was so far up their ass all the time! I've been to Motörhead rehearsals in 1981 – when they were working on the 'Iron Fist' songs – as a punter, absorbing and learning the vibe. That's what made me realize I wanted to do this shit myself."

Metal up your ass, as quicksilver, raising the temperature, boiling conventions, familiarizing through provocation. Kill 'em all, which all? Maybe the others. Maybe those that oppose the freedom of choice, the choice of that first naming of the album. Where the first title spreads its own congeniality, or at least can cut several ways, the second and final title sets up, in disgust, an adversarial situation. Us and Them.

This continues on the third cover, where you see the name Metallica untouched by the strings attached to all the crosses, the army of death being held by the hands above, the all in Metallica freely suspended on the cover, the whole Metallica name hovering like a spaceship above the rows of crosses, the energies of the M and the A, the pointed letters, spreading out over the cemetery. In alchemical terms, you are beginning to see the hands of dogma and authority holding you to the ground, institutionalized order prevailing. You begin to see the strain of this living, always wearing the helmet of death (left side of cover). In chemical terms you feel you must begin to change, a dying to a fixed regime. In political terms you feel it's time to speak up.

Doris arrives (bound and cracked). The fourth album thus introduces Woman, the female everywhere that gives solace to sailors and roadies. And more, woman as Justice, as the call to justice, for all. This all now of a different kind, the call to justice all-embracing, the slow realization that we are in this soup altogether or all together, the laws of desire, of buying and selling, the laws of legality, of favoritism and legal fees (see Putterford, p. 29), the tipping of scales, of green cards, red cards.

Black is next, the fifth album, the word in the alchemical tradition is nigredo, from Latin, the blackening of the metal, "a black blacker than black" (quoting from Jung), the stage of putrefaction that must take place before a purer metal is obtained, the transformation towards a lighter form, towards mercury, the ongoing transmutation of ignorance, a shedding of veils. In rhythmic terms it's the opening up towards blacker modes of play, having been enlisted for years, maybe for centuries, in a different, more mechanic pronunciation. In alchemical terms the snake on the cover would be the dragon, of deep-rooted confusion (both fierce and stubborn), that must be seen through, slain, the word drako being Greek for serpent, snake. In rhythmical terms, the snake (front and back cover) would be the coiling movement of the blues, like Blind Lemon Jefferson's 'Black Snake Moan.' On the cover of one of my EPs (with several versions of 'Roam' plus a live 'Battery') only the "all" of Metallica is seen, way up in the right corner, across the cover.

The latest album, then, is this process continued, both extended and turned inward. Blood and semen coming together in Serrano's poignant photograph, the marriage of male and female forces, the processes of union, its steps and stages known in alchemy as coniunctio (king and queen, solar and lunar sides, etc.). In terms of rhythm: a further vitalization, in that a continuation of less restrictive patterns opens up the entire field of play, the music breathing freer, the pulse flowing more organically. The word Metallica, on the cover, now more porous, the M pointing its point into the mixture of semen and blood, the A pointing into a breach, an opening bay. The logo, formerly with its arrows aiming only outwards, is seen in the lower left corner on the back cover (and on the CD itself, its metal): now turning some of its energy inward, the four sides of the assembled star turning also on itself, arrowpoints touching other sides, leaving a situation rich in possibilities, a variety of future ways, not without its risks of internal fractures. How do you read the logo? How do you see the cover, the series, in retrospect?

James H., quoted in Pepperford's book, May 1990: "Things are so deep and people are always trying to read shit into things that are real simple. Some people try and tell you what the songs are about and it bores me to death."

Concerning the in-between, between albums, between holes. In *Modern Drummer,* Nov. '96 issue, Lars is quoted: "... I don't like to be pigeonholed, and I really like that people never really know what's going on with Metallica. We set the tone for that going all the way back to "Ride the Lightning," which was a lot different than "Kill 'Em All." There's a certain side of me that likes messing with people's expectations of what Metallica should be."

Between beats, between drums and guitars. Lars, same issue, same page: "... you have to understand that for ten or twelve years the only thing I had on my monitor was James Hetfield. The only thing coming into my head-phones when we were recording was James. The drums and the rhythm guitar were always the backbone of this band, unlike most bands where the drums and bass are supposed to be the backbone. With us, the bass was almost an afterthought; we fit it in wherever there was a space left in the mix. You take a record like "...Justice." There wasn't very much space left.

'"Load" was the first record where we cut the drums and then the bass, so we actually had the rhythmic foundation on tape before we cut the guitars. It gave us that solid foundation we'd never quite had before. It's also the first time I felt that Jason and I were really starting to lock in at the level a drummer and bass player should, in the traditional sense of rhythm players. There's more of a connection and vibe going between us. There's more eye contact now and we're both more aware of what each other is doing.

"When we first met Jason and brought him into the band, his ears would always go to James' left hand. What we tried to do was get him to forget about James' left hand and focus more on my right hand. It was very hard to get him to do that, especially coming from his speed metal background, where the two guitars and bass are almost as one, whereas in the traditional hard rock that I was brought up on the drums and bass were more hooked up. But in the last couple of years, I think Jason's really come more into my camp and it's made an incredible difference in how the rhythm tracks hold together."

The tracks between the rhythms, the tempos. This would be the point where we might link up again with Steven Wiig's good lines in volume 3, issue 3 of SO WHAT!. I'll extend the quote to the paragraph as a whole: "'Sad But True' is without a doubt the heaviest it's ever been. With the tempo held back just a bit, the weight of the song triples. Kirk's in tune with the crows (and his guitar) like never before. Tossing and hammering his guitar around like a crazed magician, he is full of eye (liner) contact and makes a huge impression on all of us."

Being in tune, with the crows, with the tempo. When the tempo is held back just a bit, the weight triples. Here's an area where I think there're possibilities for development, relating also to Lars' comments above concerning his and Jason's coming together: taking the tempo to its rightful place, its full potential. Obviously that's never a fixed place. Yet to experiment a little with taking it down a notch, or up, will change the whole fiber of a song, open it up to a richer texture and pull. And the solo work on top of such a changed foundation might then, again, in its turn be influenced, inspired. The Count Basie band, from early on, seemed to make an art of just that, the tempo as such.

The in-between as such. There's a kind we haven't mentioned, which is a little related to the above: the in-between between songs, when one song is ended, and the next is not quite there yet: the interval on the playlist, so to speak. In those spaces, I feel there's also room to work, how to time and play with these silences, to move the whole thing along, while the applause etc. rises and waves out. To prepare, in (non-scripted) sound and silence, a chord, a cymbal, an anticipation, a rest that's still alert to its further direction. The one who impressed me in this area was Courtney Love, I heard her with Hole, striking a stand, some sliding notes, a hurling of insults, building a tension up to the release of the song itself, I thought she did that so well.

Finally, the word cover of course has several meanings, cover as protection, shield, and also, in music terms, cover as mimesis, to cover a song, adding a seal of one's own. Thinking again of Courtney Love, and the coming together, on "Load," of the seminal juices, this possibility then: to hear her version of "Where's Your Crown King Nothing."

Finally, back to the alleys. Between Metallica and the Internet, between the band and its most vocal and loyal supporters. This is what we picked up, here in Seattle, just as we were putting an end to the story. Signed by one Steve and dated Sunday Nov. 17, America Online, the subject being "Re: All I Want For Christmas," it read: "The hell with Metallica, I want a Tony Smith action figure!!!!!!!!!"

We all join in saluting the Editor. ●

META METALLURGY

When the tempo is held back just a bit, the weight triples. Here's an area where I think there are possibilities for development.... taking the tempo to its rightful place, its full potential.

WHIPLASH

THE BAND ANSWERS FAN QUESTIONS

Lars, what kind of diving equipment do you use? What is your highest qualification?
Dom C., Port Jervis, NY

LU: I'm a rescue diver. I'm 4th level of the PADI system. My equipment is mostly Scuba Pro and I have a U.S. Diver's computer.

Kirk, out of your whole toy collection, what do you consider to be your most valuable item?
Rafael M., Boston, MA

KH: A Frankenstein head radio speaker.

James how do you make those mean faces? I have tried many times, but I freeze my face up when I do it.
Ezra K., Northridge, CA

JH: Think of redoing drum tracks.

James, have you had your tonsils out yet? Will you ever have your old Hetfield beard again? Do you like lima beans?
Sarah M., Orange, TX

JH: No, but I had them chromed. I sold it back to Lemmy. Yes, accompanied by a tender kitten fillet in toenail sauce.

Q. Hey Lars! How come there's no Metallica logo on your stix?
Helena J., Bar Mills, ME

LU: 'Cause I know what band I'm in.

Have you ever been concerned about the audience's security/safety during a show, for example asked them to calm down?
Erik V., Norway

JH: Oooh yesss, I ask them how the fuck they are doing all the time.

Kirk, I was wondering, seeing as you're such a horror fanatic, how in the hell, other than a silver bullet, do you kill a werewolf?
Mary H., Perris, CA

KH: Nuclear bomb.

I have a song called 'Sucking My Love' on a bootleg released by Totonka. Since it's a bootleg, I wanted to know if this REALLY is a recording of Metallica. It sounds like James' voice, but at such an earlier age, it's hard to tell.
Jason M., Indianapolis, IN

JH: That's back when I was a little dude of metal. LU: It's probably a recording from spring '82 of us rehearsing with Mustaine and McGovney and before James' balls dropped.

Jaysun and Jaymz, could you guys please give me some advice on face making and growling?
Dan T., Burnsville, MN

JN: Be the bass, Danny.
JH: Sit on the toilet with mirror in hand.

If Cliff could see the music you make today, what do you think he would think?
Dan F., Hudson, OH

JH: I'm sure he does hear it and I know he is proud that we've never compromised what we want to do for anyone.
LU: He would think we're all a bunch of short haired sell-outs!

I've heard that some bands employ guest musicians to play some parts at the recordings. Does Metallica do it this way sometimes?
Jochen S., Germany

JH: No way! Except for 'Zamphir; Master of the Pan Flute' on "Damage, Inc."

Hey James! Why is it that you always sit down to play 'Nothing Else Matters?' I have seen you live twice and seen numerous videos and never once have you stood up through this song! Any reason?
Mark D., Richmond, VA

JH: Hey, Lars gets to sit down the whole show. No, it really helps set the mood for me and it's easier to finger pick that guitar part.

I was wondering what kind of wood James' Explorers are made out of. I played a Gibson Explorer the other day for a half-hour and afterward I could barely stand it was so heavy. The Gibsons are made out of mahogany and I was wondering if James' were made out of a lighter wood so he could play those 2+ hour sets.
Phil B., Kirtland, OH

JH: No, full-on mahogany, duder.

Did Cliff wear bell bottom pants every day or just on stage and for photo sessions?
Arturo A., Los Angeles, CA

JH: He even wore them swimming.

What the fuck is this BEEP! noise on track #9 'Poor Twisted Me' that can be heard in the left speaker at about 1:30 into the song on both the CD and cassette? Something weird and sinister is going on here.
Ron A., Franconia, NH

LU: How dare you call the mighty Hetfield's masterful fretboard movement NOISE!!??? It's art man!

Kirk, where did you get the idea for the Ouija guitar?
Jeff M., Effingham, IL

KH: I got the idea from (you'll never guess) a Ouija board!!

Jason, my hair is all fucked up like yours, but do you get your hair to grow down?
Matt H., Stillwater, MN

JN: Piss off Matt. My hair is lovely. It has to get heavy and greasy to lay down. Good luck – ha!

Are you guys ever going to make another thrash metal oriented album or is it going to be more diverse from here out?
Chris D., Garland, TX

LU: One of my few shortcomings is that I can't predict the future.

Kirk, do ya think I could get ya to tell me your famous (or infamous) Bombay Sapphire Blue Martini recipe that was so greatly hyped by everyone in Tuktoyaktuk?
Aaron E., Ellensburg, WA

KH: Gin with a microscopic splash of vermouth.

Jaymz, how did it feel to meet Jaromir Jagr one day and then watch as his team handed your team an unforgettable ass whipping?
Tommy P., Jacksonville, FL

JH: I told him to take it easy on the boys, but see what hearing a new song does for people?

James, in 'Seek and Destroy', what word do you say before you start with the first verse?
Bill K., Brick, NJ

JH: Aaah, I'm burning!!... No wait, that's 'Fade to Black.' I think it's the absolutely brilliant ad lib, 'All right.'

Jaymz, how old were you when you first started playing guitar?
Paul W., Portola Valley, CA

JH: 15 years old. (Ya think I'd be better by now.)

When was the last time you guys were jammin' together and one of you said, 'Hey fuck it, lets play 'Escape'...?Do you even remember how to play that tune? A better question should be: do you even remember that tune?
Chad P., San Diego, CA

KH: Isn't that a Journey album?
LU: Last time was in... oh, say '57 or '58 and half the band remember how to play it just to annoy the other half.

Lars, my drums are almost exactly the same as yours, how the hell do you tune your drums so they don't resonate? I'm having a bitch of a time tuning mine.
Dave M., Canada

JH: You need a 'Flemming'.
LU: I don't... I have a 'Flemming'.

Recently I saw a movie about yachts. I don't remember that movie's name, but on the American yacht's flag was the Metallica snake and the words 'Don't Tread On Me.' What the hell is it? Did they buy a license from you or is it a new USA flag?
Marius M., Lithuania

JN: Marius, the 'Don't Tread' flag was an American flag of sorts in the 1700's.

Jason, at the Astoria, I think I saw red LEDs on the side of the necks of your bass guitars. What are they for?
Fred B., France

JH: Shows him which note to play.
JN: The red lights are for cheating. It's good to know where the notes are when the stage is 'Blackened.'

Kirk, what is your favorite Lovecraft story?
Dustin S., Bradfordsville, KY

KH: 'Rats in the Walls' and 'Mountains of Madness.'

If you guys were stranded on a deserted island and could only have one album to listen to over and over again, which one would it be?
Mike S., Cleveland, OH

LU: Alice In Chains "Dirt."
JN: John Coltrane "Giant Steps" or Bob Marley "Kaya."
JH: "The Soothing Sounds of a Deserted Island" CD.

Lars, a couple of kids in my percussion class at school were saying that you used a triple foot pedal on your bass drums, so when you hit, it would hit three times. Is that true?
Dan M., Sterling, VA

LU: Absolutely not. But if someone ever invents it let me know, so I can rest my left foot once in a while.

I'm an amateur bass player and I noticed you don't have a bass book for "Garage Days." Is there any way I could get tablature to 'Crash Course In Brain Surgery'?
Moogan L., Bellevue, WA

JH: Just go 'boo da lee doot doot' a lot.

I noticed in a past issue of SO WHAT! that Lars graduated from Back Bay High School. I was wondering if that is the school in Newport Beach/ Costa Mesa, California overlooking the bluffs.
Steve L., Newport Beach, CA

LU: That is the very one. ●

...And now, a word from our sponsors

STUDIO "QUOTES" OF THE DAY
OR BABBLINGS RESULTING FROM LOSS OF OXYGEN TO THE BRAIN (OR WHAT'S LEFT OF IT.)

"Martini; liquid vibe." .... KRK '95
"It sounds better to me when it's louder!!" .... Zach '95
"Up another more." .... Rand '95
"It's a touch hair too high." .... Ol' Rand again '95
"It's a little too damp damped." .... Yet again Rand '95
"Bob is sharing his dinner with the toilet!.. .... Larz '95
"If you're going to talk to yourself, do it a lot quieter
    cause you're confusing me." .... Bob '95
"I'm too metal for mono." .... Jayson '96
"Bob Rock: The Lone Producer of the Apocalypse." ...... Zorak '96
"An open mind is like an open wound. Susceptible to
    bacteria and disease." .... Het '95
"Hey, I wouldn't make fun of people's talking." .... Rand '95
"A little chunk never hurt no one." .... Dobbs '95
"Let's hear it at full metal bloody semen hard-on level!" .. KRK '96
"Does a battery work with only a positive?" .... Jmz '96
"She may be a pig, but she's my pig." .... Anonymous
"Are these guys gonna jam or are they buying art?" .... Rock '95
"Martinis and hammers for all my friends." .... Jmz '95
"If you want happy, go buy ice cream." .... Zach '96
"Will it hender the Fender?" .... Kent '96
"Can I hear this there... you fucking fuck twat!" .... Bob '96
"I'm getting a snare tumor." .... Rand '95

STUDIO BLUES...

Wow... I can "sleep with both eyes open."

We gotta be done by when?!

Yeah!! I finally made guns, the Raideretts, beer and trucks fit into one sentence.

Ah Ha!! I've got it!! "We're off to never never...? Wait, that sounds familiar.

Hmmm... What's another word for synonym?

Damn it!!! What rhymes with ephippiorhynchus senegalensis?

SHRUNKEN GUY

NO LEAF CLOVER

AND IT FEELS RIGHT THIS TIME
ON HIS CRASH COARSE WITH THE BIG TIME
PAYS NO MIND TO THE DISTANT THUNDER
NEW DAY FILLS HIS HEAD WITH WONDER..BOY

SAYS IT FEELS RIGHT THIS TIME
TURNED IT 'ROUND AND FOUND THE RIGHT LINE
"GOOD DAY TO BE ALIVE," SIR
"GOOD DAY TO BE ALIVE," HE SAYS

THEN IT COMES TO BE
THAT THE SOOTHING LIGHT
AT THE END OF YOUR TUNNEL
WAS JUST A FRIEGHT TRAIN COMIN' YOUR WAY

DON'T IT FEEL RIGHT LIKE THIS?
ALL THE PIECES FALL TO HIS WISH
"SUCKER FOR THAT QUICK REWARD, BOY"
"SUCKER FOR THAT QUICK REWARD," THEY SAY

THEN IT COMES TO BE
THAT THE SOOTHING LIGHT
AT THE END OF YOUR TUNNEL
WAS JUST A FRIEGHT TRAIN COMIN' YOUR WAY

THEN IT COMES TO BE

SAY HELLO TO MR. STEELTOE

OH NO, A METALLICAN

AHH, LOOK ITS BUN BUN

ere's that Superglue?

HAPPY EASTER !! HA HA

While You Were Out
For Jaymz
Date 12/96 Time
MR. Your Liver
Of
Phone
AREA CODE   NUMBER   EXTENSION
Telephoned ☑   Please Call ☐
Came To See You ☐   Will Call Again ☑
Returned Your Call ☐   Wants To See You ☐
Message Fuck You!
Signed
ADAMS BUSINESS FORMS

While You Were Out
For JAYMZ Urgent ☐
Date 7/96 Time
MR. SANTA CLAUS
Of NORTH POLE
Phone
AREA CODE   NUMBER   EXTENSION
Telephoned ☑   Please Call ☐
Came To See You ☐   Will Call Again ☐
Returned Your Call ☐   Wants To See You ☐
Message Stop shooting at
my riendeer or I'll
send the elves 'round
to Rough you up!
Signed JH
ADAMS BUSINESS FORMS

BREAK

TOP TEN THINGS CHRISTMAS
MEANS TO ME   (JAYMZ)

10) GETTING A DAY (X-MAS DAY) OFF FROM TOUR

9) CLEANING OUT THE GARAGE SO
THE FAMILY HAS A PLACE TO SLEEP WHILE
VISITING

8) LEAVING BEER & PRETZELS FOR SANTA

7) DRESSING UP LIKE SATAN CLAUS (THE DYSLEXIC
SANTA) AND SCARING THE KIDZ

6) INCLUDING THE NEIGHBORS BY UNSCREWING ONE OF
THIER X-MAS HOUSE LIGHTS, SO ALL THE LIGHTS
GO OUT AND THEY CAN'T TELL WHICH ONE IT IS.

5) FILLING THE FIREPLACE SO FULL OF COLORED WRAPPING
PAPER THAT EVERYONE FLEES IN TERROR.

4) SPIKED EGG NOG.

3) WRAPPING THE SMALLEST GIFT IN THE HUGEST
BOX AND WATCHING THE FRUSTRATION.

2) ALONG WITH THE WRAPPING PAPER, ACCIDENTALLY
(ON PURPOSE) BURNING THEIR INSTRUCTIONS TO
THAT ELABORATE CONTRAPTION GIFT AND WATCHING
THE HELL UNFOLD.

1) SHOOTING THE DAMNED CAT OUT OF THE
CHRISTMAS TREE. (AGAIN)

...UNDERESTIMATE THE POWER OF THE PASS"
AMN...
APR. '97

WOODY'S BEER COUSUMPTION SINCE AUG.
18 BEERS A DAY = 500 KEGS

ACTUALLY NOT A QUOTE
JUST A FACT

PEOPLE ARE EXPENSIVE

CAN'T WE JUST PAY TO
IT WORK

JAYMZ (HOMY)
APR. '97

I THOUGHT ID DO SOMETHING NICE
FOR THE BAND...
ILL HANG MYSELF
JAYSON
MAY '97

Sock it to me

(HAVE A DAY OFF?)

MOTHER   **MAY   I**

JAYMZ

<table>
<tr><th>SUN</th><th>MON</th><th>TUE</th><th>WED</th><th>THU
TRAVEL DAY</th><th>FRI
TOUR BREAK</th><th>SAT
TOUR BREAK</th></tr>
<tr><td colspan="4"></td><td>1
TRAVEL DAY
Ft. Worth
TX</td><td>2
Tarrant County
Convention Ctr
Ft. Worth
TX</td><td>3
Tarrant County
Convention Ctr
Ft. Worth
TX</td></tr>
<tr><td>4
TOUR BREAK
Myriad Arena
Oklahoma City
OK</td><td>5
TOUR BREAK
TRAVEL DAY
Enroute To
RENO
BAR-B-QUE</td><td>6
TOUR BREAK
DAY OFF
Reno
NV</td><td>7
TOUR BREAK
Lawlor Events
Center
Reno
NV</td><td>8
Boise State
Pavilion
Boise
ID</td><td>9
Arena
Spokane
WA</td><td>10
DAY OFF
Portland
OR</td></tr>
<tr><td>11
Rose Garden
PORTLAND
OR</td><td>12
DAY OFF
Seattle
WA
DUDES</td><td>13
Key Arena
Seattle
WA</td><td>14</td><td>15
DAY OFF
OFF</td><td>16</td><td>17
GM Place
Vancouver
BC
FUCK'N
PARTY</td></tr>
<tr><td>18
DAY OFF</td><td>19
Saskatchewan
Place
Saskatoon
SK</td><td>20
Olympic
Saddledome
Calgary
AB</td><td>21
Coliseum
Edmonton
AB</td><td>22
GO HOME!!
THE FUCK</td><td>23
CHILL OUT
WATER SKIING</td><td>24</td></tr>
<tr><td>25
INDY 500</td><td>26</td><td>27</td><td>28</td><td>29</td><td>30</td><td>31</td></tr>
</table>

C - YA

SHOOT VIDEO

LOGGIN
BOOT
SHOPPIN

OFF

WARNING
BURN HAZARD
KEEP AWAY FROM CHILDREN

85

"DIDN'T I JUST DO THIS 6 WEEKS AGO" FULL FUCKEN RIGHT ARM LIST:

Breathing
Playin' my ass off on the last couple of drum tracks
Tryin' to write 1 or 2 different last songs
"Femmes, Enfants, Animaux"
Seeing an end to this record
Seeing live dates on a piece of paper for after this record
Putting "SO WHAT!'s" together every 5 minutes
Alice In Chains "Over Now" track 48 hour hang in Seattle
Pizza with chicken, provolone & feta cheeses,
garlic and perochini peppers
Mick Jagger interview in Rolling Stone
Oasis "Wonderwall" track
"Situation of a Central Figure"
"Casino"
Not drinking for 36 days
Drinking again
Mad Season "Long Gone Day" track
48 hour hang with Steven, Paul, Leo(ron),
Sammi, Neil and P____
Guinness
Alanis Morissette "Hand In My Pocket" track
"Personage dans la Tempete"
New York
"Mighty Aphrodite"
Johannes Vermeer in D.C.

Natalie Merchant "Carnival" track
Kinda watching football on Sundays
"The American President"
2 hour hang with the Pittsburgh Penguins
Black Grape "Shake Well Before Opening" track
"Personage au Costume Rouge"
MTV's "Singled Out"
Being above the fog
Vanity Fair
Jammin' on Motörhead songs
72 hour blur in New York, brownnosing Oasis
Down "Stone the Crow" track
Putting the FanCan together
Black Grape "In the Name of the Father" video clip
Wild ginger
Seeing Nine Inch Nails crush David Bowie
Mark Leialoha's pix
"Fool Moon"
Havin' Bob say "It all depends on the vocals!!"
Havin' Jaymz in my car for 30 minutes, forcing him to
listen to Oasis
Havin' a hard time doin' vibe lists
Havin' Tony share in my hard time doin' vibe lists
Havin' a much better time breathing

Lars

Hey man, we survived Lollapalooza!!!!

Actually, it wuz very cool. A nice way to kick shit off again. Now let's get down to some real touring!!

Too many days off!! But, you know what, looking back on it here in mid-August, it was the perfect way to start things off on this here cycle... outdoors, summertime, the States, short(er) set and plenty of humidity to sweat out the previous night's indulgences. After the shitstorm/debate that was brewing up 'til the first gig, it was great to finally start playing and seeing all the hoopla calm down and people just takin' it for what it was supposed to be... the next in a line of Loolapaloozaz that hopefully will continue to be as varied and as challenging to folks as this one was and some of the past ones have been. We made a lot of new friends and saw a lot more new faces than I'd thought!! I think the coolest thing for me, was how many people came up to me and professed/admitted that Metallica was a lot cooler and different than they had thought. I think it was also the best we have ever played in terms of energy and attitude. Sure it was a little ragged during the first few (it's been close to 2 years since we last toured!!), but the energy level was higher and more consistent than I can ever remember and I think people feed off that a lot more than they used to. Obviously this had a lot to do with the shorter, pummeling, more "uppity" set that we played, but the fucken energy exchange was huger than ever. There was also less circus atmosphere than I had thought, and it was pretty fun to flip around out in the crowd completely unnoticed. My favorite other band was definitely Rage Against The Machine, who very hangin' for about 8 shows. Soundgarden got better and heavier, and started playing more older shit, as the tour went along, which wuz cool. But, to be honest, I can't wait to get going with our own shit. We haven't played indoors in arenas since the fucken spring of '93, and I'm dying to go, man. On a day off in July, we all went and saw Kiss indoors in Pittsburgh, and as we stood and watched the festivities, it dawned upon me, that playing indoors in arenas seemed a fucken lifetime away and how cool the vibe and the containment of the energy was... So let's fucken go!

Highlights were actually the LA shows, where Lemmy and Jerry C. paid us some visits on stage, and I thought we were the best in Indy, the first New York and the second LA..!! There you go... enough!!!!

What else in Metalliland??? Shot the video for "Hero" a few ago and that wuz definitely the most fun vid we've done. Got to act out all these silly, goofy scenarios. You'll see. Fun!!! As for the single, we decided to throw in a bunch of the Motörhead songs from rehearsal in December last year as the B-sides. There will be one overseas format that will have all the Motörhead stuff on, kinda like a tribute EP, so check her out, eh???!

Now we head out on the longest European tour anybody's ever done, and then start up in the States, indoors, in mid-December. The first batch of dates should be printed somewhere else in this here fine rag, and will probably change 200 times before we start, but it will give you an idea of what the fuck. After that, next summer(?), the plan is to try and finish the rest of the songs leftover from the "Load" sessions(!!??) and have the second half out before the end of '97! (sure!!). This will probably also change 200 times, but for now it seems like a "doable" plan. Then more touring to places we haven't covered yet, like Japan, Australia, Pacific Rim, South America, your neighborhood pub, the living room in your parents house... you get the fucken picture.

Well, 'fuckers, that's it for now. Most of the rest of the shit is fairly well(?) documented in other, much lesser rags. I'll see all your pretty faces out there on the "Poor Touring Me" tour or whatever we decide to call our little outing,

C-Ya in a bit,
Lars

A lot of you guys (and magazines) always ask what's the latest superduty unknown cool shit I've been listening to, and you know what??? Lately, it's been kinda grim, well, apart from the Soundgarden and some roughts of the new Suicidal (due in June), so howz about some cool older shit that still holds up real fuckin' well and has helped me get through these hard times of no activity (!?!?!?!?!?!) And we are talking strictly heavy shit here!! (I can bore you with my Edie Brickell and Bob Marley hardons later!!)

BUDGIE: 'BEST OF BUDGIE' – This came out in '75(ish) and has all the best shit from the first 5 albums, thankfully leaving out all them ballady things they polluted their early records with. Some of the heaviest riffs this side of Sabbath. 'Stranded' and 'Guts' are fuckin' outstanding.

BOW WOW 'SIGNAL FIRE' – As far as I know, this was their 3rd album and surfaced around '77. These guys were from Japan and made five albums before changing their name and fading into crapdom. But on this one they hit something. The whole fucker roars, specially side 1 and the latter half of side 2 (skip 'Rainbow of Sabbath!!!' With a title like that...). 3rd track in 'Silver Lightning' is one of the best metal trax ever, has one of the best ever guitar solos in it and on numerous late nights (after 47 beers) has been thrown around as a possible Metallica cover song (if it weren't for those sometimes silly lyrics!!!!) Anyway, one of the greats.

ACCEPT 'ACCEPT' – Yes, that Accept! Well, this first album from '79 (some times referred to as the 'Chainsaw Lady') was a far cry from where they ended up a few years later ('Metal Hea_ _'). An incredibly consistent album, all 10 of these trax smoke, especially 'Sounds of War' and 'Helldriver' (which some of you might recall as one of the early candidates for our band name!!! Now you know...). Actually, come to think of it, very few albums (ever) are this good all the way thru... no weak moments... well, maybe the pictures on the back (yawn).

WARRIOR SOUL 'LAST DECADE, DEAD CENTURY' and METAL CHURCH 'THE HUMAN FACTOR' – Two bands who we've had out with us, who we've roared endlessly on about and who don't need further space, but these are fuckin' major all-time metal classics. ON each of these, both bands seem to hit something they didn't quite reach on their other albums, especially Warrior Soul with 'Charlie's Out Of Prison.' Fuck yeah!!!
Well, that's the main heavy (Heavy!!) shit I've been ragin' to lately, at least the more obscure stuff that you guys might not know!! Then there is always Thin Lizzy, Alice In Chains, Thin Lizzy, AC/DC, Thin Lizzy, Motörhead, Thin Lizzy, etc.

I am off to bed, C-Ya

LARS' CHRISTMAS WISH LIST

1. Endless year-round supply of "Tuborg Jule Ol"
2. Denmark to prevail at the World Cup 1998
3. Taco Bell as my neighbor
4. All lyrics written for next album
5. Thin Lizzy to play a gig in my house
6. Play a part in "Pulp Fiction 2"
7. Hadn't given Tony those fuckin' baby pix
8. Health and happiness to all the other guys in the band, actually everyone I know, wait... even everyone I don't know and last and absolutely least, the 12 inches of Danish dynamite I lug around in my pants, to be... oh...stop it!!!!!

Fuuuuuucckk yeah, muthafucker!! I just finished another drum track. I think that makes 7!!!!!!! In case you don't believe it, the unthinkable has happened since we last spoke (and also the main reason for the slight (cough!!) delay with this issue), Metallica are actually recording new fucken songs in the studio!! Aaaaarrrrggghhhh!!!! Yes, my friends, it's going down and it's going down big!! Down on fucken tape that is!! The team is re-assembled, the family re-united. Big Bob Rocker, Ragin' Randy Staub (and his alter ego, Vinnie), the president of the known universe (and more)... Zach Harmon, Fisheatin' Flemming, Puckplayin' Paul De Carli, Young Buck (without crutches!!) and ol' Kent there, on dat watch, among other things...

In early May, we moved ourselves and our shit into the studio and started rehearsals / preproduction / gettin' sounds / gettin' a vibe / gettin' drunk / remembering, relearning and polishing up on the songs / the mood / the interaction / the sweating / the playing and the war faces...!!!!!!! We spent about 2 weeks jammin', loosening up, gettin' used to playin' with headphones on and shit, and generally hangin' together for the first time in a while. You see, when we are writing, me and Jaymz kinda isolate ourselves from the rest of the world, so a big part of the deal becomes the hang and the vibe (without sounding too "LA"!!!). Bob Rock had suggested that the way to avoid freaking too much about "The First Big Day Of Recording In 5 Years" was to do the last rehearsals in the studio, hang, be relaxed and one day just press record and see what would happen. The main thing we wanted to do with our new songs and kinda where our heads are at right now, is to try and capture something looser and livelier and not be so fucken stiff and anal in the studio (believe me, this is where we feel we needed to improve the most!!). So there we were happily jammin' away, when out of the blue on May 15th, Bob said, "Let's do her, eh!!??" (Canadian producer talk for "Let's record") and off we went on nailing the first batch of songs. Only problem was the San Jose Sharks were kickin' some major Calgary ass, so every couple days the sessions were abruptly put on hold to flip down th the "Shark Tank", have 17 beers, a couple of martinis and watch some fucken full contact play-off hockey!!! The days after these festivities were also sometimes slightly less productive, since at least 50% of the band were nursing severe hangovers, but lo and befuckenhold, we really have some shit in the bag. Actually, right now is a week after I started writing this piece, so now we have 10 drum tracks down, Jaymz is fiddling with his guitars and I have 5 minutes to tell you guys what the fuck is going down!!!

Yes, I know you want answers (what does it sound like, song titles, style, number of tunes... blah...blah...blah...), but obviously we are still keeping most of that stuff to ourselves. I can tell you that we have written more songs for this record than ever before, which kinda surprised us, since we usually just write a specific number of songs. This time the shit just kept pouring out and actually delayed our projected start time in the studio by quite a while. The other thing I'll let out of the bag is that the looseness these songs seem to call for, is definitely happening, which is great, not only for the overall feel, but it is also making us record faster, this new thing of not having everything so note fucken perfect and just going more for a feel, that perfection!!! Enough about the damn recordings. I'll let you know next time, what the fuck and remember then when the info is ready to be spewed, you will get it here first and not in the other rags!!

What else?? Oh, yeah, that fucken gig up there somewhere by the Arctic Ocean. So they call us up a few weeks ago and go, "Howzabout playin' up in Bumfuck under the northern lights for 500 contest winners over labor day weekend????" "Yeah, okay, call me back when the drugs wear off." But, they were actually serious, and after thinking about it for about 2 minutes, it seemed like a fun thing to do and a cool way to break up the sometimes monotonous thing of recording a record!!! Also it would be a shame to not play any gigs this year, so... look, we got one!!!!! So after a few days rehearsal we'll bring out the gloves, ski-goggles and whatever else and head north into the great white unknown and see what the fuck happens!!?? A word of warning. I have been told, there is no roads that lead into this joint and all the air transportation has been "booked" by the powers (Molson), so I guess what I'm tryin' to say, is that I don't think it is very feasible to make some of you try even more. I either case, try our competition also, apart from the official one, and hopefully we'll see ya there. Dress warm!!!!!!!

Well, I got's to get back to the tunes. I just realized, that this is the first update from me in a while, where I haven't blabbered on about the fucken lawsuit, and it's real fucken nice that that is safely behind us. Once again, thanx for all the cool metallisupport on that one!!

Fuck 'em up...

C-Ya in a bit,

Lars

The Lemmy Birthday Bash – Dec '95

Featuring Lemmy, Lemmy, Lemmy, Lemmy (and (& by) Lars)

"Lars, someone named Todd Singerman is on the phone!!" "I'm tryin' to make a fucken record... (part 63!!) take a message!!"

The calendar reads something like late November and we have just finished trackin' the last coupla tunes Jaymz and me wrote out of left field a few weeks prior, and now the much feared "crunch-time" looms around the corner!! "Hmm, Todd Singerman??!!" I'm thinkin!! I remember a few weeks ago some request to partake in some Motörhead shindig came thru the office, but since I was deep in the bowels of drum-hell, that fax is probably resting comfortably in the "I'll deal with this later" pile, which by the way is way bigger than the "I've dealt with this already" pile, but that's a whole 'nother story!!!!

Soon, in a brief moment of tranquillity (rare), I actually call the man back (rarer) and god damn, it turns out that ol' Lemmy is actually quite old, havin' a 50th birthday coming up and would we be interested in takin' part in the festivities one way or another!!!!???? Well, apart from the small fact that we are so busy tryin' to finish this shit, we don't even have time to look at a gin bottle, let alone empty one... but my few brain cells keep churning!!! Give Singerman credit for persistency (something I know a lot about!!), 'coz over the next few days the phone never did stop ringin'!! Anyway, his idea wuz simple. A Motörhead gig at the Whisky... would we be interested in jamming!!?? God, I hate that fucken word!!!!!

Jamming!! Aaaaarrrggghh!!! "Well, who else would be involved???" I ask. "R____ S_____ among others!??" is the reply. "Eh, I think I have to take my dog in for a haircut that day!!" Well, we threw these vibes around for a few and came to the conclusion that it would be cool to pay our respects to the ol' Lemster, but playin' "Ace of Spades" with a bunch of washe... eh, you know what I mean!! Big dilemma!!!!! What to do??

"Hey man, I got an idea. Why don't we support Motörhead and like... eh... not tell anybody??" I throw this out into open forum a few days later and as usual the shit flies back and forth. We eventually come to the somewhat unusual decision, that since we think we know their shit pretty well, us playin' a bunch of Motorhead songs while supporting Motörhead would be pretty fucken cool. And if coupled with the hopeful low key-ness of the whole thing, it would also be a fucken cool surprise for Lemmy. Wow man!!! Into the CD library, dig up those old discs and get some cool shit happening. My vibe was to not play the obvious ones, but more the weirder obscure shit that still had a vibe to it!! Cue December 10th as we are about to start our first quick rehearsal at the studio and I immediately jump on the double-bass intro to "Overkill", which I keep going for about 15 seconds 'til I fall off the stool, out of breath!!! Oops, it's been awhile!! Playin their tunes turned out to be one step tougher than initially expected and I quickly developed another newfound level of respect for them. We plow our way thru' "Damage Case", "Too Late, Too Late", "Stone Dead Forever" and "(We Are) The Road Crew" and even thou' it's not quite the cakewalk I thought it would be, within a few, we once again get it together, at the expense of extra amounts of sweat, sore wrists and a heartbeat rate in the high 100's!!!! Revelation: recording does not keep you in shape!!

The night before the shindig, I finally spill the beans to Todd Singerman, who up 'til this point thinks we have blown it off. We are coming, we would like to support/open for Motörhead, play for about 30 minutes and oh... also keep it a secret from Lemmy!?? Not quite knowing if we are being to pushy, Singerman none the less vibes on this full on and I think we have the basis for the most fun escape from the studio since Donington 4 months prior. In the last run-thru' we all of a sudden decide to throw in "The Chase is Better Than the Catch" and we are now armed with 6 Motörhead songs to play/fuck up. Let's go!!

The next night as I walk into the Whisky for a brief "sound check", the first thing I stumble upon, is the sheet with the evening's set times, which sez that Metallica plays at 9:15 pm, between the opener and Motörhead!! So much for keeping it a fucken secret!! On top of that, our band name for the evening, "The Lemmys" is sadly nowhere to be found. Oh, well!! By the time we get to 'check, they have already started lettin' kids in and as we play our way thru' "Overkill", there are a few stunned faces staring in disbelief, wondering what the fuck we are doin' up on stage!! End of the 5 minute sound check and ol' Lemmy comes over to say "Oi!" And even thou' the secret's out, he does seem genuinely pleased his boys are there.

A couple of hours later up in our dressing-room, Jaymz breaks out the wigs, the mirrored shades, the black dress-shirts and the Sharpies(!) (for the tats!) and off we go on our mission of becoming 4 x Lemmy. After some initial hesitation, I also don the wig and shades (try playin' Motörhead songs when you have a 3 foot black wig on and can't see shit!!), and as we walk towards the Whisky stage (for the first time since supporting Saxon in 1982!!) the fucken look on peoples faces... classic... I wish I wuz out in the crowd... anyway, once again I start "Overkill", this time for real, immediately swallow half the wig, but... who gives a fuck and off we go. Total blur!!! Lemmy is of course standing about 3 feet away, staring, but as I glance over, he does look very... eh... what's the right choice of word here... pleased!! We actually play pretty good, even thou' someone (???) is slightly out of tune here and there, and as we get further thru' the set my wig etc. kinda falls to the wayside. When we get to "Road Crew", I do a quick double take as the real Lemmy is now out on stage between Jaymz and Jason, doing his infamous stance, rockin' the fuck out. Wow!!!!! Jason is singin' and Lemmy is 8 inches away. Ha!! We keep the jam at the end going, while Jaymz wanks off his solo and I think to myself, this should not fucken end... but it does. Aargh!! 30 seconds later up in the dressing room, it seems half the club is in there, with loads of buddies and potential drinking partners amongst the masses and the real, self induced blur of evening begins... Fuck, that was fun... Thanks for calling Todd...

C-ya in a bit,

Lars

Lars' "He Is Off His Tits" List For Early/Mid '96

Motherfucker part 1 is done!!!
Being happy about motherfucker part 1 being done
Gettin' ready to tour, play and sweat soon
Havin' a dream that the press tour wuz cancelled
Hangin' in New York
"Fargo"
Terror Twins on the Loose
Rage Against the Machine "Evil Empire"
Playoff hockey, especially the
Penguins and Jagr
Nick Cave "Murder Ballads"
Melatonin
The Whiskey Bar, Spys and American Trash
Running Central Park in the 50 minute region
Gakk Records
Alice In Chains unplugged taping and hanging
Soundgarden "Down on the Upside"
Shootin' the vid, especially the jam part
Black Grape live in N.Y.
Trippin' in Port Jefferson
Nobu
D.P.

Filter "Short Bus"
More Corbijn shit.
Jammin' with Chris S.
"Executive Decision"
Alice In Chains "Again" video
Much Music hang all rotted
Meeting Andres Serrano
Krays photo shoot
3 lost days in Copenhagen
Returning Mac's serve and a couple of
times passing him
"Flirting With Disaster"
Running every day/night in a different
European city
Hearing new C.O.C shit, all rotted at 4
in the morning
Soho
Vodka/tonics (G&T's take their toll!!)
The "other" songs on the Alanis album
Not having to go in and work on the
new album tomorrow
And definitely not last or least... S.S.

Motherfucker's done!!!!!

Lionel Hampton's playing on the radio and there is a few minutes of downtime on the video set (surprise!!), so I thought I'd get my blurbs done that Tony has been pestering me about for weeks. It's Monday morning, October 20th and we are hangin' in L.A. shooting the vid for "The Memory Remains" single and things are a fuckin' blur. Here is what I can tell you......... "Re-Load" is done!!!! It was really fucken close in terms of finishing..... first time I actually didn't think we would get done on time and I am usually the most optimistic. Good energy though, the last few weeks. We really took the bull by the horns (hey, cool song title!!) and churned her out. We had 2 mixing rooms and a tracking room all going at the same time and we were rotating thru there like crazy, but what was cool was that things moved so quickly that all the musical aspects became really instinctive, and I think that gives the songs an edgy feel. Cool creative chaos. And very few arguments by the way, which actually got a little boring. Bob, Jaymz and me would just sit there and talk through our differences, instead of putting the battle fatigues on like the days of old. One time I actually called Mensch and asked him if he thought it was a bad thing that there wasn't any more creative tension, and if nothing else, at least it wound him up. Being locked up in the studio for

only a few months, finishing material that wuz written and mostly recorded a few years prior, definitely helps the burnout factor, which is usually what

starts the shit flying in the first place. And most important of all, which I was the most worried about, the 2 year old material did not seem dated or stale, but holding up rather fuckin' well, thank you very much indeed!!!!!!!! Hope you like it kids!!

ELOPING... MOTHERFUCKER! 'NUFF SAID!
January 27, 1997 (4:15 am!!?)
Las Vegas, Nevada

Oh, by the way…
"**Sling Blade**" is the best picture in fuckin' ages.
Billy Bob Thornton's **performance** as Karl in "**Sling Blade**" is the best in fuckin' ages.
Billy Bob Thornton's **screenplay** for "**Sling Blade**" is the best in fuckin' ages.
Billy Bob Thornton's **direction** of "**Sling Blade**" is the best in fuckin' ages..........you get the idea!!!

So November 17/18 it is, Metallica album #7 (or rather #6, part 2). The single comes 2 weeks before, with the usual 63 B-sides that nobody cares about and then it's a round of promotional shindigs the 2nd week of November that should be both unusual and fun!! "Saturday Night Live" early December, and then the calender says downtime 'til March, but I'll believe that when I see it!!!!!!!!!! Actually, we really need some time off!!! We haven't had more than 4 weeks off in a row since the fall of '94 and it will be really good to go fuckin' disappear for a while. We should then hit the road again in late March and we'll see all our friends in the Far East, with dates being booked in Australia, New Zealand, Japan, Singapore, Thailand, etc. for April/May, outdoors in Europe in May/June, sheds in the U.S. over the summer, hopefully Latin America in September, blah, blah, blah....... and all this will change 50 times between now and then and I will look the dick as usual, so what's new, right!!??

Anyway enough babbling, I gots to go look cool in the video and focus on something visually.....????? You'll see,

C-ya in a bit,

Glenn Hughes, Tony Iommi, Brian May, Steve
Harris and a few other "heroes" checking out
the rock show
San Jose Sharks off to a good start, then...
Dries Van Noten & Costume Homme
Drivin' fast(ish) in Germany
Not flyin' in turbulent weather
Basing in Copenhagen
Anton Corbijn doing another video for us
Caleb Carr "The Alienist"
Jason being in a better mood

And as usual... Skylar, of course in
        general, and
      also more specifically,
    for helping me thru'
  a very long European
tour. TLF!!

MY NEW FRIENDS,
HERE IS A FEW SNAPS
OF THE FIRST FEW MONTHS!
HAPPY X-MAS ETC...
LOVE,
MYLES

Lone Ulrich
1930-1998

The motherfucker's done!!!!!!!!!!!!
Well, if you really wanna be technical, I'm lying!!!
But considering it's minus 6 days and we're right
on course, the fact that you are actually reading
this means that it's done or else you wouldn't be
reading this (follow!!??)...........

It's been a bit of a ride, you know a year
and a couple, lotsa songs written, almost as
many songs recorded, a few gigs, a few ligs, a
few days off (actually now I am lying, okay, lotsa
days off!!!!) And, let's not be modest, a shit load
of fucken work!!
By the time you read this horseshit, the record
should be on the way to the record stores and
hopefully in your possession within a few, and
then it's up to you… It's out of our hands for
good, it's yours to deal with, to tear apart, to
wonder about, to salivate over, to barf on, to
be challenged by… Have you ever read such
bullshit in your life????

Anyway, the motherfucker (part 1) is done,
look for motherfucker part 2 soonish (by our
standards) and thanx for your patience and
enough!!!!!!

On to tour shit!!! In the last issue we
printed what was at the time, the accurate dates
on the Lollapalooza deal. Since then they have
changed almost on a daily basis and I just want
you guys to understand a few things about that
shit. I have said it before and I'll say it again,
this is not a Metallica tour. What that means is
that we are not in charge of where it goes, what
cities it hits, what rural areas it hits and where
it doesn't. Just understand that we have done
our best to help advise, to point, to hint, and so
on to make this the best it can be and I truly do
believe, it will be by far the best Lollapalooza
you will see, but there are certain things that are
out of our powers, like where permits get granted or revoked, where the festival can play for
logistical reasons and shit like that that changes
whenever the wind does… I mean, right now
there is a chance that we won't play our home,
Northern California, for logistical reasons and
it is not something we are happy about, but we
have no fucken choice. The bottom line is we
are headlining Lollapalooza '96, it will play as
many places as it can and we will all make the
most of it and end of story. And remember this
is a Metallica magazine you are reading, so I
would say there is an above average chance we
will hit your area sooner or later in some capacity. Enough tapdancing!!!

Autumn thoughts:

I am tired, stressed and feel like shit. Thank you. Ok, let's see, is there anything
else!!??

Hmmm, I wonder why so many people ask me if the reason we put out a record full of
cover songs is we have run out of our own ideas?? No, the fucken idea is to do a record full
of cover songs. Geddit?? Thank you!! There are so many cool movies around at the moment
that – eh… it's really cool!! **'HAPPINESS'** takes the crown as the most twisted fucked
up picture for a long time, with 'CELEBRATION' right behind it. **'LIFE IS BEAUTIFUL'**
is fucked up in an entirely different manner and **'LOVE IS THE DEVIL'** is actually
so dark that it almost doesn't work, saved mainly by the performances. Keep your eyes
out for a picture called 'HURLY BURLY' which should be out around X-MAS and that is
really fucken dark and very claustrophobic. Speaking of claustrophobic, the plane isn't big
enough, he sez and Tony and his manifest bullshit is like … eh - you know!!! I actually saw
something on M-TV EUROPE I liked and wanted to buy, but this morning when I woke up, I
couldn't remember what they were called and nobody else does, so now I'm fucked. It's bad
luck to be superstitious, according to one Kirk Lee Hammett. One day it could be really fun
to make a record without having a release date locked in before you start. If you want to try
something surreal, form a band, kick around for a while, get asked to perform at the Playboy
Mansion, and then, while you are up on stage, watch Hugh Hefner kick around to your
music, with a couple of Playmates on each arm. That is fucken surreal. Speaking of surreal,
an eight piece Salvation Army marching band at a Polish airport, playing the 'UNFORGIVEN
II'. Have you ever heard of a band called TURBONEGRO?? Neither had I until yesterday,
but they actually exist and they even make records. If we ever consider a name change,
I'm going to put that at the top of the list. Coolest eyes of the year belong to Vincent Gallo,
who also happens to have directed, starred, scored, shot, probably catered etc…, one of
the coolest films of the year, namely 'BUFFALO 66'. Alcohol is my/your friend!! I like a lot of
things that I was going to tell you about over the next few paragraphs, but Tony "I don't need
any sleep" Smith is hovering over me saying something about deadlines and if I don't finish
this, the magazine will be delayed and you definitely don't want that now, do you?? My opinions will just have to wait!!

Love,

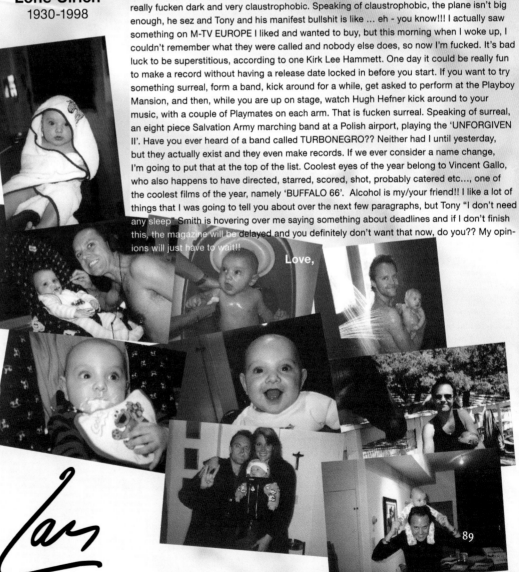

89

Here's the new tattoo I got myself for Christmas!!
Don't even ask if it (it hurts like a motherfucker) hurts!!!

Kirk

KH: Hello connoisseurs of fine music! This is Kirk, and I'm here to tell you about my favorite places to check out while out on tour. Now, before I get heavily into this subject, I need to clarify one thing. Being on tour consists of spending a large portion of time traveling, not to mention the constant barrage of dressing rooms and hotel rooms. This cycle of traveling, dressing room, stage, hotel and then more travel goes on for weeks, months, and then, before you know it, YEARS!! It can be frustrating, because you can never stop to take a look around at wherever you might be because you are just too TIRED!!

There are instances where you have to take time to see a certain place and the time usually comes out of your sleep schedule (I usually sleep from 4 a.m. to 11 or 12 p.m.). Interviews start at about 3 in the afternoon, and when these are done and out of the way, it's time to go to the gig. So, if you want to see a city or go out on a sightseeing trip or bike ride, you have to plan ahead, so I at least try not to drink the night before!

Anyway, I prefer big cities, I grew up in a big city, and I am a total urbanite. So, not surprisingly, I have a penchant for places like New York, London, Amsterdam, Tokyo, Paris, Sydney, Mexico City, Bangkok, S.F., etc. The one thing that I find interesting and attractive is culture, especially cultures that are different from my own. I think that it is really important to learn about and appreciate other societies and peoples outside Western culture; Westerners have to learn to appreciate diversity! Fortunately being in a band has allowed me to do all this. So, without further adieu, let me tell you about my FAVORITE PLACES!!!! (This is in no particular order.)

1/ Paris – Amazing!!
Great architecture everywhere. Great food everywhere. This city has done a remarkable job in preserving its past. It was one of the few places in Europe that survived WWII intact. Paris is a museum unto itself; for museums, the Louvre has the Mona Lisa (which is actually quite small) and the Pompidou has an incredible Dali collection. Even the cemeteries here are cool!!! It is very easy to just imagine yourself traveling back a few centuries because the surroundings aren't very modern. Paris is just an amazingly gothic, romantic place just to hang out and sip wine by the gallon, while listening to a jazz band at a local tavern…

2/ Southeast Asia
– or more specifically, Indonesia, The Phillippines, Malaysia, and Thailand. These places are by far the most interesting places the band has ever played. What we saw and experienced really opened my eyes to what the so called "third world" is really like, and, quite frankly, it was breathtaking as well as depressing. It was disheartening to see countries that have had their natural resources tapped by Western countries without any concern for the peoples or the economies of these places. It was especially important and personal for me to go to these countries because my heritage is Filipino. These countries are so beautiful and full of traditional culture that it makes you think about the USA's foreign policies (as well as domestic policies) that have been executed and sacrificed many ancient and important civiliza-

tions. There are also millions of positive things to be seen in these places; different lifestyles, people, Buddhist Temples, great food, curios to be bought on the street, etc. The traditional dress and music are very exciting also.

3/ Tokyo
– Have you ever seen the movie *Bladerunner*? If you have, remember the scene of the city skyline with tons of neon signs and sculptures? Well, that is what Tokyo looks like at night. This city is amazing, everywhere you look, you see the most up-to-date electronic devices available to the consumer. Everything is slightly more compact as far as living space is concerned, and everyone seems a lot more punctual than what I am used to. I love sushi and sake, and people are very friendly there. There is only one drawback, this place is EXPENSIVE!!!

4/ Barcelona
– Architecture is the main appeal of this great town, and if you appreciate towering structures of beauty, go there now! Antonio Gaudi designed many of these masterpieces, and I had gotten my lip pierced in one of the towers of the Sagrada Familia, a huge church in the middle of Barcelona.

5/ Amsterdam
– If you are a big fan of Rembrandt and Van Gogh, this is the place to be. If you know about the coffee houses around here, and you are into that kind of thing, this is paradise!!! This city is a great place to just sit around and sip your drink all day. I feel like a complete slacker in this town!! The canals are very intriguing, and the window shopping at night is equally intriguing. Make sure you catch the red light special when you are there. . .

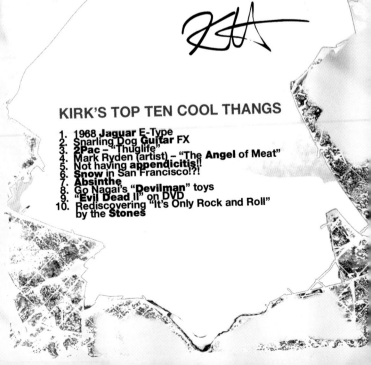

KIRK'S TOP TEN COOL THANGS

1. 1968 **Jaguar** E-Type
2. Snarling Dog **Guitar** FX
3. 2Pac – "Thuglife"
4. Mark Ryden (artist) – "The **Angel** of Meat"
5. Not having **appendicitis**!!
6. **Snow** in San Francisco!?!
7. **Absinthe**
8. Go Nagai's "**Devilman**" toys
9. "**Evil Dead II**" on DVD
10. Rediscovering "It's Only Rock and Roll" by the **Stones**

90

TRIBUTE
KIRK'S VICE LIST

1. MUSIC (I PUT IT BEFORE EVERYTHING... I MEAN EVERYTHING)
2. SEX (NO EXPLANATION NEEDED)
3. DRINKING (NOTHING WRONG WITH A MARTINI OR TEN)
4. SMOKING CIGARS (MY NEW FAVORITE PASTIME, GOOD FOR CLEARING OUT ROOMS AND UNDESIRABLES)
5. GAMBLING (CARDS, DICE, OR THE WHEEL GETS MY ADRENALINE GOING)
6. STAYING OUT TILL DAWN (I'M LIGHT SENSITIVE)
7. VOYEURISM (I SEE NOTHING WRONG WITH IT)
8. DRINKING (ANOTHER MARTINI???)
9. NEIL DIAMOND (MOTHERFUCKER CAN SING, BUT THAT EYEBROW IS GETTING SCARIER AND SCARIER)
10. SWEARING (ALL THE OTHERS ARE SO HARMLESS I HAVE TO HAVE A REAL VICE!!!)
11. BEING SINGLE ('NUF SAID!!!)

ADULTS LOVE IT TOO!

HOURS OF FUN!

KIRK'S 5 NEW YEAR'S RESOLUTIONS
1. Don't eat meat
2. Stop worshipping the devil
3. No more crack or PCP
4. Keep ignoring the little man who lives inside my head
5. Wash more often

A Day in the Life of Kirk, Lani and Darla
photos by Lani

91

This is what I did on my summer vacation, better known as Lollapalooza (a.k.a. Dollopaloozers, Metallapalooza, Lollapasmooza, etc.). I recently purchased a digital camera and went a little crazy. What you see here is a bunch of very candid stuff shot backstage, on our little flying casino (better known as our plane), and in the dressing room. It's a nice little behind the scenes look into what we are up to when we aren't onstage…

Once upon a time (1971–1973 to be exact) Kirk and his family owned a 1956 Dodge Coronet. They used to have such a wonderful time in that car going to drive-in movies, picnics, and sometimes just cruising around town.

The family sold the car in 1973 much to Kirk's dismay. However, many years later and after a lot of detective work, Kirk found the car in a vacant lot, up on wooden blocks, rusted and trashed. He bought it for $500.

Kirk and his family worked together to restore it, and after one and a half years, their hard work paid off. They preserved the original finish and the original interior. After putting in a new engine, the transformation was complete!

HERE'S A SCENE FROM THE WEDDING!

The Car That Wouldn't Die!!!

KIRK'S TOP
10

1. Captain Beefheart
   Everything & Anything!
2. Judas Priest
   "Hellbent For Leather" & "British Steel"
3. Morcheeba
   "Big Calm"
4. Jerry Cantrell
   "Boggy Depot"
5. The Stones
   "Exile On Main St."
6. The Stalin
   "Bug" from the album "Mushi"
7. Aerosmith
   "Get Your Wings"
8. Beatles
   "Revolver"
9. Gov't. Mule
   "Dose"
10. Lee Morgan
    "Standards"

Since I've Had Some
Time Off I've Managed
To trip On

My toy collection
Vintage horror movies
Old school metal
Fritz Lang
Serrano's "Blood Pope"
Rank Frazeta, Virgil Finlay & Basil Gogos
(Horror/Fantasy Illustrators)
Yoga!!
Fluxtone Amps
Sir Lord Baltimore
And last but not least - Marital Bliss!!

Jason

JASONS'S VIBE LIST

LATEST CHOPHOUSE PROJECTS
Barn **M**onkey
Th**E**e Thaw
Quartetto da Pin**G**a
Tree of the **Sun**
Blastu**LA**
Turd Ben Polished
Tele**PA**thetic
El Rone

MUSIC
All **C**eltic Frost
All **KING** Crimson
All **FU**gazi
Ziggy **M**arley - Free Like We Want To Be
Fudge Tunnel - In **A** Word
Me**SH**uggah
Alice In Chai**N**s
Do**WN**
New Sepul**T**ura Tunes
Be**S**t of **D**ischarge
Coolio
Mud**HON**ey
Bone Th**U**gs N'Harmony
Fear Factory
Han**K** Willia**M**s Box
George **J**ones Box
Fi**LT**er
Sa**M C**ooke's Night Beat
Essential Po**G**ues
Iggy **POP** - American Ceasar
Chris Issak - Forever **B**lue
Magic Slim -- Gr**AV**el Road
Toni Tony **T**one -- The Revival
Naughty **BY** Nature
Go**D** Flesh
Me**LV**ins -- Stoner Witch
BAD Religion
Stanford **P**rison **E**xperiment
Social **D**istortion

FILM &TV
Throne Of B**I**ood
Menace II Society
Once Were Warriors
Too **Y**oung **T**o Die
Man Bites **DOG**
TALK Soup
Singled **OUT** on MTV

MISCELLANEOUS
Jerry Jones **6** Bass & Boss Twah
Red **C**urry Thai Vegeta**B**les
Boddington's **ALE**
Optek Fretl**I**ght Instruments
Boss Racing **BMX** Bike

Howdy y'all — What's up friends?

Whew! We've been extremely busy with finishing the "Load" album and are now in the middle of our promo/press tour. After which, we will be sharing the new, loud, ugly, and most importantly, <u>live</u> 'Tallica experience with yooz guyz and galz!! Yyeeoow!!!

As many of you out there know by now, outside "projects" of self-indulgent musical explorations take up almost all of my down time.

Quite a few inquiries have come in pertaining to the hows?, whats?, whys? and future intentions of these experimental sessions, I'm gonna clear it up now, and then y'all can stick to 'Tallica questions.

Over the past 3 years (since the completion of the infamous "Chophouse"), an array of players, singers and performers have collaborated to create hundreds of hours of beautiful and/or ugly music.

Some of the names you may recognize from heavy favorites, members of Sepultura, Voi Vod, Machine Head, Kyuss, Exodus, Melvins to psycho avant-garde jazz stylists and far beyond. Including the five combos that were recently formulated in N.Y. (during the 8 weeks that we spent there finishing the record) with some seriously snappy younger cats at our 24-hour rehearsal pad. Some of the names that you see in this month's "Projects" list, mostly blues based heavy-heaviness.

The plan is to seek out players from all styles and worlds and languages and continue these manic recording adventures as we continue our career traveling the **GLOBE**

Howdy y'all...

Whew!! Summer just blazed on by once again.

In the time since we last connected, we've been hard at work on the new record. Ideas are flowing madly and I'm extremely stoked on the sounds that are coming forth. We're doing lots of experimenting and fiddling with old pedals and stuff to achieve the most metal tones ever.

My new motto for these sessions is; "Happiness and joy through pure evil." (Translation: "The scarier and uglier the sounds, the happier it makes you and me!) I think y'all will really dig it! So, in a couple more months it will be time to overdose on a new load of 'Tallica metal.

On the homefront we've made an addition of happiness to our family with fuzzy new metallisprouts. Kobie and Kaya are two 12 week old Rhodesian Ridgeback pups. They are tons of fun and responsibility. We've really got our hands full now.

Oh yeah, things are moving fast now, just like we like it. Before ya know it, we'll be rocking together in a shed near you. 'Til next time...

These collaborations are purely for freedom of expression and musical comradery with the main intention of building myself in a healthy manner to strengthen my link in the Metallica chain. (This music will not be available for anyone to hear apart from the individual performers.)

What it comes down to is this... It's about learning, opening your ears in order to open your mind. It's about not judging the book by the cover, but instead to see people shine when given the chance and the right chemistry.

I don't play because I have to. I play and strive to learn about all music because I want to... because I need to. Listening and playing is my way of seeing...

I'll be <u>seeing</u> you soon,

Howdy Metallifreaks!!

As you guys know, we're headed into the studio once again. Usually in the days and weeks leading up to recording, our off-tour every-day life becomes filled with busy-ness and a certain cool, grinding, unnerving Metalli-tension. It's about this time that I dig back into the fundamentals of my instrument and turn to the music that guides me in that the best. I'm also going to start a series here with some of the first and most important blue cats that formed the building blocks of true, dark grooves and the basis and roots of the heavy music we all dig so much. Jump in and hang on! C-Ya.

Blues Dudes

Charlie Patton – Born in 1887, Charlie Patton was one of the creators of what is known as the Mississippi Delta Blues. I chose Charlie first because he was the most influential artist of his time and region. His unusual guttural, gruff and barking vocal along with unheard of guitar prowess set the standard for what was to come. Recorded on Vocalion 1930-4.

Leadbelly (Huddie Ledbetter) – A huge man in stature and in the history of black American folk song. He composed and recorded many ballads, blues, dance songs and children's songs. He accompanied his massive voice with 12-string guitar, accordion, harmonica and more. He most likely would have been recorded prior to 1933, but he spent many of his middle years in prison for assault and murder. There are over 200 pieces of Leadbelly music in existence for us to enjoy today, recorded for various labels 1933-48. Check out Library of Congress recordings.

Son House – My personal favorite acoustic blues performer. His amazingly mature recordings are unsurpassed in their unity of voice and instrument. His hand strength and coordination, cut-to-the-bone slide style, and chilling, God-fearing vocal preachings are unmatched in my opinion. Son House 1930-42 Library of Congress recordings are brilliant. (There is also great video available of this guy, if you ever get a chance, do yourself a favor…)

Robert Johnson – Regarded by many as the "king of the Delta Blues," Robert Johnson has become incredibly well known 60 years after his mysterious death, and with good reason. A visionary artist whose charisma carries on strong through his inventive, suave, boo-gie-based music. A "student" of Charlie Patton, Willie Brown, and Son House, and "teacher" to Muddy Waters, Elmore James, BB King and scores more to follow. His importance as a transitional figure between country-blues style and Chicago and other styles cannot be stressed enough. His effect on music specialists, musicians and listeners is being heard and felt as hauntingly as ever today.
(The complete recordings from Vocalion are superb.)

I can't close this first episode of the Blues 'n Grooves with mentioning these other greats of the time!

Blind Lemon Jefferson
Leroy Carr
Lonnie Johnson (Kirk's fave)
Honey Boy Edwards
Furry Lewis
Big Bill Broonzy
Blind Willie McTell
Scrapper Blackwell
Brownie McGhee
Sonny Terry

GIVE 'EM AV EAR IF YOU GET THE OPPORTUNITY!

GENERAL PLAYLIST

Beatles – "Revolver"
Led Zeppelin – "Physical Graffiti"
Motörhead – "Bomber"
Los Lobos – "Will The Wolf Survive"
Black Sabbath – 1st 5 albums
AC/DC – 1st 5 albums
Mountain – "Best of Mountain"
Kiss – "Hotter Than Hell," "Love Gun," "Alive"
Riot – "Narita," "Fire Down Under"
O'Jays – Best
Jackson 5 – 3rd album
The Police – Box
Sly and the Family Stone – Anthology
UFO – All
The Clash – "London Calling"
Thin Lizzy – All
Venom – All

AUDIO

Metallica
Loudmouth
Fu Manchu
Natacha Atlas – Diaspora
Lee "Scratch" Perry – Arkology
David Byrne – Feelings
Tony Levin – Iron Mountain
Charly Garcia – Filosofia
Baka Beyond – The Meeting Pool
Maxwell – Unplugged
Devin Townsend – Ocean Machine
Erykah Badu – Baduizm
KRS One – I Got Next
Wes Montgomery – Verve Jazz
Punky Bruster – Cooked On Phonics
Puff Daddy – No Way Out
Jimmie Vaughan – Strange Pleasure
Coolio – My Soul
One World – Rounder Collection
The Roots of Sepultura
Voi Vod – Phobos

PRINT

The Monks of New Skete Dog Books
Smithsonian Mag

VIDEO/TV

2 Pac – Thug Immortal
When We Were Kings
Toy Story
Ben Stein
South Park
Animal Planet
The Daily Show

CHOPHOUSE PROJECTS

Kitshicker 6
In-On-In
Papa Wheelie – Tread
Buttoutski
Hilltop Habeneros
Kiniption

OTHER SIMULATION

Kobie and Kaya
Hog's Foot Bass Boost
Roland Groovebox
Jaymz "Special Blend Stubble" Bash
Reading Festival
Blindman's Ball

95

IN·ON·

HILLTOP HABENEROS

JULY 1·97

ZACH AND THE KING SETTIN' UP SADOWSKYS.

JULY 8·97

AUG·97

EVERYTHING LOUDER THAN EVERYTHING ELSE!!

JUNE 30·97

JULY 97

WEAPON "HAPPINESS JOY AND PURE EVIL."

SURF'S UP DUDE!

HOW MANY BASS 7#s

BUTTOUTSKI

EVERYTHING INTO EVERYTHING !!.

8·10·97

KITSHICKEN

Wazzup Peoples?

My head is spinning! I've been going crazy… playing wild music, traveling, and exposing my ears to tons of sounds; new and old.

…As much fun as it has been to get away for a bit, I am itching to get back on the move with Metallica and take some heavy music to the people. We're scheduled to play a number of very exciting shows with some great bands. We will also get the opportunity to perform in a couple of places that we haven't played before (and that's always super-cool!)

Oh yeah, don't forget about the symphony gig, man – that will be weird! So, I am looking forward to more great learning experiences all summer long! I hope to see yooz guyz and galz out there somewhere.
'Til then – shake yo' rump to the bump…
Cheers!

GOOD FER MY HEAD
AUDIO

James Brown – **Star Time**
Massive Attack – **Mezzanine**
DJ Shadow – **Preemptive Strike**
Morcheeba – **Big Calm**
Tricky – **Angels With Dirty Faces**
Soul Fly – **Soul Fly**
James Brown's **Funky People**
Funkdoobiest – **The Trouble Shooters**
Material – **Hallucination Engine**
Talking Heads – **Sand In The Vaseline**
Sneaker Pimps – **Becoming X**
Afro Cuban All-Stars – **A Toda Cuba le Gusta**
Bjork – **Homogenic**
The Crystal Method – **Vegas**
Slayer – **Diabolus In Musica**
DJ Cam – **The Beat Assassinated**
Bobby Byrd – **I Got Soul**
Bobby Collins – **Back In The Day**
Reubén González – Introducing
Jai Uttal – **Shiva Station**

VISUAL

Suburbia
Harvey Sid Fisher
Thelonius Monk Quartet

OTHER STIMULATION

Bulls NBA Champions
World Cup
King Sunny Ade Live in S.F.

This is Bob Schafer _ the man behind Flotsam & Jetsam & the key player in the cultivation of my career. 91 years young this March.

HEY JASON,
YOU TOLD ME LAST WEEK
THAT YOU REALLY LIKED OASIS!
WHERE ARE THEY?? I DON'T
UNDERSTAND?? THIS REALLY HURTS!!
Love, Lars

JUNE 30 97

'OL RAND SELF-PORT.

8·9·97

PAPA WHEELIE
FEATURING MC SIK RICH

AUG. 1. 97

BRAIN   J·BONE.
I MONTH INTO OVERLOAD + LOVIN'
IT!

music
Sepultura – Roots
Mar**c**us Miller
Voi Vod - Negatro**n**
Mad Season - Above
Wes **M**ontgomery
Any Ellip**s**is Arts Music
The **W**hite Room Album
Junio**r** Brown - Ju**n**ior High
Fran**k Z**appa - Strictly Commercial
Pinetop Perkins - A**f**ter **H**ours
The **G**oats - **T**ricks Of The Shade
Mud **S**hark
Midni**g**ht **O**il - Diesel & Dust
Brujeria - **R**aza Odiada
And**r**es Segovia - A Centenary Celebration
Che**m**ical **B**rothers
Naked **C**ity - John Zorn
Eno/**W**obble - Spinner
Jaco Pastor**i**us - The Birthday Con**c**ert
Sacred **R**eich - Heal
A**p**he**x** Twin - selected works '**8**5-'**9**2
Me**s**huggah
Wax Tra**x**! **B**lack Box
Front **L**ine Assem**b**ly
Rah**s**aan Roland Kirk - Bright Moments
Fugazi - In On The Kill Taker
Tom Waits in **O**akland

reading
Future **M**usic Ma**g**
The **E**mperor We**a**rs
N**o** Clothes
|| Literature **M**ag
Rock & The **P**op
Narcotic
Q Ma**g**
Down **B**eat
The **S**haman
Second**s** Ma**g**

latest chophouse projects
The **G**natballs
Fopdoodle
Earthburp
Tar **Rat**
8 F**r**ostee Pops
Cacafu**e**go
de **C**repitus
Wrestle**y P**elvis

97

MUSIC IS MY WORLD

5

And it's a total metal attitude

SUMMER INSANITY '97
METALLICA TERRORIZE
•••EURO•••
FESTIVALS!

Right as Metallica are finishing their "Re-load" album, someone decides it's time for a challenge. 'How about three European festival gigs in three days? Belgium's Pukkelpop, Germany's Blind Man's Ball and England's Reading festival?' says said-person. 'Why yes!' reply the members of Metallica, 'we enjoy such challenges.' Bob Rock's face drops and, errr, Bob's yer uncle, here we are in Europe!

THREE FESTIVALS IN THREE DAYS... FEELINGS

"This trip has been a big blur, you get up and play," he laughs, that voice booming, yesterday it felt like we were jamming, I could tell in Lars' eyes that he was still asleep or somewhere else... I guess he'd got three hours sleep and I'd got thirteen, so whether you have too much sleep or none you're still fucked. We just decided not to worry about it, just get up there and jam." **JAMES**

"...The Reading thing was another big fucking obstacle, it was a pain in the butt and the only thing that suffers, in terms of time, is the record. So just before they left I told them 'cancel your lives'... really." **BOB ROCK** (producer)

"We knew that coming over this quickly, this thing right here, you can become easily dehydrated because of the six flights in five days, up and down, compress, decompress and all of that, and whilst doing that it's very important to consume gallons and gallons of water. Especially when it's very muggy, like these shows, you lose gallons and gallons of fluid so that is the main thing, to make sure that you keep hydrated. The MetRx and other stuff, vitamins, a lot of stretching which is really important if you're only doing a few shows." **JASON**

"I just walked into Clawfinger's dressing room and instantly smelled that they were Scandinavian! I mean, I suppose I should say we're not angels when it comes to that! But these are the real festivals, all the hype and crap about Lollapalooza, 'gee does Metallica belong on this festival, gee, how will all the fans get along' and all that bullshit. At these festivals there are all types of age groups, people, music lovers, just dirty, drunk fucks sleeping in the mud, using cow shit for pillows!" **JAMES**

"Something that Lars said a long time ago, but that I wasn't convinced was true until now, was 'you can practice as hard as you think possible in rehearsal but it's still not going to be harder than when you go out onstage and do it for real.' That 110% comes when everything is right on the stage and ready to go." **JASON**

"Playing shows in the middle of doing a record is a challenge, but it did help. Especially with this album, it seems like we all four have our own fucking room or studio. Sometimes one guy doesn't even know what's going on on the other song, you do your part and after that you don't know what goes on it. So it's good to get together and play songs as a unit." **JAMES**

THE TALE OF "RE-LOAD"'S BIRTH

"All the basic tracks for "Load" or "Re-Load" were cut between May of '95 and November of '95. In between that we kept writing, played shows in Europe, we stuck our toes and played shows in the Arctic Ocean, some of us went hunting and some of us went chasing after Oasis. There were a lot of agendas in those seven months, but we recorded 27 basic tracks in that time frame. Most of them were developed between the Fall of '95 and the Spring of 1996. We had a meeting in January of '96 where we decided that "Load" was not going to be a double album: until that meeting, "Load" was to all intents and purposes a double album with 27 songs on it... at that point we'd been in the studio for 9 months and had been working on the songs for 16 months, so there was a potential burn-out at the end of the tunnel. We (also) got the chance to do 'Lollapalooza' and we wanted to do that. We realized that by doing that we would not have time to finish the 27 songs, so we took these 13–14 songs that were the furthest along. The other factor that played into separating the songs into two records, was that I was very adamant that we would have two records which would balance out with each other, not be an A record and a B record. They would

...e two records you would be able to put up against each other as strong, equal records from one songwriting and recording session." **LARS**

TOO MUCH PRESSURE?

"This time it's really tight for real. We have a deadline that is 16 days away, and in the past I've said that statement 'oh I dunno if we're gonna finish it' perhaps for a reaction or compassion, and this time is the first time I actually believe it. So this time it's gonna be close. I'm starting to get a little perspiration going for the first time." **LARS**

"The homework I have to do is extensive. The vocabulary of my guitar licks that are documented now, what I mean are the ones that are on the previous six albums, are used. I can't recycle them, I can't re-use the major themes of those solos. So you have to come up with something completely different." **KIRK**

"When you're away from home finishing a record, what we call crunch time, and what most Metallica fans should understand as 'crunch-time' is when we have two mixing rooms going, James is finishing his vocals and Kirk is finishing his leads, somebody's doing a bass fill, somebody's doing a percussion over-dub, and somebody's doing a re-arrangement, that turns into an 18 hour a day deal. When you're away from home, it's easier to get the most out of crunch time I'm discovering than when you're home..." **LARS**

"...I have had no control over these guys at all, I gotta be honest with you, none whatsoever." **BOB ROCK** (producer)

"I've been working at home on solos all the time because I know I don't have the luxury of two to three days to get one done. I have to kick one out every session, which is eight to ten hours. On the last album we were able to do all the solos and when we started mixing I only had two left to do, which left me more there for the mix. But because we're recording and mixing at the same time, songs are being mixed while I'm at home working out solos or even while I'm recording them. I wish I could be there when they're doing the actual mixing, but that can't happen because of scheduling." **KIRK**

"I just hate the fact that those guys say at the end of the day it all comes to the lyrics, the melody, what you're gonna do. It's like fuck, fucking hate that. Fuck you, we're a fucking band. You could have some awesome lyrics and put them on some shit song , it still might be good but this is a band effort. I don't like the extra pressure it puts on me.

"I don't wanna write shitty lyrics, that's for sure, but sometimes it's not quite so important what's being said as to how it's being performed, (certain) sounds and vowels that come out work better sometimes. I put things together that are not right. I can't spell for one thing, which doesn't really matter because there are a few people who spell-check stuff before it goes on the record. Putting words together the wrong way to make it come out right... I don't give a fuck, I'll take as long as necessary to get it done, and sometimes that will go right to the day before recording. That happened on "Load," there was one song I just couldn't get anything. The day before I was singing, I was still writing it, and it turned out to be 'King Nothing' which doesn't suck and is pretty good. So that pressure sometimes helps." **JAMES**

"I put a lot of unnecessary pressure on myself, I stress at stuff I shouldn't be stressing on...I do a solo, come home and work on the next one. I hope they don't think I'm just sitting around the pool fucking off. I haven' been going out at all." **KIRK**

...BUT THE STUDIO RIDE GETS SMOOTHER

"Let me explain this fairly simply, this is the simplest analogy of how i works. When Kirk records I'm there with him all the time, throwing idea and so on. When Jason is recording James is there with him, throwing ideas out. So I kinda deal and work with Kirk, and James has somewha the same kind of relationship with Jason I think. James has never been in the room when Kirk has been recording a guitar solo and I'm rarely in the room when Jason is recording a bass track.

"I have sat in the same room as Kirk Hammett when he's been re cording his guitar solos since the first day in Rochester in May of 198 when he put the first solo on "Kill 'Em All." I have always just sat with him. James might have been hung over or sick or writing lyrics or some thing like that, and I was there from the beginning offering a creative opinion, and that has stuck ever since.

"I think with Jason, in the earlier days when we were trying to ge Jason to play more with the track, between the "...Justice" and "Black album, when we were trying to get the bass back with the drums more instead of being with the guitars. And when Jason got comfortable with that, and playing that way on stage, it's something that I don't necessar ily need to sit down and babysit so much, it comes down to what note to play and James is much more qualified to give that kind of advice than I am." **LARS**

"This is a very abstract way of making music. You already have the drums there, this thing's already mapped out. We're familiar with the songs in our heads, where the notes go and we're laying on top of this perfec foundation because he (Lars) puts them through a computer. It makes i very cool to play to, everything's exactly where it should be and it makes it real cool to put the groovin' bass lines down on. So that added to the comfort, hugeness and pleasantness of it all." **JASON**

"OK, listen, revelation one: everything comes down to a question o age. Of course it does. I can relate any question to age, I love grow ing older, I see it in the people around me, I see it in Bob, I see it in James. I could talk for 15 minutes about how much I love it and hov much it attributes to my mental state right now. So we understand tha sitting around and being pissy, immature little rock stars is not going to get the record done. There's just the thing of understanding, and dialogue." **LARS**

"We don't think too much in advance. The deadline is put there by someone else. It makes sense to release it at Christmas, it's not a nev idea. But we have a few weeks to get shit done and, fuck, why bothe arguing about little things? We look back at previous records and thin 'why was I such an asshole there? Did that part really have to be there and I don't even listen to the song anymore.' Or you don't even like it." **JAMES**

"Three weeks ago we're sitting there saying 'we're gonna start mixing which is the potential shitstorm, because everybody on this record ha...

worked in the initial development of their own recording of the parts that were written... we are now nearly half-way through mixing the record, there have been no major blow-ups, no major irrational arguments or anything like that. We sit down, we talk about parts, I help them give an outsider's perspective on some part that means a lot to James that he cannot see from another person's perspective, he helps me with things I'm maybe too close to, Bob's in the middle as that friend in the middle... I hate to sound so hunky-dory, but compared to what it's been it's really strong right now." **LARS**

"I think Lars has let up a bit, and because he has I have as well, and we're just not as hard-headed. As we get older we realize that, fuck, there's four guys in the band and you can't please just one guy and leave the other three unhappy." **JAMES**

LYRICAL HEART OF DARKNESS?

"The man (James) may smile on the outside but there is evil lurking within that body at all times. Well, evil and darkness in the Hetfield way; when I say evil, I don't mean he goes around kicking dogs and things, but like I say, he smiles on the outside. Lyrically, and I'm sure everyone will argue with me, but he just gets better and better..." **BOB ROCK**

"I'm more and more into just sitting down with pen and paper and seeing what comes out. I get a cool line and see where it goes. They're a lot darker – if we can get darker that is – a lot sadder in many ways. It's not just me, it's seeing a little more of what's going on around us. There's songs about being down and out and not accepting pity. The song 'Fixxxer' was pretty sparse and had some particularly evil tones in it. The word 'voodoo' kept on coming up in my head, so I started looking up voodoo shit a little more. Doing research doesn't necessarily help though, in the end you're gonna write whatever words come out and sound cool. It's not like all of a sudden you say 'well I'm knowledgeable on the subject and I'm gonna let you know about it.' People don't give a fuck, they don't wanna be educated by it, they wanna hear some cool words that fit together. So voodoo dolls and pins started to figure into it, y'know, people get jabbed by something every day. When things are going right, fuck, there's another pin in ya and nothing goes your way all the time. And that's just life my friend." **JAMES**

METALLICA RIGHT NOW

"My concept of Metallica at this point is that it is what it is, and whether I say we're heavy metal, we're pop, whether I say we're jazz-funk-fusion is fucking irrelevant... I can't emphasize that enough. When I go in a heavy metal magazine and say we're not heavy metal, it really is to try and stir up some shit. I think shit should be stirred. I think people should understand how silly all this is, in terms of these categories and interpretations of somebody's music. I find myself trying to add to that is by stirring up a little bit of shit, a little bit of dialogue and a little bit of conversation about it. I'm not irrational, of course I am aware of the fact that most people on this planet consider Metallica a heavy metal band. And of course the minute you get a reaction out of it, it becomes kind of fun, the minute you start winding somebody up and they start biting on it, it becomes fun." **LARS** ●

Perspectives: Thoughts on each other by each other

Metallica on James Hetfield

JASON: Hetfield brings the pride. He stands a very tall and strong guy over all of, not just the music, but all of what is Metallica. The name Metallica.

LARS: Obviously, somewhere between most and nearly all of everything that goes on with lyrics and stuff like that, at least ends up in his head… and God knows what's goin' on in there. But the beautiful thing is that it ends up in these songs and that's obviously a great thing.

KIRK: For me, just watching how he approaches his instrument and how he conducts himself. As a person, it's great for me to observe, because he is so different from the way I think. Watching him do his thing with such a different perspective forces me to see it his way, because he has such a different slant on things. It forces me to look at things a little differently myself.

LARS: I think he's definitely a lot less guarded than he's been. I think most people consider him more approachable than before. I realize now that he's maybe never been as guarded as everybody though, he just more played it to kind of avoid contact and stuff like that and kind of be the cool one. But I think he's definitely let that issue down a bit more. I think most people feel that he's a lot warmer than he used to be.

KIRK: James has definitely loosened up. He's a lot more open-minded than he used to be and he's a lot less conservative than he used to be. He definitely has gotten a lot better at communicating with people.

JASON: It seems that he's always able to do everything he's called on to do and he doesn't complain about it. He just gets it done. He goes and sees the kids, he gets his gig done, he does interviews, he writes songs. He holds it all up and just protects it, as if it were his child.

Metallica on Kirk Hammett

LARS: Kirk creates… I mean, Kirk basically came up with the riff to 'Enter Sandman,' but really didn't know it, because Kirk sort of comes up with a lot of flashes of brilliance that need to be kind of molded just a little bit and turned into something. He comes up with an incredible amount of ideas, but most of 'em have to be molded slightly from how he spits 'em out. But a lot of songs, I'd say in the '90s, actually have their roots in something that was created on Kirk's guitar.

JASON: Kirk is the "don't-give-a-shit" guy. Although he's a passionate and very emotional person, he really likes to wind people up and to shock people and to get reactions out of people and to fuck with people. He's not afraid to say ANYTHING to ANYBODY. He's not like a scrapper or nothin', but he still will speak his mind and fuck people a lot and really try to get 'em to think weird shit. He loves that.

JAMES: Obviously Kirk brings some goofiness to the band, which is definitely needed. We've always been not the most serious band, but when it comes to the studio, sometimes it gets a little heavy. Kirk brings kind of a "not-give-a-fuck" attitude in a different way. Obviously, his attire, his fashion sense, he legitimately and truly does not give a fuck and it's cool. And it's a total metal attitude, which I totally love. He's always been a little… I don't know if eclectic is the word, but a little 'out there,' and it's coming through on his second skins.

LARS: He's also probably the least guarded one of the four of us and I think he's always the one that is the most easygoing and also he's probably the most… level of the four of us. His moods, if you have a curve on mood swings or ups and downs or things like that, his is probably the one that varies the least. He's always, and I'm talking in the last 10 year's time, I'm not talking in the last week's time… he's generally the one that is usually the most approachable and he's the one that there's the least issues with, apart from one time frame in 1994 where things were a little out of control with him, and he, himself, admitted that he was sort of caught up in some kind of relationship that was really steering him fucked up and we kind of had to take him aside and have a talk with him. Apart from that, I'd say that he's the one that varies the least, in that he's always the most approachable.

JASON: Some people would maybe call it 'flighty' or something like that, but it's not really that, it's just how Kirk is. He's just an eccentric musical artist. He's just very different and very unique in that way and that's what makes him special. He has a lot of great opinions about a lot of things. In that manner, I respect him a lot for his book smarts, as far as having a lot of literature under his belt. He always seems to be real advanced in that kind of stuff. I have a lot of respect for that. He seems to keep in touch with everything.

Metallica on Jason Newsted

JAMES: Jason is definitely the live dude. He's always up for a show, no matter where or when it is. He's very regimented in that way. He has to eat at this time and take a certain vitamin and drink his super power drinks and all that shit. But, whatever works for ya is definitely a good time... pretty good theory; whatever works for ya.

LARS: He's a little more up and down. I find that he's been a lot more 'up' lately. Me and him have a very workable, very positive thing going now that really centers on what needs to get done, which is, me and him show up and we play drums and bass in Metallica and then we go off stage and do something else. It doesn't really cross or connect when it's off stage, but I think he's made an effort to make the time on stage or the time around Metallica, and around what needs to be done around Metallica, work better.

KIRK: Jason's a lot more comfortable with his role in the band now... a lot more comfortable. That's a great thing. Y'know, he had some big shoes to fill. He basically waltzed into a perfect situation and I think he was a little overwhelmed by all of it, but he's grown into it very well.

JAMES: He obviously greets the fans here and there. He'll stop anydamnwhere... fuckin' Winnipeg, thirty below, he'll stop and get out and sign some stuff!

LARS: I mean, it's clear, it's not just a joke or anything. He's definitely the most, sort of, manic about what we do – the most wound up about it. And I don't mean that necessarily in a negative way, both positive and negative. He's the one that will not leave the building until each autograph is signed, which I think is a great thing, but some of us have been signing autographs for eight or ten longer than he has, you know what I mean? So that's not a good or bad thing, it's just the way it is.

KIRK: He has just a great attitude and he's really good at playing the devil's advocate too. When all of us agree about something, he'll disagree just to get some sort of perspective again.

JAMES: He's got a lot of energy. If we're all in kind of a down mood, he's always out there doin' whatever it is to get his energy going.

LARS: He's always the first one into the building. He's always the last one out of the building.

Metallica on Lars Ulrich

JAMES: Drumwise, I think he's got the most endurance of an fucking drummer I've known... and I don't know many drummers! Ha, ha! He can play all fuckin' night and it blows me away. He dedicates himself. The fucking guy jogs, y'know? Sorry, not jogs, he RUNS. Jogging's a bad word I guess. Endurance, both physically and metally, the guy's very good... and you know, we always are challenging each other.

KIRK: Lars has a lot of energy. He provides a lot of the driving force. When everyone can't find the energy to go on sometimes, whether it's because we're tired or just fed up or uninspired, a lot of times he'll push and we'll find it within us to do what we have to do, and I admire that from him. That's a really, really great thing. Plus, he's a good monitor when it comes to the business side of things. He monitors a lot of stuff and he makes sure that everything is within the best interests of the band. Plus, he's my drinking buddy!

JAMES: Lars, there's no doubt about it, he's the business dude. No matter how far or how much he tries to get away from it, he's still the business guy. Whether it is Metallica or something else, he likes the business sense of all that.

JASON: He gets bored quickly. He always has to have constant stimulation.

JASON: Lars and I clash quite a bit sometimes about certain things and then we learn from each other because of it. That's probably a good thing. Sometimes it's too late, which is kind of fucked up, but that's how we've learned in those areas... certain pictures that were taken or certain things that were said or certain clothes that people wore and people regret it now. We learn from each other when I told him when it was happening, 'dude, don't do that,'... and now he goes, 'why did you let me do that?'

JAMES: When there's problems, or when a problem arises, he's the guy to kind of jump in and try and fix things. He's better at it than the rest of us are.

KIRK: Lars isn't as snotty as he used to be. He was a fuckin' snot! He also has better hygiene these days.   ●

WHIPLASH

THE BAND ANSWERS FAN QUESTIONS

What do you do when there's nothing going right for you, when you feel depressed or unsure about how you're living your life?
Jean P., Candler, NC

JH: Talk with friends about it. Focus on what you're good at.
JN: Try to find some beauty in something – music, books, someone special, an animal, and work from good spirit as you can.
KH: (A) meditate on the positive potential of human beings in general. (B) drink.
LU: (A) I never have that problem (cough!!?) (B) stop drinking.

What's the weirdest thing you've ever had thrown at you on stage and did you stop playing?
Steven P., Burson, CA

JH: A pig's head followed closely by the feet and other miscellaneous parts, obviously a successful bar-b-que at our first Donington festival.

Lars, what do you think about drum triggers (live or studio)? Would you recommend them as good as miking drums?
Matt V., Stillwater, MN

LU: I'm certainly not against them. Finding the right balance between the two is fine.

Kirk, I'm 12 years old, how old do you think I should be in order to get a tattoo?
Stephanie R., Orchard Park, NY

KH: You should be very careful about decisions like these. What you like now isn't necessarily what you might like (or hate) when you are 25. I suggest you wait till you are 18 to get a tattoo.

Kirk, what is your middle name?
Kelly D., Sherwood, OR

KH: My middle name is 'Mack Daddy.'

Have you ever had to stop a show because of crowd trouble?
Steven M., Scotland

JH: A few times when the thoughtful crowd decided to trash the place to get back at the security and promoter, when actually it was our dime and it jeopardized our return as well as any other concerts there. Also we don't play very well when we have to constantly watch out and dodge thrown objects obviously meant to hurt us. So some brilliant people throwing things want to ruin the show for you.
JN: Steven, I do recall one time on "Monsters of Rock" '88, L.A. Coliseum, a questionable power failure stopped us in the middle of 'Whiplash.' I think it was in some attempt to regain control of the crowd.

Lars, are you a Godfather to anyone and are you going to have kids anytime soon?
Dee M., Oskaloosa, IA

LU: Yes, I'm the proud owner of two Godchildren, one in Denmark and one last seen cuddling a human teddy bear in Knoxville. Little Larses in a few years? Scary, but ultimately a nice thought.

Do you ever get tired of people 'Metalli-sizing' everything like 'Metalli-car' or 'Metalli-fukerz or whatever, coz it bugs the shit outta me.
Mike R., England

JH: I didn't know you felt this way Metalli-Mike from Metalli-England.

James, you've mentioned many times about your feelings on video making. Did you have input on the "Until It Sleeps" video? What was going through your mind when you were smearing mud all over yourself, and being trapped in that rib-cage like thing?
Paul S., Ellensburg, WA

JH: The antlers were my idea to make it like a disease (me), in a rib cage or hands holding me. I was thinking of sick voodoo hatred while being transformed onto the war painted set of "Apocalypse Now" and then wondering if they had a shower.

Kirk, what did you think the first time you saw yourself with your new look?
Angel S., Portsmouth, VA

KH: It wasn't a 'new' look. It was something that evolved over the course of 2–1/2 years. I'm a freak. I know it!

Did the band ever have a concert filmed professionally when Cliff was in the band? If so, would you consider releasing it on video, or is the "Cliff 'Em All" video the only one you'll ever release?
K.J. E., Wales

JH: There were only three so-called 'professionally' shot clips that I can remember. The Stone, The Oakland Day on the Green, and the Chicago footage. All are in the 'Cliff 'Em All' video. Because of the lack of footage we scoured the planet for footage shot by fans so everyone could get a chance to see and remember Cliff. I think the bootleg footage adds to the vibe and mystique of the early days.

James what kind of strings do you use, and how often do you change them?
Holly P., Riverview, MI

JH: Ernie Ball .009. I never change them, but Andy does every show.

What the hell were James and Kirk doing on Space Ghost?
Andy E., Brookings, SD

KH: Traveling through space.

What do you guys think about while you're playing on stage at a show?
Danielle C., Los Angeles, CA

JH: Playing on stage at a show.
LU: Not playing on stage, not being at a show.

James, what's your favorite fruit?
Mary M., Dallas, OR

KH: I'm his favorite fruit.

I'm 14, if I start guitar lessons after this summer, how long do you think it will take to have enough experience to start a band? Then after I have a band, what's the next step?
Dominic S., Springfield, IL

JH: With today's music... about a week. Next steps... fuck chicks, breakup, and o.d. (Just kidding.)

Lars, when Metallica first started, did you ever think that you would ever come this far?
Nicole M., Sugarland, TX

LU: We haven't come as far as Sugarland, Texas yet, but we're workin' on it.

James, you said in some guitar magazine that Stryper's "To Hell With The Devil" was the album that changed your life. I bought it and listened to it, and it's pretty good. But still I can't understand what about it was so fuckin' special that it changed your life?
Gene S., Randolph, NJ

JH: It sparked a hatred that will forever scar me. I can't bare to see striped spandex jumpsuits to this day.

Kirk, how do you change the different effects that you use on stage? You don't have a footswitch?
Yann G., France

KH: I use mental telepathy.

James, I was very pleased to hear that you now snowboard. What board do you ride and where do you like to snowboard?
Nadine S., England

JH: I've done it for about three seasons now. I ride a Burton Custom 59 and Superfly II 68 anywhere there's snow. Mainly Tahoe, California and all over Colorado.

Are there bongos in the song 'Bleeding Me?' If so, who's playing them, and why did you decide to put them in?
Brian G., Wyandolte, MI

LU: Yes, there are bongos in 'Bleeding Me.' The same percussionist friend of Bob Rock's, who made a brief appearance on the studio seg-

ments from the "A Year And A Half..." video, is playing them.

Jason, how do you headbang for show after show so aggressively without having a stiff neck? Do you do neck exercises?
Chris P., England

JN: Lots of stretching is the best thing for lots of banging and metal.

James, when you're singin' on stage, where do you look at? In the eyes of the first row guys, a fixed point in the crowd, or at the back of the concert hall?
Arnaud G., France

JH: Anywhere and everywhere the energy is, and sometimes at my guitar to see if I'm playin' the right song.

I was reading an article on the Internet the other day that said Jaymz was going to be in a commercial for the NHL. Is that true?
Jonathan G., West Jordan, UT

JH: Yes, it was a promo for the Stanley Cup 1997. 'Get Cup Crazy' with 'Nothing Else Matters.'

Lars, who are your favorite tennis players?
Sarah Y., Oxford, IA

LU: McEnroe, Vilas, and my dad.

I love the song 'Hero Of The Day' but who is your hero of the day?
Jean-Louis R., France

JH: The song to me says how children are leaving, or looking outside, home to find heroes when their parents are right there (sometimes).

In a recent move my "2 For One" video was damaged. I went to the mall to buy the video again. On the label it says "Interview With Lars... Sale price is $9.99." When I went to the counter to buy it, I was charged $22.48 for it! I'm not a millionaire. My question is what do you think of these assholes charging over double the price to your fans? Is there something that can be done about it? I don't expect a refund, I just wanted you all to be aware that we are being ripped off.
Jared H., Houma, LA

JH: An interview with Lars? I wouldn't pay $9.99 either.

Jaymz, have you ever blown out your vocal cords and couldn't sing anymore?
Nicholas B., Baltimore, MD

JH: Once during the recording of the "Black" album. It freaked me out. That wuz when I decided to start doing vocal exercises.

Kirk, when you travel from country to country do you have trouble with your piercings setting off the alarms when you walk through the detectors?
Neil G., United Kingdom

KH: My fake leg gives me more trouble than anything!

Kirk, which type of vegetarian are you? Lacto-vegetarian, lacto-ovo vegetarian, or vegan?
Carrie T., Chuluota, FL

JH: Intergalacto-ovum voodoo veggie.
KH: Lacto-ovo. It worked the best for me, and my girlfriend said it made my sperm taste better.

What is going on with Lars? Last I heard, none of the guys in Metallica would even consider smoking cigarettes. Why all of a sudden had Lars taken up this nasty habit? I don't want to sound like a momma's boy, but what the hell!!??
Dave P., Palatine, IL

LU: Cuz I really like it... wish I had started earlier. I'm trying to catch up on 32 years of not smoking. Joe Camel worked for me!!

Jason, having seen you play a variety of different stringed basses, I was wondering if you happen to have a personal preference, and on average, how many different basses do you incorporate over the course of recording a single album?
Joel S., Wausau, WI

JN: Joel, my main basses for live are handmade by Roger Sadowsky in NYC. For recording I use two main instruments; a '58 Fender Precision and an '82 Spector. Five strings is best for me.

When did you decide to play those songs at the EMAs and did you get in trouble with the MTV bosses afterwards?
Tim J., England

JH: Five minutes before goin' on. Fuck 'em.

James, on COC's new album there's a song called 'Man or Ash.' During the chorus, the vocals sound exactly like you. Was that you singing or did Pepper just do an incredible job sounding like you?
Brendan H., Tolland, CT

JH: Wuz me. Shhhh, don't tell the record company.

Which songs do you consider were your hardest or most difficult to learn?
Tonya D., Brandon, VT

JN: Some of the quicker and/or longer songs from "Master" and "...Justice" are still a challenge to try to play evenly and consistently (i.e. 'Battery', 'Damage, Inc.', 'Dyer's Eve'). ●

Timpani and tubular bell, that's all you need

Bill's off to China so I'm going to stand in for a day.

If I Were President for a Day

Lars Visits the White House Late June 1998

Let's change this to guitar shaped.

We'd better get these changed to Lars & Skylar.

This looks like a perfect spot to hang my picture.

We'd better get the Danish flag brought in here.

Interesting statues, but where's the one of me?

Nice movie theater. Let's roll that Roswell footage.

This is me trying to pass a law to make all Danish drummers exempt from income tax.

So this is where the intern interviews go on??

Oh well, it was good while it lasted.

112

A REAL GARAGE BAND

FROM THE BEGINNING, METALLICA JAMMED on tunes written by their favorite bands (they can still be heard breaking into the odd bit of Deep Iron Sabbath riffery during pre-gig warm-ups). They've also made it somewhat of a habit to record covers on a fairly frequent basis for use on 'B' sides and what have you; this, of course, is how 1987's "$5.98 Garage EP" release was born. As well as offering fun, escape and light relief, these covers provide much-appreciated exposure and remuneration for the likes of Motörhead, Discharge, Diamond Head and Killing Joke.

So when the decision was made to re-release the "$5.98 EP" with a collection of 'B' side cover tunes, the guys decided to add to the pile with a whole slew of new ones, these perhaps reflecting slightly more eclectic tastes than before. The final result was the "Garage Inc" double album, heaving with all manner of jams, twists and interpretations. Here, the band discuss the project and the catalysts which led to it happening...

Editor – February 2004

114

JAMES HETFIELD

Let's start here by being honest in saying Nick Cave is an unexpected choice of artist for you to be interested in.

"I'd heard his name mentioned here and there an immediately thought 'oh yeah, some fucking junkie.' Then Bob brought in that "Murder Ballads" and I just thought... how lovely. Nice songs, singing about 'and the little bird few off the carcass' and getting stabbed in the neck with a penknife after a nice, long kiss. It reminded me of the Misfits in the way it had really poppy modulations, riffs and vocal patterns but him singing about horror and ugliness. It was similar in a way."

When you all got together at Kirk's house for the initial rehearsals, you must have run through some other more established cover material?

"Yeah, but we didn't just wanna do regular covers. Sabbath's okay, but when it gets contemporary, like your Def Leppards, Iron Maidens, you don't really wanna go there. We though about doing 'Prowler' because we goof around with it on stage but it's just too close, too much of the same time we were around. But Fate was cool because not many people know about them anyway, plus those riffs are fucking awesome. And Thin Lizzy was far enough back."

Was there ever talk of guests?

"I would have loved to have brought in a piano for 'Astronomy' but we didn't need it. We were talking about a big string section in 'Turn The Page' and it wasn't really necessary. If we had more time it'd be great, but we didn't have the time and it sounded fine. 'Tuesday's Gone' is the only one with guests; it was live from the radio show we did last year and so there's all these people singing out of key. We gave Randy (Staub) the tapes of it and said 'here, mix this' and he was like 'holy shit.' There are 20 guys on it, and it had a great vibe. That song lyrically also felt good for us."

Do you think doing Neil Young's Bridge Benefit back in the fall of '97 had anything to do with finding the bravery to take on weirder covers such as Cave, Seger and Skynyrd?

"It was a big deal, sure. Especially 'Tuesday's Gone' because we needed another song for Neil Young's all-acoustic benefit. We started goofing on a Skynyrd song and it felt good. We'd considered 'Ring Of Fire' by Johnny Cash, but 'Tuesday's Gone' just felt good and it was one of those songs that everyone could jam on. Doing the acoustic stuff might have helped us feel a little more comfortable doing 'Turn The Page.'

JASON NEWSTED

When you come back from collaborations to "Garage Inc." it must be good. Talk about what you helped these guys see when approaching off-the-wall stuff.

"When we first talked about these, everybody was meant to bring in songs. Everybody came, but as far as the group thing it needed to be 'Metallica would do...' Diamond Head made immediate sense. Nick Cave is evil, so that worked, the Bob Seger thing has words that are pure Metallica, they all made sense.

"MY choices for songs... I didn't even bring them up. The main one I wanted to do was Bill Withers 'Who Is He and What Is He To You?' because I thought it could be happening and heavy metal. Every one of these songs is either about being in love with your baby, kill for you, die for you baby, or Satan. It's either Satan or 'I love you.' So that wouldn't have been that much of a lyrical drift from those places."

Does your scope of influence come from osmosis rather than direct comment?

"It's very much a thing where I have to plant a seed long before anybody pays attention to its seedling, or whatever. The only thing I can do is let the music do the talking, there's no other way I can penetrate the core, get any attention or prove a point or to be taken seriously. I have to apply myself to my bass.

"Like 'Loverman.' I know the song but I'm not into it like Tom Waits' songs, I had the record but I'd never studied it. I focused on the bass part, making it the best I can and leave everything else.

If they read this, it'll be the first time they'll even have heard you wanted Bill Withers?

"Yeah."

Any others?

"I mentioned artists, no titles. Tom Waits was my first choice. '16 Shells From a Thirty-Ought Six' I thought would've been cool. Some of the other stuff off 'Raindogs' too. All artists in name and I never mentioned songwriters."

I'm surprised Tom Waits didn't fly?

"Me too. But the Nick Cave thing came together real well."

One or the other?

"Probably because of the same vibe I guess that everybody leaned towards the 'Loverman' thing because the chorus is so abrasive, which is a good thing."

Which metal stuff?

"Well, the Fate stuff was fun but Black Sabbath are my favorite band of all-time, ever. Geezer Butler is my favorite bassist of all time, so needless to say, that was the shit and the one that I tried the hardest to pay the most attention to be ultra respectful on. My once chance to give a shout out to Geezer, I played my style with my five string bass a bit different to the Black Sabbath song sounds because it's Metallica doing Black Sabbath. So instead of it being a wall of sound, it has the Metallica enveloping bass which pulls everything in. The low strings, you don't really hear the notes, only the stability of it pulling everything in."

KIRK HAMMETT

Go through some of your favorite moments making "Garage Inc.?"

"I don't usually call it The Plant, I call it 'Purgatory.' But there have been so many fucking high points in the studio; it's been amazing. I keep on telling people I haven't felt this good since "Re-Load!" Recording 'Loverman' at 3 a.m. all burned out and just kind of somber, capturing the mood the band was in and it was a perfect vibe to do that track. It had so much mood and atmosphere in the cut, we decided to go for it. 75% of my guitar parts were played at that time, no overdubs necessary. I was playing slide guitar, playing the piano part on guitar and a lot of different stuff. We felt we'd nailed it, it was getting late, we thought we'd be pretty useless but we got a lot out of that. Definitely a high point."

Do you feel you've let go of your inhibitions

"I feel like I've let go of a lot of my inhibitions. One example of that is my slide-guitar playing which I've grown much more confident about. It pushed me to go other places with the slide that I didn't think I could pull off. During 'Turn The Page' the original is a very sparse arrangement. We knew we could keep it light or totally fuck with the arrangement, make it heavy and put some dynamics in there. It didn't answer what I'd do during the sax part, so then I thought I'd play slide and then I felt maybe I should play slide through the whole arrangement for that extra mood. I strove for it, I let go of my attachment of what I thought good slide playing was, what should or shouldn't be in the song, I said 'fuck all that' and just let-it-goooo."

LARS ULRICH

I would imagine that, on "Garage, Inc.," the Mercyful Fate cover holds the most interest for you, true or false?

"...Settling down and heading into the Fate stuff was a challenge. It was a lot of fun, very hard, and for me very exciting because it's something that's very dear to me. I think it's dear to all of us. We realize 15 years later how tremendously influential they were and what a motherfucker it was to execute. Just realizing how those guys were such brilliant musicians and have such a great thing going, I know a lot of people turned off to MF because of the whole thing with King Diamond, his vocal style and Satanism; well if you take that away and just listen to the music, it's really challenging and a lot of fun. Of all the 11 songs, that was both the most challenging and fun for me."

A lot of people will find it a surprise to hear you talking fondly once more of 'old metal' given your recent apparent antipathy towards that school.

"When you talk about old metal, that's a very general term. There's a lot of old metal that certainly holds a place in my nostalgic heart but doesn't necessarily age all that well, or is something we feel particularly interested in diving into. But when we came around to listening to the MF stuff this summer in various Midwestern hotel rooms playing poker at 1 a.m., it really sounded incredibly fresh and very strong. It's aged very well to my ears, especially that earlier stuff. Some of the later stuff I have reservations about, but songs like 'Evil' and 'Curse Of The Pharaohs' have just aged tremendously. Maybe the Fate stuff would've been easier to nail 10 years ago, when we were in the "...Justice" phase and the progressive aspect of playing and writing.

OK. In Metallica, there's one guy who's approaching in a looser fashion and another guy who has a more concise approach to the studio? Who are those people?

"That's really not an easy question to answer. With every song everyone has a different opinion on where to take it. The Nick Cave song for example was something James really pushed for, and was close to his heart. It's something I appreciate but don't have a long-term relationship with. So when we went in and played it, I'd have been happy with take four or five of it, I felt we'd nailed it. And then other guys wanted to redo their guitar parts, I though James sang a brilliant vocal off the floor and he wanted to redo all the vocals, where I was happy to leave it. So I think it has a lot to do with who pushed for what. I'm very protective of the Mercyful Fate thing, the Diamond Head thing, James is very protective of the Nick Cave thing, the Misfits thing, so to sit down and generalize about who's loose and specific isn't easy. It varies.

"I think I could've been happier with leaving more stuff from off the floor generally, but once you start sitting down and changing guitar parts and redoing new vocals, then I found myself thinking 'well if they're doing that, maybe I'll go into the computer and do some drum fills.' I wouldn't say I have more of a right approach, I'm just saying it started somewhere and then we started sliding back into the direction of how we make our own records with everybody getting a bit more specific."

Projects like this must be a great re-bonding experience, helping to bring people closer together.

"This whole project started some three or four months ago, because even though we didn't start playing anything until we were at Kirk's house, the bonding process started on the summer tour, sitting around and shoving shit at each other in terms of different songs, and ideas, directions and there were a lot of good moments in late night hotel rooms around the country. James saying he'd like to do some Tom Waits stuff, and him giving me a CD, I sit and listen because I don't know him that well but I know James likes him so I'm trying to find stuff that would work for us.

"Then there were bands like Blue Oyster Cult where we felt they were really fucking cool, they had a lot of material that was suitable so it was a case of sitting down with four or five BOC albums in a room one night, so you sit down and listen to 'Astronomy' or 'Dominance and Submission.' If you go back to 1975 and BOC, who else was relevant with the time? Cheap Trick, Kiss, Robin Trower, Aerosmith, Ted Nugent and I think of all of them, BOC are among the bands from that time period who aged the best. So the bonding happened all summer. It's been a lot of fun sitting and hearing Fate, Thin Lizzy and stuff like that again. There's been a lot of sharing, sitting around and saying 'here's those five Thin Lizzy songs, why don't you take a tape with you tonight and we'll talk about it tomorrow.'"

What material got close to the mark?

"I think with the Misfits we sat down with half a dozen of them, 'Ghoul's Night out,' 'Astro Zombies,' 'London Dungeon,' and we ended up with 'Die Die My Darling.' One of the last songs to be picked out was 'It's Electric' and sitting down and having an idea of how the project was shaping up, it was pretty clear that one thing we were missing despite the 12 minute Fate thing, was a shorter more concise NWOBHM underground metal song. We had the Segers and the wacky stuff like Nike Cave, but in terms of a 4-minute straight-ahead metal song there were three Diamond Head songs we tried, one was 'Streets of Gold.' We were listening to a Sweet Savage song called 'Eye of the Storm,' a Jaguar song called 'Backstreet Woman' and 'Dutch Connection,' there was a song on my record by a band called Witchfynde called 'Leaving Nadir' which is a great fucking song and one that I would really like to cover one day because I think it sounds like we could do it justice. But that song ended up sounding more in the BOC '70s feel.

How important was that Bridge Benefit in gaining the confidence to move even further forward on more offbeat stuff?

"I think when you sit down to write the history of this band one day, you will have to say that that was a major cornerstone, and a pretty interesting one. The decision to play the show was reached with no effort at all. We were doing a photo session with Danny Clinch in San Francisco, we had some downtime, we discussed the request and everybody kinda jumped at it really quickly. I was a little bit surprised, and that was maybe six to eight weeks before the show. And then a couple of weeks later, phones started going off and guys were on telephones saying 'why are we doing this? We cannot go up and play acoustic in front of 20,000 people?' Wait a minute, we had made the fucking decision and whenever we'd faced a challenge in the past we've taken it on and fucking done it. There were one or two people who were pushing it to the point of pulling out and saying we made a mistake, it wasn't for us and was something we could not pull off. So we had to dig deep. We got together the day after we mastered the "Re-Load" record over at Kirk's for one fucking day, we had no idea what songs we were going to end up playing. All of a sudden James started playing a Lynyrd Skynyrd song, that came together, 'Poor Twisted Me' and 'Nothing Else Matters' came together really quickly. And there was this spirit that afternoon over at Kirk's house of 'y'know what? Maybe this isn't going to be a complete fucking bust after all.' Then when we went out and did it in front of 20,000 people for two days, it was almost like another chapter had opened. It was a case of 'wow, there's a whole other side.'

"The cool thing we got from that, more so than the whole physical aspect of playing acoustically, was reinventing older, earlier songs, reinventing songs, taking songs we'd played to death for 75 years or whatever, taking a song like 'The Four Horsemen' and completely reinventing it. Knowing that it was okay and fun and challenging to sit down and re-address, re-arrange and re-fuck with old stuff. Then slowly over the course of the last year it's become more comfortable doing it in front of people, doing it as part of the Metallica set. And I will say it is now a genuine part of what Metallica has to offer, sitting down with acoustic instruments and playing some of our songs in a different format." ●

Metallica talk about indulging in a little "S&M"

Orchestral Maneuvers

On April 21st and 22nd 1999, Metallica collaborated with famous classical composer Michael Kamen (who sadly passed away in 2003) and the San Francisco Symphony to perform two shows at the Berkeley Community Theater in Northern California. The results were spectacular; when this melding of metal and orchestra worked, it really, really worked... and when it didn't, you knew it! Being archivists supreme, Metallica recorded and filmed every last minute of the performances, and the result was a double album entitled "S&M" as well as a DVD of the event.

Editor – April 2004

Making the marriage work

"Basically it's been two years since Michael Kamen came to San Francisco and initiated the project. So to me it has been through three distinct phases. The first started with the preparation from a year and a half ago with Michael, then there were those four days in Berkeley, which were another kind of vibe, and, thirdly in the studio. We had a very focused week of rehearsals leading up to the show, the vibe was great with the band and with Kamen too. The rehearsals were good, the warm-up shows were very strong and I don't ever remember feeling wobbly about the band or my role in this. There were certainly very exciting variables in there with regards to the audience, and the interplay between us, the symphony and Kamen. But Metallica were about as lean and clean as we had been for a long time, and were certainly ready and prepared to step up that extra notch to the challenge.

"While the first couple of days in rehearsal we might've felt a bit awkward with the symphony, by the first show there was a real vibe going on. And by the second show, which was the fourth night of playing together we were practically old chinas, exchanging war stories, memories and thoughts." Lars

"We were very adamant on that point (of interaction) because we didn't want the orchestra to be some backdrop behind us making noise. We wanted to be part of it. So in certain songs I was sitting in there, Jason was running by knocking music stands over, sheets flying, you could go into a section and rock out with them a little bit. If I'd have had the stuff in my ears too, it would've been complete sensory overload. So I didn't get to enjoy the full monty that night, I kinda had to just see afterwards how the pieces of the puzzle came together...and it was a puzzle." James

"I think 'Ktulu' is the one that sums it up, but lots of songs, (not just the old ones) 'The Outlaw Torn,' 'Hero Of The Day,' 'Bleeding Me,' those epicy things really came alive, they were thicker and deeper with all the orchestral color. But 'Ktulu,' sure, that was the one we were trying to be an orchestra ourselves." James

"They (the orchestra) were really up for it! Considering the mixed ages and points of origin and education in music, it was amazing. You had your Eastern bloc kinda cat, white haired kinda conductor guy, scarf over one shoulder and you're thinking 'dude, will he even talk to me or will he think we're shite?' So when that cat, for example, finally smiled it was a great thing. The primary cellist was a major Metallica fan, totally hip to what was going on and most of the guys who sat in the primary chairs knew what was going on. But there were some people who, y'know, weren't quite sure what to think when you were sweatin' on their paper. And just watchin' those faces on the first night when the kids suddenly started just screaming 'FUCK YEAAAAHHH' and 'METALLICAAAAA' was great, because they're used to 'hello, good evening' y'know? And by the end of the second night you saw the cellists holding their bows like this (metal sign) and they had the tuxedo tees under their jackets having blown off most of the convention by then." Jason

"That first night, maybe more so than the second night, was absolutely magic. There was an incredible feeling of coming through and making it happen. Even though there was an anxiousness of wanting to get on with it, I think it was more a case of welcoming it rather than fearing it. That first hour and a half of the first night was just magical... we really were in a situation we'd never been in before. And carrying the weight I was carrying, plus the rest of the team carrying their weight, that was truly sharing an experience." Lars

"In April it was a shot in the dark. Nobody had ever done it before, there was no point of reference, there was no video of a band who'd done it three or four years ago that we could've checked out just to see how they'd done it. The only band that ever did anything close was Deep Purple in the '70s – I wasn't a big fan of that – and they weren't doing their own songs, John Lord had written this original music specially for the orchestra. But in retrospect it was super-exciting, it sounded incredible and it was just this amazing feeling being able to weld the power and grace of the symphony with the power, passion... and grace of our band. I think the big question mark in all our minds was whether this would be cohesive and seamless or would it be a big collision.

"It seemed like after the first couple of rehearsals our insecurities gave way and we felt much better about it. There was also the thing about what would it be like played in front of an audience, how would they react and obviously that's such an important dynamic because we feed off the audience's reaction. So when we all actually did it, and saw that it turned out pretty much fucking way-cool, then it was an amazing thing." Kirk

"I mean, mixing this thing! There's so many melodies going on, Kamen came out with so many great parts and you don't hear 'em until you turn the orchestra up loud. Then you can't hear the band. With the orchestra you've got so many more colors with all these cool instruments going on. You're creating those crescendos, and live Michael Kamen was doing it, he's the guy who 'mixes' live, that's his gig. But when you get it all back here on tape it's 'what do we do?' So Kamen's assistant James has been out helping us with the mix from the orchestra perspective. Kamen was out here for a bit too, but both of them have helped us work out, for example, where certain instruments need to be grouped together. There were so many melodies going on, not just in our melodic parts but generally, people were jumping in holes to do a riff. So we had to really pick which melodies were best for that song, and those were the things that got turned up and highlighted. But every damn time you listen to the song you hear something new, 'aww man, there's a great little flute part, maybe we should turn that up.' And you get to learn what you like in the symphony. We realized that glockenspiel is not the most important thing in an orchestra for Metallica, but French horn plays a major part and obviously the bow strings and my favorite, the timpani. Timpani and tubular bell, that's all you need." James

"The cool thing about the "S&M" DVD, is that you'll be able to isolate the orchestra from the band and hear each group separately from each other. Generally I am notoriously lax on these advances in technology and for a lot of people I'm sure it's exciting. I mean, James is pretty excited, but for me it's something I'm not that passionate about right now. So far, my initial DVD experiences have been largely pornographic..." Lars

"There's been a bit of fixing up here and there, some of the strings were really out of key simply because it was so loud and they couldn't hear what they were playing. We didn't have amps on stage but there's also usually not a giant Big Mick full-roar PA in the symphony!" James

"I mean look... Kirk re-played a couple of bits that were out of tune, James re-sang a verse in one of the new songs and all things considered, when you're trying to put two hours and 20 minutes on a CD and film, and considering all the elements that were going on, we're dealing with a very strong situation." Lars ●

From Woodstock to the Millennium

As Metallica made their way towards the New Year's Eve show in Detroit's Pontiac Silverdome (plus a few 'Metllennium gigs afterwards), they 'summered' in South America and Europe as well as taking in Woodstock on July 24, 1999 in Rome, New York.

and shit, then a press pit, then a security pit and whooaa man, it's not about connecting with the crowd at all, we were more or less playing for the TV… which is fucked up. I love playing wherever it is, and I just think we could've done better. I'm sure that really it wasn't that bad, but when I notice a few things then it becomes pretty magnified for me personally. I can tell when I'm not at my best or running on all cylinders." **James**

"Going to Bogota, Colombia was pretty big. I saw a kid's t-shirt and it said 'Bogota Is Not All Just About Violence'. And in our case it turned out to be so, the show transcended all the bullshit and political gangland violence and racketeering. We did have extensive security, yeah, because there's a big kidnapping ring down there which targets corporate American figures or just about anyone who could cough up a hefty ransom. And we weren't about to second

PEACE OFF

On Festivals and Woodstock…

"I think the European Festival tour was a little difficult because certain playing wasn't up to snuff and 'what's going on? I'm out on tour here… in Europe… and we gotta do our best every night. I'm on tour to play those 2.5 hours and I want them to be good, and there were a few times that they weren't so good.' So we re-arranged the set, did a few things to make it exciting. But it's true that when we got back to the States, Woodstock in particular, there is more of an element of competition involved. I thought it was probably the worst gig we played all summer, the tempos were all fucked up, vocally there were fuck-ups, the stage was a piece of crap.

"The whole day we'd had some arguments. It was fine when we got there, a good vibe. I went up to watch Limp Bizkit because I hadn't seen them before. To get on-stage to watch 'em… the stage was so packed with poseurs for the cameras that it would've been easier to have walked out front and seen them. So, fuck, OK, whatever. I gave that a miss. So for our set 'oh, you've gotta have all these people on-stage for your set, it looks good for the cameras and the vibe of Woodstock.' I said, 'y'know what? I don't give a fuck about Woodstock, we wanna play good. And I cannot do that if I cannot see my roadie or my monitor guy so you've gotta clear these poseurs off now.' I mean, we do all these festival shows, and we come to that one and it's completely different. There's film crew all over the fucking place, the crowd is a mile away because there's train tracks of cameras

guess anything, so we had a security team that did it right. I really didn't expect anything to happen, and we were all hoping that the music might transcend the bullshit and it did. The audience were amazing, they knew all the songs and they were just so-damn-HAPPY that we were down there. You could tell by the look on their faces. It was a small miracle, both for them and for us." **Kirk**

"At Woodstock you go up after the Limp Bizkits and Kid Rocks and Rage Against The Machines, and people think they know what you're doing. So you continue to try and outdo yourselves for the other bands, the business fucks and backstage poseurs, and, most importantly, yourself. Some of the things we've done this year have provided some great moments, and shown people that we still are a force very much to be reckoned with. We continuously coast through these sorts of things, but it was very nice to prove points to all of the above, and I was very proud of what we did at Woodstock.

"Ultimately it's about proving it to yourself, proving it to the other three guys in the band and to me, a big thing about it is staying relevant to your peers backstage. Y'know, 'look here comes Metallica with their Gucci clothes and nice haircuts, do they still have the tenacity, energy and anger thing.' And I think we can always find that anger, energy and… hatred. It never ceases to amaze me how easily the hatred comes back, wanting to fucking upstage these other cunts, at least for me. I went out at Woodstock with one mission, which was to play harder, more furiously, more venomously, angrier, grittier and with more war faces than ever." **Lars**

On the Millennium show in Detroit and future plans
"There's no-one else I'd rather be with more on this planet than Ted Nugent and Kid Rock! I mean, it's another year to me, all the zeros look cool and all that. I mean, is it renting a barge and going out to Greenwich where the time changes or whatever, be the first band to play in the year 2000, all this crazy shit, or instead... Detroit! For Metallica in the States it's strongest around the lakes I think, Detroit, Chicago, all that area. And since you're out, it's like 'what the hell, do a few more dates after...'" **James**

"James and I talked up at my house recently, and January 10th in Minneapolis will be the last show. And we both agreed that when we wake up on January 11th, we don't wanna have a fucking schedule in front of us. We'll stay in touch on a weekly basis, and when the urge becomes too much to suppress, then we'll get together and get on with it. I hope we do take, at least, a 6 month breather. I'm really at peace with that, but at the same time, I'll be ready to get going with the album when the right time comes.

"I personally want the next album to be really brutal and harsh and fucked up and ugly. Those are the words that come to mind when I think of the next record, especially 'brutal' and 'harsh'. I wanna make a really harsh record, I think we've done enough of the blues-based English riffage, that we've been having so much fun with for the last three albums. For me, that's out of my system. The "Garage Days" album was a lot of fun, it showed some things we're still capable of doing in terms of recording under certain time-frames. And this project here has been very, very rewarding. But the next Metallica record is one that I want to be brutal and fucked up.

"I think we have a good system in terms of how we develop and create the music: the thing that will make the big difference is the process of recording the next record. I don't wanna do another record here (at The Plant), I wanna go somewhere else, and I don't think we need to leave the Bay Area to make that record. And also, as Bob Rock was pointing out the other day, the way technology is going, we don't even need a recording studio. Maybe we could rent a house somewhere, a factory space, a warehouse, a garbage dump, whatever." **Lars**

"There's a few ideas we're throwing around about the record and we'd love to do, bringing it on the road. You add stuff you wouldn't in the studio, can we get everyone on a fucking bus and just do it? I'm sure we could. Can we play these gigs without someone bootlegging them on the internet? Probably not. But it's important not to be so comfortable. This place (The Plant studios on Sausalito, CA – ED) is pretty comfortable. We're talking about maybe getting a house together and bringing a desk in. That'd be fun. Could it happen? Dunno, there are variables with families and all that. But we've gotta try something fresh, we know that for sure." **James**

"It's been so long since we've written songs, and I think there've been so many advances in terms of sound possibilities and technology, that I really look forward to embracing it all and trying something new with regards to sounds and approach. For me, there's a tenacity which insures that when Metallica puts out a record in 2001, we'll still be contenders, relevant and viable, at least in our own minds. I'm really looking forward to that. I'm anxious to do it..." **Lars**

"It's always been about satisfying ourselves first and foremost. To take on the challenge of satisfying the entire world

is unrealistic, and you have to think about it in those terms. Another part of it is redefining ourselves. I don't like saying 'reinventing', because it's redefining ourselves and our sound. Finding different ways to channel that energy and aggression we have, taking a few different creative roads that we haven't taken. Let me put it this way. I don't think there will be any drum loops or sequencers, not that I can foresee at this point; we're not about to become the next Fatboy Slim. But manipulated sounds, guitar sounds and samples definitely have some room in our future." **Kirk**

"If 'Minus Human' and 'No Leaf Clover' are signs of what's to come from Hetfield's hands and head, there's gonna be some good, well thought out music. It's all about technique and he's really good at that slight of hand thing. The changes I would like to see are lessening of the rules and removal of many many rules as we know them now, plus way more open minds from everyone to do some crazy shit. I'd like to see things like James playing drums and me singing – maybe on the song he plays drums on. I dunno, just some different shit.

"James and I have already had words about all this and I feel really good. He said he wants me to come with real songs, that I have great ideas and a riff here and a riff there... dude, is that the green light? Yes it was. So that's all I needed. I mean it's been a long time since I had to think about putting a real riff tape together... five years. So part of what I mean when I talk about changing rules, is that maybe I'll just go to James' house and work on some shit before he gets to Lars' dungeon. We just really need to take some different approaches and channels, I mean, even if we stick with the same production team, we need that new approach." **Jason**

...and finally, the very first Metallicomments on MP3s
"My take on it is, that it's still too early. Anyone you ask will only give you a speculative answer. I think people are waiting to see where the chips fall, and with Metallica we've been aware of where it's going in terms of communicating and selling records directly to the kids, that type of stuff. What role does the Internet play for an established band? A lot of people are saying that record companies will be extinct, and I don't think that's true for one reason: there will always be a need to develop artists, there will always be a need to finance artists and there will always be a need to find $100,000 to make a record with and a $100,000 to promote that record with. You have to speak clearly in distinct terms about the established artists and up and coming artists when talking about this stuff. I think Metallica could probably survive without a record company and could potentially be it's own record company, and not need the umbrella of big machinery or finance. But I think the MP3 ilks of the world serve a great purpose, because you and your son can start a garage band and have your music out to people immediately.

"I was talking to my travel agent the other day, and it's amazing how much this Internet stuff is affecting people. Travel agents are becoming extinct, because people are buying more tickets over the Internet: imagine where the Internet is now versus where it's going to be in 100 years. Compare where the car was 100 years ago and where it is now. So people only know they're part of the infancy of some kind of major revolution in communications compared to what we've been used to in the 20th century. For our grandchildren it'll be a completely different thing." **Lars** ●

125

SSSSSSSHHH!
don't mention Bambi!

JAMES HETFIELD
Hunts in Patagonia

Hunting has never been my 'thing'... it never did float my boat. So to receive an invitation from James to report on a hunting trip he was making in Argentinian Patagonia during the 1999 South American tour was intriguing. I knew I would be 'hunting,' but I also knew of Hetfield's respect for the whole endeavor, as well as his extensive hunting knowledge. I decided only a fool would turn this opportunity down, and besides, I really wanted to understand what makes this pursuit so engaging for the people involved. Thus Hetfield and I spent three days in one of the world's more beautiful patches of turf, with many more pairs of eyes watching us than the other way around. Between the long, silent walks through rich Patagonian forests and the venison stew heartily eaten 'camp' style in the small, rustic lodge kitchen, this was one of those assignments that you never forget. Perhaps the most interesting thing looking back, is how quiet, respectful (of others and surroundings) and completely immersed in the 'land' Hetfield was. It was obvious that this was his sanctuary, his escape and his chance to leave behind the guy in Metallica and get back to the core of Hetfield, the man himself.
Editor – February 2004

His Father's Influence "My Dad was always full of hobbies, there was always something going on. Seeing my dad cleaning guns and seeing deer hanging in the garage are instant memories. Seeing Pops go hunting maybe once a year made an impression. I had a little set of antlers that was my little trophy he gave me, he made rings out of some of the antlers which I'd wear to school, but they'd break because they weren't very strong. He'd also take me skeet shooting at the skeet range, it's basically practice for hunting birds. But he never really introduced me to a gun, though I don't know why. He made me rubber-band guns and I had plenty of sling-shots, so I don't really know why there weren't guns.

"One week he was making his own bullets, pouring hot lead into the mould, packing his own shells, then the next month or two he was tying his own flies for fly-fishing. We were always outdoors. Every summer we'd go and live on our boat for two or three weeks and live off the fish we caught in the lake. So camping, being outdoors, eating fish off the lake, that was all part of life, and it was the right thing to do because we were doing it with our parents.

"I don't recall whether there was an actual time where he sat down and told me what happens when things die or explained the food chain. I think the religious (Christian Science – Ed) background was part of it all, you're taught that the body was just a shell and your soul lives on. And that things are here for a purpose, as well as that whole Darwinian theory of strong surviving and so on. So I didn't really question if there was a birdy heaven or a human heaven or what."

The Reasons Behind His Hunting "It never really was for me just about drinking and hanging out. For that you'd take your .22 and shoot cans, targets and whatever. Shooting crows off the telephone wire was never fun. It was about the challenge of stalking, seeing how close you could get, it was never just about the thrill of killing. It's a combination of things. The thrill of the chase, the kill, the meat, being away, being outdoors, being in the clean air, seeing how much your body can take as well so far as hiking. You don't think you can hike 'that' mountain, and at the end of the day with a guide you've actually done it, you've hiked that mountain which isn't something you'd necessarily do without a guide. He's kinda pushing you along too.

"I'm not just a meat hunter and I'm not just a trophy hunter. I want to go off and find the biggest rack out there, the animal who's the smartest, the most cunning, the one who's survived the longest and that's the challenging part. And you get to keep the meat too, so as you can 'feed your family' or make winter stew, clean out the freezer and get your buddies over."

First Kill "It was a rabbit somewhere, and it was shocking. You put human emotions into it, into the animal and you over think it, which is not, no matter how much you think, animals aren't created equal. We are the top of the food chain and sometimes we have the ability to think too much and we get ourselves into trouble. I think we have thought too much, we put human emotions into animals and you cannot."

The Patagonian Hunt "We were on our way to another hunting site, and from the truck we saw a couple of does and a buck. So I put my hand up to gesture I'd seen something, Martin (the guide in photo on facing page – ED) took a look and said one was do-able. I popped out of the truck, they ran 40 yards and I followed to a clearing. So it was a running shot initially, they were running and I thought I'd gut-shot him but it was in the hindquarters.

"We got our bearings and started tracking them as they got away. I didn't even know if I'd hit him, the bullet didn't make a sound, there was no real blood, they instantly split and we had to follow the right tracks. Bucks have four imprints with two back little heels. We followed those, started

finding tiny trickles of blood, we were looking down at the trail, looking for blood and then suddenly about 15 minutes later he popped up the other side of the hill looking straight at me. Right then I knew he was injured because he didn't take off running, so I popped him a few more times and within 100 yards he fell. We fetched the truck, had to clear all kinds of debris away to get the truck in and then there was the fun thing of two guys trying to haul a 350 lb. beast into a Datsun! He parked on a hill so we could yank the buck up into it. We had to cut little finger/hand holes into his leg to dig in and pull him up, you cut into the skin there near the Achilles tendon and it's like a handle."

Game Management And Beyond "There are many people who don't understand game management. I have heard of people trying to put condoms on deer, or birth control, instead of taking advantage of the animals that are there and providing meat for people. It's a way of managing the human/animal ratio. People are getting killed because deer run into the road and hit their vehicles, so why not extend the hunting season. 'No, let's just give 'em condoms!' It just doesn't make sense.

"Everything on the planet has natural answers, and population management of deer by life higher in the food chain is a reasonable and natural answer. You get deer and other animals who are over-populating and before you know it there are coyotes roaming L.A. killing cats and dogs. So it becomes a case of managing the herds. Every time there's a kill (in North America) you have to report to a station on the way out, they note what was killed, what sex, they estimate how many animals were harvested and how many are left so as the next time they can sell the appropriate amount of tags to keep things in good shape, say 70 (hunters have to buy permits known as 'tags' which are priced according to the animal. It is a strictly regulated affair, and hunting without tags is prohibited). The money from those tags, which isn't necessarily cheap I can tell ya, is funneled back into wetlands, the national parks system and specific preserves which allow species to breed under relatively protected circumstances."

"I am no drum beater for hunting. It's something I like to do but I wouldn't go out there and campaign for it. But as for hunters being crazy, I think people who don't understand where meat comes from, the people who think everything just 'arrives' at Safeway are the crazy ones."

"Funny thing is, the true hunters are some of the most dedicated environmentalists you could ever know. By managing a species like that, and by to a lesser extent weeding out the weak, you are guaranteeing the survival of that species. It saves getting the military going in and slaughtering everything at once, why not let it happen naturally and open up more to the public?"

Dealing With Alternate Options "Some people go out of their way to block freedom. Take me, coming back from a hunt in Colorado with a nice elk rack in the back... people honk their horns and wave their thumbs as you go through the state, to say 'good one.' When you hit California, people honk and offer another finger. It isn't like I'm out there flaunting my freedom every day of the week, 'look at me I'm taking advantage of my freedom to kill things' and have meat dripping off the bumpers of my truck. But it seems that many of those folks are the same people who loudly promote their own choices publicly. I just don't think anyone should throw their choices into other people's faces. If that's what you like to do then great, go do it, but don't go criticizing people for their choices. The world is huge and everyone has a different way of living, and you can't put down different ways of life. People should just be left alone to pursue their own way of living, and ultimately, like-minded people tend to hang with each other and get on with whatever it is they wanna do." ●

WHIPLASH

THE BAND ANSWERS FAN QUESTIONS

I'm probably gonna regret asking this, but why do you give such smartass answers to questions that people honestly want the answers to?
Dawn M., Des Moines, IA

LU: To avoid having to suffer agonizing deep self-examination of our psyche – when most of the answers are either obvious or available elsewhere!

How did you first come up with the name Metallica?
Denis L., Jackson, NJ

JH: Black Sabbath was taken, so....

Is 'Outlaw Torn' the sequel to 'My Friend of Misery' James? It's great that you quit drinking. Do you ever go to A.A.? Have you ever been too drunk to play?
Brian Y., Alex, VA

JH: "Not a sequel. 'Outlaw...' is seeking for that someone that never comes. No need for A.A., but AAA towed my truck once. Never onstage, but too hung over – yes."

I got this band and we write our own shit and pump out a lot of Metallica, but we don't have a name for our band. Any suggestions?
John G., Pittsburgh, PA

JH: Shit Pumperz.
JN: Shitpump?
KH: Tape Recorder, or Chocolate Anus.

In 'The Unforgiven' video the young man writes 'yest' on the wall in his blood. What does that mean?
Jason L., Greeley, CO

JH: Add 'erday' to it.

"Say yes. At least say hello." This is a line from "The Misfits," Marilyn Monroe's final movie. Was this the source of the cryptic dialogue at the end of 'The Memory Remains' and if so, whose idea was it to use this?
Julia K., Glen Ellyn, IL

JH: Marianne Faithfull chose a few of her favorite movie one-liners to add to the feel of the song.

Did any of you sell your hair to wig companies when you cut it?
Hank B., Nevada City, CA

JH: They wouldn't take it. They said it was too abused and smelly.
KH: No, but I thought about gluing mine to my chest.

Jaymz, how did you get to be so amazingly perfect?
Kim G., Lowell, MA

JH: Minutes of practice.

"This is a clean band. The closest thing to debauchery will come after the show, when Ulrich daringly sips a cup of chilled Chardonnay." Is this true? Request Magazine, February 1998 issue.
Daniel S., Kimball, NE

LU: Don't believe everything you read! They were just pissed 'cuz we wouldn't share the crack pipe.

Do you guys wear the same shirt every show or do you wear a new one?
Travis L., Oelwein, IA

JH: No, we all have our own.
LU: I wear whatever shirt the representative of our wardrobe staff gives me that night. It's somewhat dependent on conditions, i.e. temperature.

Is it just me or are all your songs about drugs, death or misled emotions?
Brian Y., Alexandria, VA

JH: Hey, fuck off or I'll kill you with my hypo-needle.

James, what have you got against Ford?
Chris R., New Hudson, MI

JH: Gerald or Harrison?

Kirk and James, how do you all change from clean tone to distortion on stage? I've never seen any pedals around, except for the wahs.
Jason A., Tuscaloosa, AL

KH: Mental telepathy.
JH: My trusty roadie, Andy, has finally learned the songs after 12 years.

Kirk, is it true that you've got a piercing called a prince albert? Do you wear it all the time?
Virginie B., France

KH: I don't have a prince albert. It makes pissing while standing a problem.

If someone were to make Metallica into action figures, what would your special features be?
Samantha H., Summerville, SC

JH: Forget lyrix.
JN: My action figure would have 'rotating neck action' and the 'bass neck grip'.
KH: Endless guitar solos, stun guitar solos, guitar solos that make you tell the truth.
LU: Svend the Danish Thunder God.

Kirk, I'd like to know what does Lani do for a living?
Jean F., New York, NY

KH: She drives a cement truck.

Hey, I wanted to know if you have any videos or CDs of you guys playing in your garage or anywhere that the public has not seen, and could you send it to me?
David D., College Point, NY

JH: Would you like wine with that?!

What do you guys think of Marilyn Manson and Korn?
Mitya R., La Crosse, WI

JH: They make a lovely couple.

15 years ago did you think you would be writing songs like 'Hero of the Day' and 'Low Man's Lyric'? I could not picture you guys playing them 15 years ago.
Joe R., Lavallette, NJ

LU: ... and the stuff you'll hear on our records 15 years from now, I cannot picture writing/playing right now!

Kirk, it goes without saying what a great guitarist you are. Did you get where you are today with tons of practice, or were you also blessed with natural talent?
Mark W., England

KH: I practiced a lot and sold my soul.

James, what guitar effects (pedals, etc.) did you use while recording "Kill 'Em All"? Of all the new songs that you guys have done, which ones would Cliff have liked the most?
John D., Russellville, AL

JH: A Boss Rat distortion was all I had. I think Cliff would love 'Outlaw Torn', 'Carpe Diem Baby', and 'Fixxxer'. The more epic feel.

You guys, especially Kirk, have taken a lot of flack about your image. Strangely so did Cliff, mostly from you guys for his bell-bottoms. But his stubborn attitude never wavered. Did you look upon this as a source of strength or inspiration?
Christopher K., Greenville, ME

JH: Wow, good observation. We're all a bit stubborn.
KH: Cliff taught me to not give a fuck what others thought.

You guys put instrumental songs on the first four albums, but not on the last three. I enjoy the guitar riffs and solos on these immensely! Is there any chance more will be on your future albums?
Joel C., Charleston, WV

JH: What, lyrics get in your way Joel? Seriously, we haven't felt that fancy lately, and I've got lots to say.

James, I love the song 'Unforgiven II', but since these are very abstract and awesome lyrics, could you please tell me what they are about?
Sebastien T., France

JH: Forgiving no one and ending up alone.

Do you guys have any new material left after "Re-Load" and what's the chance of a new record before the year 2000?
Steven W., Australia

LU: Starting with "Load" we're running at one a year.
JH: Unloaded all the loads of "Load" material. Can't wait to write again. Start that in '99. 2000 might be pushin it, but soon after.
JN: Steven – you will hear some 'new' 'Tallica stuff, maybe not a full album though.

Jaymz, is it true that you once asked Les Claypool to join Metallica?
Chris B., Oaklyn, NJ

JH: He tried out after Cliff's death, but he didn't fit in. He was too good.

When you were on SNL, did you try asking if you could appear in a sketch?
Brian Y., Alexandria, VA

JN: Yes, we tried to get involved in a Goat Boy of Metal skit, but I think the powers that be got scared. Maybe some other time.

James, my brother heard on MTV that when you play live someone backstage plays your guitar part and you just fake to play and sing. Is this true?
Jason L., Greeley, CO

JH: Well, you got me. It's some guy named Ted... somethin'... oh yeah, Ted Nugent.
KH: Yes, it is true with all of us. Actually, Pantera play backstage.
LU: It's me doing James' vox and guitars. We have a look-a-like drumming.
JN: Jason, that is not quite true. On television, however, pieces of music and background vocals are often pre-recorded.

Lars, is there a special reason you drink Evian water, or is it just good?
Dan R., Southgate, MI

LU: It's the most neutral tasting bottled water. It's always good to set off alcohol dehydration by chugging lots of water.

Jaymz, when you wrote the song 'Fixxxer' what were your feelings
Hannu J., Finland

JH: Comparing ourselves (humans) to voodoo dolls not in control of our own fate. When all seems perfect, something or someone pushes a pin to make you struggle again.

Why is 'Escape' Metallica's least favorite song, and who wrote it?
Markus H., Sweden

LU: It's the only time we've written a song for a specific purpose. Kirk's riff with Lars' push and James salvaged it.

I was wondering if any of the guys have ever had a paranormal or supernatural experience, and if so, what kind?
Alexis C., Spiro, OK

KH: I had a vision you would be asking me this.
JH: I have deja vu every once in a while. I have deja vu every once in a while.

James, what is 'Ain't My Bitch' about?
Matt H., Gilbert, AZ

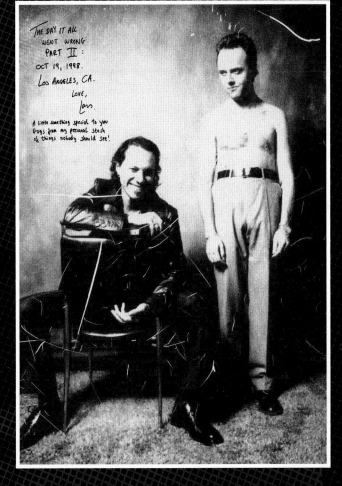

THE DAY IT ALL
WENT WRONG
PART II:
OCT 19, 1998.
LOS ANGELES, CA.
LOVE,
lars.
A little something special to you Guys from my personal stash of things nobody should see!

JH: Complainers and how they'd rather complain than enjoy what they have.

I have been fortunate enough to get backstage passes at two different shows. Each time Jaymz and Jason were the only two guys of the band that came out for the meet-n-greet. I have spoken with other fan club members who have said the same thing. Kirk and Lars, what's up?
Tommy W., Charleston, SC

LU: We have our own fan club. While Jason and James take care of Metclub, we take care of our own club – it's very exclusive.
KH: Unfortunately, the fan club members come at a time when I am right in the middle of my pre-show warm-up.

Kirk and James, do you guys think it is important to do good in school? Did you guys do good in school? I personally just say fuck it.
Ben D., Taylor, MI

KH: School is a stepping stone to other things. You should study what you truly would like to learn.
JH: Well, that's where I met my first band mates (Obsession). ●

Midriff-glockenspiel-fucking-pot-bullet-fart

There's a couch.
There's a band (Metallica).
There's a cheap psychiatrist
in the house (Steffan Chirazi)
and there's odd words flying
around. It can only be...
the not-so-annual, but
very special, round-table.

I**T WAS JUST ABOUT FOUR YEARS AGO**
that Hetfield, Hammett, Ulrich and Newsted all
gathered around a dining room table at The Plant
Studios for an interview idea that threatened
to be fun. Termed a 'round-table,' the idea was
that I would throw out questions and they would
bounce answers off each other, perhaps engaging
in a little light conversation here and there, a
few polite jokes to be exchanged and general
jollity to be shared by all.

It ended up being something like that.

Things were said that hadn't ever been shared.
People admitted things they hadn't previously
admitted. Eyebrows were raised
by all towards all, and the
outcome was Metallica's most
revealing, and intriguing,
interview ever, an evening
which became known to the
band as 'therapy.' I'm still
not sure that they enjoyed
the process more than just
sort of accepted it
as 'being.'

GLOCK-FUCKING-ULET... FART...

Color photos taken on location in San Francisco, October 1999.

But you liked it. We know that because even the back issues sold out and much correspondence was received on both the session itself and when the next one might be.

Needless to say, I have pushed for more therapy on an annual basis, the response always being that it was something which shouldn't be overdone, a format which owed as much to good timing as simple execution. I didn't always agree but, frankly, that wasn't important as it wasn't me who was under the microscope or making the decisions.

Which is why I am proud to say that as we end the year and go into the next phase of Metallica's career, a round-table was not only agreed to but executed within the space of 12 days. It happened during rehearsals for the symphony shows and took place in San Rafael on the evening of November 11th at 8:30 p.m.

There was a tremendous amount going on: "S&M" shows were imminent, various families were in town for a last visit before promotional duties in Europe 48 hours later, and a full technical load-out was happening next door.

When everyone filtered in shortly after 8:30 p.m. to sit down, I sensed some trepidation. Not that I should've been too surprised... after all, there's no telling what these situations bring out.

Over the past three years, could you pick out a favorite moment from the whole "Load" era?

JH: The last round-table, hahaha.

JN: Two days ago in rehearsal I figured out the new chorus to 'Battery...'

JH: ... Er... instead of Bud-weis-Er, it's Batt-ER-y...

JN: That was a good time, everybody was lovely, Lars was doing OTT background vocals and we were jamming!

KH: A personal highlight for me was when Lars and I stayed up the whole night on the 1996 tour with nothing better to do than cinch up the "Garage Inc" album that wasn't going to come out for another two years.

And that was just simple honest fun I'm sure, a few too many coffees!

KH: Well there was more to it...

JH: They stayed up late because of the coffee!

KH: ...I ended up with about two hours sleep and I had to do an interview for German TV, I was doing the interview and it's a good thing I had sunglasses on because I was falling asleep between questions, hahaha... (general hub-bub and laughter)

KH: ...but that was just a personal highlight. I mean, there have been many professional ones.

LU: For me, Woodstock was...

JN: What, this last one?

LU: Yeah, probably one of the highlights for me...

KH: I think selling out Giants Stadium was another highlight.

JH: Glad you added 'Giants Stadium'... otherwise 'selling out...' heh heh heh. For me, touring with

bands like COC was great and personally going out on the road and having fun again was cool.

Do you all feel as comfortable with your respective roles in the band as you did 10 years ago?

JH: Well, yeah, I got one and a half now... (cue belly jokes and much staring at midriffs).

KH: I'm actually happier with things in the band now than I've ever been. I dunno why I just feel more comfortable.

JH: I wanna play glockenspiel now.

KH: Cool 'cos I wanna play trombone.

JN: Awesome you guys.

Are you happy with everyone's input? (directed towards a very reserved Lars)

LU: Uh... yeah. I think the fact we're still sitting here is amazing.

JN: So do I.

JH: The fact that we can be forced to be in a room together to be interviewed and still do it is great!

LU: (moving on swiftly)... I was watching Rage Against The Machine the other day, they were doing the RATM interview hour on MTV and three members of the band were in one part of the studio together and the lead singer was talking by himself in another part of the studio. They weren't actually sitting around a table together like we are now. And when you see stuff like that it makes you realize how lucky you are to be able to co-exist like that and the fact you can even just sit in the same room as each other is great.

Is that a surprise?

LU: No it doesn't surprise me regarding this, but what does surprise me is seeing how fragile everybody else's relationships in our peer

groups are, how much you hear about the shit in other so-called peers of ours through the grapevine about the problems they have. So because of that I feel things are very good.

Do you all agree with that?

KH: (who has put on an absurd pair of sunglasses at this point) Steffan, I actually look forward to hanging out with these guys.

Careful now, you're wearing the truth glasses so the truth WILL come out.

KH: Let me rephrase that, I still look forward to hanging out with everyone.

Was there a time that wasn't the case?

KH: Maybe when things were getting a little hectic on the "Black" album tour, show number 183 and I just wanted to go home.

If you would each explain what you think each other's role is in this band, each other's strength (at this point, Lars has the glasses, general low-level hub-bub is breaking out). Is it a nerve-wracking thing to do this?

LU: Strengths? No, I mean I don't think you'll find many surprises in the answers to that though. I look at Jason I see stability, I see probably the most musically grounded and focused of all of us, in Kirk I see – y'know, those clichés that everyone always mentions – (interrupted by laughter and various quips jumbling together). No, I mean Jason says Quirk Hammett and Kirk brings the element of quirkiness and fun, the light-hearted approach with no negative connotations; it's about being happy playing music, in James I see weight, focus and creative spark... What I'm trying to say is there are no new revelations, there's no new side of James or new side of Kirk, it's pretty much how it's been for the past couple of years.

JH: No-one's got any better, that's what he's saying hehehe.

KH: We've all stagnated together!

JN: But our tolerance levels have all gotten much much better. It's true for myself for sure. We're all just as good as we are and we've learned to accept that, whatever a person can or cannot do there's a magic that happens when we come together and a bunch of people dig it. Somehow we put up with it, because anytime you mix shit up in bands, Lars was talking about a singer here and a band there, or a member changes whenever that happens the magic changes, it's gonna have to. So our tolerance levels went up because we finally realized, both as individuals and collectively what this all means. Taking the good with bad and the bad with the good.

LU: The key word is tolerance. I think we're all fully aware of each other's strengths and weaknesses, including our own, and we don't need to hide, we don't need to push the strengths and hide the weaknesses.

JN: Everyone's really good at flexing the right muscles when it comes to stamping the name 'Metallica' on something, especially with the live shit. We can fuck around all day long but when it comes down to it everybody always steps up because they know what we are representing. That's why we have the tolerance.

JH: It was pretty apparent with the symphony stuff the strength of us. We've never really let a lot of other musicians be in the Metallica world, either in the studio or live. Even when we did 'Nothing Else Matters' with Kamen scoring it, it was 'shit what do we do? We don't want all those musicians in here!' and not only was it a time constraint, it was the intimidation factor. So we sent the fucking thing off and left the 'schooled musicians' to put the shit on. It came back and 'cool everything's done and there.' Slowly we got a little more confidant with ourselves on the "Load"/"Re-Load" stuff. One of the engineers played fiddle on 'Lowman's Lyric,' we had dude Dave the hurdy-gurdy man come in. Then when we went for the symphony thing, it was pretty much as extreme as you could with these schooled musicians, and we were a rock band up there...

JN: Totally exposed –

JH: Right, and our strength was... us, y'know? Take us individually and we're not brilliant, we're not brilliant virtuosos at anything, vocals, singing, drumming, bassing whatever, but when you put us together it's a force to be reckoned with, no doubt.

JN: Put in a situation like that where we are somewhat vulnerable we really look to each other. **Maybe we don't speak it, but we take pride in each other when we're up against that kind of a challenge, we stick together as a brotherhood up against this 'thing.'** We've been against a lot of challenges in tons of different ways and come through it, but this time it was all actions and reactions from 90 other people up there and we've never been put in that spot before.

JH: The Bridge School stuff started all that as well, looking inward going 'fuck...'

LU: I think that was a key moment because there was a lot of reluctance to do that and I think we

kind of agreed to do that without really thinking about what it was we were doing until a couple of weeks before. There was a lot of reluctance in doing it, and when we walked on that stage and then walked off it 30 minutes later it was like 'fuck somehow we managed to step up to the plate and pull something off – '

JN: Right –

LU: That probably none of us really thought we could do.

JN: It started out as a good-hearted collective motion to help that thing out and also to be a part of the Bay Area thing.

LU: I think it was a very key moment like James was saying because I think we felt very vulnerable before that and felt quite intimidated by the company we were in and I think that somehow when we came off stage we had proven to ourselves that we could pull that shit off.

So there was a point there that despite having sold 15 million copies –

LU: 65 million. *(Much laughter again)*

Indeed, 65 total but 15 million of the one, and let it be noted I am referring to the "Black" album –

JH: *(dryly)* Our peak!

Yeah right, what I'm trying to establish is that even after that album sold what it did there was a feeling within you all that you weren't respected outside a certain genre and that you wanted to grow, push out and do that.

LU: I think one thing you're saying that's relevant to me anyway, is that as "Load" came out we were a band that could do wrong. Before then we were the band that could do no wrong. When "Load" came out we were suddenly doing things that people were questioning and that brought us closer together, a tighter unit who were weathering the shitstorm, and we looked for strength in each other.

KH: I know I draw strength from our very strong foundation. Every time we are challenged by a situation, or whenever we need to step up to the plate, I look to the band for strength most times.

JH: Y'need something lifted over at your house?

KH: Yeah, you guys wanna come over and help me lift some stuff up the stairs? *(laughter)*

Is there any accuracy in thinking that maybe you wanted to invite some negativity to feel the fight, push and chal-

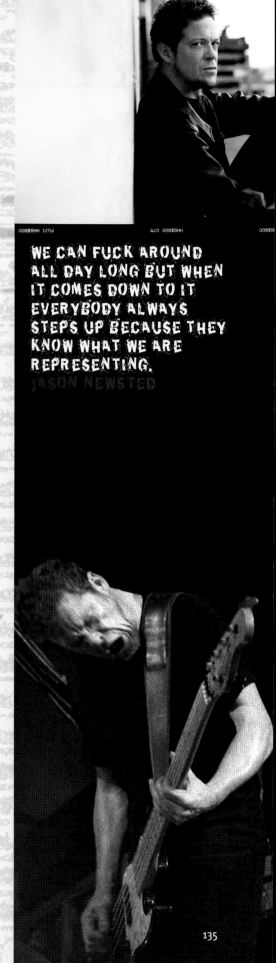

WE CAN FUCK AROUND ALL DAY LONG BUT WHEN IT COMES DOWN TO IT EVERYBODY ALWAYS STEPS UP BECAUSE THEY KNOW WHAT WE ARE REPRESENTING.

JASON NEWSTED

135

lenge? For example, when you first came in James and – let's go back to the infamous haircuts that kill era – and saw some of the changes that had happened visually, did you think 'fuck this is too much but I need to tolerate it for the good of our long-term future?'

JH: Definitely not. I mean I don't think about that shit. Hindsight's 20/20 and it'd be nice to think it was that thought out but it wasn't; it just happened. I mean there's a fun in being hated, it puts a fire in your ass and it gets fucking boring to be loved by everyone and it's good to get some negative shit coming back. In all the albums and tour programs we've done we've highlighted all the negativity, quotes from people saying all this shit, it's fun. At the end of the day it gets to you a little bit somehow and it ricochets off ya. But stuff like that we're out to prove wrong in the long run. The shit that someone says in print, someone like a Nikki Sixx who's eating crow for breakfast, lunch and dinner now, that makes you feel kinda good sometimes.

Was there ever a time during that reinvention and rejuvenation or whatever that any of you felt things were going a little too far?

JN: I was very uncomfortable with all that shit for a long time.

KH: For me, Steffan, you can never push anything too far. I'm looking for more mileage to push.

JN: Like you kinda said, it wasn't how I pictured Metallica. I tried to look at it really from another place, a fan's, and I felt that 'what the hell's going on here?' I felt that maybe my man over there (Lars) was kinda caught up in that New York thing and I think it affected some of the decisions that were made about things like photographs and stuff like that. I felt very strongly about that.

How do you deal with that as a band? Do you discuss it or just carry on doing your own thing trusting it will all come out in the wash?

JN: I didn't want to fight it, I wasn't fighting it for fighting's sake at all, it was just something that didn't seem to be the right representation of us. I agreed to go along with it because of the band thing, these guys really felt strongly about that and the photos and all that.

LU: I don't think it boils down to photographs per se…

JN: No, that's just an example and I think that has to be a certain part of the roots of it.

LU: … but I think the whole thing, y'know, Metallica'd been away for five years, a lot had changed in our personal lives, we'd all gone through a lot of things individually and I just think there was a fear of repetition, at least from my perspective –

KH: Definitely from my point too.

LU: A fear of stalemate and repetition. You can always sit and look back on that shit, and no matter how you might feel about it three years later, at that moment it felt like the right thing and that's key. You could sit and look at 10 other things we've done in our career and you've just gotta sit back and find the peace in your mind to know that no matter how stupid it might seem now, then it was the right thing to do. Listen to the "…Justice" record 10 years later, for me it's unlistenable, but at that time it seemed right, d'ya know what I mean? Personally I try to find peace that way: when I make creative decisions, am I being truthful to myself, am I being truthful to what my creative heart and soul tell me, and if you are then it's almost like you can't go wrong no matter what.

JH: Very true, but the thing is you're dealing with more than one person. You have to deal with four people who have to feel the same way, which is difficult sometimes. It was easier in the earlier days when you were all living in a room in an attic at Sweet Silence Sound in Denmark somewhere, you're living there, you think the same, you grow as far as the places you go together. Obviously you then become more and more individuals when you aren't roommates anymore. It comes down to how you think in life: do you look back and think 'fuck that was stupid but there's something kinda cool about that?' or 'God I wish I'd never done that!' There's never been a point where – at least for myself I dunno about the other guys – where I've thought 'fuck I wish I'd never done that!' You think about the moment it happened and the fun shit that went on with it.

The thing with all that ("Load" era stuff) was trying to have fun together trying something new. I remember seeing a picture of Venom in some fancy three-piece suits holding wine and thinking 'what the fuck are they doing?!' From spikes and a beach in Newcastle to fucking sipping wine in some mansion, it was like 'whoooo.' Nobody gave a shit about that. It comes down to also poking fun at the top guy.

JN: I'm all for no repetition, but there can be a level where you take it too far. There can also be a spot in between it somewhere that's still… y'know?

JH: Some people worry too much about consequence: we don't.

LU: It's been talked about to death. I think we're very comfortable that there are guys in this band who have different points as to how far they'll push it. At that point we might have been taking it one step too far, the spirit of the band now is one more of balance but at that time it was right.

JH: The element of danger was cool. This is dangerous…but hell, how dangerous is it dressing up in a fuzzy jacket? Heh heh, I dunno…

JN: I still look back at that (speaking over laughter from James) and I think 'I'm not happy that I did that.'

LU: I'm happy…

KH: During that entire period I was just being myself. I was already there, there was no stretch… (general conversational overflow and laughter)

JH: There are certain parts in the life of Metallica where certain members, uh, come to the surface more than others.

LU: Right, the pushing and pulling, the back and forth. How much pushing back then that he might have done was taken on board? Let's take it back to fuzzy jackets (James laughs again at mention of this)…

JN: I wasn't wearing no fuzzy jacket, I was just standing in the picture when he was wearing a fuzzy jacket.

JH: Heh heh, there's only one fuzzy jacket and y'know who wore it!

KH: Wait a minute, I wore a fuzzy jacket…

JH: The WHITE fluffy jacket, the white leather jacket, the white fuzzy fluffy leather jacket…

KH: It definitely was a situation where the three of us were pulling Jason along –

JH: Well I definitely cut myself out of a few pictures as well!

KH: Well OK, two and a half of us.

In terms of performance first and spirit second, are you able to spot low points in each other these days and how do you deal with it? (For some reason James laughs loudly again before exclaiming 'wow!') Let's say, James, you look at Kirk and know this guy's not had a good day… maybe he's kicked a flight case…

JH: I've never seen Kirk kick a flight case or be mad… except that time we broke into his house.

KH: Yeah, right at the time I was having a major 5.0 earthquake argument with my ex-girlfriend.

JH: I dunno why he got mad, I mean we broke into his house and started jamming in his studio!

KH: I was on the third floor arguing and all of a sudden I heard this faint music emanating from my basement and I was like 'WHAT THE FUCK IS THAT?'

JH: There's this little square window in the door, and we couldn't hear anything Kirk was saying 'cause we were jamming and he's goin' *(whispers and motions)* no, no!

KH: I kicked 'em all out, ha ha! But anyway, getting back to your original question, I think we all know each other well enough to where we can read each other and know when to back off. We've lived with each other so long that we just know when someone's had a bad day or just has a bad hangover, and uh, we do what we do to make it through the night. Sometimes you feel like putting in the effort to lift a mood, others you know when to back off.

But I imagine that now maybe you'd inquire as to what's up whereas before not a word would've been said?

LU: I think it's down to us knowing that back-off point. We can tell when it's serious and when it's a bad hangover. When Jason's got his brows on or whatever. The key is we all have major mood swings, we're all moody and sometimes need to be left alone. There's sometimes a couple of days when you don't wanna talk to anybody. For me the most difficult thing is when you're going through a bad period and you just wanna be left alone, yet there's always somebody to talk to. But we know each other and when we need to back the fuck away.

JN: The second key is to try not to take it to the stage with you... which I'm not good at. You have to try your best not to take your shitty attitude up there otherwise sometimes shit won't connect.

KH: When Lars talks about mood swings, you have to understand when one of us is feeling really shitty we're almost in a situation where it's bi-polar, we have incredible highs and lows. So when the pendulum swings it swings wide.

LU: The worst thing is when you have one guy who's out and the other three guys are flying high.

JH: Then it's a fucking slaughter, heh heh heh.

KH: Like WWF, one guy on bottom and three guys on top.

JH: There's some beauty in fucking feeling good when someone else is down for some reason, it's fucked up but there's something about that human nature that feels good... *(At this point,*

Jason makes his first motion to leave.)

Is he off?

KH: He has a date or something?

JH: He's got more important things than the Fan Club magazine...shouldn't that be a quote?

Alright. Then each of the three of you, where does Metallica need to go?

KH: I think we just need to bring the Metallica thing into the new millennium. I know it's a cliché but I take it personally on a musical level. I think that since it's a new millennium there are new avenues for us to explore and the timing is appropriate for us right now to go out there and see what's out there for us to grab on a musical level.

JH: Musically y'just see what happens, what comes out of your fucking head when you start writing. You try not to foresee or say what you're going to do next because you disappoint yourself and others. Trying new things? We're definitely all up for that but we know what we do best and y'don't HAVE to stay cutting edge just to stay afloat, that's just fucking stupid. You wanna write good songs man, no matter what advances in technology there have been, no matter...

KH: That's what it comes down to, writing good music together.

LU: I agree. It all starts with the songs. What I'm looking forward to is the fact we haven't done anything for five years, I feel that the last couple of years have been kind of being in a twilight zone where it's been very repetitive, playing a bunch of songs over and over and over again. I'm just really looking forward to writing something, it's been five years since we've sat down, written a bunch of songs and done a creative project from scratch, so I'm really excited about that. I think that with everything all four of us have learned and the different inspirations that all four of us have had over the past four years, it's been pretty exciting.

When you hear from Lars and James, and I'll put this to you Jason (who has returned for a few more minutes) and hear 'we want you to bring a tape of 10 songs' when you sit down and put that material together do you try to work out what they will like or are you doing what you wanna do? Do you feel more confident than ever that what you offer will be liked, I mean, how do you approach the situation?

JH: *(background)* That's a good question...

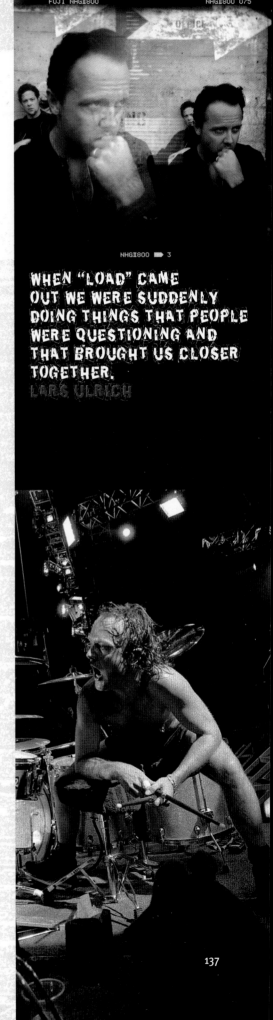

WHEN "LOAD" CAME OUT WE WERE SUDDENLY DOING THINGS THAT PEOPLE WERE QUESTIONING AND THAT BROUGHT US CLOSER TOGETHER.
LARS ULRICH

JN: It's always very intimidating, absolutely, without even trying very hard to think about it I do think about it. About what they would dig or what they would say is interesting; I want them to go 'that's pretty fucking cool.' So that's definitely been an element, but some years have gone by and I've had a chance to play with some other songwriters with good ideas, so...

JH: I think that hearing you say that now, some of the stuff that we have liked is probably the stuff you didn't think we'd dig, you know what I mean. Some of the, not so much 'out there' stuff, but the less typical stuff.

LU: I think that the musical adventures all four of us have gone through outside the band have brought a whole other level of confidence and calmness...

(At this point Jason is running late, apologetically insists he has to go when I insist he give us five more minutes here as we're into something directly related to him: he sits down for a bit longer.)

LU: I just think that about five years ago when it bottomed out that you 'can't go and jam with other people' and it hit that low point, I think everybody's just more comfortable and confident about themselves and their abilities and that's what I sense, that everybody's more musically fulfilled.

Bottom line is, if he (Jason) or Kirk brings a tape in are you going to open a bit more from the parameters of expectation you've had in the past...

LU: If anybody anywhere, and I am speaking only for myself, thinks that I try and say, 'well that's Jason's or Kirk's'... look, the last time me and James spent a week up in my office listening to everybody's tapes, I can guarantee you it was with completely neutral ears and I feel completely pure about that. So if there's an imbalance in the songwriting credits it's got nothing to do with any kind of judgements other than what we think the music should be at this time. And I hope these two guys don't think any different. I know guys in the press like to try and highlight that, but it would really surprise me hand-on-heart if these two guys felt that.

KH: For me, I pretty much try and write music whenever I play guitar. I know what plateau I'd have to reach before I put something on tape, even though it might not sound like it to you...

LU: Yeah but it isn't up to me.

KH: I know I know, just hear me out. I know what level of quality these guys are looking for and I try to shoot for that every single time I write something.

LU: For me, **the way we work creatively it's not about bringing a song in, it's about having a musical spark, something that ignites...**

JH: Yeah.

LU: ... it's also about having a musical spark, it's not just about bringing a song in, it's about something that ignites. Jason might have something on a tape that starts something, that gets taken to another level and we all just embellish it.

JH: That can even be just a 'feel,' a 'feel' that someone's trying to capture that's not quite there and then someone else...

LU: Turns it into something.

JH: Right. Or it can be two notes together that spark something. It networks through three other people to become something even better.

LU: It's not kindergarten anymore, and whenever we get around to this next year I know that it'll be really pure.

Do you feel your preconceptions fading away?

JN: Oh yeah, it'll be different the next time. It's been a lot of years between the last time we sat down.

JH: 'Submit your tape to...'

Where does Metallica need to go for you personally this next time?

KH: Alaska!

JN: It needs to be listenable, musical, thick, heavy it has to just... we need to take some chances, really make it sound like it was fucking fun when people listen back, make it live... sorry man, gotta go, thanks. (Jason exits on his date: I think it went well.)

JH: Going way back to the very first question tonight, I'd have to say it was fun in Alaska when we all went out, that was fun.

What happened?

KH: Some big fat guy gave me a whole bag of fucking pot!

OK, an inevitable question: have any of you felt that you've been pushed to an absolute breaking point in the band where it's felt like 'fuck this!'

KH: I think I have a higher tolerance than anyone else. I can take a lot of shit before I need to turn around and walk out which I've never had to do in the entire time I've been in the band. Now whether that's just down to my personality or the way things are I don't know, but I've never ever felt that.

JH: I think that's definitely part of your personality, heh heh. I think maybe – no disrespect – but the amount of pressure on a person as well, it all varies between the four of us. Yeah, there are times, especially on the last tour, there were times when it got really hairy, especially between Lars and I. Y'know, it's your way of telling each other 'let's step up to the plate and fix things.' And each one of us deals with things differently. Some of us work up to a certain point and some of us just fucking DUUNK! it's there, in-face. We all operate differently and we all take that into consideration when we're dealing with each other.

LU: The main thing for me that's changed the past couple of years is the sameness of touring gets harder to live with definitely. Trying to find balancing points for what our various needs are, and for me the sameness of touring is starting to get to me more.

KH: The monotony?

LU: Hmmm... the sameness of it, the machine that we're locked into when you tour gets to me more and more. I'm definitely the extreme and I'm comfortable with that, I think everybody knows that...

In terms of?

LU: I wish we could fuck it up more, I wish we could fuck it up more often and be more spontaneous. I'm the extreme of that.

JH: As in the touring, the staying in hotels, the set?

LU: Mostly the musical thing. The hardest thing for me is the sameness of the musical vibe. Music to me is about chances and interaction, with each other and the crowd. I think when we get into stuff like (the sheds last summer???) the human side of music gets lost and it becomes very machine like?

How could you fuck with that?

LU: The way I try to fuck with it is to fuck with setlists and fuck with songs and stuff like that and I have a tendency to do that nine minutes before we go onstage. Of course other people's needs are that they need three days to know about that so as they can practice it whereas I'm the opposite, 'let's go out and play a different song tonight.' I understand, though, that everyone has different needs but when I look at the clashes we've had over the last year or two, they've mostly been to do with that. And they get taken out in different ways.

JH: For some of us there is certainly a need to be well rehearsed. And that's how we get our strength. And if Lars is looking for some kind of new spark or strength – he's probably the guy who plays the least of us off the road and as far as getting rehearsal stuff together, I don't think he feels the need to be as rehearsed as we do, and I think I'd rather NOT show that side that we could fuck something up. It doesn't make me feel good when we fuck something up, and he looks at it more as 'wow that's the human side of things.'

LU: Or the spontaneous thing. To me, and it's very clear we differ on that and that's totally cool, but what makes rock'n'roll totally exciting are those moments of danger and spontaneity where it can go in all sorts of directions, and you can grab it and make something cool out of it. Confrontations come as much from frustrations as anything else, y'know, Jason gets pissed off because I botch something up continuously because I'm looking at the lighting rig, and I get pissed off because I think these guys are boring old farts and don't wanna take a chance...

JH: Yeeeaaah, because they don't wanna fuck up with him! I mean, spontainuiety...

LU: (chuckling) Spontain-U-ity?

JH: ...I'm all for that shit, I love it. When you're up there and rehearsed then you can fucking jam. That's when I feel best. I can sit here 10 times over and never play it again, that's a different kind of 'spontain-U-it-tay'! I think he's talking about a different kind, where you jam on a song and if you fuck it up, oh well ha ha who cares except for, maybe, the crowd.

Do you, Kirk, ever come in and mediate this?

JH: The first person who gets between us is Kirk, heh heh.

KH: I feel like the human partition...

JH: The bullet shield!

KH: I'm like 'hey I'm here guys, let's just get on and play the fucking song!'

LU: He is, of course, completely invisible.

JH: Heh heh.

KH: They don't even see me even though I'm between them because it's the heavy stare down.

Obviously you get past these problems, you have to because you're still here, but does the respect you have for each other (James and Lars) come from history or is it rooted in the 'now'?

LU: The scariest thing is that if people could hear how quickly me and him apologize to each other after we've been in each other's faces then they'd puke. I'm in there five minutes later saying I'm sorry, and vice-versa. I look at it all as frustrations which come out of the pressure we allow ourselves to get into through these schedules

and so on. The major difference between now and 10 years ago is that we would sit on the hatred a lot longer, y'know, looking back on the "Black" album and some of the arguments and differences of opinions when we wouldn't speak to each other for weeks. Looking at this summer, we reconciled very quickly, and that comes out of a respect for the relationship, respect for the destiny of the relationship and also stupid things like we're all in our mid to late 30's and it's easier to be adult about these things. It's easier to see, at least for myself, when I'm out of line.

So you now see a right and wrong?

LU: I try and move out of who I am and see what an asshole I was from somebody else's' perspective, and it's easier to see that whereas 10 years ago I wouldn't have seen that.

JH: I gotta say that you're a fool to think that none of that's gonna happen or ever gonna happen again, I mean it's gotta happen, it's part of being a human. Some other bands though just don't know when to stop or they just got bad, bad attitudes and the wrong ideas about it all, and the fact that we all know we need each other is the thing.

Is that an instinct or has history told you that?

JH: For me I can't meet someone and tell exactly what they're all about, it takes me a while, and I'd say 20 years is enough to figure these guys out. So definitely history... we got history between us man.

KH: It's easy to figure out. You've come this far and accomplished this much together and it's really stupid to throw it all away over a stupid squabble.

LU: And there's a certain amount of pride in sitting here and saying we're the last men standing in a way, and in some way we probably all feel that a little bit. So it's really cool to be able to give a big 'fuck you' to everybody who's fallen by the wayside that we're the last men standing.

KH: That aspect of our gang-mentality that we had when it was all about that and really really strong, has still survived. That one aspect of it, the last ones standing, the battle of the bands thing that was there for years.

LU: And there's definitely an argument for saying that, y'know, a lot of other people who evaluate us from outside and in comparison to other units, that there's got to be tension. If there's no tension it loses its nerves and energy, there's got to be a push and pull, a creative tension and in some way even though it gets to us sometimes we all know it's a valuable thing to have.

I THINK WE ALL KNOW EACH OTHER WELL ENOUGH TO WHERE WE CAN READ EACH OTHER AND KNOW WHEN TO BACK OFF.
KIRK HAMMETT

139

That suggests that you might occasionally take it upon yourself to toss a scenario in there if it's been a bit mellow.

LU: No.

KH: That's a particularly evil thought: 'things are going rather too well I'd best toss in a nasty vibe to get things going...'

JH: 'YOOOOOOOOOO SUUUUUUCK!' Heh heh...

Perhaps I am overthinking a bit there. OK, Kirk, a question for you. What has fatherhood done for James and Lars in terms of character changes?

KH: I definitely have seen these guys showing more patience, compassion and consideration. When things get particularly hairy, I've observed that they're not as quick to fly off the handle as in the past. They're quite a bit more patient. I cannot say whether parenthood's done that, but I've noticed a bit more consideration for where that person might be coming from and little more empathy as to what that person might be feeling. I think over time that'll even grow as they...

JH: ... become more and more fathers, heh heh.

Fair comment? Do you notice that change in yourselves, particularly in your band dealings?

JH: I dunno. You've got these two lives and you wanna make 'em work together. You're on the phone with Q Prime while you're trying to e-mail something and your kid's smashing the computer. Five years ago it would've been 'get the motherfuck–' you'd have lost it, whereas now it's 'here dear... play with this knife instead... 'I'm joking, it's a fork! But yeah, it's definitely a test of your patience no doubt about it, especially as they get older. When you're a kid you get counted to all the time, 'come here on a count of three' and I'm counting myself all the time 'OK, to ten' and then I'm cool. You do learn to take that step back on a lotta stuff.

LU: I wouldn't say I disagree with Kirk, but with all due respects I'd say it's a little bit of cliché. It hasn't changed the business side of what I do to get shit done that much at all. The main thing it's done for me in my life is make evaluate how I spend my time, and I think that I let things go, I don't need to see that movie, I don't need to... *(Lars' cellphone is ringing)*

JH: ... take that phone call.

LU: ... take that phone call...

JH: HEH HEH, it could be your kid man!

LU: ... or those types of things. *(He consequently breaks to take the call).*

JH: But it's true, you do sit there thinking 'I'm sitting here dealing with this bullshit and I could be at home sitting with my little girl, there's some bonding that could be happening. I never used to think so much about this 'time is money' bullshit, but time is worth something. And it's worth something to that little person, which matters big time.

If you could get rid of one fault from each other, looking around, what would it be?

JH: That's something man...

KH: When he's (James) pissed off he gets REALLY loud! And it's kind of nerve-wracking. He's pissed off and he's screaming, and you think 'fuck man, he's screaming really loud, can't he just talk regular?'

JH: *(grinning, albeit surprised)* Wow, maybe it's true. I'M NOT FUCKING YELLING!

(Laughter from everyone.)

KH: I think he does have one of the loudest voices of any person I know...

So it would be, for James, the scream.

KH: Yeah, the Hetfield bellow...

JH: It's got us this far! *(More laughter)*

KH: OK OK, I admit that wouldn't be too conducive to our day job so maybe I should take that back! But y'know, one thing I can say about all of us is that I wish all of us weren't as moody as we were. I think it's the nature of our situation being in a band, the long hours, what people expect of you and that kind of stuff.

JH: I don't really wanna get rid of anything because that's who the person is.

I know, but imagine there really is this one thing you could change.

JH: Uhh, I mean, a lot of it is directed towards Lars, really. I mean, the other two guys I can deal with pretty much. But Lars and his control freakiness, it kind gets to me. When you're on an airplane he's sitting up there with the pilot – arrgghh, just relax! – he's such a control freak. I mean you've dealt with something and he's always got to have the last checkmark or signature or change a little something just to say he's done it... he doesn't have to change just for the sake of 'I've controlled something.' But there is this control aspect about it. And I wish he'd give a shit more about rehearsal.

KH: I'll agree with that... I wish Jason didn't parade all these women in front of us married men. That really fucking gets my goat! *(Much laughter)* It's like he's totally rubbing our noses in it. *(Lars comes back into the room from his call.)*

LU: Hello.

(Repeating for Lars...) The question is, if there was one thing you wish you could get rid of in any of the others, what would it be?

KH: I wish Lars wouldn't always call me up and say 'c'mon let's go out' and I say 'not tonight' and he says 'you never go out' when in truth I've gone out with him for the last four nights in a row!

LU: OK, let me do my three. I think the main fault with Kirk I have at the moment is I don't understand why he was fucking smiling through the whole fucking "S&M" video! When I saw it the other day I saw you've got this fucking shit-eating grin on your face all the time...

KH: I'm just so fucking happy to do that, weren't you?

JH: C'mon man, he was wearing a suit!

LU: Jason... I think the major thing I would like to eradicate in him is a better sense of, y'know, in rehearsal situations and music and stuff that we all know we can step up to the plate when we have to and pull our end of it down, but we also have what seems to be a need to fuck around and be silly and goofy once in a while. And sometimes he doesn't necessarily see those moments in the same way that I do. With James... the thing I probably despise... *(Much laughter)*

JH: Oh, it's become 'despise' now eh? Not softly eradicate...

LU: OK... I'd like to softly eradicate the fact that James Hetfield is probably the worst person I know... *(Even bigger laughter)*

JH: OH WOW! Period. Tape runs out...

KH: End quote!

LU: *(continuing outwardly unruffled)*... at returning phoning calls. That's what I would say, returning phone calls. And I know that sometimes he does it on purpose just to annoy me.

JH: Now I will!

LU: I'll call up and say 'dude, there's something going on and we need to make a decision on this' and I don't hear back from him for four days. And when I finally call him again four days later there's no acknowledgement of the fact I called four days ago.

JH: That's because I've forgotten.

LU: And I know he's sitting laughing at my message while I'm saying 'dude, we've gotta make this decision, we've gotta do it now...'

JH: There are definitely times when it's like

you're in total business mode and it's like 'fuck, you're gettin' the shit done de de de de' and the other guy isn't? That's tough.

LU: For me it's tough. That gets under my skin more so...

JH: Most of the time I really am not there to hear it.

And is there a fault in yourselves you'd change?

LU: Myself? I would say the thing about myself that probably irks the guys the most is that I don't tend to work that well with time tables. It's not like it's on purpose, I'm not sitting around watching TV. It's like today 'OK, I gotta be there (at rehearsal) by 4, I was walking out the door at 3:40 and my son woke up screaming from his nap, so I took 10 minutes out, then I couldn't find my cellphone and... my fault is that I feel it's never my fault. And, of course, at the end of the day it is my fault because I should start looking for my cellphone 30 minutes before instead of 20 minutes before. So I always find a way to convince myself it's not my fault. If the reason I was late is that I couldn't find my cellphone, then I should start looking for it earlier.

JH: The dog ate my cellphone.

LU: That's probably the thing I wish I could eradicate the most for these guys.

JH: But for YOU. That was the question, what is it about yourself that you'd most like to eradicate?

LU: For me? Hmmm...*(long pause, some muttering)*...I think that hmm, probably, just letting go in terms of control. *(There is much nodding and musing from James and Kirk, who themselves had mentioned this very point when Lars was out of the room.)* I find I take the same mentality in the way I do business and apply it elsewhere: I'm really bad at cutting off the business side.

You're a last word kind of person?

LU: No. I'm doing business all day, and then all of a sudden my wife is there and I bring the business end into things. That is probably the worst thing. My dad's been here, so I've been on the phone for six hours and I suddenly find myself talking to my Dad the same way I've been talking on the phone. That annoys me.

KH: Sometimes I feel Lars is talking to me like he's doing an interview.

The session could easily go on for another couple of hours, but schedules and the time (after 10:30 p.m.) dictate that the meeting will shortly self-adjourn.

OK then, finally: what are the things you'll never say to each other?

KH: I love you man...

LU: I think we've had moments when we were there. Some of most heartfelt conversations me and him had ever had (James) was a couple of days after my Mom died when we spoke on the phone for a couple of hours each day. Sometimes I feel we're kind of guarded with each other, and apart from being drunk or something, that was the most unguarded, vulnerable and naked conversation we've had. So I think we've been through all the different things from all the different extremes, so I don't think there's anything we'd never say to each other. It's always easy to say when people are fucking up, but is it easy to dispense praise?

I MEAN THERE'S A FUN IN BEING HATED, IT PUTS A FIRE IN YOUR ASS AND IT GETS FUCKING BORING TO BE LOVED BY EVERYONE.
JAMES HETFIELD

And so it ended, prematurely in my opinion, as there seemed to be plenty more to say and no shortage of confidence in saying it. I must admit, when Jason said he had to leave for a date, I feared the worst. The extra five minutes he ended up staying proved to be the most important of the evening, providing the genuine breakthrough into some of the most open conversation I've heard between the band members anywhere; makes you wonder what might've happened had Jason been flying solo for the night.

As everyone left to pack for the trip to Europe, this round-table struck me as another timeless landmark documenting the band's history. It showed that at this time, Metallica have never been as comfortable with each other or themselves, and consequently nobody's hiding anything from anyone. Of course this leads to some genuinely edgy moments... when you decide to be comfortable with yourself it will lead to stronger opinions and greater debates.

But what makes Metallica unique, is that they can ride such issues and differences out knowing that there are so many positives between the four of them, not the least of which is their enjoyment of the music they play. In summary, the evening proved to me that the cliché, 'what doesn't kill you makes you stronger' perhaps applies to this band more than any other.

Until the next one then... ●

BAND COMMENTS

I READ THIS AND THINK "WHY CANT THAT JH GUY ANSWER A QUESTION SERIOUSLY?"

JH 3/04

I THINK WE WERE IN A BROOM CLOSET! THIS WUZ DONE IN THE BUILDING THAT NOW IS OUR HQ .... A HINT OF THINGS TO COME!

IN RETROSPECT I AM SURPRISED HOW INTIMATE WE WERE WITH EACH OTHER, BUT THE EARLY WARNING SIGNS SEEMED TO BE RIGHT BENEATH OUR SURFACE AS A HAPPY-GO-LUCKY ROCK BAND. UNFORTUNATELY, THIS WAS PROBABLY THE LAST TIME THE FOUR OF US WERE ACTUALLY COMFORTABLE IN EACH OTHERS PRESENCE BECAUSE SHORTLY THEREAFTER, THINGS WENT SOUTH!!

3/04

142

SUMMER SANITARIUM TOUR 2000

143

JAMES WHO?

The "Summer Sanitarium" tour was going to be easy. A month of stadiums, a few dozen thousand friends and some pals. But then it all went a bit pear-shaped. James Hetfield aggravated an old back injury one hour before showtime at the 50,000 sold Atlanta Metrodome, and nobody knew what was going to happen next. Support acts Kid Rock, System Of A Down, and Korn came together, Metallica's remaining trio ran through some tunes, and so it was that somewhere in Atlanta at around 1 a.m., a certain band member answered the question of how things were panning out with two clear, monosyllabic words: James Who?

44

"I was so busy making sure everyone else was playing everything right that I was fucking up! I've played 'Nothing Else Matters' a million times and I fucked it up... (but) you can't critique it because everyone's just doing it... That was pure anarchy! I can't wait until the album comes out! I thought it was so great the other bands could rise to the occasion and help us out when we were under-staffed." KIRK HAMMETT

"I've never been so nervous. It makes you realize what that man takes on his shoulders... 12 or something people tried to fill the man's shoes and no-one could quite manage it." JASON NEWSTED

"That was all right, huh?!" LARS ULRICH

NAPSTER

and beyond

THE CENTRAL POINT OF THE NAPSTER BATTLE

"What I'm fighting for is my choice. I was never asked if I wanted my music traded on the Internet. I was never asked if I wanted my music traded on Napster. Well, 'we're Napster, we have all these wonderful sites with emerging artists' and all this type of stuff. Fine, yes you do, because the artists gave you their permission to have their music. So, the bottom line is really that we know that they have the technology, to remove Metallica recordings that we don't want traded, we know that technology exists, they've copped to it...

"... For the record, let it be officially known that I have no issues with a company like Napster's right to exist, but if the only way that I can pre-vent my music from being 'swapped' on a Napster-like service is to shut them down, then I'm sorry. They came to us many, many times over the last few months and said, 'what can we do to settle this?' It's really simple, you can block our 96 songs from being 'swapped'... Everybody's happy.

"But let's not forget, Hank Barry and Napster are not doing it as some kind of charity, they're doing it because ultimately they believe that one day if Napster becomes the standard – almost an AOL-like company on that frontier – that they will have a company worth billions and billions of dollars."

THE BIGGER PICTURE BEHIND THE BATTLE
"... We've been fighting this as a direct legal action against the company Napster, but at the same time, the bigger picture is really trying to get people to understand what it's about, to understand the enormity of the issue and to understand what it really means... what's going on is basically that you had an issue which is 'should people be allowed to freely share anything they want on the Internet that is copyrighted?' The idea of 'do you want to live in that kind of society where the mob rules mentality becomes the main thing' and that 'because the technology exists then it's OK.' The Napster thing is increasingly more of a sidebar that is ultimately out of our hands, because it's being played out in the courts of California. So what has been taking up my time, and what I think is really much more valuable right now, is getting people to really understand what this is about and trying and get people away from the selfish ignorance of, you know, 'he's just taking my ability to download a song off the Internet.'"

PRO-RECORD COMPANY WARRIORS? ERR, NO...
"One issue that comes up a lot is that because of our stance on Napster that we are pro-record company. That is not true. I'm not particularly pro-record company, I'm not particularly anti-record company. I'm pro-Metallica, and at the end of day I'm doing this because I'm pro-Metallica. That's the only thing that I really care about. In 1994 when we sued our record company, we were basically wanting ownership of the songs that we wrote. We felt that by us not owning what we created, the possibilities for our songs to be used for something other than what we wanted later on was there. One of the clearer things that sparked it off, was when some of the Beatles songs were made available for Nike commercials in the early '90s, outside of their willingness because somebody else owned them. So we felt that we didn't want to see 'Leper Messiah' end up as background music in a toothpaste commercial *(laughter)*, unless it was something that we wanted and the choice came from us. So now we retain the rights to any master recordings we have ever made, master recordings basically being any songs that we have written and that have appeared on our studio albums."

THE IMPORTANCE (HOWEVER) OF MARKETING IN MUSIC
"For every successful record that a record company puts out, there's fucking 19 unsuccessful records that nobody ever hears about, and there are a lot of good people and a lot of passionate people that work at record companies, who are really pushing and trying to help artists and to get artists out there. The problem with this whole analogy of making the record companies disappear because they're 'evil,' and then turning what the record companies do over to Napster-like services, is that Napster-like services don't promote, they don't market and they don't build any kind of awareness of bands. There are some basic facts here. It is a fact that there is no band that has ever really broken, or become successful, through the Internet alone. There's this thing some people say that everybody's music should be equally available on the Internet, which I don't in theory have any kind of problem with, as long as the artist chooses and the artists are part of that choice. But the reason that Korn becomes successful and the reason that Limp Bizkit becomes successful, the reason that all of these other bands become successful, is because record companies sit there and pour hundreds of thousands and millions of dollars into making videos and into marketing them so you hear about them. They spend lots of money giving them tour support and slots on fucking tours so you hear about them. The bottom line is that no band will ever really break from the Internet alone without the aid of some kind of record company. There's only 24 hours in a day, we talked about this before, and people do not have enough time to sit down and listen to every single posted file on the Internet..."

THE MISUNDERSTANDING OF METALLICA'S POSITION
"This whole thing about 'Lars sues his fans' type of thing. That is just completely out of context. You have to remember, once again, that Napster were the ones that sat there and held up their arms and said that 'we're not doing anything illegal here, but if you can come to us with proof of people who are downloading your songs, we will be happy to remove them from our service' fully well knowing that they could come up with that information themselves. It wasn't about suing the fans, it was basically 'OK, you want to play that kind of dare game with us, then here's the information.' Certainly in the beginning of this process I said some things that were out of line... I did an interview with BBC where I said some things about 'yes we will go after the fans directly' or something like that... this has been a learning process for me also. I said some very arrogant and aggressive things about our fans and so on, and I calmed down a little bit and tried to be more just, y'know, standing up for my own rights and be more neutral, sticking to the facts and so on. We actually reinstated 35,000 people because we found they had only been trading live recordings, which is something we have never objected to.

ATTACKING THE SPOKESPERSONS

"If people want to poke fun at us, that's fine, I don't have issues with that so much. What I have issues with more are levels of ignorance. I have issues with, like, when *Rolling Stone,* for instance, reports on the scene and then they print three response letters, all three of the response letters are 'what the fuck are Metallica doing – these greedy, multi-million-aire, rock stars, arrogant assholes?' There's no reason that the response letters have to have the same tone. That's editorial. Do you know what I mean? It doesn't bother me that much if we're the only ones out here with balls big enough to take this on and say what has to be said on behalf of everybody who agrees with us; that makes me proud. That doesn't bother me so much and the whole kind of paylars.com and all of that stuff that we're talking about, silly cartoons and stuff, that's really no different than somebody telling us to fuck off because of Lollapalooza, because of haircuts or because of Bob Rock or whatever. That's just outside criticism.

"I certainly never anticipated to get into this, and all this crap about 'Lars Ulrich poster boy for artist rights' and all that. I don't need any more publicity, and I don't need anything else on my plate, but what happens is that it becomes sort of like a snowballing thing. It becomes something that fuels itself. You sit there and you do something, and then somebody else responds to it, and then you try to restate your position and then somebody else says something that's so complete horseshit that then it becomes this thing that escalates. Once in a while you have to take a deep breath, and I've been so caught up in so many emotional things in the last couple of months where it gets to a point that you call up Cliff and go 'I'm so fucking both pissed and annoyed and it's like I don't even know if I can do this anymore' and then you sit there and have your pep talk and it always comes back. I look at it almost more like what a radar screen looks like. You have sort of a present position, and then you have hundreds of miles of the sweep that goes across and monitors weather in front of you, and you end up going all the way out 200–300 miles in front of you and feeling the stuff that's out there. And then you become so emotionally distraught at what's out there that you have to take a step back to your present position and remind yourself what you're doing. You start over again, and you sit down and go 'the reason I'm doing this is because I have a right to control where my music goes, including the Internet. That right has been taken away from me end of story.' So, you have to sort of keep coming back to the original starting position, and that is what makes it possible to sort of keep it going. Because, there has been a lot of times over the last couple of months where I have been so frustrated that I just wanted to walk away from it."

A LESSON IN MUSIC BUSINESS ECONOMICS

"Look, it costs Metallica a million dollars to make a record. Forgetting about what it does for Lars, James, Kirk, and Jason in terms of time, there's also physical cost in that. It costs us money, we employ dozens of people. We hire a studio, which is a small business that profits from us making a record there. We hire tape operators, we hire assistants, we hire runners, we hire recording engineers, that whole livelihood depends on us making records. Costs us a million dollars. So, the minute you make all that music available for free – forget about Lars, James, Kirk, and Jason, we're fine, we're set up for life thank you very much for supporting the cause for 20 years we're fine – but you're going to put that studio out of business, you're going to put that recording engineer out of business, basically there's an industry here that is not just about those fat cats that run the record companies on the 52nd floor. That is what people also have a tendency to overlook, and they have a tendency to forget about how many people this really affects. It affects everybody who works at Tower Records. The road is littered with, you know, a lot of small record store owners, especially around college campuses and stuff like that, who are complaining about how their sales are down.

IS IT REALLY 'SHARING'?

"Let me just clarify another thing, which is this whole thing about the use of the word 'sharing.' We really feel that using the word 'sharing' is not right. Look at it like this: I'm a Napster user and I have a Metallica record. I trade that whole record away, I 'swap' it with somebody else and I gain Soundgarden's "Badmotorfinger." So I'm not really 'swapping' my Metallica record, I'm basically duplicating for somebody else and then I've gained "Badmotorfinger" by duplicating. But I still have my Metallica record when we're done swapping. If I swap stamps, if me and you sit down and swap stamps, I give you a stamp and you give me a stamp. I start with one stamp and when me and you have swapped stamps I'm left with one stamp. When me and you 'swap' Metallica for "Badmotorfinger," I turn my one record into two records. So basically what we're trying to point out to people is that instead of buying "Badmotorfinger" for $16, you're basically using your Metallica CD as currency. Your Metallica CD replaces the $16 in the way to gain the Soundgarden CD. So basically, what we're trying to make people understand is that Metallica's records are being used to gain something else. This is not 'swapping,' it's duplicating... (And) doing it on a shitty little TDK analog cassette tape with your friend down the street is very different from having access to first digital copies with 20 million users all over the world. It's just not an analogy that works.

INTELLECTUAL PROPERTY

"I want to go into an analogy that 15 year old kids might understand. What does a 15 year old kid own that could be comparable to intellectual property? Their homework. You write a term paper on U.S. history.

You write that, it's yours, it comes from your mind. So, I'm 15 years old and I write a term paper on U.S. History. It's something that I create, it's something that I write, it's something that, for all intents and purposes, is mine. Now, let's say that somebody got access to that term paper and put it up on the Internet for all of the other kids in my class to download and copy. You would be pissed because it's your term paper, you wrote it, you put a lot of time and effort into it. You wrote it – it's yours! Should you not have the right to decide who copies that term paper? If you want to give it to one of your friends, that should be your choice, but if somebody stole it from you and put it on the Internet and copied it to everybody in their class so people could just download it for free, wouldn't you be fucking pissed?

METALLICA MUSIC AND THE INTERNET DOWN THE ROAD
"Ultimately, we want to get into making our records available to stream on **metallica.com** We want to be able to sell our records on **metallica.com,** but not while the other guys are giving it away for free. We want to be able to share live concerts, share all kinds of crazy stuff that we come up with through our Internet site and so on. We're starting to get there. We're starting to think about it." ●

IF I SHARE
MY SANDWICH

On July 11th, 2000, Lars Ulrich attended a Senate Judiciary Committee Hearing on the future of digital music, his invitation arriving as a result of the pioneering stand he and Metallica took on the file sharing company Napster. It wasn't a pretty road to hoe; Ulrich received the vented spleens of various angry people worldwide as Metallica's concise argument got twisted and turned like a flag braving gale force winds. But there was at least a sense of vindication at receiving the committee invite, Ulrich and Metallica happy that the issue of downloading albums for free on the Internet was attracting such weighty scrutiny. And y'know what? In the end you'd have to say that the boy did good!

Editor — February 2004

"I'm not fucking doing it!" Lars Ulrich, Washington DC, hotel room, 9.22am on July 11th, 2000 semi-naked and dripping wet.

"Sharing means we each get something... like, if I share my sandwich with you, you get half and I get half." Lars Ulrich to Senator Orrin Hatch, Senate Judiciary Hearing on The Future of Digital Music, 10.48am, July 11th, 2000

"We have tried to hold discussions with Napster, and despite the good faith on everyone's part, I think there's just too much a gap to reach an agreement." Lars Ulrich

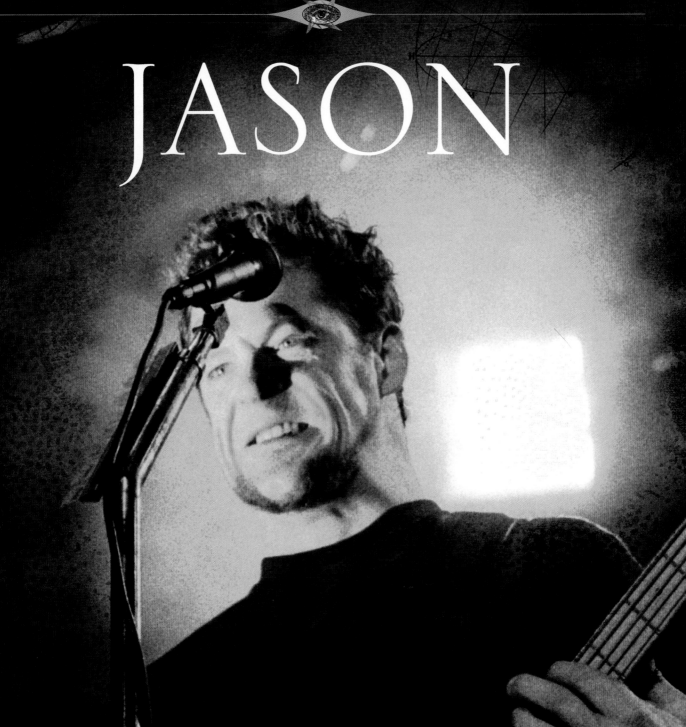

JASON

During 2000, Lars, James and Kirk took it in turns to sit with Jason Newsted and interview him. No-one else was present or sat in on these conversations, the idea being that such privacy would generate deeper discussion. The resultant (edited from the original) conversations reflect Lars, James and Kirk uncovering topics and issues which usually remained both undiscussed and unknown.

Editor – March 2004

JASON & KIRK

KH: HOW DOES IT FEEL TO BE JASON NEWSTED? WHAT GOES ON IN THE HEAD OF JASON NEWSTED? WHAT'S THE DAY TO DAY, THE 24-7, THE WEEK TO WEEK, THE MONTH TO MONTH, THE YEAR TO YEAR?

JN: I think generally inside I'm a pretty happy person. I might not show it always on the outside, but I think I really am. And I am very thankful for everything that I have, and I try not to take things for granted too much. Even though it's very hard for us because we have so much shit and everything available to us, I still try to be really thankful for all of that stuff. I think that's an everyday thing for me. That's something that I think about all of the time when we go into a nice hotel somewhere, I get treatment, I still feel really cool about it. When we get on our plane or when we do special things, even get in a big car or stuff like that. I try not to take that shit too lightly.

KH: I WOULD SAY OUT OF ALL OF US, YOU ARE THE MOST CONSCIENTIOUS PERSON WHEN IT COMES TO THINGS LIKE THAT. I MEAN, IT SEEMS LIKE YOU'RE MUCH MORE APPRECIATIVE OF OUR SITUATION THAN THE REST OF US ARE.

JN: To put it very simply, you get out more than I do and you really expose yourself to a lot of different higher grade type of things and social activities that involve those kind of things. So that plays a part in the way that you look at those things. It's not that you don't really appreciate them, because you do, it's just that you've been exposed to them – it seems like really a lot more. You know, you're used to going out and seeing things and doing things and these very gregarious types of activities, and I think that has a lot to do with the way you look at that stuff. I don't think it makes you any less appreciative, it's just not as uh, maybe not as... you can't see it as plainly or something like that.

KH: HOW DO YOU DEAL WITH SUCCESS?

JN: I think that I have the same type of answers that I have been having, just about trying to keep it all in stride. There was a time, I think for all of us, that we got sucked in too deep. Pats on the back and the success and the dollars and the shit and the rock star thing. I think all of us have been victims of it at one time or another. Some of it hasn't left yet, but you know that time in '91 or '92 or whatever, the "Black" album was hitting and I was SOOO guilty of all that shit and I totally fell right into it, you know? Fortunately, I was able to pull myself out of it and still retain myself.

KH: HOW DO YOU SEE THE BAND IN CONTEXT WITH THE REST OF YOUR LIFE?

JN: Pretty much for me it's everything. It seems to permeate everything. I think about it all the time. Like when I'm out and walking my dogs, and really feeling like I almost let go of everything and was able to turn everything off, I still think about what are you guys doing right then. I find myself thinking, "I wonder if Hammett's on his bike," you know, "is he doing what he's supposed to be doing or is he just partying?" I do think about that kind of stuff. It's kind of weird being able to keep each other in check like that. It's something that's so ever-present.

KH: HOW'S YOUR KARMA?

JN: I would say... I am a bit crafty I feel. Maybe sometimes too much for my own good. Therefore, it would create some negative Karma.

KH: DO YOU DO ANYTHING TO AMEND THAT?

JN: I think that my good deeds, for lack of a better word, as far as sharing my time. My special quality time with people. I think that Karma, the 150 people that I talked to yesterday and looked into the eye, and all of the 150 all that I talked to today and looked in the eye and said I want to shake your hand; the Karma that is created there, I think is so hugely positive and overwhelming that the negative things that I do create with my carousing as it were can be defeated by the positive. So I would say for the most part, the Karma that I do create is peaceful, loving and positive.

KH: UH-HUH, GOOD.

JN: Thank you Mr. Hammett

KH: OH WAIT... THERE IS ONE MORE QUESTION... WHAT'S YOUR FAVORITE COLOR?

JN: Blue, no red... AHHHHHHHHHHHHHHHH!

JASON & LARS

LU: WHAT IS IMPORTANT? NOT PARTICULARLY YESTERDAY OR TOMORROW, BUT WHEN YOU THINK ABOUT THAT RIGHT NOW, WHAT IS IMPORTANT?

JN: *(thinking, sighs)* There's a cool thing, it's the most important... to have a connection with the people that are actually here... you know? It's unconditional acceptance and non-judgmental love and that kind of thing. So that is absolutely the most important thing, and after that I don't know in what order they would go but, friends and pride, stand-upness or that kind of thing. The real truth. Some things you are always going to fool yourself about – we know what those are. But other things that you absolutely will be truthful to yourself about, and you have to be, it's really important being able to perceive that in yourself.

LU: SO, I JUST ASKED YOU WHAT WAS IMPORTANT AND YOU MENTIONED OBVIOUSLY A BUNCH OF THINGS THAT I WOULD FULLY AGREE WITH. YOU DIDN'T MENTION THE WORD MUSIC. WHERE DOES THAT PLAY INTO THE WHOLE THING?

JN: Today. You asked about today. You didn't ask about yesterday or tomorrow. Today it really doesn't play that big of a part.

(Ed's note: the following quote refers to the time right after Jason was invited to join Metallica back in early 1987).

LU: I REMEMBER ONE OF THE GREAT MOMENTS OF THAT WEEK, WAS BEING DOWN AT THAT REHEARSAL PLACE WITH YOU AND MRS. BURTON (Cliff Burton's mother – ED) AND ALL THAT. WHAT WAS THAT LIKE? DO YOU HAVE ANY MEMORIES OF THAT?

JN: Absolutely. It's very, very clear. I could draw that for you too. I could make you a movie and print the script out for ya. Your Dad, I just remember right away, just like he always is everytime he greets anyone, was very warm. And this comes before he touches you, he's warm, you know? And his hand shake, I remember that. I can't remember exactly what he said, but it was all really cool, all positive. I was so nervous. I was actually more nervous right then than I really had been meeting you guys or meeting James and playing for the first time. When the Burtons came in, and Mrs. Burton came over, I was actually most nervous. She said, 'you must be OK because they know,' or something like that. And 'just be yourself, just be yourself'... at least two or three times she said that. That's what I remember from her words, and then just them gracing us, and just these two incredibly vibey people, you know? That hits you before they touch you too, you know? Still to this day, Ray (Cliff's father) is that way, sunshine just comes out of him, like PAHHHH! Those people are very special people. Cliff must have been something, I tell you.

LU: WHEN YOU BUILT THE CHOPHOUSE INITIALLY, WAS THE INTENT THAT IT WAS GOING TO BE THIS GREAT OUTLET OF ALL THESE THINGS, OR DID IT START LIKE MORE OF A PRACTICE ROOM OR A JAM ROOM?

JN: I always had a Chophouse, but I didn't have a physical building until about '90. But even in apartments, or especially in the house in Richmond that we rented, I had a room that had everything set up. There (were) micro-phones and the guys from Exodus would come over and the guys from whatever fricken bands were going on then *(laughs)*. They called them-selves the mix and match of San Francisco thrash guys, they would come over and we'd play in there and do things and make tapes and all that from way back. So, that would have been all the way pretty much ever since I joined Metallica.

LU: SO, THIS GOES WAY BACK BEFORE METALLICA.

JN: And then it kind of got enhanced by the Maxwell thing (a ranch belonging to the Martin family, old friends of Cliff Burton). Jim and Lou told me that they always recorded everything up there and that and that just really sparked me. I'm like, 'man we always liked to record all of our stuff in the desert and everything, so that's great with me, you know.' And that kind of sparked me to do it out in California and then the brothers Martin dubbed that building the Chophouse and from then on, they always come up with good shit. As soon as it was built, we christened it on Elvis' birthday in '92 and that was the first time that we actually made a real tape with a machine and all that. It started out with the idea of being a jam room, and then as time went on we wanted it to be more of a studio in mid-construction, so some of the wires that are in the walls and things like that aren't necessarily what you would call 'studio code' you know? It's just a project studio really. But the whole idea was for it to always be someplace where people could come and just do whatever and always turn the mic's on and do as few overdubs as possible.

LU: TELL ME SOMETHING. TELL ME, YOU HAD SO MANY GREAT PEOPLE IN THERE. TELL ME SOME OF THE PEOPLE YOU WISH YOU COULD HAVE HAD IN THERE? I'M TALKING ABOUT STUFF LIKE 'I WISH JOHN COLTRANE WOULD COME OVER'... CLOSE YOUR EYES, DRIFT AWAY, LIVING OR DEAD. GIVE ME FIVE OR TEN NAMES THAT YOU JUST WISH YOU COULD FUCKING SPEND 12 HOURS WITH?

JN: Stevie Ray Vaughn, spend at least a couple out of the 12. Hendrix, it gets crazy now...

LU: GET CRAZY!

JN: Billie Holiday, Bob Marley, Jeff Buckley (thinking)... geez!

LU: OK, WHAT DO YOU THINK WHEN YOU HEAR THE WORD METALLICA?

JN: For me, 'wow!' How's that? 'WOW!' That's my first answer absolutely. I want to do it (answer) as an outsider, I want to do it as a fan. I look at Metallica as legend, that's true. I guess integrity, and this thing that people, whether it goes up and down, people like them or don't like them. There's nothing that really goes by (in our lives) that Metallica doesn't connect to, that we don't relate to or we don't think about somehow in the back of our head. We know that it's all relating to it. I don't want to say Metallica's everything because there are so many other things that we have now created that we are as people and collectively too. So it's not everything, but it's a big part of all of us. A very important part, but maybe a little bit different than it was some years ago.

JAS N & JAMES

JH: All right, Jason Newsted, bass player of Metallica... Goddamn... the real reason you started to play music?

JN: I think that it was seeing people in the church and at different church camps and social activities. There would always be one or two acoustic guitars, and a lot of C, G, and D songs, and there was always at least one kind of hippy trippy person that played guitar and made songs and stuff. As a little kid I spent a lot of time in those places with my family, those kind of church surroundings and settings, and I was always really impressed by those people and attracted to those people, even if they were older and things like that. That was probably the first reason I got an acoustic guitar for my ninth Christmas, I got an acoustic guitar and played – no left hand stuff, only right hand stuff. I didn't know how to tune it or anything, but I would just write my own songs.

JH: Awesome. So church and family are very important?

JN: I'd say that the morals that were instilled in me from that, even though I didn't want to get up – no way did you ever want to get up and go to it (church). You know? Nobody does... Sunday morning? Are you kidding man?! But discipline... there was no choice, that's just the way it was with the family.

good things that you and I both know and are able to taste everyday and feel and, you know, positive energy from people, and– FUCK – cut it with a knife! It's just fucking so, so apparent and so real because that is what we work so hard for, for feeling that feeling. You know, that's what we do all that shit for man, no matter what. So that's the good part of success for me.

JH: Where do you go for true advice? Not band, not business, like, good for your head stuff? If you have a serious problem, who do you go to?

JN: Wow, well, let's put it this way. If I got in a car accident and you were with me, or one of my closest friends or whoever was with me, and I was freaking out half in shock, the first person I would call would be my father and I would say, "Dad, this is what has happened man, what should I do?" no question about it. I would do it in shock when I wasn't able to think straight, and when I was out of shock when I was able to think straight. And when it came down to, I guess, a really serious financial thing, I mean really big, I would also talk to him because that was his job for many, many years – it was working out money for big things and he knows what's up with that kind of stuff.

JH: Absolutely. Good stuff! Where do you go when

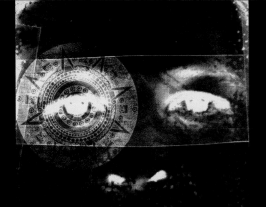

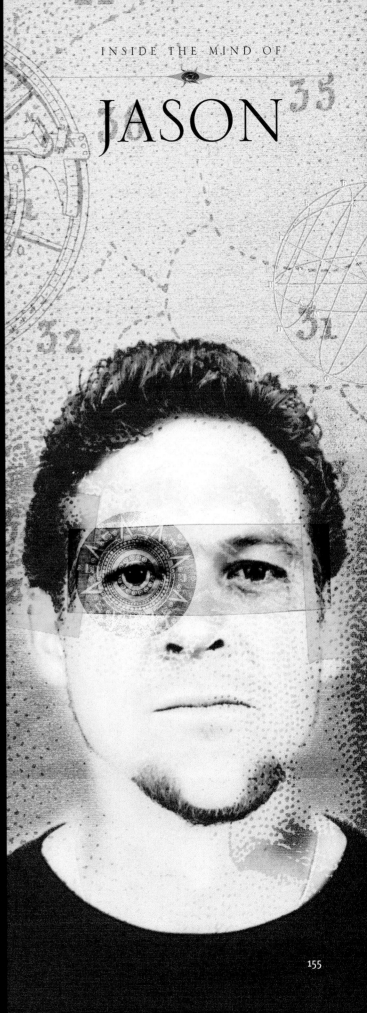

the writings of these people? How much can you believe? They were artists, they were poets, they drank a lot of wine, they came up with a lot of stuff. 'He walked on water... yeah write that one down, that's a great one.' For real, how much... some of it is incredibly heavy and so believable and fuck yeah man, wow, really, really incredible. But some of it is not believable, and so this is also stuff to think about... how many colors and flavors and shapes and sizes and everything... beautiful things, so many different people, etc. And that book is so limited in color to white people – we are a minority if you add up all the people on the planet, there's less of us than everybody else, you know? And so that kind of thing is just not fair when you are looking at the world, and that's how things need to be looked at. Once I got in this band I was able to see things in a world's view, which is better than just a view of Michigan or Arizona. That's when I was able to see that that book couldn't be absolutely true, because it didn't involve all of the people that do exist and even would have existed at that time as well. And the people that wrote the fucking book were far darker skinned than you or I. There's got to be some way maybe that our spirits, who have created positivity, are able to go on, and people who are negative and were killers and did crimes against children or things like that, they do not get to go on; that's all. I don't have an answer for that.

JH: WHAT'S THE MOST ROCK STAR THING YOU HAVE EVER DONE?

JN: The most rock star thing... I'm so mad at myself for doing it because it may seem minor, but I was at a show in Phoenix at that place outside... the Compton Terrace it's called. I was going to see Flotsam opening up for Sepultura or something like that. It was during the time of the "Black" album and I was already getting caught up in the rock star shit anyway at that point. I felt that was the only time that I felt I had to deal with it and pull myself back together, but it was in that zone and this guy at the gate in the back – a security guy and he's like, "You can't come in. Where's your pass?" and I go, "Don't you know who I am?" that's the most rock star thing and I don't... I mean those words to me are just fucking real bad, real wrong. I don't want to ever catch myself saying that again... I just don't dig it. There might have been some more obvious things like things in a car, posing, or doing blow with Van Halen or some other rock star thing. But to me that was a fucked up rock star thing to do. ●

155

WHIPLASH

THE BAND ANSWERS FAN QUESTIONS

Hey, Lars, do you guys ever keep in touch with the very first members of the band back in the beginning, and how does playing live in Nashville, TN rate on the list of must-play cities?
Sean W., Westmoreland, TN

LU: I speak to Dave Mustaine fairly often, and he shows up at gigs here and there. Ron McGovney I never speak to but he has a tendency to show up at gigs depending on where he's living at that time. Nashville is definitely my favorite place to play in North Central Tennessee.

Have any of you ever jammed with the people who inspired you to become musicians?
Chris C., Erlanger, KY

JN: Chris, I'm in a band with three guys that inspire me and inspired me as a younger musician.
JH: Ozzy, Gary Rossington, Queen, and Ted Nugent.
KH: I have played with Carlos Santana three times, and it was the coolest thing because he is such a major influence, I grew up listening to his music ever since I was a wee lad!
LU: I'm still looking for people to inspire me to become a musician; in the meantime I'll settle for this dead-end I'm in now.

Lars, is it true that you keep a record of each and every performance? If so, please comment on the concert I went to August 28, 1998 at Irvine Meadows, CA.
Emily L., Santa Ana, CA

LU: Yes, it is true I keep a record of every performance. I keep it stored in the safest place I know – inside my thick Danish head. The particular performance you are inquiring about was on a hot Friday evening, it was the first show back from a three and a half week hiatus in which I became a father. The gig was pretty good, probably somewhere around a 7 on a 10 scale, since we hadn't played live for a while and sometimes the L.A. crowd can be rather passive in their display of emotion.

James, you have said that the lyrics to 'Until It Sleeps' refer to cancer. I never realized how true

those words are until my dad was diagnosed with cancer in May of '99. Even though I am into my 40's and Dad is in his 70's, he has always been my personal "hero." Do you have advice on how to cope with a loved one having this awful disease?
Laurie J., E. Freetown, MA

JH: Whether the disease is terminal or not, listening, bonding, getting closer will be gratifying for both.

Will 'Human' and 'No Leaf Clover' be on a future album? That'd be the shit, to hear 'em both studio recorded!
Cliff D., Claxton, GA

JH: Sorry, no. But you can hear a band-only mix (no orchestra) on the "S&M" DVD of those two songs as well as the whole show.

Lars, what's your most and least favorite thing about fatherhood?
Crystal H., Columbia, IL

LU: My favorite things about fatherhood are so numerous and so personal that it's probably best to say that there are a lot of them and that most parents out there can figure out what they are. My least favorite thing is when he (Myles – this question came pre-Layne's birth-ED) hurts himself, cos I freak out tenfold to what he does and when I have to go away for an extended period of time and he seems to know that.

Why haven't you guys done an all-instrumental since Bob Rock came to the band?
Bryan L., Faribault, MN

JH: Too many awsum lyrix zzzzzzzz.
LU: Since Bob Rock came on board, we haven't had the need to put filler material on our records.

When you were growing up, did you do your homework on time?
Shane K., Berlin Center, OH

JH: No, my sister ate it.
JN: I pretty much did my homework until I got really interested in music and then everything else kinda didn't get done on time or otherwise. I don't recommend u follow those steps.

KH: I'm still growing up and I'm still waiting 'til the last minute to do my homework...
LU: Define 'on time'...I always did it for what I consider 'on time.'

What is the first song you ever sang and how old were you when you sang it?
Jessica S., Albion, MI

JH: Two years old, happy birthday to me.
JN: The main one I can remember was 'Pick A Bale Of Cotton' Sonny Terry & Brownie McGhee, soon followed by the entire Jackson 5 third album.
KH: 'Baby U Can Drive My Car' when I was about four years old.
LU: 'Can't Buy Me Love' by The Beatles around five or six.

Where in the world do you dudes get your songs from?
Amanda W., Marietta, GA

JH: Kid Rock.
JN: Melting down old Black Sabbath albums.
KH: Napster.
LU: From 'The Metallica Song Bank.' We make a withdrawal there every couple of years.

Do you think you guys will ever break apart or have you even thought about it?
Bobby Joe Martin III, Stillwater, OK

JH: After every tour we break apart and un-break apart for the next tour.
JN: Whether we're together or apart Metallica will always be.
KH: If I was dropped from 5000 feet I would break apart.
LU: Yawn... when the above mentioned 'Metallica Song Bank' runs dry.

Kirk, since I saw you on the "S&M" documentary video, I was wondering if you believe in God, or Jesus Christ whatsoever? Or do y'all believe in satanic religions?
Casey P., Ft. Worth, TX

KH: I believe that there's a supreme energy that's in everything and everyone and everything is ruled by cause and effect.

156

Lars, my shins begin to cramp up while I drum, what can I do to stop that?
Jerry M., Round Rock, TX

LH: Stop drumming (Editor now asks if there's a serious answer for this poor, beleaguered, crippled young drummer... Lars agrees on condition of first answer standing.) It sounds to me like you could be suffering from shin-splints, you should consult your physician.

James, how do you memorize the lyrics for all of your songs because it seems like music artists can go through a concert and sing a number of songs without ever looking at them?
Brandon M., Landark, IL

JH: They're written down on cheat sheets... when you've sung songs for 20 years it's hard to get them out of your head. I'll try to forget them but they won't go away... please make the voices go away!

Jason, what one person do you wish your school would've taught you about in school?
Alex J., Roseville, MN

JN: I would say more about Da Vinci and modern heroes like Medgar Evers, a civil rights activist. There are so many things people don't know about now that people should learn about. There has to be more of a world scope than just traditional Anglo-American history.

I was wondering if you had any tips for being damn good? What do you do when you have writer's block?
Ben S., Elberton, GA

JH: Stop writing. I don't believe in writer's block, you just continue writing crappy stuff.
JN: For the writers block I'm having a hard time coming to a conclusion...
KH: Yeah I got a tip: always make sure you wear clean underwear because you never know when you'll be in a car accident and this could be a reflection on your upbringing; that's what makes a Mom damn good.
LU: Have blind faith in yourself and your abilities.

Lars, what does that "Re-Load" picture represent?
Emily L., Santa Ana, CA

LU: One of the basic ideas behind abstract art is that it represents whatever the viewer wants it to represent.

What do all of you think of Britney Spears and Staind?
Katie M., Lancaster, NC

JH: I don't know but I'd like to leave a stain on Britney Spears.
LU: I think they have a right to exist.

Is James' hand made of plastic?
Marcelo M., Argentina

JH: No, just my tits.

What made you decide to stop printing the lyrics in the CD jacket?
Rick W., San Clemente, CA

JH: Writers block or eye kant spel.
KH: More room for pictures...
JN: More room for pix of me and Kirk, and of me balancing Kirk's $10,000 Strat w/my pinkie...
KH: We fought for an hour about that afterwards because I was so pissed off. I still get mad when I see that pic...
LU: Obviousness.

What sort of music do you guys chill out to when you're not playing or working?
Stuart J P., New Zealand

JH: Me snoring...
KH: Music gives me a headache.
JN: Kirk's guitar solo tapes...
KH: Hey, you must have 15 tapes of ours from 10 years ago...
JN: Kirk's guitar solo tapes when drunk... and Barry White.
LU: Good music.

James, how do you sing and play guitar at the same time?
Al S., Gibsonia, PA

JH: Open mouth, move hand up and down.

What is the song 'Welcome Home Sanitarium' supposed to mean?
Brad C., Blackfoot, ID

JH: It's based on the movie "One Flew Over The Cuckoo's Nest."
KH: It's about my dog named Sanitarium when it came home from the vet after having had its colon dilated and wouldn't stop scooting... the unscoopable skid mark.

LU: It was named for a potential future tour's title...

Lars, what are your drum set measurements?
Tara T., Alleghany, CA

LU: Ask Flemming (Larsen, long-time drum tech).

The editor has asked Flemming and now here they are:

Bass drums – 2 each, 22 x 16, Rack tom – 9 x 10, Rack tom – 10 x 12, Floor tom – 16 x 16, Floor tom – 18 x 16, Snare – 6.5 x 14, Cymbals: 17" median crash, 18" median crash, 19" median crash, 18" china crash, 20" ping ride, 18" median crash, 19" custom china, 14" high hat (Dynobeat Z).

James, with your wife being Argentinian and I suppose speaking English and Spanish, do you speak or understand Spanish? And what about Cali and Castor (when he's older)?
Asun E., Larrondo, Spain

JH: Why not have your children speak another language when they can, as long as they don't talk shit about me. Cali's already translating for me, I've tried but I'm too stupid to learn.

James: Are you anti-religion and were your parents devout Catholics or something? I noticed a lot of your songs have a negative religious connotation to them. Did they turn you off to it?
Deb G., Polk City, FL

JH: I was raised a very strict Christian Scientist which alienated me at school and places where I needed to be part of a team. All our songs deal with my youth in various ways.

I wanted to ask Kirk Hammett if he still collects old toys like G.I. Joes, Hot Wheels and stuff like that.
Jimmy Ambush V., Manitowoc, WI

KH: Yes. But I don't collect G.I. Joes, Hot Wheels and stuff like that. I collect monster toys from the 50's, 60's and 70's. Got any? ●

Kirk's sweaty underwear

IT'S BEEN AN EVENTFUL START

TRUE

TO METALLICA'S 20TH YEAR.

FAMILY

LARS, JAMES AND KIRK

VALUES

SIT DOWN TO DISCUSS

A HOST OF ISSUES WITH THE EDITOR

INCLUDING THEIR FEELINGS,

 THE JASON MATTER

AND THAT PLAYBOY INTERVIEW.

Photos taken at Kirk's house
in San Francisco on March 1, 2001.

PEOPLE ALWAYS ASSUME THEY'RE BEING LEFT OUT. When Jason Newsted announced he was leaving Metallica in January, people nearly trampled each other in the rush to state 'the' reason, why it signaled the end of the band and to also inform us of whose fault it was. Some said it had been in the works for months, others that it was a marketing plot designed to create interest and havoc. Both were wrong. It was a relationship that had been going through problems for a while. Those problems one day proved irreconcilable. That happens in life. There doesn't always have to be 'a' reason.

Then, just as a dignified dust had settled allowing both parties to continue with their lives until a point later when they could discuss matters more liberally, came the Playboy interview. Done during a series of separate interviews starting last October and concluding last November, the author of the piece found himself in the middle of a band whose foundations were being tested. Subsequently he heard a few moans from member to member. And ultimately, these were collected and fashioned into a story which made it appear that the band was in huge turmoil, unable to slay inner demons and on the precipice of collapse.

Partially this was true. There were problems. There were issues. Some of you would've noticed during Jason's discussions with Lars that he wasn't the happiest camper in the wagon. But one thing must be made clear. That was then. And this is now.

When the Playboy interview surfaced in March 2001, it seemed like 24 months had passed in terms of where Metallica stood with itself and each other. I had never witnessed a band go through so much hard work to turn a corner and make their communication work on a level it never had before.

The part of the story which rankled with me personally was the cheap character portrayals. James was painted as a dictatorial redneck, Kirk as a zen-warrior, Jason as a chip-shouldered, hard-done-by victim and Lars as a Hollywood-style showbiz dude. People are never that simple, and thus the portrayals failed to offer proper dimension. And from this came the idea that one issue (Jason's side-project) was the main reason for the split. A 15 year relationship doesn't end over one thing. It was the culmination of many matters, most of which the band have agreed to keep to themselves. Jason has his own reasons too, and when he feels the time is right (if ever) then he will be the one to offer them. That is, and should be, his right.

What concerned me most was that the fans would have a warped view of what was going on. So I chatted with Lars, James and Kirk, saying I felt we needed to have a round-table discussion to clear the air, offer the facts and let you all know exactly what's been going on up to the end of March 2001. They agreed.

And so it was that the four of us sat down for lunch at Salute, an Italian restaurant in San Rafael, for the hour-plus discussion which follows.

Let it be noted that there is a jovial mood at the table.

Let me just start lightly, I mean obviously people would like to know, this is an anniversary year and it's a pretty quiet start to a Metallica anniversary year. I don't think you would have expected this.

JH: Is it really 20 years?

Technically it is. Technically it's 20 years.

LU: I went over this with Cliff Burnstein the other day and he was saying that most people count the 20th anniversary from when you release your 1st record. So, I think a lot of people feel that it's not our 20th anniversary until 2003.

So, is this like the millennium argument?

LU: I guess so.

KH: We're not going to be eligible for the Rock and Roll Hall of Fame until 2008. Is it 25 years? So, wow that's a big year for us!

Well, this one's not inconsiderable. (laughing) Let's deal with this one first! (laughing even harder) All right, so there's not really any anniversary thoughts or whatever? You haven't sat down and thought, "well in the summer we're gonna have the big anniversary jam?"

KH: I think there's going to be a big cake and ice cream party sometime or another, right?

JH: A two-kegger!

KH: A two-kegger! (laughing)

JH: I just think... I've never paid attention to anniversaries and things, but we should do something very cool. Any band that's been together this long, whether it's 19 or 20 years, deserves to at least fucking have a drink together. (laughter of everyone)

KH: Acknowledge it? Yeah!

Would you say that since November you guys have probably seen more of each other off stage than in the last 10 years? Would that be accurate?

KH: For a break – yes! Because when we go on break I never see, well I NEVER see James. I always see Lars, but it's between the hours of 10 o'clock at night and 6 o'clock in the morning. (devilish laughter) So, it's nice to see all of these guys during break times when...

JH: (interrupts) We're uglier in the daytime.

KH: YES!

And I mean there is a reason for that, obviously which is that...

JH: There's more sunlight! (laughs)

KH: Because we're growing together, rediscovering our friendship with each other in a different capacity.

Right. (To Lars) Do you have anything to add at the moment?

LU: Uh, no it is nice.

Are you guys ready?

All: Yeah!

All right, let's get back to the whole thing of hanging out and so forth. Maybe you want to address why people who have toured for three years in a row don't immediately hang out with each other off stage. Because I don't think some people understand what that's all about.

JH: When you are in confined spaces with someone, like in a bus, airplane or dressing rooms, all that... small stages, you know like the "Load" tour. *(laughs)* But anyway, you're with these people all of the time and when you get off tour you don't necessarily call them up a day later and go, "Hey, I miss you, let's hang out!" We kind of use that time to cultivate our own individuality. With that you start to lose touch after a while and then on the breaks you start to kind of freak out like, "what's the band feeling?" and you start to not know each other again. When you get back together it's an instant bond, but you haven't really caught up with all the other stuff that everyone's going through that brothers should know. Then you start to get a little – built brick by brick – a little wall between you. We hadn't taken the time, road or studio, to break the walls down again. That's exactly what we're doing right now and it feels great.

What's been the precipitating point for that? What's the main reason?

KH: You mean who's sacrificed themselves to get to this point?

Right, I mean has it basically come down to the fact that with Jason's departure, you realized that the wheels needed to be realigned?

JH: Well, he basically just built the biggest wall. So, when that couldn't be hurdled anymore, that just made us discover that there are little walls between us that don't need to be there.

KH: Basically, what I get is that it sounds like all four of us were wondering the same thing and not really communicating that 'wonder.' We were all wondering what the hell we were doing, but we had just kind of... we wanted to give each other personal space during a tour and we were always hesitant to reach out and communicate.

I mean it's going to be quite bizarre for people to read that you guys were reluctant to contact each other. Because if it was a kid, he would be reluctant to contact each of you, but you were feeling the same.

KH: Well, I can really just talk about myself. *(quiet laugh)*

JH: Especially when you've got your own family and things, you're kind of... you're so adamant about focusing just on your family that you kind of forget about your Metallica family too.

Right. You've been quiet Lars – at the moment.

LU: I'm just taking all the love in.

No, seriously putting sarcasm aside...

LU: How do you know it's sarcasm? *(laughing)*

Let it be noted that it's come to a point where I am having trouble deciphering sarcasm from the truth! I mean were you one of the people, when Jason split, that said, 'look, we need to sort this shit out!'

LU: No, it was Cliff Burnstein. (management)

KH: It started actually before Jason made the statement.

"ANY BAND THAT'S BEEN TOGETHER THIS LONG DESERVES TO AT LEAST FUCKING HAVE A DRINK TOGETHER."

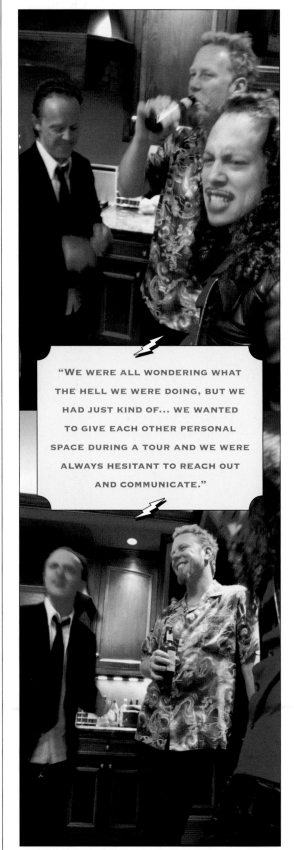

"WE WERE ALL WONDERING WHAT THE HELL WE WERE DOING, BUT WE HAD JUST KIND OF... WE WANTED TO GIVE EACH OTHER PERSONAL SPACE DURING A TOUR AND WE WERE ALWAYS HESITANT TO REACH OUT AND COMMUNICATE."

LU: What statement?

KH: That he quit the band. That he actually quit the band. Or did we start on that day?

JH: No, we started chatting...

KH: Before.

JH: Well, he told us that day, but...

LU: Well, what happened was Cliff Burnstein thought that it would be valuable if there was another person in the room with us other than the four of us and other than our managers – somebody neutral. So, when we realized that this thing with Jason... that something was going down with Jason, we called a big meeting in the first week of January to figure out what was up and talk about the rest of the year and talk about the state of life in Metallica. Cliff Burnstein suggested that there be a mutual party in there to mediate...

JH: *(chuckling)* Make sure we didn't kill each other.

LU: Right. I mean just sit down and talk our shit through. This is eight weeks ago now and what's happened, to make a long story short, is that we have worked with this gentleman named Phil Towle who has really re-energized the band and re-energized the relationships. We have basically spent six to seven meetings within the last eight weeks meeting up with Jason and without Jason, even after Jason left the band. And we continue to see Jason in these types of surroundings – it's been awesome.

Is that to mend fences that were broken from years of...

LU: I don't think that 'mending fences' is the phrase I would use. Like James was saying, what we sort of ended up doing is calling this guy, the connector, basically to reconnect us again. To help us sit down and focus on the reasons why we are together, why we play music, why we have this great love for each other, why it's been so difficult for us to share that with each other. Like James was saying, because we haven't spent that much time together off tour, we have a tendency to... it's like human nature gravitates toward the negative instead of the positive. And so it's like you sit there and think the other guy's a fucking CUNT for not calling you up or whatever, and you don't sit there and realize what his needs are or what your own needs are. So it's been a lot of that type of stuff.

So, it's a lot of getting lost in your own world?

LU: Yeah and your own insecurities and your own doubts and your own questions about where you are, how you fit in the big scheme of things, trying to find the right balance between what your own needs are, what the bands' needs are – all that type of stuff. Over the last couple of years, a lot of that stuff has just really never gotten communicated and the whole Jason thing brought that out in us finally. So, it's sort of like 19-20 years later we sit here now in a perverse situation where we lost Jason...

JH: We know where he is, but...*(laughs)*

LU: ...and, at least speaking for myself, I have a stronger relationship with Jason than I ever had when he was in the band. I really feel closer to him than I ever did when he was in Metallica, but also James, Kirk, and myself have a stronger situation than we probably ever had. So, it's sort of like a strange crossroads in that we lost a member, but in the same way there's a great energizing of all of these relationships that in some way makes it more tolerable. It's like in any relationship, if you can truly break up as friends – true friends, then it makes it easier to break up in some ways because everything has been dealt with. We have dealt with everything with Jason and it's been awesome.

Right. Let me ask...

KH: Anything lingering in the past won't come up or affect the separation.

Has he been forthcoming in these meetings by telling you exactly what he's repressed for years in terms of feelings? Do you feel that you're hearing the full extent of his disgruntlement?

JH: I don't think it can ever get to the full extent of anything with any talks. It's always an ongoing thing and you're all discovering things and going, 'oh, I forgot about that.' It's not so much detail stuff than more of an overall feeling. We understand where he was coming from, but I don't think it's ever all out there.

I should switch it as well. Do you guys feel, looking at each other, that there is stuff that will come out?

All: Absolutely. Yes. *(no hesitation)*

JH: And I hope it does.

Right. So, there's still...

LU: Each time it comes out it's like a cleansing. There's a real sense of re-energizing every time something gets talked about and dealt with. It's really cool, with Jason, with the way we're feeling about what we're going through with Phil Towle, because we've probably had three of the worst months that we've ever had at the end of last year. We talked about it, it's not a process that particularly has an angle to it. May 1st, we're done with that and, I think we all feel that this will be an awesome thing to have as part of Metallica.

So, this chap is going to have an ongoing function?

LU: I certainly hope so.

JH: I look at him as any other kind of person that's a witness, more like a producer really. You work with a producer until you've learned what he's got, and then you move on. You'll probably never ever get as deep into the psyche of a human as Phil does, but what I mean really, is that I would like to learn as much as possible from him and use it all of the time. I don't really see a point when he wouldn't be used, but hopefully you can take it a few steps further yourself when he's not there. It's not like you have to have this guy with you all of the time. I mean, one of the most valuable things he's taught us, I think, is listening. Actually shutting the fuck up, listening to the other guy, letting him finish the sentence and get his point across and actually looking at each other and communicating, seeing how the guy really feels. Learning to sympathize with certain situations.

KH: I think the greatest thing about Phil is that he's brought out a level of intimacy between us three that we've never really experienced before. And he's also brought out in us what we really, truly feel about each other, how we feel about the band and our own fears and, you know, strengths. Just being able to vocalize that with these other two guys in the room and finding out they are pretty much on the same page, I mean just hearing that gives me a huge sense of security. It gives everyone a huge sense of security. If there was any wonder on whether or not there was another potential Jason in the group, I think we've put all those fears to rest.

Can you tab this moment right here, right now, attitude wise? Does it go back to, 'this is what it was like in 1987-88' or is it just like, 'new deal, uncharted band territory?'

JH: You could never go backwards, just for the fact that we've been somewhere else. We've been really far down and we've been really high, and so now we're to this other place. When you start out you don't know the extreme lows or extreme highs. I think we're wiser.

So, this is uncharted territory pretty much for you. Is it weird sitting here right now with you three doing a roundtable with....

(everyone says no)

No strangeness at all?

LU: We've done 30-40 hours of this in the last month and we're totally comfortable with each other. And the greatest things about these sessions is that we get to these points when we have these moments and stuff like that. Like when Kirk was saying there is an amazing sense of intimacy, an amazing sense of brotherhood, an amazing sense of love, it's an amazing sense of just being with guys you've been with for 20 years and continuing to discover new things about them that you didn't know. Hearing stories, thoughts, emotions, what they feel about certain things, hearing childhood experiences and crying together and all this stuff. It's really, really powerful.

Is there one thing that each of you have learned about each other that you want to share right now.

JH: I just think that we've all got weaknesses that we were never willing to show or wanted anyone to see, but showing the guys your weaker side has made you stronger. That someone else knows... I don't know how to explain this, but through some of this... becomes a huge strength. I mean it might sound funny to other bands that 'they're hugging and weeping' and all this crap together, but at the end of this, this shit is making us as bullet proof and as strong as it ever has been. The strength coming out of this, and the trust, and the just pure kick ass of it all, is pretty amazing.

KH: I'll tell you one thing. After reading that *Playboy* interview yesterday...

(laughing)...which is where I was just about to go.

KH: I mean if you compare that capsule in time to where we are right now, I mean we are just miles away. I mean FUCKING MILES away. I hope that people don't read that *Playboy* interview and think that's where the three of us are still at. That's just not the case.

JH: To me it doesn't matter...

LU: It doesn't matter...

JH: Because I don't give a shit. That's where we were at that point and that interview occurred when we were the most disconnected from the band that we had ever been. And he (writer Rob Tannenbaum) really exploited the fact. I mean a lot of those things that he said, we just sit here and laugh about them, we've always laughed about them. Those aren't major shocks. Those aren't things that are, 'ooh, he said this about ME!' That's shit we say to our faces all of the fucking time, so people that really know us know that that is not a big deal. The real fans know

> "I THINK THE GREATEST THING ABOUT PHIL IS THAT HE'S BROUGHT OUT A LEVEL OF INTIMACY BETWEEN US THREE THAT WE'VE NEVER REALLY EXPERIENCED BEFORE. AND HE'S ALSO BROUGHT OUT... HOW WE FEEL ABOUT THE BAND AND OUR OWN FEARS AND, YOU KNOW, STRENGTHS."

the stuff that everybody's talking about is really cool, because it will almost serve like a testament forever of that time where things were at the lowest point. You can almost look back on that and gain strength from that...

KH: That time period.

You'll be using that as a reference if matters go there again?

LU: I think so. Again, I thought the piece was quite well written actually and I think when you've got four guys sitting there and saying four different things, he (Tannenbaum) should fucking exploit it. That's what he gets paid to do and that's what people want to read. So that doesn't either anger me or surprise me, but I think that where we're at now is even more special, because what people read in this *Playboy* thing that came out this week, they think that's where we're at, and if that's so we will continue to be one step ahead of where everybody else is and that's pretty cool.

So, when it got to the level of websites like Yahoo! News it's, "Whatever!" There has been a bullet proofness that has come around in the last few months that kind of protects you all from that.

JH: In all honesty, like Cliff always used to say, 'Truth is the mightiest hammer.'

KH: He'd say... sorry man.

JH: It's true. You're getting interviewed in a dark moment of your life and a lot of people wouldn't want to do that. I think it was later, when the Jason shit started happening, that I got a little worried, saying, 'should we pull this *Playboy* interview or make it go away?' Later I thought, 'why?' If it's us, it's honest, it's where we were at that time. If people want to think that's where we are all of the time, that's too bad. I mean, if you interview someone after their dog dies you are going to get a certain thing, and after they get a new dog... don't take this as a direct comparison or anything. *(laughs)* But you know what I'm getting at. You have dark points and you've got great points in your life.

KH: When you share really intimate moments, like with these sessions we have been having, you kind of get a deeper understanding of the person and you get a deeper understanding of why or how that person, or personality, acts or reacts. I think we've learned a lot from each other in that regard.

JH: It helps each other. If you know that a certain personality is a certain way, when something is happening with him you can support him the way that he needs it.

So for example, if someone needs some support and help when the chips are down, you guys are open to asking each other. If you want to be left alone, now you guys know that's....

KH: Or support or whatever on whatever basis. We're basically better equipped now to support each other.

I guess we should bring this whole communication thing around to the primary reason that you guys are together, which is music. I would imagine that it opens up all sorts of corridors for musical communication, right?

KH: I definitely feel less musically inhibited now, even though we have yet to go into the studio. *(laughs)*

JH: It can only be better. We know how to do it (communicate) the other ways. Any new way, anything you learn on how to do something is great.

Kirk, do you feel more comfortable bringing ideas to these guys? Will

that we are strong enough to take that kind of criticism even though there's a little truth behind it and I just think reading that and being where we are now, I'm really comfortable with it. It makes us feel even better that we've made such progress. I mean, I read that thing and I think it's just so stupid sounding. There's some funny stuff in there, there's some little digs that are funny, but he's trying to make us sound like we're complete assholes to each other all of the time and that's absolutely not the case.

LU: Let me say also that if everybody else out there thinks we're in that portrayed mental frame of mind in that *Playboy* interview, it makes what we have now even cooler. Because it's sort of like our little thing and nobody else really knows about it and that's like really, really cool. I think that the *Playboy* interview is really good. I think it's really well written and I think that you feel more comfortable in saying, 'listen, I have a good fucking riff and I want you to listen to it?'

KH: My problem in the past was… I always felt comfortable about showing these guys my ideas, I just didn't feel very confident in them (the ideas). So I would hold myself back. Now I don't feel like I have to, which is a big plus.

Right. Let me go back to the Jason thing for just a moment. Open communication, everything's friendly. Will it remain that way? Will he still go to shows and so on and so forth?

LU: I hope so.

JH: We certainly hope so, there's no reason to not be like that. But we've gotten to the point where any press things that come out, we know that it's not really good to read. We can communicate with each other and not through the press, putting stuff through the press is stupid.

(Author's note: at this point I decided to raise one of the cited reasons behind Jason's decision to leave, James' disapproval of his side project. Obviously this was one of many contributing reasons that each party has which led to Jason's departure, some of which will remain personal between them. I asked James about this particular one, because it was the most discussed reason).

So let me ask you bluntly. Was his side project the major reason, do you want to address that?

JH: What's that?

Do you want to address the whole matter of his side project? Was that the straw that broke the camel's back? James, are you the great dictator that the Playboy stuff appears to portray?

JH: I certainly had views on it (the Echobrain side-project) and they stemmed from other things. I felt the band was becoming weak that way, and that was always my way of keeping the band together and not fracturing any kind of family strength. That's pretty important to me I guess, and I felt when Jason was doing his side project that it was taking away from his family, his brothers. And I've come to realize that it's absolutely crazy to try and limit anyone on what they want to do and you've got to find the family strength other ways. I think, I don't want to put words in Jason's mouth, but he's realized what I was going for as well – trying to keep things strong and family like and what not. So in the end, we've really both kind of met towards the middle and understood what one another were talking about. So, as far as I'm concerned, there's not really any hard feelings – we just had two different opinions.

So, let me ask this question and put this to rest.

JH: Will I play on a solo project? (laughs)

Two-part question. 1: if the situation of members doing solo projects were to come up again, would you be equipped to deal with it? Let's say Kirk turns around to you guys and says, "You know what? I'm going to release a blues project." Now, have you reached a point where you would say, "I may not necessarily agree with it, but I can see that stuff has to be done?"

JH: I think I'm to the point where it can happen.

KH: Not that it's going to happen anytime soon.

JH: We'll find strength in other ways.

And the second part of that question: if in October or September you are still a three piece, all right, let's say it comes to June and someone has offered some gigs you want to do…

JH: …would Jason ever be welcomed back?

KH: My opinion on that is that it's still too soon.

LU: That's a tough question.

KH: That is a tough question.

LU: Very, very brilliant, brilliant journalism!

KH: The only way I can answer it is that it's too soon.

LU: As far as the whole bass player thing, when I tell you we haven't talked about it and we haven't thought about it, that's not just the party line kind of thing…

Well, you did discuss Keanu Reeves!!!!

JH: Not in a bass player way. (laughs)

LU: We have not looked at time frames, we have not looked at people, we have not talked about any of that stuff. We're at a point right now, I think for the first time that I certainly can remember in Metallica, where there's nothing marked on the calendar in front of us. There is a great freedom that comes with that. I think that we're all really enjoying what we're doing, which is getting to know each other better and exploring our relationships and all that type of stuff. And when we get together and start jamming, whether that's tomorrow, next week, or next month, the energy that's going to come from the first five minutes… somebody better fucking tape that! There are a lot of possibilities with the record and with writing and with playing some shows, you know, the whole… I just feel so free because the three of us will make the decisions together. You know, we don't have shit going on in the business side, management or anywhere. And if for some reason Jason shows up as part of that somewhere, I don't know. Right now, I'm just really psyched that he and I had a 10 minute phone call where we didn't talk about Metallica – that's, like, the first time in 15 years. He's got a lot of stuff that he's got to deal with.

Look, let's not make it so one-dimensional here… I think all of us at various points have been frustrated. A great deal of that sense of frustration comes from the fact that in the 1st couple of meetings I really feel that we all got closer to both Jason and each other. And it was very frustrating, because it seemed to us that Jason had some kind of agenda, and I think that we feel that Jason had planned his departure for quite awhile. And we, for instance, looking back now on the interview that he and I did for SO WHAT! three or four months ago, I think that a lot of that stuff was already seeded at that time. So, there's a great deal of frustration that in all that goodwill, and in all of that wonderful shit that came out in January and February, that he wouldn't consider/reconsider. There's a weird thing about this thing, where we part ways when it's the best it's ever been – that's frustrating, and has been frustrating, and difficult for I think for all of us to deal with at different levels.

> "...WHEN WE GET TOGETHER AND START JAMMING, WHETHER THAT'S TOMORROW, NEXT WEEK, OR NEXT MONTH, THE ENERGY THAT'S GOING TO COME FROM THE FIRST 5 MINUTES... SOMEBODY BETTER FUCKING TAPE THAT!"

KH: *(laughing)* They were fighting and there was a camera that was beaming it out to an arena full of people. (On the "Black" album tour there were cameras capturing the backstage action and beaming it out to the arena.) I was going, 'Oh shit! Here we go!' because I know when Lars means it and I know when Jason means it, but that doesn't necessarily mean that they know it. I was just like, "Oh, all right, what can I do to get the camera off..." *(laughing hysterically)*

I'm just reveling in the fact you (Lars) would throw a punch at him.

JH: Let me just say something more about the side project. I really felt in my heart that side projects were detracting from the strength of Metallica, and now that we've got a real trust with each other, that's a huge strength. When you doubt each other a little bit and a side project occurs, you think that they've got ulterior motives a lot of times and that's what I didn't like. It didn't feel as strong as it could be and that was most of the fear.

Right. You were acting on having fear and no knowledge so...

JH: So, I spoke to him and said, 'no, you can't, we've got to stay together.'

Right, right. Everyone else has made their comments about if he were to wander back into the picture, is it a picture that you would care to entertain yourself?

JH: He can wander back anytime, but being in the band would be tough because of what has gone on. To tell you the truth I'm looking forward, I really am. We're talking about this new era and it's too bad Jason couldn't be a part of it and really, he's created this new era by bringing us to the point of where we are.

Sacrificing?

JH: If we had these talks 10 years ago, we might not be where we are right now, but we might be there earlier and we might have discovered things about each other that were completely wrong and different. One of us... the band could have had different members back then, you know?

Right.

JH: Because it is... being truthful with each other. Why lie to just stay in a band or do whatever, you know? You've got to understand each other and be strong together, you know?

LU: I just want to agree that when James says there is a sense of rebirth, I think we're all really looking forward to it, whatever it is. Once again going back to what I said before about all of the options... it's pretty fucking cool. Of course in some perverse way Jason was the sacrificial lamb for that, so it's like...

JH: But really, sorry to cut you off, but there was a point at the very first meeting where he didn't have to go that far, he didn't have to quit. But it was really months ahead of time, he had... (it seems) it was a premeditated thing.

LU: We really all feel that because of what went down, he had the option of changing his mind. We talked to him about changing his mind...

JH: That should be known.

LU: Yeah. He had made his choice sometime before that. I'm not going to go on record as saying that's a fact, but he probably made his decision sometime in the fall during the black hole.

KH: You know what really sucks for me about this whole Jason thing, is that it appears that he arrived at his decision without even including us, you know? And after having so much history with the guy...

Very interesting you say that.

LU: So, that's why I'm saying if Jason offered to come back in three months, I think that we would probably not go with that to protect ourselves from being hurt again. Do you know what I mean?

I know exactly what you're saying. For the record, you're also making it known that he quit at probably the most fluent point of your relationship.

KH: It's just a shame, it's sad that he couldn't be part of this new era of Metallica because we are just growing so much on a personal level and that's bound to influence things on a musical level. That's an area that he would have just flourished and it's just a shame that he's not here to be a part of that.

LU: If I had known that the night I punched him back in '93 in Fort Myers, if I had known then what I know now, I wouldn't have punched him.

You actually punched him?

I would even agree with that, no doubt.

KH: You would think that he would at least give us the opportunity to at least consider this with him instead of unilaterally making a decision months in advance of us ever even trying to fix the situation. In other words, he didn't give us the opportunity or enough of an opportunity to fix it.

Maybe he just wasn't able to do it at that time, for whatever reason. Maybe he had the desire but just couldn't do it.

KH: What it was – is too little too late. That was the bottom line, too little too fucking late.

JH: It's not like the three of us had to fix something for him, we all had to fix it together.

LU: And fix stuff within ourselves.

JH: Exactly. And if he didn't want to be part of the fixing then that was his decision.

The stuff he has to fix, he might only be capable of doing by himself.

JH: Well, it was all internal fixing within ourselves and each other.

LU: That's the key thing I think James is saying. It's come to a point where I don't think any of us really ever realized that in order to mend relationships it's not just about trying to get the other person to see your point, it's also about how you interpret the situation and how you deal with what's inside you. And that's where I'd say the major change has been in the last couple of months, is that we all have a different awareness of our strengths and of our weaknesses and we have a different honesty both to ourselves and to each other about them. Especially about weaknesses, and that has never, ever, ever come out before and that is awesome.

JH: If you could take inventory of all the band weaknesses, all of the strengths will appear and fill those 'weakness' holes and become completely strong.

Lars. Let me ask you something on a very personal level. In the past whenever a crisis has occurred, you're the person that pops up and basically, you put a business head on, and sort out whatever has to be done to bring it through...

KH: ...he's the most eloquent.

...do you think if you hadn't have been going through your personal situation (Lars was separated from his wife for a while at the end of 2000) you might have been tempted to throw all of your energy into repairing this situation in the short term, thus dragging it out and out...

LU: Jason?

I mean, let's be honest, your tank was probably empty. You were probably like, 'fuck, I've got other shit to sort out here in my own life.' Do you think if you hadn't had that, you would have been tempted to make it all work, like, 'we've got to make this happen, we've got to keep...'

LU: Good question. In my heart of hearts I feel Jason made a decision months before our meeting, and I do not think that he would, for any-

thing in the world, change that. So I sort of felt I had an awareness of that all along, so I don't think it's got so much to do with that. I mean, it's interesting when you're dealing with it, cuz I'm dealing with two levels instead of just one. I'm not just dealing with the band, I'm also dealing with similar stuff personally in terms of what's going on with my family. So, it's an interesting correlation between the two situations and how you come to a point where you realize, and this is something I think that we all realized, like James keeps coming up with the word family... that Metallica and your own thing are not two separate entities, no matter how much you try and force that and I've been trying to do that a lot. And we are all Metallica, we all are each ourselves and all of our families are as much part of Metallica as they're not part of Metallica. And it's sort of like the strength of Metallica depends on the individual strength and the happiness that each person has in their own lives, and the balances that each person has in his own life and all this type of stuff. So, it's obviously been interesting for me in the last couple of months to deal with some of the imbalances in my personal life. It's been very awakening on many levels.

Has it been interesting for you guys to be privy to some of the imbalances in his (Lars') life that you might not have known about and thought 'wow, I have some advice for that, maybe I could offer some support?'

JH: Sure. But we didn't know before that there wasn't much communication. This whole thing... you needed to realize *first* that there wasn't communication and *then* remedy it.

LU: I think we would all tell each other what the other person would want to hear. So, now we don't censor ourselves.

KH: That's a total codependent thing – don't censor yourself.

JH: Don't fucking censor your fucking self!

LU: That's what's so awesome about the sessions and stuff that we're going through. There's a completely... there's never, ever a moment where I sit and think about what it is I want to say, I just say it. So, It's not like at this moment, what do you think the other guys would want to hear and that type of stuff. I think we all feel that at different levels, that there's kind of a naked openness about what comes out of our mouths that has never been there before, because it was always about what would the other person really think about this or other stuff.

Very cool. Back to musical matters for a moment. Any writing at all right now, anything going on?

JH: There's been individual writing, but we would like to sit down and write together. I mean, there are some approaches to writing that we haven't tried that I think are very appealing right now. So, we'd like to try a few different ways, creating more together, creating different ways, 'here, I've got a whole song, let's fuck with it that way,' 'here you've got nothing, let's start from scratch!'

LU: Everything right now is about trying to create together. We've talked about, at least for the foreseeable future, we've talked about only playing together, writing together...

So, you will be writing together?

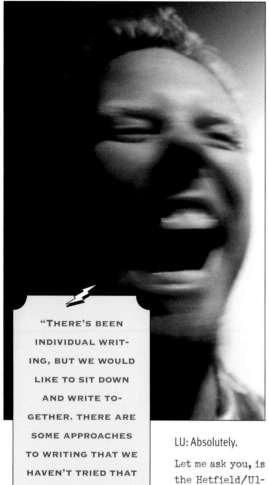

> "THERE'S BEEN INDIVIDUAL WRITING, BUT WE WOULD LIKE TO SIT DOWN AND WRITE TOGETHER. THERE ARE SOME APPROACHES TO WRITING THAT WE HAVEN'T TRIED THAT I THINK ARE VERY APPEALING RIGHT NOW. SO, WE'D LIKE TO TRY A FEW DIFFERENT WAYS, CREATING MORE TOGETHER..."

KH: It's either that or three different CD sleeves.

JH: Well, I... what we want to get at is a complete honest way of writing and before it was... well, looking back it worked completely. But, you know, if I was Kirk, I would feel like I was submitting my tape for approval and it's really weird now that I think about that.

Right.

JH: 'And who's approving this? And why are you approving it and why am I not a part of the approval process?' That's crazy.

LU: I spoke to our accountant a couple of days ago and said we should get together and have a meeting about some financial things . The accountant said, 'I should meet with you and James' and I said, 'no you shouldn't meet with me and James, you should meet with me, Kirk and James.' I think that you'll find it's really awesome all of us just doing interviews together from now on and all that type of stuff. Meetings should be all of us together and all that type of stuff.

So that's going to impact the way you record, the way you write. I mean...

JH: I mean it's only going to make it stronger. The more open it is, the more great shit comes in, and at the end of the day we all have to agree that it's good. So why not have it in there.

Right. Wow, I'm serious, this is an exciting time... this is exciting right now.

JH: Yes.

That's the key word — exciting!

JH: I'd say so.

Have you at all started thinking about what you'll be doing recording wise or is that the point... you haven't because you don't yet know.

LU: We haven't really talked much communally.

Do you guys want to start now?

LU: I'm just looking forward to getting into a room with these two guys and fucking seeing what happens when we start playing.

Right.

LU: The one thing that we've talked about, is that the approach becomes different. In the past it's always been two different processes – the writing process and the recording process have been two separate entities in two separate physical places at two separate times. We want to try and do away with that separation. We want to try and write and record at the same time in the same place and maybe even kind of do what we did with 'I Disappear' maybe write and make one song at a time.

JH: And release it... *(everybody laughs)*

LU: ...on Napster. *(everybody laughs)*

JH: Instead of writing and recording we just thought, let's record it first and then write it! *(mischievous chuckling)*

So anything could happen. I mean, nobody should be surprised if you don't choose a bassist immediately... you could play with a touring bass player for the summer if you wanted to. You could...

KH: (To James and Lars) Should I tell him about my idea about the two guitar necks?

JH: Yeah.

LU: Absolutely.

Let me ask you, is the Hetfield/Ulrich 'we are the song people' being relinquished a little bit?

JH: No. We want to add to it. We want to make it the Hetfield/ Ulrich/ Hammett song people – I guess it would be alphabetically...

KH: YEAH! Hammett, Hetfield and Ulrich... *(laughs)*

JH: No, wait a minute, let's go first names... James! *(everyone laughs)*

LU: Let's go from place of birth, east to west. *(laughter)*

JH: Wait! Let's go by height!

Let it be noted that the democracy is so great right now that they are striving for ways to...

LU: What we're going to do is go for three different versions of SO WHAT! and in each one of them we could say Hetfield, Ulrich, Hammett and you can say Hammett, Ulrich, Hetfield...

KH: See, what we're going to do is James and I are going to get double necks. Bass on one neck and guitar on the other. During the song James is going to be playing guitar and I'm going to be playing bass. And when it comes to bass solos – I switch back to the guitar neck and he switches to the bass neck, I play the solo on the guitar solo, he can play his bass and when I'm done, he switches to the guitar and I switch to bass.

You guys are already being mean, you're leaving him (Lars) out of it. Maybe he wants to be the bass player too.

KH: No, we're going to give him a whistle.

A whistle?

LU: So I can play drums and whistle. *(everyone laughs)*

So, you can play drums and whistle!

LU: I'm going to be back bathing at that point.

Oh man. Before the comedians get carried away here, I have to say that the "N" word just came up – that would be Napster. So, it's the 1st time I've talked to all three of you together about Napster. How did you feel about it as it was happening and how do you feel about it now?

KH: I feel good about it now.

LU: How did you feel about it before?

JH: (speaking the day after judges ordered Napster to bar access to certain copywritten songs) What's happening? *(laughs really hard)*

KH: They closed down. They're screening…

How did you feel about it when there was a fight to be fought and he (Lars) took it on?

JH: He was awesome. He IS awesome.

LU: Thanks man!

JH: We can't say enough about how… he's taken a lot of hits and a lot of … he's taken the brunt of the feedback – good or bad, but most of it has been bad. A lot of the good feedback is really quiet because no one wants to support you, they'll do it in back rooms but they're not going to come out and…

KH: It doesn't look as good in print. *(everyone laughing)*

JH: We've always been supportive because obviously it was a band decision. There were other things going on in our lives that didn't allow us to be as vocal as Lars. He got very educated on it and very in depth into it. None of us could really catch up to help at that point and he kind of ran with it, and we're very proud and it's great that he did that.

Would you do it again?

LU: No.

Seriously, you wouldn't do it again?

LU: It would be really difficult.

What's been the hardest bit?

LU: All of the time that it has taken up.

Has it been hard getting a good whipping from a lot of people and being told that you're an asshole?

LU: It's not that. The hardest thing has been the amount of time it's consumed. It's been about a year now and it's consumed so much of my time. That's the hardest thing. It was actually kind of nice because in November, December, January before… when it was lost in appellate court and held for three months or whatever, it actually got kind of quiet. Then about a month ago when they came back, it just all flared up like twofold. Every single day I meet some young musician who comes up and says 'I'm in a garage band, what you're doing is standing up for me, that's awesome.' The biggest misconception has always been about the money and we've already talked about that. But, there's a lot of great people out there who have given me the support and supported the band and stuff like that, but then there's been that time frame. The amount of time it's taken up where I could be hanging with my son or working on my relationships or practicing drums or bathing or whatever.

I'd personally like to note that bathing is at the lowest point of that priority list!

KH: Napster was in this for the money all along and their whole process if they had won, initially, they would have been circumventing all the money that goes to the artist and putting it in their pockets. Their whole appeal to the media and to the public was that they were doing it for altruistic reasons, they're doing it for the good of mankind or whatever. That is the biggest fucking crock of shit! And then here comes Lars, who represents success, fame, wealth – of course Napster is going to try to appeal to people who aren't as privileged or whatever – of course they are going to appeal to the people with an altruistic notion, you know? Because they (people) don't know, they're just getting music for free and they just think it's going to remain that way for the whole time, but it was always their intention to make money and take money away from artists and put it in their own pockets. That is a fight worth fighting until the death.

JH: They would become the new record company and we would be stuck with them without a contract. At least when you sign with a record company, you know what you're signing, 'OK, we'll sign this' or 'let's alter this.' They just took your stuff and all of a sudden 'hey we're going to charge you.' It doesn't matter which way it was, we're getting fucked. We'll take the hits, we're strong, it's not going to kill us, it's going to make us stronger, but all of the hits about the greediness are what kind of bugged me a little bit. Greedy? So, I'm greedy because I want to get paid for what I'm doing? It's really not greedy to go online and horde thousands of songs just because Napster might go down? It's like looting, you know? And that's not greedy at all? I mean what the fuck's that all about?

KH: That's a good analogy. Napster enabled people to basically loot the record companies, the record stores, the artists…

Right.

LU: Let me go back to what we talked about before, 'would I do it again?' Of course I would do it again, it's just I don't want to... it's been difficult and I'm not going to sit here and fucking say, 'hey, I'd do it again in a heartbeat and fuck them all.' I mean it's been really difficult and I've been very confused about a lot of it. I questioned myself, I questioned Metallica's involvement in it, I questioned the people involved around us and stuff, but ultimately, of course, I would do it again. Probably, if I had to do it again, I would want to be a little more... prepared, I guess. The one thing I wish, in retrospect, is that I could've seen the shit storm it turned into coming, because I might have done a couple of things differently in the beginning.

Sure. I understand.

LU: There was a little bit of chest beating at the beginning, which I think kind of turned people off. I think, ultimately, the best thing with the whole thing is that hopefully it will get to a point where it becomes a tolerable part of the music industry for the next time frame. But I think that the greatest sense of accomplishment of the last year was basically taking part in the education of the public. It was awesome to ride the front of that wave.

JH: It really had to happen because we were a band that stood up for that side. We could have sat back, let it slide and let the lawyers take care of it one day and said, 'let's play it safe' like most of the other people and just let it do its thing and let the courts and all that handle it.

Right, but you picked a fight instead.

JH: Yeah. We stood up for what we felt was right. It was a little confusing in the beginning and now it's come down to just total simplicity. Why is this not a law that is held up everywhere? Just because there's a new way of communicating all of a sudden the law doesn't...

... apply...

JH: ...apply. I mean, what the fuck's that? So, we love the technology and there can be some awesome things done with it if it's done properly, and it's too bad, but it took this to get where we are. It was completely unsafe for us to do that, you know? You get shot at!

Very bluntly, this music is probably going to be angrier, live-lier or heavier? Any words you want to throw out to give anyone a clue? Or it's just going to be exciting?

JH: There's definitely a lot to write about! *(laughs wickedly)*

I mean, there is a lot of anger but there's a lot of control at the same time. We have a whole range of emotions and we're learning how to get them out and communicate them.

KH: It's about learning how to let those emotions, like anger, come out in a more mature fashion and using them as opposed to being controlled by them. Channeling all that stuff into the right place. We discuss channeling all that energy, and we practice it.

LU: Y'know what would be awesome? To do a contest where the winner gets to spend time connecting with Metallica.

Anything that's surprised you in this new-found communication?

KH: I've found that James and I have a lot more similarities than I ever thought we had in my life.

JH: We are American! *(bursts into laughter)*

I have to say that this conversation has been very, very cool. I mean, I know how it's been recently and I really think having this chat right now was the right thing to do for the mag.

JH: The fans have a had a lot of stuff thrown at them recently, and I think it's been hard for them to decipher what's real and not real. I think they've done a pretty great job overall, especially in the web chats where one guy gets way out of hand and everybody beats him back, there's been so much action going on out there. I mean it's unfortunate that the biggest statement after Jason leaving has been the *Playboy* interview, it's kinda fucked up. *(chuckling)* So I'm glad people are getting to hear what we actually have to say right now. There is a lot of patience out there, and the people who stick with us belong with us.

LU: I have to agree, it's cool that so many people have been sticking with us.

KH: I'm just glad that they're still there after all this, and they'll be rewarded for their patience because when we go back into the studio, all that patience will be rewarded. ●

BAND COMMENTS

PREHAB. GETTING USED TO OPENING UP.
JC 3/04

THE SPRING OF RESOLVE!
AND THEN THERE WERE 3!
THE CONNECTING PROCESS HAS BEGUN......

BOY, WERE WE
NAIVE!! WE HAD
NO IDEA WHAT WAS
TO COME!! I'M
JUST GLAD WERE SMILING
IN THESE PICTURES!!
A FEW WEEKS LATER
THERE WOULD BE MANY
TEARS SHED! AND I'M
NOT TRYING TO BE NEGATIVE,
JUST ACCURATE!!

3/04

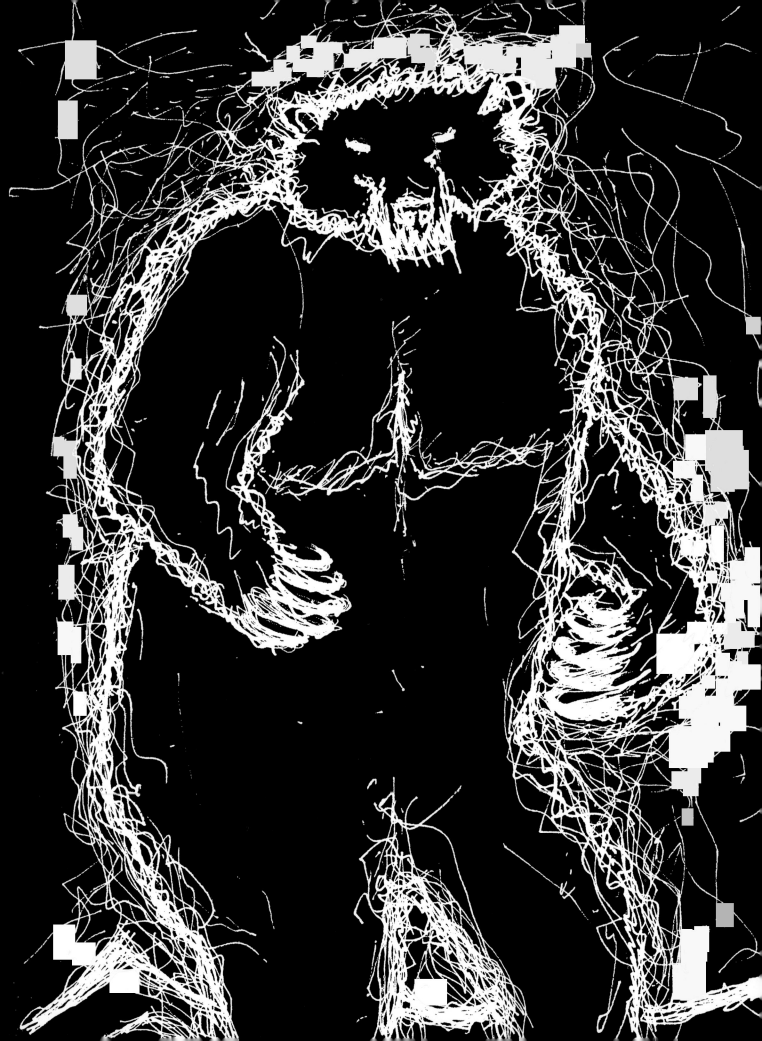

FROM RUSSIA W/ LOVE?

In May 2000, James took off on one of his periodic hunting trips, this time to hunt bear in Eastern Siberia. The trip promised to be an adventure, no matter what happened. But as time would tell, James got more adventure than he bargained for.

"**T**he flight itself was San Francisco-Seattle, Seattle-Moscow, Moscow-Petropovlav, and then helicopter ride to the hunting area, which had to happen like that because there aren't any flights going from Seattle, Anchorage, right over anymore, which is only like five-six hours. So after 15 hours of flying, it's the next day and you're burnt and you get to the hotel. The hotel itself was right there at Red Square, and they instantly take your passport away, saying 'we'll keep this for awhile.' So you ask 'OK, can I have it back,' and they reply 'yes, come back at Tuesday at seven or something.' Then they give you a little voucher. That's what they do over there. This voucher is suddenly like your passport. And then you pay! You have to pay to get your passport back, which is a lot of fun. 75 cents! It's not like it's free or $ 10.00. It's 75 cents! Everyone was really friendly and cool. Everyone looks at you weirdly though, I mean everyone is paranoid. There are a lot of paranoid people over there... On the way back, since we are talking about hotels, we stayed at a different hotel on the way back and it was on the other side of the Kremlin, and dude, it was seedy. It was nice, but as soon as you walk in there's just slot machines all over the place, people smoking, it's like a bar and then there's reception right there, people cruising around just looking at you hanging around the slot machines, hookers at noon. Well, we checked in, they took our passports and then we have to pay for our room. "You can pay for it when you leave." Ok, that's fine, do you want a credit card or anything? 'No, but you have to go to room 527 to pay your bill.' It's like an old hotel room converted into a little office, but it's somebody else running that thing, you know. Gangsters, who knows what it is.

Camp was a shed that had been there, they had been using it 20 some odd years for hunting. Really, low, low ceilings. I bumped my head a million times on the door. We slept on plywood sheets, I mean it wasn't bad at all. The kitchen and the sleeping were all in the same, there were 11 people sleeping in there. And fuck, the snoring was brutal. I mean these big dudes, the whole thing was they're going to bed. 'OH SHIT I got to hurry up and get to bed.' Trying to fall asleep quick, but it didn't work. There was a snoring section and a non-snoring section. Even though we did snore, they were louder. I slept with earplugs in every night and I've never done that... And the shithouse in camp was a hole. I mean, one there was no seat. It was just a shack with no floor. They just dug a big hole in the tundra and you just kind of squat over it. The other one had a seat, but it was square. I was thinking that these dudes would kill for a) bungee cords, cuz everything was just about wire and rope, and b) a fucking toilet seat! Everyone had splinters in their ass. That was another thing... fucking toilet paper!

There were four in each camp and a guide for every hunter, they had their own snowmobile with a sled on the back... Kostow was my guide. He was the chief guide. **HE SPOKE THE LEAST ENGLISH AND HAD THE LEAST TEETH.** And so he's in a sled in front of me and he doesn't speak English, so off we go we're off hunting on our own. They hunt on snowmobiles and that's the only way to hunt them there. It's complete barren land, there's hardly any trees. There's four feet of snow and you ain't walking around in that shit. You get up at six have some breakfast you're out by seven and you'd go 'til probably around two and the snow would start to get soft and the snowmobiles would start to bog down, you couldn't go anywhere, so you would wait from two, you would be out in this 'til 8:30 or 9 at night, just having tea and sleeping and just hanging out waiting for the snow to harden.

...Bears are creatures that I feel when you are out in the woods, they're hunting you instead of you hunting them. When they stand up, they're 12 feet tall. **THE BEARS WERE NOT EDIBLE.** That kind of freaked me out. After they skinned them out, the one freaky thing about bears is that they look really human when they are skinned. Once their claws are off, it's like hands, it's like a giant, giant monkey, hands and feet. They don't take any meat. I thought at least they would take the back straps, the filet mignon of any animal is right there in the back straps and they'd at least do

that, I thought, I guess because their digestion hasn't gone yet and there's something in there, something is a possible toxin. But they do take the gall bladder out and sell in China for sure. That's big money. So, that was the only thing they took. We took the skull, hide, and gall. You can eat bear, but I guess not right after hibernation.

Oh, it was definitely freaky I'll tell you. When we were hunting, we drove by where someone had killed his bear, he got like a 9ft 7" bear. **THEY LEAVE THE CARCASS FOR OTHER BEARS,** foxes, birds all of the other creatures that use that food in the food chain. We come up on that and you see these hands and legs sticking out and up in the air and it was like, wow. It was freaky and it felt like I was on Everest and there was, like, one of the hikers that didn't make it and I was expecting to see oxygen tanks lying around... you know they are closer to human than most other animals that are huntable.

THIS WAS THE MOST I'VE MISSED MY FAMILY EVER. I didn't get to talk to them for, like, a week, and you know there's not really any cell reception out there in Siberia.*(laughing)* I wish I would have thought about it 'cuz you can rent these satellite phones, and you can talk to anyone from anywhere on the planet now, which is pretty amazing. It was Castor's first birthday that I missed. Of course we had a little vodka to Castor, a little shot for him and everything, but I would have love to been able to get a hold of home. I wouldn't have been calling everyday, I might not have even called, but just the fact that you could is kind of comforting or they could get a hold of you somehow if something goes wrong.

When I came back with pictures, Cali said, "Hey, mommy look, the bear is dead." I mean hear her saying the word 'dead' was a little freaky actually. But what's even freakier is when, like, I'm here at the studio recording, making music. I'll tell her, 'I'm going to the studio making music...' and Cali will just be crying for da-da. 'Where's my da-da, I want my da-da...' Well where is da-da this time? He's hunting. So, the hunting thing has put a big mark on her. That's one thing that's kind of freaky to me, when I'm going away for these two week hunting trips, that's too long to be away from my family,it really is at this, especially at this time when they're so young. I get home and I get, I'll sit in bed and I'll be sad, you know. I'm at home and my daughter's just downstairs asleep and I'll just get sad that I haven't... it's so weird that I'll be sad that I've missed something or boy she's growing up too quick. It's going so fast...   ●

ITS HARD TO READ THIS AS IT IS THE BEGINING OF
HITTING AN ALLTIME LOW IN MY LIFE. FAMILY,
BAND MY WAY OF LIFE ALL CRASH TO THE GROUND.
I READ THE TOTAL DENIAL IN MY WORDS. FUNNY
ARTICLE BUT AT A HUGE COST. IM GLAD IM HERE TO
READ IT.

JH 3/04

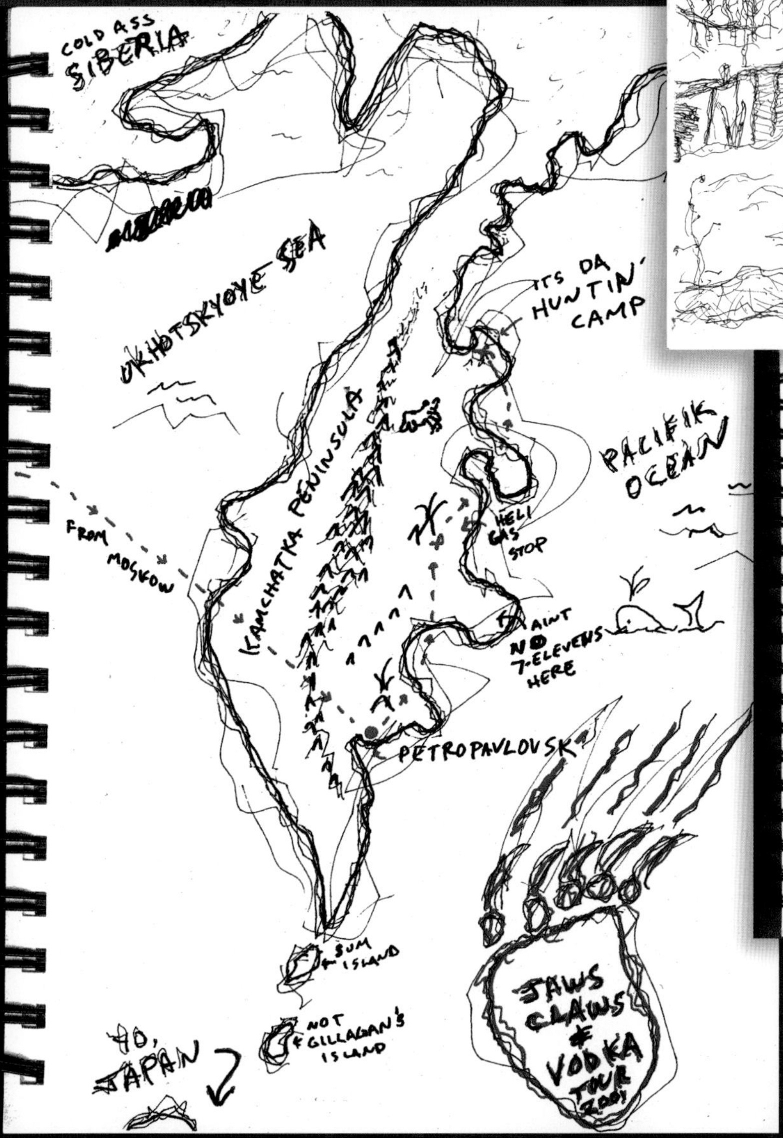

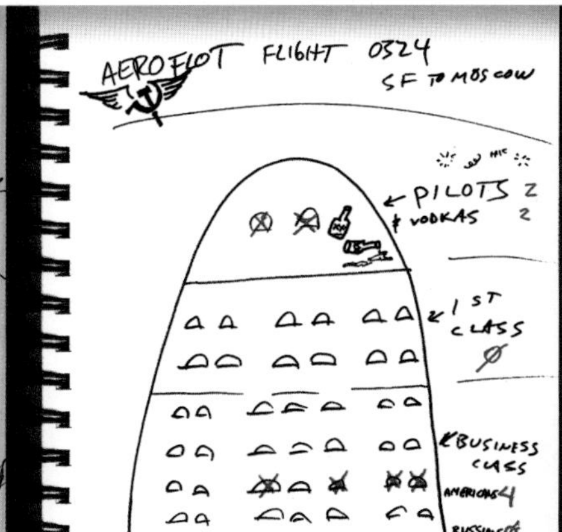

COLD ASS SIBERIA

UKHOTSKYOYE SEA

KAMCHATKA PENINSULA

FROM MOSKOW

ITS DA HUNTIN CAMP

PACIFIK OCEAN

HELI GAS STOP

AINT NO 7-ELEVENS HERE

PETROPAVLOVSK

SUM ISLAND

NOT F. GILLAGAN'S ISLAND

YO, JAPAN

JAWS CLAWS & VODKA TOUR 2001

JH 2003

AEROFLOT FLIGHT 0324
SF TO MOSCOW

PILOTS 2
+ VODKAS 2

1ST CLASS 0

BUSINESS CLASS
AMERICANS 4
RUSSIANS 0

EKONOMY CLASS
RUSSIANS YOP

the SANITY REMAINS

GUITAR MAN omic and horror movies were my life until I got a guitar when I was 15. When I was 13 and 14 years old I was actively buying music, but once I got that guitar, guitar playing became my fixation, my obsession. I remember spending countless hours in my bedroom just playing the same old stuff, not being able to play it very well but knowing fully well that if I just kept doing it, kept slugging away at it, I would be able to master it. Everything else fell by the wayside. And I mean everything! When I play, I play for myself in a more recreational way. The difference is expectations. When I play for the band there are certain expectations versus when I am playing recreationally. Being able to separate the two is very important. When I say recreational playing, for me, it is almost always playing jazz or blues because I feel I have so much to learn. On the flipside of that, every time I pick up a guitar I feel like I push myself to write something really good for the band, so it goes back and forth really.

Sometimes I am at home and I come up with an idea and roll with it to try to develop it for the band. I feel that in the heavy metal specter of music I have not completely mastered it but do feel that I am at the top of my game. When inspiration strikes you have to act upon it, because you don't know if or when it will happen again. Sometimes there are long periods between being inspired and not being inspired. There have literally been times when songs have been pouring out of me, and then there will be a dry spell of two or three months. It can get kind of scary. I get kind of nervous. So when the inspiration does, in fact, come, you have to act upon it and capture it and do something about it or else it is lost. I cannot tell you how many times I have thought up great riffs which have been lost because I have not been able to record them.

The Horror! As soon as I began to make any real money in music, by real money I mean money I could spend outside of rent, food and transportation, I started buying comics and toys again and I started to buy a lot of things that I couldn't afford when I was a kid. Of course they were a hell of a lot more expensive by then because most of the toys were from the 1960's and it was already the late 1980's when I got the financial freedom to buy, but I just dove right into all of it. Now I have the best of both worlds. One feeds the other. Actually I get a lot of inspiration from horror movies. The dark aspects of horror are very intriguing to me and a lot of times I watch a horror movie and get a certain feeling, which I try to capture musically. Sometimes I will watch a horror movie and turn off the sound and play to what is on the screen. I haven't done that in a long time, but I should try it again just to see how it works nowadays. It was always a lot of fun to do.

why Art + Horror = Hobby It is a lot of things but nothing in particular. It is really hard to describe but I just have always gravitated toward it. I just have such a love for all this stuff. It is so many things. It is the imagery. It is the fantasy aspect of it. It is the dark, moody atmosphere. It is death-obsessed, which I am a sucker for. I love the mysticism, the mythology that many horror movies have. Not to mention I have read many horror novels and books. Unfortunately however, all I read these days is like 50 magazines a month and if I am lucky one book... I really like the movie posters. I love the toys from the 1950's and 60's. I really like the toys because they are very '60's, a bit campy but cool. Much of the stuff brings me back to a time when I was young and very innocent. Part of the reason why I like all this stuff is that it brings me to a point in my life when I was innocent, untainted. I will be honest; I had a really rough childhood. I was abused on a number of different levels. It didn't really kick in until I was old enough to be aware of it. All the abuse didn't really start manifesting itself until I was 10 or 11 and I have been collecting since I was six or seven, so in a way it brings me back to a time when I wasn't tainted. Psychologically it helps me and I find refuge in going into a room with all my stuff around me. It is like a nice warm womb to me I guess.

Toys vs. Trophies There are things that I should recognize as being cool, like Grammy awards for instance but where are my Grammys? Half are on top of the freezer hidden in the basement and the others are upstairs in a room where I never go. And it is not just the rare hard to find things from fifty years ago that I like. For instance, I love the idea and image of little plastic skulls. I love them to death. A little Satan bobbing head is great. I found two plastic spiders the other day and I just thought they were the coolest things. I flipped them over and they cost like $1.75 each. I am very proud that simple things like that can still get me excited. There are just too many examples of people that are in this business and just get so jaded that the simplest things won't move them anymore. I am happy that the simple things still matter to me... And it is definitely not important to have the best collection. It is not an ego thing for me. I know a lot of collectors who seem to base their whole self worth on their collection but I have never been that sort of person. Every time I buy something I buy it to keep it. I might trade up or something but I really want to keep this stuff. Money is just not a motivational factor in this or really in anything I do because I don't necessarily believe in money. You can do an immense amount of good with money or an immense amount of harm with it so my whole attitude toward money is a bit ambivalent. I don't believe in hoarding money so I have no qualms helping our family and friends with money. I just have a weird relationship with money. I have seen money change people and I hate money for that. I've seen people alienate themselves and all because of money.

coming home   There is this thing that I call Post Traumatic Tour Depression that sets in whenever you come home from touring. I mean when you are on tour, if you think about it, you are constantly moving in a forward motion and doing stuff. You are living really, really fast. And when the tour ends it is like hitting a brick wall at 60 miles per hour. There is some real mental baggage that goes with it. It is the sort of situation where it is very easy to become an alcoholic or a drug addict, you know, because this depression just sits inside of you and you don't really know how to deal with it. There is no instruction manual or anything. No book of rock and roll that will tell you how to deal with such things. You kind of have to deal with it yourself.

I can turn it off now but it still takes time to turn it off. Having an understanding wife helps a lot. I am pretty much a fitness nut now. I go to the gym at least three times a week. I run, bike, swim, surf, do whatever I can to stay active. All of these things help to alleviate that stress and make the transition from a person on the road to a person coming down to a more realistic way of living.

I have more of a life to come back to now. I have a wonderful relationship with Lani and I have all these family members around me and animals and such and that makes a big difference. It is a big consideration even when I am on the road. For instance, when it gets close to me coming off the road I consciously try to slow myself down and mellow out a bit more and ready myself for time off of touring. Even if I have been to a city a million times I still like to go to places and to see my friends. So I never get tired of that.

eastern philosophy   I have always had an inability to relax and I am finding out now that that has everything to do with my childhood. I realized early on that not being able to relax was not healthy and not conducive to my fitness program so I looked up alternative methods to help me learn to relax. From there I got into transcendental meditation, better known as TM. I got into a routine every morning and every night. It would help me to clear my head and help me focus... then my mother in law who is a Buddhist, gave my wife a book called the "Tibetan Book Of Living And Dying." She read it and thought I might like it. I read it and it really perked my interest in Buddhism and different Buddhist philosophies.

The more I read the more it made sense and the more I started incorporating certain practices into my life. I would have more and more profound results including a significant change in my overall outlook on life, my personality and the overall way I treat people and every living thing. I was always known as a mellow guy but this made me a mellow guy without all the cynicism and sarcasm. I was a bit of a nihilist in the past and now nihilism is just a bad thing to me.

Before, I was looking for meaning in everything. I was essentially wondering why things were the way that they were. Why I was in my situation. Why I was with the people I was with. I was trying to find my connection to the bigger picture and to society as a whole and to life as a whole. Buddhism pretty much laid it all down in front of me. A lot of profound things came out of it. Like my fear of death. I have always been obsessed with death and Buddhism basically teaches us that death is not the end but is actually just another phase of life and birth.

SURFING BIRD   Surfing is all about freedom. Complete freedom. You are chasing a rush that is very similar to the initial rush that you have when you walk out on stage. The feeling that you have being able to hit a power chord and move 10,000 people. When I am not touring, I miss the atmosphere of walking out on stage and knowing that all that energy is directed toward the four of us. I miss playing live, at least that aspect of it. Surfing is kind of that same rush. You are trying to catch a wave and once you catch it you ride that motherfucker and it is just such a great feeling. Plus there is always a possibility of getting killed or drowning or getting bit by a shark that adds to the whole experience.   ●

the Sanity remain

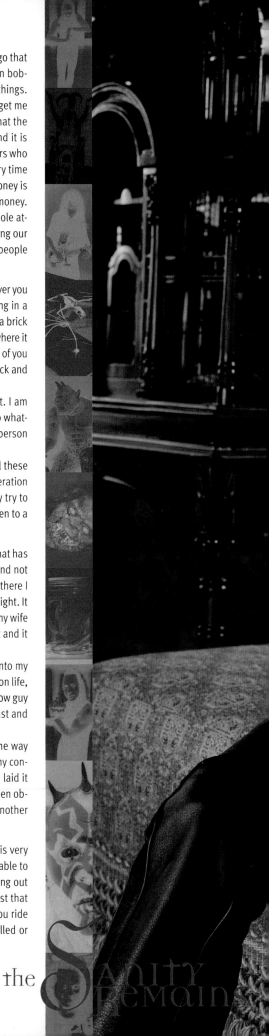

WELL, I CAN'T COMMENT TOO MUCH ABOUT THIS OTHER THAN I THINK I'VE TAKEN THESE SEEDS (EASTERN PHILOSOPHY, SURFING, MY RELATIONSHIPS) AND HAVE GROWN WITH THEM!!

3/04

181

Endless Summer

...or 'how Kirk spent a portion of his summer vacation in Hawaii with Metclub webmaster Niclas Swanlund.'

KIRK: It was an incredible time, seven days in Hawaii, seven surf sessions. Saw a lot of waves, caught 'em, did a lot of paddling. My back is about to fall apart but it is well worth it. We came here at a certain level, and left much better than we came.

NIC: Which was your favorite day?

KIRK: Chun's Reef, on the North Shore, chest high, clean waves and a lot of juice, did really well, it was great. Yesterday was really good too. A little bit bigger that than the last time we were there.

NIC: Do you remember your best wave, did you have an "epic" one?

KIRK: Yes, at Chun's Reef. A nice big wave, peeling nice and I was just riding it on top of the world. It had a lot of speed and I totally felt in control of my board and of the wave. What can I say, we have to come back!

NIC: And the next trip is planned for?

KIRK: Mexico, Santa Barbara, Costa Rica, Fiji, Bali or wherever...(with a BIG smile on his face). You name it, we will be there!

"That's a bit of a shit sandwich isn't it?"

by Lars Ulrich

Somehow the most commonly used phrase on this trip seems at its most appropriate right now. I am about a third of the way in on the Going-to-the-Sun Road (Glacier National Park, Montana). On my left behind me is Heaven's Peak at 8987 feet. On my left in front of me is Going-to-the-Sun Mountain at 9642 feet. In front of me on my right is a great big fuckin' lake. From where I am right now in my Suburban, that fucking lake looks — and more importantly, FEELS like it's at sea level — you do the fuckin' math. I'm driving with my family what feels like inches away from a straight vertical drop down of thousands of feet on a road that feels like, and is probably not far from, six feet wide, built 65 years ago. I'm feeling a bit dizzy wondering what the fuck I'm doing here.

Me and my big mouth. Me and my bright ideas. Let's go exploring. >>>

'm getting off an airplane in Salt Lake City being greeted by a tall skinny guy with black hair and thick southern accent going: "Hi, I'm Jeff. I'm your driver."

Almost 15 minutes later, we were in some nondescript parking lot outside the airport staring at the blackest, biggest, shiniest, most 'fuck you,' over the top tour bus I'd seen (at least paid attention to) in years. It turns out this fucker (the bus, not the driver) was two weeks old and was basically on its maiden voyage. There were more bells and whistles in this thing than you can fuckin' imagine; from walls that extended, ceilings that raised, DVD players and satellite TV blaring away on 50-inch color monitors, refrigerators, toilets, beds, bunks, blah, blah, blah... a little overwhelming for a guy who has a hard time accessing his e-mail, but paradise on earth for a three-year-old who instantly takes over every bunk and turns them into Fort-something-or-other; and for a mom who wants to sit with said three-year-old's new little brother and read all about solving medical problems facing mankind. In other words, this looks like it has all the potential for a good month of family time.

Fast forward two weeks, and the fuckin' bus isn't fucking allowed in Glacier National Park. Who's fucking bright idea was this? Actually, that's a bit of a stretch of the truth. It isn't allowed on that particular part of Going-To-The-Sun Road. Thank fuck for my friends Steve and Trish following in my Suburban close behind, in case, you know, in case... ehhh... the fucking thing's too big, too wide, too OTT. And boy, does it ever attract attention. I think I conveniently forgot about that part of Tour Bus Travel. It attracts attention. It might as well carry a banner that screams "come follow the Metallica guy around on his vacation!"

All right, no complaining here. It's all good, as they say. Just trying to paint the whole picture for ya.

A short shift. The idea of doing a day-by-day diary repulses me (those can be found elsewhere in your wonderful fan club magazine), so to live up to the reputation that somehow precedes me, I will instead proceed with some more verbal diarrhea (not unlike what you have already read) of some of the high, low and sidelites of the trip over the next few pages. The other thing I will not do is caption any of the pictures which somehow seems very trite to me at this moment in time. So here goes...

If you ever find yourself in the middle of a big fucking lake, stuck with a jet-ski that has become inoperable, here's what NOT to do: Do not tow the jet-ski behind a speed boat with a rope tied around the jet-ski's steering column! It will get dragged underwater immediately as far down as the tow line is long. I

can confirm this, because it happened to me one wonderful afternoon, while water-skiing/jet-skiing on Flathead Lake in Montana. Oh, and by the way, second piece of advice: do not go over water-ski tow-lines with your jet-ski, because they get sucked into the inner bowels of the machine, never to be seen again, and in some indirect way make the above mentioned scenario possible.

There we were, innocently enough enjoying ourselves, when in the space of 20 minutes, the following shit went down: Your moronic drummer and his friend Steve were horsing around when the moronic drummer, in the excitement of the moment, went right over the tow-line with the jet-ski, got the tow-line tangled in his jet-ski engine, was unable to go anywhere, decided to let the speedboat tow them into shore, tied another rope around the steering column of the jet-ski, sat on the jet-ski, and as the ski-boat started moving, within seconds was at least 10 feet underwater in Flathead Lake. I mean, it was really amazing. As soon as we started moving, I went straight down. I came up first, followed a few seconds later by an upside-down, water-filled jet-ski, which presumably would currently be residing at the bottom of Flathead Lake if it wasn't for the fact it had been tied to the boat. I will say in retrospect that one of the more interesting sights on this trip was the look of disbelief, bewilderment and a little bit of 'are you completely out of your fucking mind?' on the face of the jet-ski's owner's son, when he arrived at the scene of the crime about an hour later, wondering how he was gonna explain this to his dad. Pros at work!

You know what's really whacky (I'm sure some of you parents out there can relate to this)? It's really whacky when you're on a five mile hike up (UP!!) a mountain and your oldest kid, who weighs 41 pounds, decides about half-way that he doesn't want to walk anymore. That one always gets me!! The reasonable question of course would be why anybody with half a brain would wanna hike up a mountain with a three-year-old, but on that particular morning, hiking up Big Mountain, in Whitefish, Montana seemed like the right thing to do. You know, I guess it's what people do on ski hills in the summer. They hike up and take the fucking gondola/ski-chair down and everybody's happy. But man, carrying Myles up a fucking downhill ski run on my shoulders was a bit more than I bargained for, when I agreed to Skylar's request that morning. Like I said, it was a five mile plus hike, mostly along blue and black runs and about halfway up, he said, as would most three-year-olds with any sense, "Fuck this!! Daddy, carry me!" At that point you're stuck with two choices, getting on with it or not moving. It should be noted here, in all fairness, that Skylar was already ferrying Layne (our three-month-old) in a Baby Bjorn, as part of her "post pregnancy workout"

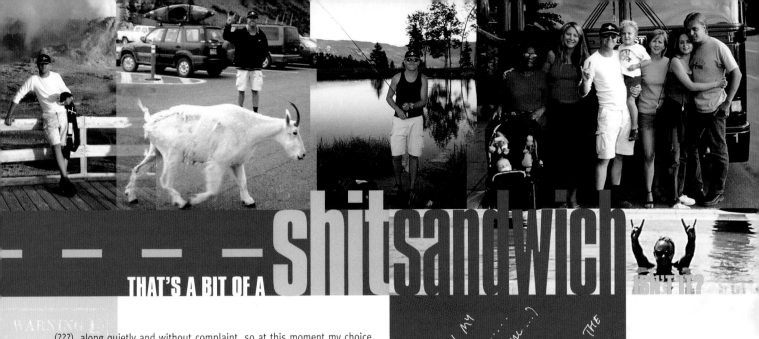

(???), along quietly and without complaint, so at this moment my choice was...not really a choice! A few hours later we made it to the summit, greatly in need of never doing this again. I can say I've never ridden down (DOWN!!) a mountain in a ski chair, but this was the first time and I was damn proud.

I could (also) tell you about the merry-go-round in Missoula; I could tell you about the desolate downtown of Butte, Montana; I could tell you about hanging out with the guys from Teton Gravity Research, getting up to very little good; about tree swings in Idaho over a lake that made me and Skylar feel like 14-year-olds again; about a full-on authentic rodeo in Jackson, Wyoming; about the beauty of the moonlight reflecting on the bus in Bumfuck, Idaho courtesy of the Salmon River; about how fucking hilarious it is to walk around amongst mountain goats in parking lots at the top of nowhere; about the tackiness of the zebra-striped bedspread in the tour bus; about how cool it is for a guy like me to drive in this tour bus across great big deserted flat lands at the foot of the Rocky mountains and literally not see other vehicles for 30 minutes at a time on a state highway; about how cool it is, once again for somebody like me, to wake up in a Travelodge hotel at some place in Western Montana not knowing where you're going to bed that night; about sneaking Vodka tonics into Montana's largest water park and spending hours on the 'rollercoaster bullet speed slide;' about going horseback riding in the Wyoming wilderness and wondering what would happen if we got trapped by the ginormous thunder storms that looked like they were going to envelope us at any time; about using Myles' love for Taco Bell and McDonalds as a cheap excuse to eat there myself; and about a friend of mine who has an amazing piece of property in a secret location in this tri-state area that I can't even give you a hint about... BUT I WON'T!

I think we've taken up just about enough space with this nonsense. What I will tell you though, is how awesome this experience was, how many great places we saw, how fucking cool people in this part of America are and how great it was to be back in a tour bus again, even though we pussied out and never actually stayed overnight on it!

Thanks to the cast of shady characters: Jeff, our magnificent bus driver, my friends Steve and Trish, Merle, Lynette, Francine, Layne, Myles and Skylar. But this article is dedicated, with love and appreciation, to the most invaluable member of the team, who as I'm writing this right now is probably only minutes away from his daily ritual of praying that I never, ever decide to undertake a trip quite like this again... Mr. Richard Joseph.

C-ya in a bit,

WHAT I DID ON MY
SUMMER VACATION.......
(ASIDE FROM EAT TACO BELL...)
OR ALSO KNOW AS...
THE METALSIGN ON TOUR IN THE
MOUNTAIN TIME ZONE...

LARS & KIRK

THE SO WHAT! INTERVIEW 2001

T he following chat with Lars and Kirk took place in Hammett's basement games room during late November 2001. It had, indisputably, been an annus horribilus for both of them. Jason Newsted had officially quit as the year began, and steaming progress had then been achieved on a new album before James Hetfield suddenly announced he was taking off for rehab and didn't know when he'd be back. Furthermore, due to a sense of uncertainty within themselves, Lars and Kirk hadn't been speaking about the band or anything publicly, leading to strong rumors that the band was close to breaking up. This was the first time either had spoken at length about Metallimatters since James had entered rehab.

Editor – January 2004

So, January 2001. How did you expect the year to pan out?

KH: I thought 2001 was going to be a great fucking year, you know? I thought 2000 was pretty good for us, you know, moderate, good, had a lot of time off. I thought 2001 would be very fruitful, but it's all turning into a big pile of shit! We were going to do it all! We were going to record, we were going to tour, we were going to continue as a band as usual, go on our merry way and do things like they always had been going...

Let's back up a bit and discuss some of the events which led up to this strange year. Obviously the Jason departure is perhaps the main one.

LU: ...From when we played the last of the six make up shows in Dallas, Atlanta, and Kentucky (late summer 2000), there were only two times that the four of us were together in one space. The third week in September, when we were doing the 'Black' album thing (a TV documentary was being filmed about the making of that album – ED), and then again in Los Angeles in late November when we were doing the VH1 Awards thing. Those are the only two times we were together. It was clear from the unfolding of events in Los Angeles for the 'Black' album thing that there was some serious stuff that needed to be resolved, because that was basically when the whole thing came to a head between James and Jason. So, when we started the year in January, we had a lot of cleaning up to do, and I think it was unclear for me what the long-term picture of the band was. What was clear for me was that we were at a point where, in order for things to move forward, there had to be a lot of resolving. And then at the same time, I'd say the worst two months in my personal life were November and December of 2000. So in January the band things were just starting to turn the corner, but I was still very wrapped up in my personal life.

KH: You know, I could feel tension in the air when we were down in Hollywood doing the "Black" album thing. I could feel the tension between James

and Jason and it was kind of a scary thing, you know? Because in the past neither of them had very much success communicating properly, and this was a much more serious thing than any of the issues that they had failed to communicate about in the past. So, frankly, I was a bit nervous because Jason came up to me at one point and said, 'James wants to speak to me' and Jason was pretty freaked out. I mean, he was practically shaking. It had everything to do with Echobrain and nothing else. And so I left, I had to make a couple of stops before I got to the airport, but when I got to the airport I saw Jason in the bar and I went over to him and said, 'hey man, how are you doing?' He goes, 'I'm doing all right, our flight's delayed by two hours.' So, he proceeded to sit down and talk to me about the meeting and it was pretty depressing, you know. Hearing Jason's perspective. And he was very, very bummed out. And that kind of set my mind racing and in the next few months when I saw everyone again for the VH1 thing in November, you know, frankly I was nervous to see all four of us in one spot. I was nervous to see what sort of... what was going to happen, what this thing was going to parlay itself into. And we all kind of got the word from Cliff and Peter that we were going to have a band meeting, a management-imposed band meeting so that we could talk things out. But after the VH1 thing, Jason just left and I was very hurt by that and I know James was pretty hurt, too. I mean, if I remember correctly he was pretty floored by that and I knew Lars was pretty hurt by it, too. And by the time the holidays went by, New Years went by, I knew that we were heading towards pretty stormy waters. And, I knew that the next six months or so were going to be interesting.

LU: I think there was one thing that happened, which was my real first involvement with any of this nastiness... in some perverse way, it's sort of interesting how little I had to do with this whole thing, and I have to tell you it puts a rare smile on my face... but anyway, in mid-October, we were offered to play this new VH1 award show. And I remember that Peter Mensch called, and all of us individually said 'yes,' except Jason. He told Mensch 'no,' he didn't want to do it. That was the first indication that there was something sort of amiss. So, I called up and had a nice chat with him and he agreed to do it. But it was pretty clear that something was not right, but what WAS going on, was that we all knew that we had to deal with these issues at some point. **(Lars addresses the following to Kirk – ED)** The only thing I'm not sure of is when you said that there was a management-imposed meeting, I'm not sure. I'm still trying to remember if that is correct or not.

KH: Yeah, that's fuzzy.

LU: I can't remember if the idea of this meeting was something that Jason called, or we called, or whatever, but the whole idea, and this is where it gets a little tricky, is that we knew something was amiss and we wanted to sit down and deal with it there and then. But Jason specifically did not want to have a set meeting until after the holidays, because he did not want to have the meeting...

KH: Ruin our holidays.

LU: Ruin everybody's holidays.

So, of course that leaves you guys hanging in the air?

LU: Look, I'm not agreeing/disagreeing with that. Probably, in retrospect, it was not such a bad thing, but with the whole VH1 thing, where things got rapidly worse... he didn't want to do it in the first place, I had to talk him into doing it, and then the whole thing that went down when he was there... I remember when me and James came off stage, it was at some point in the next 30 minutes following the performance when we had a moment together, just me and him, and we sort of looked at each other and locked eyes, and we acknowledged to each other that that was probably the last time we ever played with Jason Newsted live in front of people. And we both knew from the fact that he didn't walk in with us, the fact that he didn't sit with us, the fact that he basically was just a physical presence, except for the performance which was obviously required of him, we knew that something was terribly amiss. But he purposely did not want to deal with any of this until January.

Let me bring it to early March, when we did the chat for issue one of 2001, and you guys were roaring at that point. How much of that was bravado, how much of that was you taking for granted that Metallica was an indivisible name and force that would continue regardless and then how much were you completely floored when the James situation arrived?

KH: Well for a start, it wasn't like all of a sudden one day we grouped up and decided to go into the studio. I mean there was a lot of groundwork that was laid down before that. We had gotten some outside help with Phil **(Towle – the performance coach hired by the band to help mediate all matters business and personal – ED)** and kind of laid out to each other what we really felt and what the band really meant to us... and how it felt to be without Jason and how much we missed him and how much it hurt, and we spent a lot of time just kind of working that part of the situation until we felt comfortable enough to actually feel good about playing. And as soon as the opportunity came, and the Presidio came along, and we got the studio up and running, we were in there, literally, that night.

And by the time we went back into the studio, and I can only speak for myself, I felt totally re-energized. I felt so happy to be with these two other guys and playing music and have Bob Rock on bass just filling in, I can't say just filling, because it's more than that, but just to have Bob on bass it was a great thing, it felt like we had some semblance of normalcy back and it was an amazing era. I think it's some of the best stuff we've done in the last year or two. *(laughing)* In the last six months! *(laughing hysterically)* No, I think it's very, very inspiring music and it's not like anything we've ever done and our whole approach to it had changed and I thought it had really shone through. It really came through.

LU: I think you were hinting that the lunch we had in San Rafael that day (last round-table conversation)... that you felt maybe we were trying to hide something, and that what we were saying that day was just hot air... I think that so much of the year was just... you know, a big part of making music together is also being together and acknowledging and celebrating and applauding those relationships that exist within the three of us. And I think we realized that there was a lot of work that needed to be done on that front. So, in order to get to the point of being comfortable playing music together, there was some sort of process and some sort of thing that had to happen before that. Nobody could put a time frame on it, it wasn't something that was easily marked on a calendar, it was more about when the time was right, when we would feel it. We were in the thick of that when we saw you in March in that restaurant, and that continued for a while.

There was one event in early May that put the only time frame in our calendar, and that was the birth of Ulrich baby number two. That meant that in the middle of April, when we were starting to get to the point where playing music was only moments away, all of a sudden it was like 'wait a minute, we're not going to do anything much this month because of this birth happening...' So, it was either we would start right then or we would

FROM A FAN PERSPECTIVE IT LOOKS LIKE WE'VE TAKEN A LOT OF KNOCKS, AND GRANTED WE HAVE TAKEN OUR SHARE OF KNOCKS THIS YEAR, BUT THE SACRIFICES WE HAVE MADE ARE ULTIMATELY FOR THE GOOD OF THE BAND.

wait another six to eight weeks 'til we were on the other side of this birth. And that's when there was a great moment where, I think in true Metallica fashion, the troops rallied and everything got turned around literally within a week. We found a place to play with The Presidio building. The headquarters building that we had been working on for the last year was still not ready, and when you've gotta play, you've gotta fucking play! So, this interim place ended up being everything that it needed to be, which was great. But the key thing was, that we all felt that there was a lot of stuff that needed to happen before we were going to be in a room playing together.

A LOT OF BAGGAGE TO BE CLEARED BETWEEN...

LU: No, no, not 'baggage.' To me that word has a negative connotation. To me the baggage was out of the door by late January, mid-February and then it became about emphasizing the positive, embellishing the relationships, taking it further, re-getting to know each other...

KH: Reconnecting!

LU: ...Reconnecting, re-opening up at a whole different level to each other in terms of our vulnerabilities... and being completely void of any kind of barriers or facades to each other. In retrospect, I think it was the closest we've ever come to not having any of that stuff with each other.

THAT'S WHERE I HAVE TO ASK, FROM THE WORK THAT YOU DID WITH PHIL, DID ANY OF YOU GET ANY INKLING OF WHAT WAS AROUND THE CORNER WITH JAMES' SITUATION?

LU: Once again, I have to go back to the same answer I gave you before... can I answer that question without knowing what I know now? I think in retrospect the seeds were all there. It was going through that process... especially for James, exposing himself to these different ways of thinking, and being more and more comfortable throughout the spring time... being open about one's own perception of one's weaknesses and somebody else's interpretation of their weaknesses, those are two very different things by the way...

THAT'S A GOOD DISTINCTION.

LU: Right, through the course of that, the groundwork and the seeds were sort of sown for him to really go away and re-address everything in his life from a new perspective. So, in retrospect, I would say that when he walked into the studio that day I was not that shocked. **(The day JH told the band he was going to go to rehabilitation—Ed.)** I had sensed that in the maybe three to five days leading up to it, his head was not in the same place that it had been since we started writing and recording. We started in mid-April, took about three weeks off for Layne's birth, but the three days

before he went away in, I think, mid-June, there was something that was amiss in his eyes. Other than that, there were really no signs of what was up.

KH: Well, you know with our conversations with Phil, we had these sessions where they were very, very open. I mean we were just really, really brutally honest, talked openly about our childhoods, how they affected us as adults and as a group and there was a lot of groundwork that led up to each one of us dealing with our own individual issues and how that related to each other as a band. You know, I could see it clearly now, but back then we were all kind of dealing with our individual issues, and I think that kind of got the ball rolling with all of us. It especially got the ball rolling with James, which led him to, I think, coming to his conclusion. But there were some events that leading up to that that made it very evident that there was something wrong in the Hetfield camp. He was silent, he was a bit distant and I think we all know James enough to know that when he's like that something is brewing. You can definitely sense it and at one point he stormed out...

LU/KH: ...he stormed out of the studio!

KH: And we were all kind of shocked because we had been working for the past seven or eight weeks toward not reacting like that...

LU: Yeah, it was like Hetfield 1988.

KH: Yeah, it was a total regression and we were all blown away, but then he came back and we talked it out, and then a couple of days later he told us what he needed to do. To a certain extent I was surprised, but I wasn't so surprised because we had been headed toward that direction. Things had been revealing themselves, and to me it felt like this was just like another thing being revealed in a time period where we were just learning a lot of things about ourselves.

LET ME ASK YOU, ONE OF THE THINGS THAT YOU MIGHT HAVE LEARNED FROM THE JAMES SITUATION...

LU: Can I just state the ultimate irony, and in the process, stop this from turning into a totally somber affair... that there are two members of Metallica present for this interview, which in some very surreal way means me and Kirk are the two functioning members of Metallica. ME AND KIRK!

KH: Exactly.

THE MEN WHO ONCE SHARED A KISS ARE THE ONES HOLDING THE FORT UP. (LAUGHING)

KH: Exactly. *(laughing)*

LU: Sometimes things are not what they seem, boys and girls, ladies and gentlemen! No, but seriously, it's an interesting thing to me, because I

I REMEMBER WHEN ME AND JAMES CAME OFF STAGE AFTER THE [VH1] PERFORMANCE. WE HAD A MOMENT TOGETHER JUST ME AND HIM. WE LOOKED AT EACH OTHER AND LOCKED EYES AND ACKNOWLEDGED THAT WAS PROBABLY THE LAST TIME WE WOULD EVER PLAY WITH JASON NEWSTED LIVE.

think it proves how shallow perception can be, and proves just how false some of the narrow definitions people in the hard rock world embrace, and cling on to, are. I would say that it certainly was a bit of an annoyance a few years ago, when people were sitting there talking about dividing Metallica into these two separate groups…

KH: More the metal guys and then the non-metal guys.

LU: The metal guys and the more free spirited.

KH: Very well put, Lars!

KH: Not only are we the two standing members…

LU: Outstanding. *(laughing)*

KH: Outstanding members… *(laughing)* BUT everyone would have thought that he and I would have been the main nominees for rehab, you know? That we would be the first in rehab…

Right. Right.

LU: Not that we probably shouldn't have gone many times! (laughing)

There we go! All right. Were you afraid that he (James) was going to split completely and the band would not stay together? Did you learn to live with that fear? And then what has your communication been like with James?

KH: (getting philosophical) The band could split apart tomorrow…

SC: In relative terms, OK?

LU: I would say two things. Yes, the band could split apart tomorrow. I would also say that it's not a decision that has solely rested in James' hands.

Great, great.

LU: Do you understand that?

Yes, I do.

LU: So, I would say that there definitely have been moments where I started numbing myself to that potential reality, and started trying to find ways of being comfortable with it. I wasn't sure where James was at. I wasn't sure where I was at, I wasn't quite sure where Kirk was at and nobody seemed to be really sure where the band was at. In the darkest moments of post-June and James dealing with his issues, nobody really knew what the future looked like. So, for me it became, 'if the future looks this way,' that's one option, and, 'if the future looks this and that way,' then maybe I'm not interested in being part of it. Do you know what I mean? It's about feeling that at all times you have an awareness of your own role in that equation…

What I do feel now… for me personally, it's behind me. I now feel much more optimistic about Metallica, because I feel much more optimistic about James. After looking him in the eye, hearing what he has to say, re-examining how I feel about everything that has gone on this year, my time spent with him and my interpretation of the things he said, I feel really positive. I feel great. A couple of months ago it was very difficult for me, on a personal level, to deal with not knowing what was going on, not being able to affect what was going on. It was difficult enough to be riding this incredibly creative wave for those couple of months, and one day for James to say, "I'm going away for five weeks." "OK, James, go away for five weeks and we'll see you at the end of July and we'll just continue right there." Fair enough. But then it became something more. We were holding some live dates for the Fall, the studio was sitting there literally with the power on, people were on standby 24/7, we had the web site launch

party, all this type of stuff, and then one by one these things just started dissipating to nothing. And James kept staying away longer and longer, and there was very little communication. And, by the time he got back in September, there was even less communication and things just got really frustrating. But since then communication has been re-established, and we have learned to not just be dependent on reacting to how he's doing, but also learning to cope and learning to readjust and re-align how we are doing ourselves with our own lives… which had become this really secondary thing. It was always about 'how is James doing, how is James doing, how is James doing??' And nobody ever sat there and said 'well, wait a minute how the fuck are you doing? How's Kirk doing? How's Bob Rock doing with all this? How are you guys dealing with what's going on?' Because we were, I think, just supposed to sit there and be completely un-phased with everything, just sit there and go, 'we are fine, we support our brother and whenever he is done with what he's doing, we'll be there.'

And of course in the bigger picture that is how we feel, and should feel. But it's impossible to go through the kind of ride that we've been through this year and not have thoughts, emotions, questions and feel bewildered dealing with the aftermath and the effects of all this stuff.

KH: My initial outlook was that he was going to disappear for five weeks and at the end of five weeks come back and everything would be great and we would start back up again. But of course that's not how it turned out, and when it looked like that wasn't going to be turning out the way it seemed I fell back into my mode of 'hope for the best but expect the worst.' And, after weighing out all the possible options that could happen in my puny little brain, I decided that I should really see, if something did happen with the band, if I could continue living. So I took the time out to just examine my life and see if I had enough of a life to carry me through this.

LU: That's a great way to put it.

KH: And, I discovered that I did have a life… I could have a life outside the band. In a weird sort of way, I needed this time for my own self to discover that because I never, ever sat down and really faced that. I used that time to find out that yes, I did indeed have a life outside the band, and when I found that out I came to a sort of peace with myself. And I realized that for this to happen James needs time, and I'm fine with that and I will continue living my life and whatever happens I will be ready for it and I'll deal with it accordingly. But in the meantime, I'm not going to sit there and ruminate about everything and drive myself crazy, which I have done during different situations in the past.

LU: Can I just say that I really second that. That's very eloquent and I really agree with that… for me there also came a point a couple months ago when I realized that I was not afraid. And when I was not afraid, when that fear factor of feeling uncomfortable went away, I felt confident enough in myself as a person, as a father, as a partner and as a creative human being to be able to not only survive a Metallica meltdown, but also rise from one and shine in my own way.

Do you think that has helped James in the long run?

KH: I told James that I was using this time very constructively. Like I said, I have every reason in the world to be thankful for this time because it brought me to my own kind of… it brought me to the crossroads and I made a decision. I mean, separate all of this stuff and that in itself is very liberating to me and so after that I was just fine with whatever happened. Over the course of time I felt angry, and a lot of that anger stemmed from the fact that we had these golden eggs that are the songs, the Presidio songs, and we couldn't act upon them, we could not see them through to full blossom.

LU: Yet.

KH: Yeah, yet. But other than that I was completely at peace with it and I relayed that to James. And when we had our conversation about that I instantly felt more optimistic about the future and it quieted down a lot of my fears. I knew that there was, indeed, a future for the band. It just gets better and better. I saw James, we both saw James last weekend, and he looked incredible. His eyes were clear, he had a serenity about him that I had only seen in his most relaxed times and it was surprising because we were out in public, and if you know James when he's out in public, in a public situation, he has his guard on...

HE'D SQUARE UP A BIT...

KH: Yeah you know, see the wide leg stance, the crossed arms, we all do it you know, but it was surprising, I was surprised to see him so relaxed, and again it told me a lot. Just in being in his presence spoke tons, more than words can say, and as cliché as that sounds it was just that.

LU: One other thing while we're talking about this important stuff today, and I believe I speak for Kirk also... I've never really been around anybody who went away to rehabilitate themselves.

KH: I've never had anyone so close to me go into rehab.

LU: I know a lot of people in a lot of bands that have been our peers have a lot more experience with this sort of thing than we do... and that in it-self was a difficult thing to deal with, even just in terms of what your own appropriate behavior in these types of situations could be or should be. Speaking for myself, I was definitely struggling a bit with my own role in this, whether to move closer and to try and help, push and instigate or to move back a few steps, to be passive and let the events unfold in front of me. And as at least you are probably aware of, my nature *(laughing)* is to do more of the former...

(LAUGHING) HAVE A HANDS-ON ROLE?!!

LU: Yeah, and try to help and instigate, you know, make things happen. So, sitting around watching events go on in front of me, and feeling kind of helpless about it, is not something I have a lot of experience with. So that was once again an eye-opening experience and, in retrospect, I'm happy to say, a precious and enriching one. So, I think there are so many ways to slice and dice everything that has happened in the last year. I don't want to be one of these people that sit and try and make only good stuff out of it all in interviews. If people out there think that we've had a shit year, I can see that. But I'm talking about experiences here that have been so enrich-ing on so many levels... that are maybe quite foreign to most of the people that just sit there and look at whether we released any, quote, 'product' this year, or whether we have performed live or whatever the fuck we had our hands in. In order for us to hopefully exist another 20 years as a band, we have to have these human experiences on this fucking journey, and we have to take time out for ourselves to fully realize these things and see them through. We have our own terms and our own time frames and our own ways, and people have to be respectful of that, people have to understand that...

KH: We have done a lot of band work, it's just not been musical.

LU: We've probably done more band work this year than in most of the last five... ●

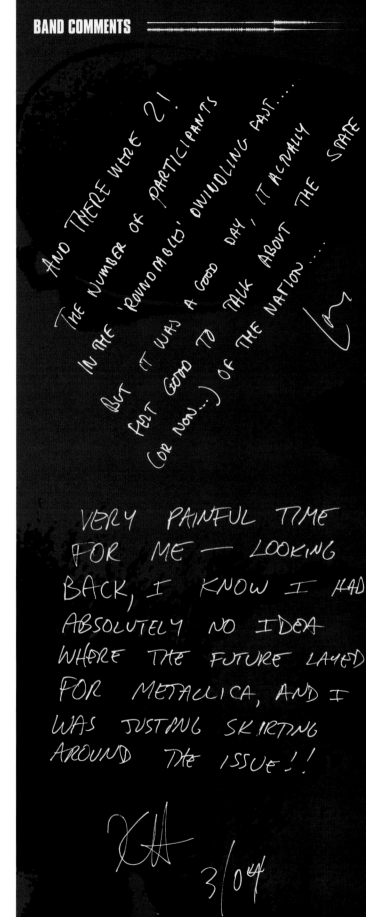

AND THERE WERE 2!.
THE NUMBER OF PARTICIPANTS IN THE 'ROUND ROBIN' DWINDLING FAST....
BUT IT WAS A GOOD DAY, IT ACTUALLY FELT GOOD TO TALK ABOUT THE STATE (OR NON...) OF THE NATION.....

VERY PAINFUL TIME FOR ME — LOOKING BACK, I KNOW I HAD ABSOLUTELY NO IDEA WHERE THE FUTURE LAYED FOR METALLICA, AND I WAS JUST/NG SKIRTING AROUND THE ISSUE!!

3/04

WHIPLASH

THE BAND ANSWERS FAN QUESTIONS

Lars – How do you say FUCK in Danish, or any other naughty words?
Mandy D., Gunnison, CO

LU: There isn't really a comparable word with as many uses as 'fuck' in the English language. The verb 'to fuck' would be either 'at kneppe' or 'at knalde.'

Metal Gods – I just had my first gig with a few buddies of mine and I got really nervous. So nervous that I forgot the second verse to "Seek & Destroy." Any tips to combat this?
Tim M., Excelsior, MN

KH: Just pretend you're playing to a bunch of ducks, chickens or geese. It works man...
LU: Cheat sheets...I heard they work!
JH: Delete all second verses live.

Considering your success, would you encourage your children to enter the music business? What three things would you do if you knew you couldn't fail?
Kate M., Echuca Australia

KH: 1- world peace; 2- world compassion; 3- welfare (as in well being) for everyone.
LU: I would never stand in the way of anything my children wanted to do naturally. As long as it wasn't forced I'd support it. 1- world champion nose-picker; (Achieved already — Ed) 2- describe every dressing room in every venue Metallica has ever played (Achieved already — Ed) 3- be the last person on Planet Earth to know how to operate a computer (For Christ's sake man, achieved alre... Ed)
JH: I will encourage them to play instruments and enjoy music. Not necessarily the music business. 1) write music; 2) sing; 3) play guitar.

Have any of you at any stage ever met someone that you're a real fan of and been totally tongue-tied?
Sarah C., Ireland

KH: When I met Eric Clapton, I repeated every sentence I said to him twice.
LU: I feel completely comfortable and on the level with any other famous person these days, being so famous myself. (Listen carefully and you can hear my eyes rolling! — Ed)
JH: Phil Lynott of Thin Lizzy. The only sounds I could produce were caveman grunts.

I've been drinking a shitload of brew these past few years and now I have a nice gut. How the FUCK do the 3 of you drink so much and stay so thin? Maybe it's all the hell you raise across the world.
Danny R., Staten Island, NY

KH: Satan is my trainer.
LU: Balance it out with large quantities of cocaine... (Steffan, are we pushing it with the sarcasm here?) (Maybe – alarmed Ed)
JH: We get so drunk we forget to eat.

As a woman I often wonder about the "romantic" side of my "Metalli-Gods!" How did you AND where did you propose to your wives?
Gina T., New Orleans, LA

KH: I was at a restaurant and some asshole was screaming from three tables down how much he hated "Load." The people he was with were very embarrassed for him. I was just trying to eat my dinner when all of a sudden my wife proposed to me. I was so happy I started crying. But it probably looked like I was crying because the guy was talking shit about the album. When she asked, instead of saying 'yes' I said 'of course...'
LU: Which one? (We have officially hit a new low... Ed)
JH: I hid the ring under a dead elk in the garage and told her to skin it.

Lars: I know you have been a fan of a group called Diamond Head. I've been collecting classic metal bands from the tail end of 1979, which was considered the British metal invasion. Could you recommend a song or album by them?
Chris S., Columbus, OH

LU: Sure. "Lightning To The Nations" is where it starts and ends at the same time. The original version is the one to go after. There's a remixed version of that record called "Behold the Beginning." The first record they put out on MCA called "Borrowed Time" is strong, and some of the compilation albums of their early recordings, such as "Am I Evil?" are also worth having. For a general overview of the best of the British Metal Invasion may I humbly suggest the record I compiled in 1990 titled "N.W.O.B.H.M '79 Revisited" and thank you very much for asking.

Jaymz: Did you get to choose the car you drove in the 'I Disappear' video clip? What kind of car was it? It kicks ass!!!
Nerissa S., New Zealand

JH: Yup, I drove the '67 Camaro straight into my garage!

Do you guys have any REALLY embarrassing moments that happened while you were in school? Do share! Do share!
Lisa D, Long Beach, NY (or is it LA?)

JH: Wut is skool meenz?
KH: I flunked religion in 5th grade which was especially bad because I was at a Catholic school. The faculty took notice. It was a pre-requisite to all my Mercyful Fate and Venom records plus my future in metal. I was also busted by nuns for many other things that didn't jive with my schooling.
LU: In the fall of 1975 I got some platform boots that were very similar to what Ritchie Blackmore was wearing at the time, and I was very proud of these until the other kids started teasing me and calling me 'Smoking Joe.'

Guys: If confronted with the Knights of "NE," would you search for a shrubbery?
Keith B., Scotland

JH: South American or African?
KH: Only if I got to cut it down with a herring.
LU: What would The Spanish Inquisition say?

Kirk: When the Loma Prieta quake hit the Bay Area on October 17, 1989, were you all out on tour, or were you all at home? Did your homes and family fare o.k.?
Tracy P., Seattle

KH: I was lying naked on the floor waiting for the World Series to begin. It was the first time I was ever interested in the WS so I thought I'd lie on the floor naked...I won't go into it, that was 1989. When the house was shaking, I managed to run to the back of the house with one leg in a pair of pants and the other leg struggling to get a leg into the pant. Then it stopped and I was only wearing one pant leg. (Ed — but did you remember to put underwear on first?)

Lars: What's the weirdest thing a fan has ever said to you?
Ray B., Polk City, FL

LU: I think our definitions of the word 'weird' might be a little different, but somewhere in-between, 'I'd be really honored if you'd fuck my girlfriend' and 'Why are you fighting Napster?'

Lars & James – What music rocks the worlds of your little ones at this point?
Ginna D., Lansdale, PA

JH: Soundtrax to the Rugrats, Tarzan and The Lion King ... oh, and the new 'Grave Worm' demo.
LU: Anything associated with "Blues Clues." 'I Disappear' is his favorite Metallica song.

If you weren't a musician, what would you be?
Kelly L, Indianapolis, IN

JH: Some guy trying to be a musician.
KH: I don't know, I honestly don't know. A tree? Who knows. Anything I think I might have been is all just speculation.
LU: The drummer in Metallica!

James & Kirk – When your hair was long, did it ever get caught in the strings of your guitar while onstage?
Debbie P., Oak Lawn, IL

JH: Yes, that's why it's short now. It all got ripped out.
KH: Not the strings but the tuners. The worst thing is having to get rid of gum on stage because you try to spit it out and it goes straight into your hair. Then you either cut it out or sit with it.

I like to travel a lot and obviously will never get to visit all the places that you guys have been, but out of all the things you've seen and done – what is the one thing that really stands out? How did you meet your significant others?
Kim B., Richmond, KY

JH: I said "Hi."
KH: There's this bar in San Francisco that's pretty incredible and, oh yeah, that's where I met my significant other.
LU: San Francisco. 'I'm a really rich and famous rock star. Can I buy you a drink?'

What do you individually feel is your best physical attribute?
Vanessa A., Brownsville, TX

LU: Both me and Kirk have incredible 'power alleys...'
KH: Yup.

Is there a song, which at the time of writing you thought was great, but now that you've developed more, you can't see what was so great about it, and do you still play it?
Phyllida S., Larbert, Stirlingshire, Scotland

KH: I don't think any of our songs are crap but some songs endure a lot more than others.
LU: I have a lukewarm relationship with a song called 'Until It Sleeps.' Some nights I like it, some nights I question it and most nights, the only reason I'd leave it in the set list was because Jason kept asking me to take it out.
KH: I still like the song...

So Lars, The Hills Run Red, eh?
Alberto U., Malaga, Spain

LU: Nice one, good memory! That's many vodka tonics ago. That was actually 'The Hills Ran Red,' and if my memory serves me correct, it was the skeleton for the song that ended up being 'Leper Messiah.'

What other member of the band would you want to be if you had to pick one, and why?
John L., Syracuse, NY

KH: I wish I was Lars so I could write the set list.
LU: Linda McCartney, no, strike that. Um, Bon Scott.
KH: I thought it was 'in Metallica...'
LU: In Metallica? Oh...
KH: I wish I could be James so as I could bark 'hoooaarggh' all the time.
LU: I wish I could be Kirk so as I could point at people, hit a chord and then raise my right hand.

How would you have reacted if you had listened to 'Nothing Else Matters' in 1983?
Bounous Y., Cannes, France

KH: The question is how would YOU have reacted?
LU: Probably kicked James out of the band!
KH: Cliff would've loved it. He had a real melodic sense. He got us listening to Simon & Garfunkel for God's sake.

Why did you cut your hair?
David F., Swansea, Wales

KH: I didn't cut my hair, somebody else did.
LU: Incorrect use of tense. The question should read 'why DO you cut your hair.'
KH: True.
LU: Why do I shave, why do I eat, why do I bang one off?
KH: All I can say is why ask why?
LU: Dave, why were you born?

What is your birth time? I want to know your ascendant.
Bonnie L., Miami Beach, FL

LU: I believe I was born in the 4 a.m. vicinity.
KH: I was born sometime around 3–3:30 in the morning, and ascendant? That sounds like something you'd hear in an Iron Maiden song.

Jeg skriver til dig fordi jeg ikke skriver så godt engelsk, men spørgsmålet er til hele bandet. Jeg vil bare høre om man på det nye album kommer til høre noget i stil med 'Hit The Lights'. Jeg synes både at den gamle og nye stil er fed så jeg synes at det kunne være fed at kombinere de to stilarter. Men uanset hvad bliver det fedt at høre fra jer på forhånd tak.
lasse fra Danmark

LU: Tak, man. Det er sgu lidt tidligt at beskrive den nye skive, men du laeser det her først.

I read in SO WHAT! that core fans are trading Kirk's sweaty underwear. How did his underwear ever get to be traded?
Bonnie G., Miami Beach, FL

KH: On the Nasdaq or the Dow Jones?
LU: Ask some of our former wardrobe employees.
JH: I was strapped for cash... eBay/eButt... ●

9

...And now, another word from our sponsors

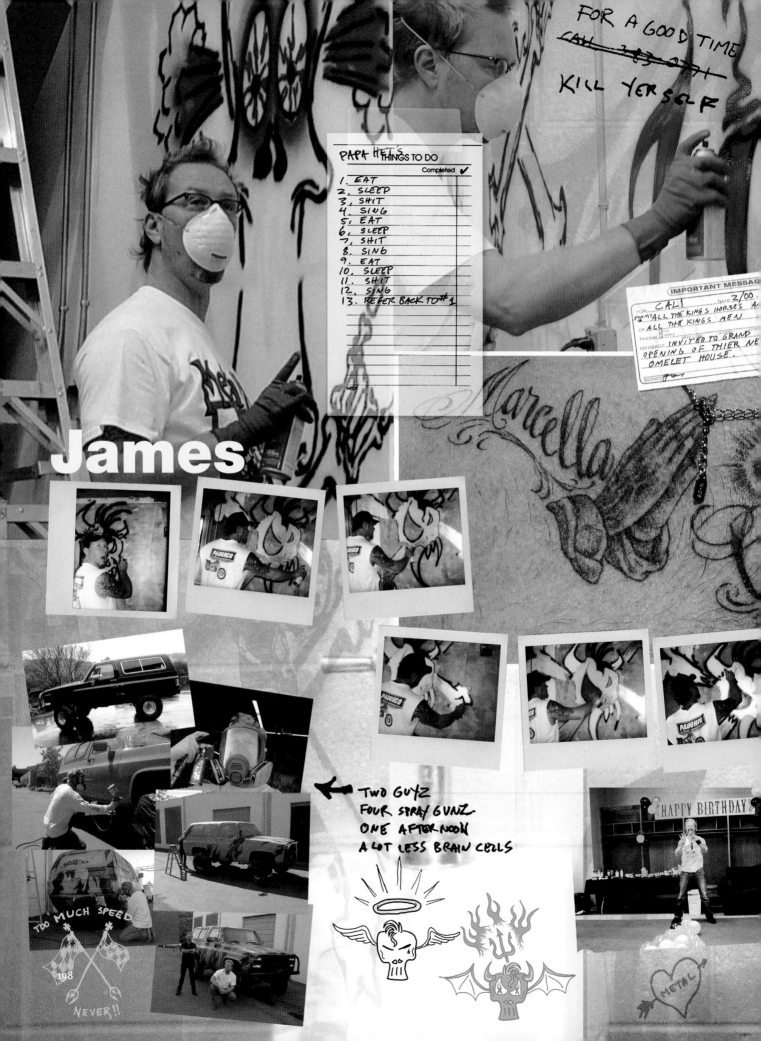

FOR A GOOD TIME
~~CALL 385 271~~
KILL YERSELF

PAPA HET'S THINGS TO DO

	Completed ✔
1. EAT	
2. SLEEP	
3. SHIT	
4. SING	
5. EAT	
6. SLEEP	
7. SHIT	
8. SING	
9. EAT	
10. SLEEP	
11. SHIT	
12. SING	
13. REFER BACK TO # 1	

IMPORTANT MESSAGE

FOR CALI   DATE 2/00
FROM ALL THE KINGS HORSES A
OF ALL THE KINGS MEN
MESSAGE   INVITED TO GRAND
OPENING OF THIER NE
OMELET HOUSE.
SIGNED

James

TWO GUYZ
FOUR SPRAY GUNZ
ONE AFTERNOON
A LOT LESS BRAIN CELLS

TOO MUCH SPEED

NEVER!!

198

HAPPY BIRTHDAY

METAL

that you want and like. Believe me, many people would ... they are not strang...

and ...

JH

I send you all my ... to see you soon in ...

2000 Die Weltausstellung 1.6. bis 31.10. 2000
Deutschland 100 HANNOVER EXPO2000
Deutschland 100 HANNOVER EXPO2000
ZENTRUM -6.01-20

... WANT ... TELL ... COULD WITH ALL MY LOVE AND SUPPORT TO GET
OVER WITH ALL YOUR PROBLEMS. I GUESS IT MUST BE PRETTY
HARD TO GET OVER AN ADDICTION, BUT YOU HAVE A LOTS OF REASON
TO KEEP FIGHTING AND KEEP GOING WITH YOUR LIFE, LIKE FOR EXAMPLE
YOUR FAMILY, YOUR FRIENDS AND IN ALL AND EACH ONE OF YOUR FANS
AND OF COURSE, ALL THE LOVE AND SUPPORT THAT YOU CAN FIND IN
EACH ONE OF US

I'm so sad to hear you're having
problems + that your recording is on hold.
Please get better soon - so you can
continue recording + go on tour soon.
Just remember how many people truly
love you + want you back!

You are a very inspirational person and I
hope you get through everything ok. I'm a huge
fan of you and your music and of Metallica
as well. GET WELL SOON!

CLEAN TOWELS

August 21-01..

Tallica James

This is for you James!

Hi James,

This is just a quick note to give you all my support and to animate you in this
difficult moments. All the Metallica family are with you and I hope that this
letter will help you a little bit, because first of all is James as person and
then, as an excellent musician.

I know that you are anxious to come back, but take your time. We will wait
for you the necessary. I hope to hear/see you soon on the road again with a
new strength, to still demonstrating what Metallica really is : the best and
biggest heavy metal band of the world (whatever critics will ever say the
opposite).

And I know that you will never quit. I know that you will never stop, 'cause
you are Metallica, man!

You will never walk alone, we always will be at your side.
Just take a look around.

Kind regards
Hugo Gallart Muñoz
Valencia, Spain

200

Luda Schumelova
Russia

08/09/01

Dear James

Let me express all my respect.
MY LOVE and support to you.
and about your problems. It influences
on my mind and worries me.

Dear James don't give in this shit to break
you. Be able to stand against this wind.

In other way you will be disappear.
I would like you know that they love

and think about you in far Russia.
Keep yourself guy. We need you.

I believe in you.

I love Metallica
I love you all.

PAR AVION

HELVETIA 400 2001

РОССИЯ 2.00 1998 ROSSIJA

Dear James,
My name is Livia, I'm 15 and I'm from Bucharest, Romania. I'm one of
your greatest fans and it would mean more than the world to me if you'd see
this.

About your problems, I'm sure you'll find a way to leave them behind
you. I mean, of course, this was the last thing you needed, but besides Lars,
Kirk, Jason, your family and your friends who are there for you, you got all
the fans all over the world supporting you.

So I wish you the very best and I hope that you'll be OK as soon as posible.
I wish there was more I could do for you, but 'cos there's not, I just send you
my best thoughts and I hope you'll be better soon.

YOU RULE!!
Love,
Livia

Love, Sunny
...love to you.

JAMES HERE & **ALIVE** AND GETTING WELL
WOW, WHERE DO I START? .... (HERE)

~~X~~ RECOVERY IS THE MOST DIFICULT AND CHALLENGING THING
I'VE EVER ATTEMPTED (ALONG WITH PARENTING). ALSO THE MOST
GROUNDING AND GRATIFYING GIFT I'VE EVER RECIEVED (ALONG
WITH PARENTING). I'VE SO MUCH TO SAY, I FEEL I'VE BEN AWAY
A LIFETIME.... IN A WAY I HAVE.

MY ROUGH ROAD HAS BECOME SMOOTHER READING THE
SHOW OF SUPPORT FROM THE FRIENDS WE MET THROUGH METALLICA.
I'VE ~~NEVER~~ NOT SEEN ~~AND~~ NOR FELT ~~THIS SUCH~~ POTENT ~~AND~~ REAL HEART
CONNECTING WORDS PUT TOGETHER AS THESE. THANK YOU.
THEY MOVE ME DEEPLY.

MY MUSIC AND LYRIX HAVE ALWAYS BEN A THERAPY FOR ME.
WITHOUT THIS GOD GIVEN GIFT I DONT KNOW WHERE I'D BE.
~~AND WHEN~~ AND NOW I _TRULY_ FEEL THE IMPACT AND CONNECTION

ITS MADE WITH OTHERS. STRUGGLE TO STRUGGLE. **PAIN TO ~~PAIN~~.**
HUMAN TO HUMAN, NOT IDOL TO FAN, FAN TO IDOL. CLARITY
HAS PUT ME IN A HUMBLE AND SERENE PLACE TO RECIEVE
THIS CONNECTION IN RETURN AND ~~FEEL~~ IT HELPING HEAL ME.
EVERY BREATH I TAKE BECOMES DEEPER AND MORE CONFIDENT
OF MYSELF WITHOUT MY CRUTCHES, THE LIES I'VE FILLED MY
BODY AND SOUL WITH **ARENT** ~~NEEDED~~ ANYMORE, ~~TODAY~~
THEY'RE **NOT WELCOME**. I CHOOSE TO LIVE NOT JUST EXIST.

I MISS YOU ALL SO MUCH. ~~AND~~ ~~AND~~ ~~I~~ AND I AM
AWAITING THE TIME THIS DEEPER CONNECTION I FEEL TO YOU WILL
BE IN PERSON.

LOVE & RESPECT,

NOV 2002

JAMES'S GRATITUDE LIST

* FOR MY HEALTH
* FOR MY FAMILY
* FOR MY _BAND_
* FOR MY _FRIENDS_
* FOR THOSE WHO HAVE HELPED ME LOOK INSIDE
* FOR JASON AND HIS DEDICATION FOR ALL THOSE YEARS
* FOR FANS WHO SUPPORT ME & METALLICA
* FOR FANS WHO DONT... AND WHAT THEY HELP US
  LEARN ABOUT OURSELVES
* FOR THE GIFT OF CREATIVITY
* FOR A **KICK-ASS** TEAM @ HQ
* FOR ANOTHER DAY TO GROW AND BE GRATEFUL ABOUT
* FOR THE AWARENESS TO WANT TO WRITE SUCH
  A LIST.. AND SHARE IT.

for being in the middle of time off, i'm tired…if you want a good time at the movies go see 'dancer in the dark' and 'requiem for a dream' back-to-back. both amongst the darkest, mos fucked up movies ever committed to whatever movies are committed to, celluloid maybe…wh do i find baseball's subway world series kinda interesting? i can't figure it out, but so far i've watched every minute of every game…i like it when it rains in northern california…should a 36 year old man drink as much as i do after having drank as much i have for the last 20 years?…what the fuck happened to the tampa bay bucs?…in the last month i've listened mor to disc 1 of 'garage inc.'…more than any other metallica cd in the last five years. why?…drop whatever you're doing, and go see a movie called 'the pledge' when it opens in decem- ber…what the fuck is up with the new radiohea album?…northern california has the best col- lection of radio stations anywhere in america.. here's a statistic that should tell you something about how fucked up i am. i, not counting

Lars

HEY,

JUST A QUICK LAST MINUTE NOTE ON THIS FUCKEN NAPSTER SHIT THAT HAS BECOME THE MAIN FUCKEN THING IN MY LIFE THE LAST COUPLE OF WEEKS.

YOU, OUR TRUE METALLI-FRIENDS, KNOW WE DON'T PICK A FIGHT WITHOUT A REASON AND WE REALLY FEEL THIS IS WORTH IT. I KNOW ALOT OF YOU ARE KINDA BEWILDERED AND CONFUSED ABOUT THIS SHIT AND TO BE HONEST, SOMETIMES SO AM I. BUT ALOT OF SHIT IS AT STAKE HERE. THIS IS NOT ABOUT MONEY, THIS IS ABOUT CONTROL AND CHOICE. WE NEVER HAD OR WERE GIVEN A CHOICE IN THIS MATTER AND SINCE IT'S OUR MUSIC, AND WE OWN IT, WE WANT TO CONTROL IT. SOME PEOPLE HAVE THIS STRANGE NOTION THAT THEY HAVE A RIGHT TO OUR MUSIC THRU' THE INTERNET

FOR FREE THRU' WHATEVER SERVICE PROVIDERS THEY CHOOSE AND THIS WHAT WE SO PASSIONATELY DISAGREE WITH. OVER THE LAST COUPLE OF YEARS, BECAUSE TECHNOLOGY HAS BEEN WAY AHEAD OF THE REST OF US, PEOPLE HAVE HAD THE PRIVILEGE TO ACCESS MUSIC THRU' THE NET, NOT THE FUCKEN RIGHT!! AND THIS IS THE FIGHT WORTH FIGHTING. WE WANT TO CHOOSE WHERE OUR MUSIC GOES AND WHAT HAPPENS TO IT, END OF STORY. OF COURSE THE FUTURE IS THRU' THE NET, BUT ON WHOSE CONDITIONS?? SO AS WE CONTINUE TO SEE WHERE THIS SHIT IS GOING, I JUST WANTED YOU ALL TO KNOW WE UNDERSTAND ALOT OF PEOPLES CONFUSION WITH THIS SHIT AND IN THE NEXT ISSUE WE WILL HAVE AN IN DEPTH Q&A ON THIS SHIT AND HOPEFULLY ALOT OF QUESTIONS WILL BE ANSWERED

MEANWHILE, THANX FOR YOU CONTINUED SUPPORT AND UNDERSTANDING AND TO THOSE OF YOU ARE AGAINST US, AT LEAST RESPECT OUR RIGHT TO DEAL WITH THIS THE WAY WE WANT TO, UNTIL WE COME TO A POINT THAT MAKES US, THE FANS AND THE SERVICE PROVIDERS HAPPY. WE FEEL, THAT ONCE MOST PEOPLE HAVE ALL THE INFORMATION AND TRULY UNDERSTAND THE BIG PICTURE AND WHAT'S AT STAKE HERE, THIS IS A FAIR POSITION WE HAVE TAKEN.

BEAR WITH ME 'TIL THE NEXT ISSUE,

LOVE

DATELINE APRIL SOMEWHERE I PART OF SAN F QUITE FAR F EH - PEOPLE KIRK HAMMETT THE HARDEST LAYING DOWN ON SOME WE JUST 'TA STUDI

202

Hey Kirk, I am sorry, dude! I couldn't resist! Nothing personal, you know that. Please don't be mad.

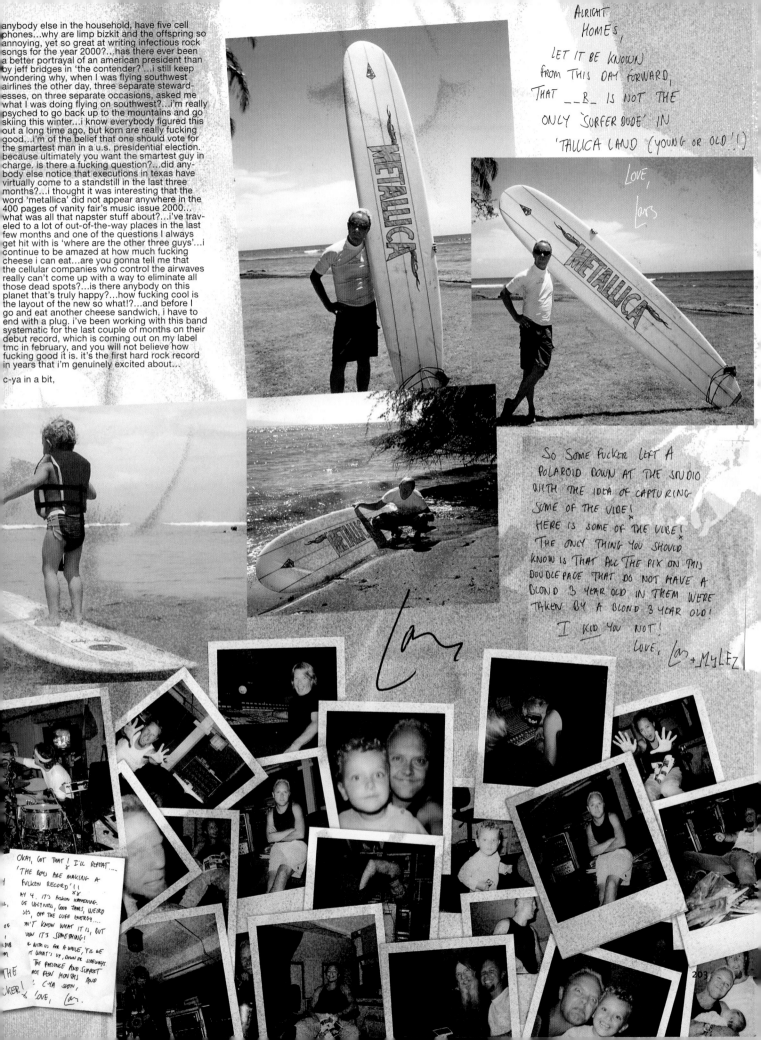

anybody else in the household, have five cell phones...why are limp bizkit and the offspring so annoying, yet so great at writing infectious rock songs for the year 2000?...has there ever been a better portrayal of an american president than by jeff bridges in 'the contender?'...i still keep wondering why, when I was flying southwest airlines the other day, three separate stewardesses, on three separate occasions, asked me what I was doing flying on southwest?...i'm really psyched to go back up to the mountains and go skiing this winter...i know everybody figured this out a long time ago, but korn are really fucking good...i'm of the belief that one should vote for the smartest man in a u.s. presidential election. because ultimately you want the smartest guy in charge. is there a fucking question?...did anybody else notice that executions in texas have virtually come to a standstill in the last three months?...i thought it was interesting that the word 'metallica' did not appear anywhere in the 400 pages of vanity fair's music issue 2000... what was all that napster stuff about?...i've traveled to a lot of out-of-the-way places in the last few months and one of the questions I always get hit with is 'where are the other three guys'...i continue to be amazed at how much fucking cheese i can eat...are you gonna tell me that the cellular companies who control the airwaves really can't come up with a way to eliminate all those dead spots?...is there anybody on this planet that's truly happy?...how fucking cool is the layout of the new so what!?...and before I go and eat another cheese sandwich, i have to end with a plug. i've been working with this band systematic for the last couple of months on their debut record, which is coming out on my label tmc in february, and you will not believe how fucking good it is. it's the first hard rock record in years that i'm genuinely excited about...

c-ya in a bit,

ALRIGHT
HOMES,

LET IT BE KNOWN
FROM THIS DAY FORWARD,
THAT __R__ IS NOT THE
ONLY 'SURFER DUDE' IN
'TALLICA LAND (YOUNG OR OLD'!)

Love,
Lars

SO SOME FUCKER LEFT A
POLAROID DOWN AT THE STUDIO
WITH THE IDEA OF CAPTURING
SOME OF THE VIBE!
HERE IS SOME OF THE VIBE!
THE ONLY THING YOU SHOULD
KNOW IS THAT ALL THE PIX ON THIS
DOUBLE PAGE THAT DO NOT HAVE A
BLOND 3 YEAR OLD IN THEM WERE
TAKEN BY A BLOND 3 YEAR OLD!
I KID YOU NOT!
LOVE, Lars + MYLES

OKAY, GOT THAT! I'LL REPEAT....
'THE BOYS ARE MAKING A
FUCKEN RECORD'!!
MY 4. IT'S FUCKEN HAPPENING...
DE UGLYNESS, GOOD JAMS, WEIRD
SES, OFF THE CUFF ENERGY...
DN'T KNOW WHAT IT IS, BUT
NOW IT'S SOMETHING!
WITH US FOR A WHILE, 'TIL WE
IT WHAT'S UP, DOWN OR SIDEWAYS
THE PATIENCE AND SUPPORT
AST FEW MONTHS AND
CKER! C-YA SOON,
LOVE, Lars.

203

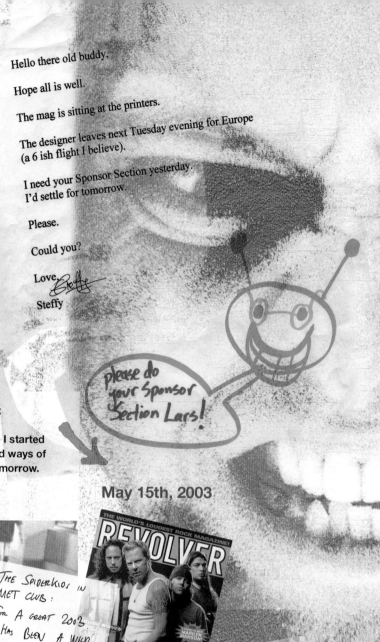

Hello there old buddy.

Hope all is well.

The mag is sitting at the printers.

The designer leaves next Tuesday evening for Europe (a 6 ish flight I believe).

I need your Sponsor Section yesterday. I'd settle for tomorrow.

Please.

Could you?

Love,
Steffy

please do your Sponsor Section Lars!

SC: Were you afraid that he (James) was going to split completely and the band would not stay together?
LU: I would say that there definitely have been moments where I started numbing myself to the potential reality, and started trying to find ways of being comfortable with it...yes, the band could split apart tommorrow.

May 15th, 2003

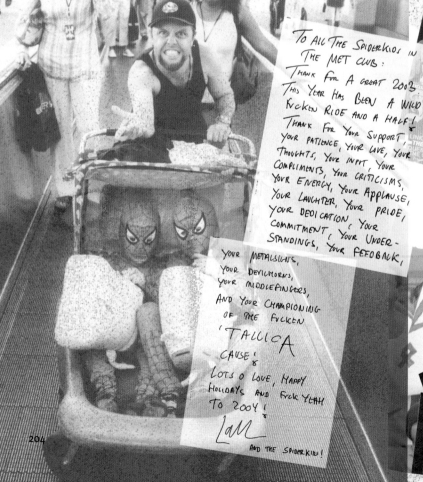

To All The Spiderkids in
The Met Club:

Thank for a great 2003!
This Year Has Been A Wild
Fucken Ride And A Half!
Thank For Your Support,
Your Patience, Your Love, Your
Thoughts, Your Input, Your
Compliments, Your Criticisms,
Your Energy, Your Applause,
Your Laughter, Your Pride,
Your Dedication, Your
Commitment, Your Under-
Standings, Your Feedback,

Your Metalsigns,
Your Devilhorns,
Your Middlefingers,
And Your Championing
Of The Fucken
'Tallica
Cause!
Lots o Love, Happy
Holidays And Fuck Yeah
To 2004!

Lars

And The Spiderkids!

A funny thing happened the other day. We were sitting around the studio and me and Bob were discussing film and the results of the 3200 B & W stock that Bob had turned me on to previously and James Hetfield, in a somewhat intimate moment, asked if he could have a look at a few of my pictures. So I showed him a few of my pictures. And that's when the funny thing happened. James Hetfield told me these were really good pictures. So we had a bit of a chat, and I told him that I was actually really enjoying a newfound creative element that came in the wake of taking pictures of my family and that it was pretty rewarding to up the ante a little and have a few somewhat 'artsy' moments thrown in there for good measure.

Fast forward three weeks. Hi, it's Steffan, where is your fu……(yawn!)." Here are some of those 'artsy' moments. Take that with you.

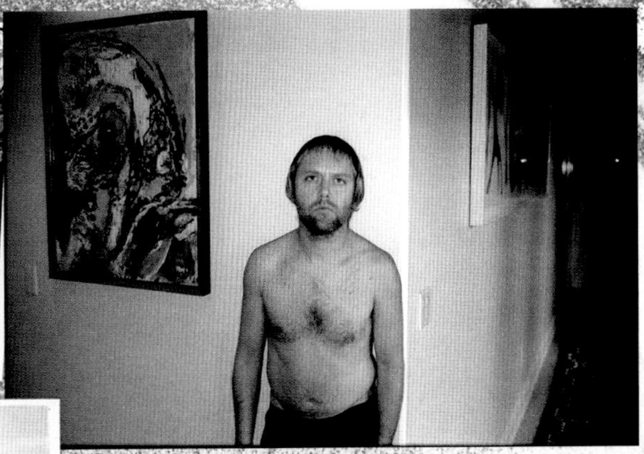

DID YOU EVER HAVE A HAIR DAY THAT WAS SO BAD, IT JUST HAD TO SHARED??

Love, Lars

205

Kirk

SUMMER SANITARIUM VACATION 2000
From the Krypt of **Kirk**!

A FEW GOOD BOOKS
The Heart of the Sea by Nathaniel Philbrick
The Church of Dead Girls by Stephen Dobyns
Hell House by Richard Matheson

SOME GOOD MUSIC
Moby – Play
Queens of the Stone Age
Korn – I really love these guys!
I Fuckin LOVE STEELY DAN and fuck off if you don't like it!!

And One Fuckin Great CAT
EVA, RIP 8/3/00

HOPE YOU
HAD A SCARY
HALLOWEEN !!
I KNOW I DID !!

KIRK'S TOP ELEVEN:

1. THE CALIFORNIA WINTER SURFING SEASON
2. HANGING OUT WITH MY HORSE RISKE
3. SURFING
4. JAZZ SAXOPHONIST CHARLES LLOYD
5. WORKING AND HANGING OUT
   WITH SWIZZ BEAT AND JA RULE
6. MY NEW ZEMAITIS GUITAR
7. DID I MENTION SURFING?
8. MY NEW WINGNUT SURFBOARD
9. METALLICA ACTION FIGURES
10. NEW GOV'T MULE - THE DEEP END
11. NEW SYSTEM OF A DOWN - TOXICITY

A TOP TEN LIST OF THINGS IN MY LIFE

1. MY NEW 9 FOOT SURFBOARD
2. MY NEW WET SUIT (THANKS O'NEIL !)
3. SMOKINGGUN.COM
4. PEDALMAN.COM
5. MY INDO BOARD (BALANCING BOARD THAT
   SIMULATES WAKEBOARDING, SURFING, SKIING, ETC.)
6. RAMONES ANTHOLOGY (GABBA GABBA HEY !)
7. JACKAL - THE COMPLETE STORY OF THE LEGENDARY
   TERRORIST, CARLOS THE JACKAL)
8. THE ZEN OF ARCHERY - PROFOUND WISDOM !
9. SWEET TEA   BUDDY GUY
10. DRINKING W/ BUKOWSKI - RECOLLECTIONS
    OF THE POET LAUREATE OF SKID ROW

SCORPTALLICA

KIRK'S TOP LIST

1. "THE SECRET HISTORY OF CONSCIOUSNESS"
   BY GARY LACHMAN
2. "28 DAYS LATER"
3. COLD STONE CREAMERY
4. SURFING W/O A WETSUIT!
5. EXTENDED VERSION OF
   "THE TWO TOWERS"
6. THE TAO OF HEALTH, SEX AND LONGEVITY
   BY DANIEL P. REID
7. "THE DA VINCI CODE" BY DAN BROWN
8. OUTKAST'S "SPEAKERBOXXX/THE LOVE BELOW"
9. ZEPPELIN VIDEO BOOTLEG - LIVE, SEATTLE 197
10. JIMI HENDRIX LIVE VIDEO BOOTLEG - NEWPORT BEACH, 19

TOP TEN

1. KAYA — BOB MARLEY
2. BURNIN — "   "
3. ( ) — SIGÜR ROSE
4. THE MIGHTY GORGA
   (SOME INTENSE HORROR MOVIE)
5. ANGELS DON'T PLAY THIS HAARP
   BY DR. NICK BEGICH
6. WWW.EARTHPULSE.COM/HAARP
7. MY SECOND WINTER SURFING
8. JAMBA JUICE !!
9. NEW VOI VOD
10. INTEGRITY

My grandmother and I on her 100th birthday celebration.
She doesn't look a day over 82, does she??

ME + MY BRO!

STOP TEMPTING ME NICLAS!

209

Jason

FISHIN AT SUNRISE

2·6·2000

·31·2000

MY FRIENDS IN MY BIKE CLUB CALL ME "THE CRUISER". #1

FISHIN AT SUNSET

2-9-2000

210

CAPT. J·BONE

SHOUT FROM JASON

HEY WHAT'S UP MY FRIENDS?
I HOPE THAT THESE SCRIBBLES FIND Y'ALL WITH GOOD SPIRITS AND RINGING EARS
METALLICA IS HAVING A CRAZY SUMMER! — I TELL YA... BETWEEN THE MIGHTY HET GOING A BIT MENTAL ON THE OL' JET SKI AND MR. LARS KICKING SOME NAPPY NAPSTER ASS,... OUR YEAR OF "LAYIN' LOW" TURNS OUT TO BE OUR HIGH PROFILE YEAR... GO FIGURE...
OTHER THAN THE OBVIOUS SETBACKS (HE HE) THE SUMMER SANITARIUM TOUR WAS REALLY COOL FOR US. THERE WAS A GREAT VIBE HANGIN' OUT WITH GUYS FROM BANDS OF THE NEXT WAVE OF HEAVY MUSIC! (KORN, SYSTEM, ETC.)
THE BEST THING WAS TO SEE HOW MANY TRUE FANS WERE AS PLEASED AS I WAS TO PARTICIPATE IN AN AMERICAN METAL FESTIVAL EVENT. THIS IS PROOF THAT OUR FAVORITE KIND OF MUSIC IS ALIVE AND WELL RIGHT HERE AT HOME!!

IF Y'ALL GET A CHANCE, CHECK OUT!

AMERICAN MOVIE
COLORS MAGAZINE
& THE TOP 5 RECORDS OF THE SUMMER! (IN NO PARTICULAR ORDER OTHER THAN THIS ONE!)

ECHOBRAIN - ECHOBRAIN
QUEENS OF THE STONE AGE - FEEL GOOD HIT OF THE SUMMER
LINVAL THOMPSON - RIDE ON DREADLOCKS 1975-77
THE LEGENDARY MARVIN PONTIAC
NO ONE FUCKS WITH VEGAS THUNDER

HONORABLE MENTION: GOLDIE - DEBUT
CURTIS MAYFIELD - MOVE ON UP

ONCE AGAIN, IT IS GREAT TO SHARE WITH ALL OF YOU.
CHEERS
Jason

PEOPLES · PEOPLES · PEOPLES —

THANK YOU TO ALL OF THE TRUE FANS OF
METALLICA. OLD AND NEW - FAR AND NEAR...
OVER THE YEARS OF SHARING MUSIC AND POSITIVE ENERGY,
MANY OF YOU HAVE BECOME MY FRIENDS, AND
FRIENDS WITH EACH OTHER THROUGH METALLICA.
I FEEL THAT THE BEAUTY AND STRENGTH OF
THAT FACT IS SO AMAZING! JUST LIKE SO
MANY FOLKS HAVE SAID OR WRITTEN TO US;
METALLICA IS MORE THAN JUST A BAND.
    I MUST AGREE, AND THIS IS BECAUSE
YOU MADE IT HAPPEN! YOU MADE US FEEL IT.
I PERSONALLY WILL NEVER LET IT GO UNFELT.
    I WANT TO THANK EVERY ONE OF YOU
FROM MY TRUEST HEART. YOU ARE MY FUEL
AND I LOOK FORWARD TO SHARING MORE
MUSIC AND KEEPING UP POSITIVE VIBES
WITH ALL OF MY FRIENDS IN THE YEARS TO COME.

                    YOURS WITH RESPECT—
                    JASON
                    MARCH 2001

211

Robert

HEY, WHATS UP ¡¿? Millenium HOODRATZ

HOWS IT?
My experience with the 'METALLIC' WARLORDS
is going AMAZING !!
THE ROAD HAS BEEN GOOD TO US.
COVERING THE NATION

MY NEW BROTHERS PLAY HARD, EACH SHOW
FEELS INTENSE, LIKE A TRIATHALON
AND I LUV IT !

KIRK AND I HAVE MANAGED a couple of
SURF EXCURSIONS (1 IN PORTUGAL, THE 2nd IN
SOUTH FLORIDA
KICK ASS BEACHES, FUN WAVES,
GREAT FRIENDS

CHEERS
MATES

Hello, Whiskey Warlord, High Octane
HOODRATZ!
OF
MID-EVILNESS

'Tis I' TRUJILLO, Who is absolutely
Totally STOKED! (NEXT LEVEL)
WITH
EXCITEMENT!
To be apart of the 'Metalli' familia
It's time to step it up!
Pump it up!
FUNK IT UP!!
SUCK IT UP!!!
Words cannot explain
ENERGY, EXCITEMENT, FURY
POWER
ABOUT THIS NEW PULVERIZING
JOURNEY!

TILL
THE
NEXT
TIME

213

The stupidest riff
can lead to the most beautiful part

IT'S BEEN A LONG TIME, BUT METALLICA ARE FINALLY BACK AND COMING TO GRIPS ONCE AGAIN WITH THE STUDIO, THE SONGS AND EACH OTHER. HERE THEY DISCUSS IT ALL IN ANOTHER EXCLUSIVE ROUND-TABLE DISCUSSION FOR SO WHAT! MAGAZINE.

BACK
IN THE SADDLE AGAIN

IT IS A BUSY THURSDAY AFTERNOON when Lars Ulrich, Kirk Hammett, James Hetfield and producer/studio bassist Bob Rock sit down for a conversation about what's been going on. As ever, the question will not prove anywhere near as easy to answer as it might seem. To the outside world Metallica took a year off, Lars and Kirk went on a few holidays and James went into rehab. The reality is rather more complex; that all parties concerned have probably been through more hard work, more soul-searching, more self-discovery and more collective damage control and repair than at any other time in their history.

There was an unmistakable, if reluctantly acknowledged, unease when we all sat down to start the conversation. This was the first time everyone had sat down to discuss matters outside the Phil Towle sessions, and the air crackled with nervous energy for a little while as we eased and slid our way into discussion. To be honest, it was the most uncomfortable opening few minutes I've felt interviewing these men in 16 years (something which surprised them all when I said as much after we'd wrapped up).

There is perhaps only one more thing to add before you get to the main course. The conversation was as honest, revealing and (in the end) free-flowing as it could possibly have been right now.

Honestly.

I'd have settled for nothing less... but what's most important is neither would they.

Editor, July 2002

21

During the last interview we did, there was a lot of talk about how Jason's departure had helped you see a lot of things between each other and helped you clear up a lot of stuff. Looking back now, do you think that was an honest assessment or did you all sense that there might be more to come?

Kirk Hammett (KH): Man, there's a lot of housecleaning to do. *(laughing)*

Lars Ulrich (LU): I'm not sure I get the question.

James Hetfield (JH): Yeah, I don't either.

At the time you were very adamant...

LU: Last time we did the round-table?

You were very adamant that Jason's departure had helped you see communication problems between each other, you had Phil in, you guys were talking to Phil, you were opening up between each other. At that time, did you see or foresee the problems that were going to come a few months later?

LU: What problems?

(exasperated) OK, let's talk about what happened. You went into the Presidio...

LU: OK.

...and then suddenly you're rolling, there's an album going and all of a sudden it stops. So, obviously not all of the problems had been blown out. What I'm asking is at the time when you did the Jason thing did it seem like they had been? Did you know...

JH: For me it felt like we were in a great place for where we were right then. I have no idea what underlying things we could work on individually, that's for sure. As a band we felt really good I think.

OK, so describe those sessions and the whole decision to work in the Presidio. I know it's a dead issue, but it happened, it has been mentioned and I think it's good to have some words about it.

LU: I think the key thing was that we felt the time was right to play some music together. It was a pretty instantaneous thing. Basically, what happened was this place (new HQ) wasn't ready, so we had to make a decision whether we wanted to wait for this place to be ready. I think, speaking for myself, through that spring of last year, we knew we would feel when we were going to be ready to play music. And one day we felt were ready to play music, and it then it literally became 'let's turn this around on a dime.'

Bob Rock (BR): It was a month wasn't it?

LU: Yeah, we turned it around in two weeks. It was pretty incredible to do that, and I think the energy at that moment when we decided to play music went into the studio with us and was felt throughout those recordings. It was an incredibly short spurt of time, it was incredibly intense...

KH: Very productive.

LU: Literally, it was like 15 days or something...

BR: 15 to 18 days, yeah but even putting the studio together. We went to see the barracks, and they were literally deserted army barracks, and from that Metallica purchased a console, I had all of my gear, so I just brought it over. We set up and they had a studio together in literally two weeks, wasn't it? They put a whole studio together and we were in there doing it! It was actually nothing short of incredible. It was also on the fourth floor or third floor?

KH: Third floor.

BR: Third floor. So, they hauled all this gear up three floors. I mean it was an incredible feeling, but the thing is, the music is very special.

From those sessions or just in general?

BR: Just yeah, from those sessions...

JH: I think there was quite an energy that was carried from at least getting over the Jason part. We felt a rekindled fire there. We had no idea how great the fire could become, there were sparks flying right then, so when we went into the Presidio, like others have been saying, we made it happen. We'd been talking with Bob about ideas around just going into a rented house somewhere and just setting up and recording there, not unlike the Peppers or some other bands that have done that, and seeing how we can do it our way.

Just working in the room together jamming, which is something in itself. You've never really recorded all together.

LU: Yeah, I think with emphasis on not being in a "proper" recording studio environment. Bob introduced us at some point a few years before that, to the idea of the beauty that could come out of chaos. Because everything had always been so perfectly orchestrated in these recording studios, in these very sterile areas and facilities, and he/we were trying to really just shake it up as much as possible and we did.

Yeah, diving into that, the idea that you were flying off the cuff and maybe not working in as controlled an environment as you had done before. Do you think that added to the spark of working and being excited to work? Did it feel weird?

KH: It just felt weird, it just felt weird that there were three of us involved when usually there'd been four of us involved. Just the fact that there wasn't another body there, for me, it was kind of weird to get used to at first, but after a few days it wasn't really much of an issue.

LU: It didn't feel weird to me at all. It felt really good.

So you were relaxed, happy...

LU: Yeah, that's not a stab at him (meaning Jason – Ed).

KH: Yeah, that's totally not a stab at him either.

LU: It just felt comfortable. That was the key thing, the intimacy and the re-aquainting of ourselves post-Jason, and trying to just get all of our shit and our laundry aired and deal with some resentments and bits of crap from the last 20 years. The positiveness of that, I think, went into the energy of the Presidio and created some very beautiful intimate intense moments. For me, at that time, it felt so right being with these guys and as I said, not a dis to Jason, but I never missed him. And I said this before too, the irony once again was that the process we ended up falling into working with was really, in a perverse way, what he had always looked for. And that will always be the most ironic thing about that.

JH: And the even more ironic thing is, I don't know if it would have worked with him in.

Right. Double irony. So James, let me go to when you came back from Russia (last summer) and that day we sat down, maybe a week after you come back, and were talking about the trip. How much do you think that trip brought out feelings in you that you hadn't had before? I think I told you this before, in my psychiatry 101 way, I sensed that you were getting pretty emotional as you talked about the trip, the hunting, the paw and all that business.

LU: The what? The what?

There was a picture of a paw (a bear's paw which we declined to print – Ed) that I mean, well, I think you said it looked like a hand… well it did.

JH: It very much did.

Did that trip have anything to do with deeper emotions coming out?

JH: To me it didn't. I was going on a hunting trip and that was pretty much it, you know? Now that I look back at it, it's like 'I'm going to Siberia. You're going to Siberia? Yeah, OK. You're going on a chopper? A Russian military chopper for four hours in the air and… OK. You're getting dropped off in the middle of nowhere where people hardly speak English and there's nothing to drink but vodka? OK. And they've got weapons and they're not extremely pro-American? OK.' Looking at it now, well, sure, a little crazy perhaps…

I guess I'm focusing on this because you had told me that you got a bear early on and that you had a long time basically by yourself in the luxury suite (it was, in fact, a shed, as illustrated by James in issue 8.2 last year) out there on the ice…

JH: MTV Cribs, right. *(laughing)*

… and you did a lot of sketching there and you, I mean you had a lot of time to yourself. That plus vodka, plus thinking, I mean bluntly, when you came back, in the back of your mind did you have issues that had built up?

JH: No. *(laughing)* Not at all. I was out there on the ice, on the tundra or whatever, just doing my escapism or my risk taking, you know? That's another side of myself that I've investigated quite a bit since though, how much can I push myself or how risky can I make life for me? How far do I have to go to get a thrill? I've been investigating that stuff.

And I'd completely numbed out to any other thing, so that was the only avenue I saw to get any feelings about life or excitement.

Excitement was the part of life I liked best. I didn't like dealing with the rest of it, so I numbed out with the rest of all of that and just looked for the excitement part, and at a lot of cost you know? To the band, family, you know? I was… in my self centeredness, looking for happiness in my life. I couldn't look for it at home, I couldn't look for it with friends, I always felt I had to find it on my own out somewhere else, and hunting was one of those things. I still enjoy it, but I don't think I have to go to those extremes anymore. It was… you know really the drinking part, falling back into drinking, it started my bottom happening again, when I bottomed out. And getting back on the drink, enjoying that brief moment of drinking for a while, and then the reality sets in, of coming home and going 'I still want to drink and I still want to do that, but I can't anymore.' You know, I started to really lose it, and it's so weird that you don't know you're losing it man. It's so scary.

KH: Wow.

JH: You just don't.

Did you guys know that he was losing it? I mean had you ever…

KH: There was no outward signs of him…

LU: No, I did not.

I mean did you guys ever think of saying to him, 'wow that's a really strange trip you're taking?'

KH: He just got back. He went to Patagonia before that. *(laughing)* So I mean going to Siberia was just in line with everything else.

Yeah, I think that the kids think that you guys would definitely be talking all the time about this stuff and you'd be like, 'hey man, you must be nuts going there.' But I think it's a surprise when James says 'well in a month I'm going to Russia' and nobody asks about it.

JH: *(laughing)* It was kind of like that, but it was more that there were little digs that I got defensive about which made me want to do it. Just kid stuff, you know, 'Oh when you bagged the bear! When the big mean bear…' So it became, like, 'I'll show you!'

Bob, did you notice any palatable difference in James when he came back?

BR: No, not really. I mean James was always James right up until the end of the Presidio sessions.

LU: I think you've got to remember that good or bad, right or wrong, that was a side of James that had been there for many, many, many years.

Right. I'm just amazed at…

LU: …Somebody said whether he went to Patagonia or Siberia or whatever, it was just sort of the next logical step, I mean I can sort of relate to it…

KH: It's right in line with what he had been doing for the last 10 years.

LU: ...But I can relate to it a little bit in terms of a period I went through in my life about 10-12 years ago, where I was doing a lot of the scuba diving stuff and pushing it to extremes and saying 'OK, let's see if I can hit 200 feet this time.' That type of stuff, like 'let's see if I can take four flights instead of three flights, is there an island further away from Palau or Micronesia?' So in some way I can relate to that, and I didn't think it was anything particularly odd.

OK, back to that night in the studio when I talked with James about Russia. Soon afterwards you guys have an argument in the studio. I'm sure there's been hundreds of studio arguments, but James got pissed, stormed out, you guys were sitting there, and I can't believe that all of you can sit in the same room and not sense that there's something building. Or was it just another typical studio row?

KH: We were playing music. That day we were playing music and there was a disagreement. When you're playing music, you're not really having a conversation over the music, so maybe if there was something building, James knows for sure, we weren't talking about it because we were too busy playing music.

OK. Great, fair enough.

LU: Speaking for myself, I can't find anything.

BR: I think I understand which incident you're talking about. Previous to going to the Presidio we had all been getting together with Phil. And so these guys were walking into the work (with Phil) they had already done, and they were becoming a lot more aware of each other, the feelings and emotions and all the issues, and they were really starting to become the friends and the brothers they have always claimed to be.

JH: And that was instrumental in all of us wanting to address more issues and being comfortable doing that, knowing that 'OK, I'm not superhuman,' well at least in my case. Knowing that I might have some support from the band addressing some other issues, you know? I'd been neglecting myself mentally for so long that this had to happen for me in my life to survive. And knowing that we were getting tighter as a band probably played a big part in that.

I'm interested to know just when you realized you needed to take off and repair for a while, how it came to a head both inside yourself and with the outside world.

JH: Well, the whole kind of boil up... Lars and I have had plenty of arguments over music in the studio and we all know what they're about. There's a bit of an ego-power struggle, and as long as we both know that we're OK with it. I think we're learning to deal with that a little more these days. And we know what each of our issues are a little more, so when something flares up we can kind of say, 'ah well that's probably that' and we'll lay off it awhile or, 'hey, let's address this because this isn't right.' But (before) it got to a point where I didn't feel like it was going anywhere and I wasn't getting heard, so I got up and I left. And the scariest thing about that was there was a guy that used to play bass who did that same thing, and so I was, of course, catastrophising, saying, 'uh oh, well that means in a couple of months

I'm going to come to the band and say guess what, blah blah blah I can't be in this band, whatever.' And of course in my extreme thinking, that's what had to happen, but it just... the correlation between the two just scared the shit out of me and that's when I got really depressed, I got SOOO depressed and really down. All the work that Phil was doing with us, and all of the progress that we had made I thought, 'oh my God it's all gone,' you know? I had never stormed out... so that was really, really scary and in a way Jason kind of opened that door a little bit, you know, it was OK to push it that far. It was like, 'well I'll do that,' not consciously obviously, but that was a moment that really scared the hell out of me and I knew that I had to address some personal issues that I had in dealing with people.

You mean feeling comfortable dealing with people? Having confidence speaking up for yourself?

JH: Well, it's so, you know, it's so deep. You start with the outside of the onion, and you peel a little of it off and then as you get down it gets stinkier and you go 'oh my God this is what's going on.' There's so many layers to it you don't know. And it keeps going, it's endless. I don't know what we end up as... just a little heart or a little soul sitting here not doing anything? But there were so many more issues that I had to deal with... OK, the addiction issue was just the vehicle for all of the other crap I had inside. It was just coming out through addictions, and you know when you go in to FIX yourself, you know the behaviors might stop, but you've still got that stuff inside which made you use your addictions. You have to backpeddle into why it's happening. I didn't want to deal with any of that crap EVER in my life. I was afraid of addressing, you know, what could be wrong up here (points to head — Ed), you know? Partly because, 'oh I'm getting good lyrics' or 'it's spurring on this great stuff' or 'this is just how I am. Maybe I'm totally fucked. I'm so unique that no one sees I'm fucked,' you know? Just building up this dream in my head, my reality was askew and distorted and there's me not wanting to listen to anybody else. It's like, 'I need your help, but don't tell me what to fucking do!' What a stuck position to be in.

It's an easy world, that of a rock star, for that to happen, right? It's an easy environment...

JH: Yeah, it felt... everything that...

You know, big rock singer, no one around you willing to tell you what is...

JH: Right. Yeah, you're right.

KH: (to James) That's the first time I've ever heard you make a correlation between that event and Jason.

(To Lars and Kirk) So, your reactions to that: fear? I mean, you get a phone call saying, well repeating, 'I need to go do this, you understand...'

LU: That's not what happened.

KH: We didn't get a phone call.

JH: Let me tell you what happened. I was there, I was in the studio and it was a scary time for me, to finally kind of take care of myself. In

another way I had been doing that all along with these hunting trips or these other things. But taking care of myself like this, saying to them 'you know, guys if I don't go away for a little while and get some help… you know, not to sound ungrateful or anything, but the band means that (motions a small pinchful) much right now.' And my whole life was at stake really. It was a scary moment to just sit and say that. But all of the stuff we'd done with Phil building up to that got me up to that point, and it was a lot easier or else I don't think it ever would have happened. So, I'm pretty grateful, extremely grateful…

(To Lars). So your reaction when you hear that… it's pretty intense. Let me say again this is twofold, because I know that it takes a situation out of your hands that you are used to having a degree of control over, and suddenly it's out of your hands and you can't do anything about it.

LU: I think that's a little black and white. I think the key thing was just the surprise of it, because as we have all alluded to, I don't think anybody saw it coming. So it was a pretty heavy thing to be confronted with, that one day when you showed up, we were just playing music and… it was just overwhelming, and there were just a fucking cornucopia of thoughts and it's really difficult for me to put into words. I can't remember clearly, *(pauses to think)* I remember, like, (to Bob) did you come over to my San Francisco place and we sat and had a glass of wine with my dad or something?

BR: Yeah, we did.

LU: Was that that day?

BR: That was the day James left and I was leaving the next day or whatever to go back home.

LU: You know, when James came in he was very, my recollection of it was (to James) you were very sort of, 'listen guys I have to do this, I have to do this for myself and I've got to go and deal with my shit.' And that was about it. So it came out of nowhere, and I guess it was hard on one level, it was difficult to gauge the level of 'where is he really at?' You know what I mean? You wanted to support, you wanted to carry, you wanted to do that sort of stuff but it was difficult, there wasn't a lot there. So, that's when the rest of us just started talking. James called me five or six days later, I remember that, he left a message and we started communicating about once a week and slowly started, I think, to get a clearer picture of the severity of his situation.

Was it scary to either of you?

KH: It was scary as fuck.

LU: The scary thing for me was just the unknown.

KH: Yeah, there was a big question mark. I've had some experiences with friends and relatives coming to me and telling me that they are about to go into an eight-week program or 12 week or whatever. And so when James told me that, I was shocked because I did not think that what he had in front of him warranted such treatment. That was kind of a wake up-call for me, because I had started asking myself… was I contributing to this? Were there things that I was doing which maybe led him to do this sort of thing? Those were the first thoughts that came into my head and it was just total chaos.

LU: Yeah, 'what role do I play in this?'

KH: (to James) You also have to remember that you told us that you were only going to be away for eight weeks right?

LU: Five.

BR: Five weeks originally.

JH: Yeah, because that's what I knew it was.

KH: Well at the end of those five weeks, it didn't look like he was going to be coming back anytime soon. So it started this whole process of Lars, Bob and I meeting up with Phil and just discussing the situation. There were a lot of words, a lot of words of all sorts that were just thrown about.

BR: It was all fear-based.

KH: Yeah, it was all very much fear-based and, you know, we really didn't have anything else to do…

But to be afraid?

KH: But to get together and talk about it because we were so afraid and we needed a forum to vent our fears and frustrations and concerns and everything else. It was just a really, really difficult time and it got more difficult as time went on.

BR: It seemed to me at first it was 'what's going on?' then it was total support for James and then a lot of anger and then it came around to love and belief.

KH: Faith. Faith.

See, that's an important word.

BR: It kind of went through these phases, we were speculating and all of a sudden we went, 'this is bullshit.' And we just stopped getting together. We just stopped completely because we knew…

KH: We were doing more damage to each other than we would have if we had just not…

And what timeframe are we talking about when you finally decided, 'oh fuck it, we have to let things take/run their course.'

KH: Early summer?

LU: No, no, no it was… you came back, what, mid-September?

JH: I was gone for five weeks initially, then I stayed an extra couple to work on some other things and then there were two other after care places for a couple of weeks. So, it was a total of seven, 11 weeks.

LU: (to James) I think you came back around early September, because I think the first time me and you had a proper conversation after I saw you in Los Angeles was September 11th. So I think we stopped our shit probably mid to late October. There was a different phase that happened. We were all, in our ignorance and our selfishness, thinking that as soon as James comes back to Northern California it's all going to be fine. **(James is laughing at this point – Ed)** Y'know, keep the Presidio on hold, it's going to be good, yeah, just keep the board and keep the power on, it's all good. So, then he came back to Northern California and the first Phil meeting after he came back, we were all going to get together, it's all going to be great, we'll be over there playing music next week. And then James called and said he was not going to come to the meeting and that he wasn't quite ready yet. Then it went to a different level, because then it was sort of like, 'wow, wait a minute...'

KH: He's out, why isn't he with us?

LU: He's out, but why isn't he here? Somebody just saw him over at the mall, what the fuck?

JH: *(laughing)* At the mall.

LU: I remember you ran into Steven Wiig over at the mall. *(everyone laughing)*

JH: In my hot new glasses! *(laughing)*

BR: And he's got glasses!

JH: Yeah, and I saw him and I was like, 'hey you're Steven Wiig, is that what you look like?!!' *(everyone laughing)*

LU: But then it took on a different thing, because now our brother was back and at least speaking for myself, since I've never been around anybody who had been through these type of programs, so in my like I said selfishness, when he comes back we'll be ready to go next week, right?! So, I was unaware of what I would call the second phase...

Why did you never just ask him? Why didn't you just say right away, do you think you'll be playing anytime soon?

KH: It was not a question that we thought was appropriate at the time.

LU: We were also at the time... I mean I had... through different, through, I don't know if it's OK to say this, but through some secondary people, I was told to not talk to James about any band stuff. (To James) And then when you came back, when that meeting went away, it was sort of once again related through other people, 'don't call me I'll call you when I'm ready to call you.' That was the worst six weeks, the next six weeks after that (James getting home), we were sitting there going kind of like 'laa dee daa.'

KH: Again, a lot of speculation and a lot of just driving each other crazy.

LU: A lot of concern, intermixed with the anger and frustration. There was also concern about, 'well, what's going on here? Is he OK? Is he really OK?' We sat there and talked about, maybe we should just go over and kick the door down and...

BR: So, many times we were just like, 'OK we're going to get our buddy, we're going to...'

JH: *(laughing)* We're going to rescue him!

BR: Y'know, 'what he really needs is to be with us, because we're so together.' Hanging on to three of us, it's like our wives won't even talk to us, they think we're nuts and we're going to bust James loose.

JH: Tie the bedsheets together!

KH: Get the helicopter.

BR: You guys take Gio, I'll get James. *(everyone laughing)*

JH: Yeah, I mean it's cool to hear this stuff, because I remember that was a really difficult time for me too. The assumptions, all of that stuff was... 'OK, they're assuming that I'm OK and I'm going to show up at the next meeting.' There wasn't that 'do you think you're OK to come to the meeting?' It was just, 'SEE YOU AT THE MEETING!' WHAT? Fuuck! Then the real issues started. It was my reintroduction to life and it had to go slow, it really had to go slow. Being away somewhere like that (rehabilitation) is...

KH: It's got to be hard.

JH: Well, it's extremely different. You're in your own world there and it's for a reason. And it's like a clean little cocoon. It's a way that you can just try and wash yourself, get down to your basic essence of life and simplicity, and then (when you come out) you start adding the little pieces of what makes up your life or what you're connected to. It's no longer one pair of pants, one shirt that you wash every night, make your own bed at five and your food's done for you just right. It's really kid gloves in there, which is great because you don't have to worry about any of the other stuff, because there's so many other things to worry about. But then when you're out, connecting back with family, connecting back with the band, with friends, I was so fearful of relapsing that I wanted to make sure that there were not going to be any flare ups or anything. Because I had no idea how to reconnect back into life. You just have to do it, you gotta do it the way you feel is best for you. And it was tough (the way I had to do it), it was really tough for everybody, I know that. And I didn't see the caring in, you know, 'come back, come on.' I saw the 'they think it's all cool now, but it's not.' I couldn't see past any of that stuff.

You definitely signed up for the accelerated program though James. People go through recovery in various stages and you signed up for one of the more intense levels of doing so. Would you not agree? I mean you put yourself through a pretty big ringer.

JH: Yeah, well I had tried it (recovery) five years ago. I had stopped drinking for a year and a half and then felt 'oh, it's cool' and went back. And all the other stuff that goes along with drinking, the erratic and distorted behaviors that go around, started to appear again. And I knew it had to take something more drastic to get through my thick skull. Also in my extreme fashion, it's a case of 'I want it all and I want it all now.' So I'm going to do the best damn recovery there is available, and give it all to me and I'll dive straight in. And it's tough to do more than just that at that moment. So it was hard to tell the (band) guys, 'I can't think about you, I can't think about anything but me right now.' And I'm sure they were sitting there going, 'well that's what you used to do except times 20 now. It's your old behavior magnified, what's going on here?' But it had to happen, and that was the beginning of me trusting my own intuitions.

So, what held it together during the six weeks where you mentioned faith which is a pretty big word. Is it trust? Is it faith? Is it history?

BR: To be quite honest, I think what held it together was we talked as much as we could and Phil stressed communication. We talked a lot... there were a lot of conversations and stuff...

LU: I think part of, a lot of, what we discovered about our fears was realizing you're not alone. And so while James was away and dealing with his stuff, we just became so much closer, probably both out of need and out of...

KH: Sanity.

LU: Yeah, we just embraced and became closer than we've ever been. These relationships... raised the bar.

So, go through that as well for the fans because I don't think they know this either. Most think it's a case of you're in a big rock band, and everyone's jolly happy, and everyone knows each other and everyone is just tight.

JH: Oh man!

KH: I can put it really simply... we thought we knew each other back then and we're on the way to really truly knowing each other now.

BR: To offer a bit of my perspective, I think generally with rock bands or any kind of organizations when they have a goal in front of them, in music, and a type of music, becomes the driving force. And most of the energy is put into that. When I met these guys when we did the "Black" album, I walked into a band that had the blinders on and had this vision. I mean they were like machines, like cyborgs, metal cyborgs that were just like 'this is what we're doing, if you want to come along you could offer your two bits, we'll just roll right over you Rock and you can come for the ride.' It was just like they were on auto pilot. Which is why they are the band they are. I think it's the price you pay for having that much ambition and that much dedication to something, so the relationships, the everything, they're all lying in the ditch and it's all about the music. And I think with the "Black" album, the degree of success, and with touring and everything else, they could finally kind of relax. "Load" and "Re-Load" were a bit of relaxing, you know what I mean? I think some of the other albums were relaxing, and then finally you know they had to start... you have kids, they start looking at their lives. They start becoming real people and looking at each other. I mean, that's really generalizing the whole picture, but really it happens to bands, it's kind of like an artist generally. They get in that zone and it's like if they are feeding off that, they have no time for each other or various other stuff. That interferes with what they are trying to do.

Right. And then suddenly things shift and...

BR: Yeah, things shift. When James left to deal with what he had to deal with, what made it really, really more difficult was that preceding that had been a realization and a place that these guys had never been and I've never been with a band. It was amazing at the Presidio! The energy, the music, everything. It was just this great experience that we all went though, and that made it even worse, do you know what I mean? It was almost like, 'WOW, everything's going right, wow, oh man, this is just, like AGGHHH! See ya in 10 months.' Do you know what I mean?

JH: I know what you mean.

KH: We got such a small taste of something really, really great. It was like you have a big cake and someone gives you just a little corner. And you're like, 'oh that's great, can I have some more?' And they're like 'no, not for 10 months.'

JH: So, I've just become like the baker.

BR: That's not directed at you, it's a way to gauge the feeling that went along with that. But now it's like having gone through this, you really realize that this is the next life of Metallica.

LU: If there was a turning point with the "Black" album then I would say that with the start of the Presidio sessions there was another major turning point. I would almost say a musical rebirth, it was like we reinvented our wheel. It felt that way and it had been something that had been, I think, felt around everybody for a few years with the last couple of records that we were making, and it happened in those 15/18 days. And that made it harder because of just that.

JH: I just want to add onto that. But that was the part that made me comfortable enough to address those issues.

BR: Yeah.

JH: So that was great that it happened.

KH: Thank God it did.

JH: The other thing about that focus, that musical focus, I think we were so driven as individuals and as a group, but we didn't even want to look right next to us, at the other guys next to us.

BR: What if you didn't like him?

JH: What if I stir something up that they think 'err yeaah!' That was the commonality that we had, all three of us were just going and we didn't want to look sideways at all.

So, are you using any of that stuff now?

JH: Sidewaysness?

The music... are you using any of those sessions from the Presidio right now in your work?

LU: We haven't as of now...

JH: We didn't lose them.

But are you working from them now? Do you know where they are?

JH: We're moving on.

Ok, so you have this brilliant thing. What's going to happen to it?

KH: Well, they'll eventually...

JH: It's part of the record that we're making.

KH: But check this out though. Some days we would go in there and write a song right off the bat, and some days we would go in there write a song, take a fucking dinner break and write another song. Two songs in one day!

Which is wild.

KH: I mean like within three hour spans. That was unheard of.

JH: We had always wanted those sessions, and these sessions, to be the same. Our intentions were when this place was being built, we're just going to record over there until it's done and then we'll just continue on and get a fresher vibe or something like that. So, yeah they weren't intended to be separate at all but they were separated by a huge profound event in our lives. But still we listen to the Presidio stuff, and what we're doing now it's pretty copacetic, they're pretty happening together I think.

Let me bring you back to the October doldrums you're talking about and ask at that point what Metallica meant to each of you.

KH: The what now?

The October doldrums, like when you guys had been talking…

LU: I think I blocked it out. *(laughing)* I just wanted to say for anybody that cares that the first time I saw James back here was at your (editor's) wedding **(which was in late October — Ed)**. So, there you go, just a sidebar.

KH: Nothing is quite absolute. I started questioning whether or not there was a future to the band, and I also asked myself if I had a life outside of the band. And to try and answer that question, I went out and tried to find if there was anything there, if I actually had a life outside the band. I totally went introspective.

Were you happy with what you found?

KH: Absolutely. I mean a lot of it had to do with Phil's guidance, but I kind of found myself in James' absence. The one positive thing that came out of that is that I realized that I actually had a life outside of the band. And it gave me a lot of confidence, a lot of self-esteem. It was just the most remarkable thing because here we are in a situation where I'm questioning whether or not I had any sort of musical future. And in that process, somehow I learned, I managed to find my own identity. So, I mean it was the strangest thing, out of all the negativity, I managed to find a positive aspect within myself. And that's basically what I got out of it, and it was a very mind blowing thing for me. I had never really sat down, I don't have a family, I don't have kids, I have animals. And for me to do that and walk away with some pretty positive things, it was huge for me.

JH: That's essentially what I was doing, you know?

KH: Basically, yeah.

BR: That's what everyone… I mean even though, for me, I had my year planned out to be with these guys and all of a sudden, it kept going… so I couldn't really get into something because my heart was really in the Presidio with these guys. So, I couldn't move on and it forced me to take a look at myself and my relationship with my family and my wife and everything. Just the same thing with Kirk, and I think with Lars too. It's just amazing what his action did for… when you're sitting there and you're reeling in this turmoil because of it, and then slowly coming out of it just made everything better.

LU: We all kept working on the shit individually and collectively. James was doing it obviously a little bit more intensely, but I think in retrospect we were all doing it. And out of his dealing with his shit came us dealing with our shit. So there was kind of a nice correlation there.

KH: I feel that I'm a better person because of it.

JH: How healthy it is to address that. It's a scary thing to think, and I was thinking the same thing, what if the band doesn't continue? What if we can't get along? What if… all of these what ifs. And what ifs are pretty dangerous, but it was healthy to think… it made me think the band isn't my life. It's a great, huge and important part of my life, but if it wasn't there would I crumble? Would I fall to the ground and be dust, you know? And that made me scared to hang onto this group for the wrong reasons. So when we backed off, I feel we all got our individual selves together, with families and feeling strong. And that meant we can get together completely healthy without any of the controlling things that we're still dealing with. But most importantly, we can hang onto this band because we're friends and because we like making music together, not because 'if I don't have it I'll die.'

Right.

LU: I think everybody's saying the same thing. For myself, I for the first time in my life, dealt with the reality of Metallica possibly not continuing and feeling that I could survive that…

And feeling that you could not control its fate right?

LU: Yeah, absolutely. You know…

It was probably a pretty big deal for you I would think right? To know you couldn't control it, that it was out of your hands.

LU: Well you know what was (a big deal)? I consider myself to be fairly active/pro-active, so the hardest thing, and I think we talked about this when me and Kirk were talking with you (for SW! 8.4) was that one part of me wanted to help James, it was like, 'what can I do to help?' And another part of me realized that, for the first time in my life, maybe I would help him better by staying away and giving him time and giving him space.

Which is kind of hard to deal with.

LU: Of course. There's no fucking road map to this shit, right, OK? There's no fucking 101, OK? Your fucking buddy, your brother, your best friend, your band member whatever, goes away, now what do you do? Do you know what I mean? So there were a lot of awakenings on a lot of different levels. But ultimately, controlling it or not, it was dealing with the realization that there was at least a chance that Metallica would not continue, and finding a way to accept that. And I think that time proved once again, choice or no choice, that I could survive it.

Did any of you ever read James' lyrics for some insight? I know a lot of the fans would read them, I know that James read back over some of them and was kind of blown away by what he had written. Did you ever do stuff like that?

LU: Can I pick that up? I would say that I didn't do that as much as

I went back and found the signs in my relationship with James, and James' behavior from the past, where I felt that I could have helped. Do you know what I mean? That was what I did more... I didn't necessarily sit down and find other meanings in the lyrics or anything like that, but I felt... I more went over our past experiences together and realized that here, maybe, went astray, here we went astray, what if I had helped then, that sign was so fucking obvious, why didn't I grab that and run with it or grab him and run with him or whatever. Do you know what I mean? I also found, as the time went on and I got further and further away from any kind of tangible situation, that I had developed a different relationship with Metallica songs when I heard them on the radio.

Which was?

LU: I appreciated them more.

That's a good band. That kind of thing?

LU: No, just thinking about it, (before) I would definitely begin changing the station when they would come on. Either in kind of an elitist way or just 'fuck, hearing something.' I started appreciating it in a different way. I also have considered myself to be Metallica's number one fan, and sometimes I forgot about that, and I think that I started being that again.

You stopped taking it for granted.

LU: Uh-huh.

Same feelings for each of you?

KH: Yeah, I mean I have to agree with Lars. Whenever a Metallica song came on, I listened that much more intently. I would think about the memories, all the good times, playing the song, playing it live and just leaving it at that. And that's basically what I did, I mean, I didn't deconstruct any of the lyrics or look for hidden meanings or anything, I just had more of an appreciation for the songs, because I didn't know at that point what the hell was going on. I was thinking, 'well this might be the last time this fucking song gets played on the radio.'

LU: It's pretty fucking scary when the fucking local rock station... OK, I'll explain. There's a station ID that they run on KSJO called 'Rock From Then' and 'Rock From Now', and they have ones like AC/DC from '...Then' and Linkin Park from '...Now.' And one day I'm driving along and they have their 'Rock From Then,' and 'Sad But True' came on.

KH: I heard that.

LU: ...Fucking 'rock from now,' Godsmack! *(everyone laughing)*

JH: It was something from last week instead of five years ago...

LU: We have become 'Rock From Then!'

JH: Well I'd like to be both dammit! They could play our songs after that too.

LU: That's right. 'Rock From Then,' 'For Whom The Bell Tolls' and 'Rock From Now,' 'No Leaf Clover.'

KH: I also want to be part of rock from the future.

JH: I think hearing the songs on the radio now, they definitely have more of a celebratory feeling to them, when before I hated hearing them because it was just past stuff. I just wanted to go forward, I didn't care about celebrating anything that was behind me. And I was fearful that if I did, I'd rest on my laurels and get lazy, complacent, and fat and, you know, just become unhungry for the next thing. And that's not the case. I would sit there and judge the song and say, 'my God why did we do that, what were we thinking?' And that would spur me onto the next thing, that this will be better, instead of 'OK that could be better, but man that was cool, we could try that again.' Just getting spurred on my negativity instead of by the positive side of that battery too. So, now there should be twice as much power. Oh God! I've set it up now. *(everyone laughing)*

JH: You mentioned the lyrics. Someone (a counselor) had mentioned to bring some lyrics along, because I had gotten into this real headspace of 'I'm a monster, I've got no feelings, I'm a Frankenstein of sorts. I've got no caring for humans and I'm just really inhumane.' So this person said I should bring in some lyrics, so I brought in a bunch and she said I should circle all of the words that were 'feeling' words. And there were a lot of little red circles by the end of the day. So, that was a little bit of tangible relief.

Can you remember when you first started feeling ready to come back and start working? Maybe a little less fearful of Metallica and what it meant to get back to work?

JH: I think just picking a guitar up and playing it was kind of scary. Like, 'uh-oh I don't want to be engulfed by music again and forget everything again.' My extreme thinking wanted to say, 'let's jump back in completely' and then the more sensible me said 'let's take it in baby steps,' pick up the guitar and see if I could stop playing after five minutes instead of eight hours or something excessive. I was afraid to pick up a guitar, fearful of what would happen. There were other things like would I not like it? Would I love it? Would I not be able to write anything cool? Would I write just recovery stuff? Would I be... what the hell is going to happen?

There was a total, real fear too. Everyone kept saying, 'are you playing guitar yet?' And you know? I would just say 'no, not yet.' I wasn't even at that place of saying, 'I'm afraid to...what if this or this or this happens?'

The tension of knowing that it's like this... a circle of people who are waiting for you to pick up a guitar, I mean you must have been aware of that. There's this whole circle of silence around you, but they're bristling with 'I wonder if he's picked it up today.'

JH: Yeah.

BR: There was some fucking bliss going on when we heard some of that crunch coming out of that (points to studio) room. Believe me. Remember?

KH: Oh yeah.

BR: I remember that day. It was the first day back wasn't it?

KH: It was in the first few days.

LU: Not that there was any pressure on James.

BR: No, there was no pressure but you know....

JH: A lot of pressure coming out of that amp though!

BR: There sure was.

JH: It felt good. It was built up for awhile.

Did you feel a release when you got on the phone to everyone, or however it worked, and said, 'well I think this will be the day I can come back?'

JH: It slowly happened, I felt I kind of had to plan. That's crazy right there, I had a plan in my life, OK, wow. It was to slowly introduce ourselves to each other again before we pick up an instrument and kind of neglect the other stuff. Music has always gotten us through tough times, but our friendship, I know our friendship can do it too. And to have both of those ways is great, and I didn't want to rely only on the music and then forget about all of the other issues we need to deal with. So, it slowly happened. We started meeting up, then Bob suggested there could be an actual mark on my calendar where we're going to start, or to push the people here to finish the studio (HQ was completed in April 2002 — Ed). And you know, I was afraid to set that date, I was afraid to say, 'OK, this is the day.' Because I didn't know if I would be ready, and at times you have to take that leap of faith that says your friends aren't going to steer you wrong, and if they see signs of wobbliness they'll be there to say 'we're there and we've got your back.'

So, then you're in, you're rolling in the studio, it's all going well and suddenly there's this shoulder injury, and I'm still not too clear on exactly how that happened or what that was about or....

JH: Me either.

LU: Are you comfortable talking about that?

JH: Yeah, sure.

I mean, when you first heard about the shoulder injury first of all, did you guys think 'oh wow.'

LU: No, for me that time, the first thing was concern because we had connected, or we had started the process of reconnecting. Or as my wife kept pointing out when I said that we're going to get to know each other again, 'well did you ever really know him in the first place?' I was just like 'wow.'

That's pretty big....

LU: Yeah, that was a pretty big moment when she said that.

She is a doctor.

BR: (laughing) Women!

LU: (laughing) Why do they do that?

KH: (laughing) I know there should be a law against that.

LU: When James called me, I was down in Los Angeles, and he had to go and deal with his shoulder and we were roughly about a month into re-acquainting, and it was just concern. I had no anger, no nothing, it was just about concern for nothing but his health.

KH: Likewise, I mean I've had problems, muscle and tendon related problems too, where I couldn't even pick up a guitar, let alone play the goddamn thing. I knew what I felt like, so basically, physically impaired, you know, and in such a way that you can't do the thing that you do the most. So I was concerned, I realized that it was going to take a lot of time too, because those things you just can't rush. You know, you just have to let it play itself out. The healing process needs to just play itself out. So I have a pretty good idea of what James is going through, and it's going to take him a long time and I'm the most patient guy in the world.

LU: I think, in retrospect, the shoulder thing probably didn't change much in terms of a time frame. It just... we kept working on getting closer, but I'm not sure that if that shoulder hadn't been there it would have been any different.

I mean for you James, did it bring up a whole other set of insecurities and fears or was it just like, 'oh well, I've been through this thing and we'll go through this, it's fine, blah, blah, blah.'

JH: Well I agree with what Lars is saying, that it didn't change the course of Metallica or healing, but if it didn't happen I'd feel a lot better. I'd be standing up playing in there (currently James is playing all his guitar sitting down as his shoulder isn't fully healed yet, thus cannot take the strap strain — Ed). This injury, as opposed to all of the other ones that I've had (Lars laughing in background) was scary. You know, even the burning in Montreal, I knew I was going to play again, I just kind of knew it. And I don't know if it was me being in denial of my whole life or everything, but having this injury, I got scared. Like you know this one feels different, this one feels like I might not be able to play again. And whether that's just me getting some reality checks now, being in recovery or whatever, it felt a lot different. I had done it just stretching my neck out. I was doing some resistance stretching and something went not snap, but it was a different kind of sound. It was some poppy kind of noise...

KH: Tear.

Snap, crackle, pop.

LU: Yeah, Rice Krispies.

JH: And you know that hurt. And then it started to swell up, and it got so bad that the pain was just brutal. I went to go get some acupuncture and all kinds of other stuff, and of course it happened on a Sunday, nothing was open and all this, can't get a hold of your doctor, but then yeah seeing some specialists and them saying that, 'hey you need neck surgery'... wow hold on man. The fact that I couldn't lift my arm past this, (motions shoulder height in a 'wing' movement — Ed) had something to do with my fear. But it's come along, and nerve damage (the main problem was nerve damage according to doctors — Ed)... you know it was another one of those things where I wanted to be in control, I wanted it to be fixed now and I jumped into that recovery too full throttle. But all the weights that I lift, all of the exercise that I'm doing is not going to make my nerve heal any quicker, you know? They're going to keep the muscles from atrophy, but the nerve has to do its thing and that's kind of out of my hands.

But you're at this point where those fears are gone and it's all healing in the way that you need it to heal...

JH: It's on course, and it is one of those things that you don't know. Each one is individual, they say the nerve heals an inch a month. And it's got to go close to 10–12 inches.

The relief is that you're playing.

JH: Yeah.

So, I guess that directly that impacts any thoughts you would have of playing live for a while.

JH: Well, it will be different, that's for sure. I mean sitting down and playing, I've certainly done a few songs sitting down and playing. I mean we've dealt with injuries before.

LU: I sit down and play all the time.

JH: He's so lazy.

Well he's always standing up and fucking going like this (motions sticks in the air) so I don't know...

JH: Yeah, he did sit down once.

KH: Playing around on stage in a chair isn't that bad. I had to do it when I had appendicitis you know...

Right, I remember.

JH: That's just another phase of being in the band. I think it's cool when you've gone and seen the band when dude was in a cast or, you know, he was in a wheelchair or whatever... you've seen a unique piece of their history.

I mean we should rephrase the question. Are you saying that there's a possibility that if you do some shows you will be in a chair, but you're not always going to be in a chair when you play?

JH: No, I don't want to be sitting in a chair.

Right. So I want to re-address that. So, it's not going to stop you from playing in the next six months if you want to, is that what you're saying.

JH: Playing live?

Yeah.

JH: Yeah, I don't know. I think my health, my physical health is not the issue, it's how we're doing mentally together as a band.

OK. And again, do they have any idea exactly what caused the shoulder to give?

JH: What brought this on? They don't know. Pulling my muscle, a ruptured disc was what it was, but it could have been built up over the years or the jet ski accident, the ATV flipping on my head, and 20 years of headbanging…

KH: The ATV flipped?

JH: Yeah, the ATV flipped.

KH: And it landed on you?

JH: Yeah, I had 40 stitches right here, right along here. On the elk hunting trip in Colorado.

LU: *(sighs and smiles)* It's pretty amazing. I've known you for 21 years and I have no idea what you're talking about.

JH: What? No way.

KH: Yeah, I didn't even know that. I did not know that. An ATV flipping over and landed on your head! Man, those things are like fucking 7–800 pounds. Jesus.

JH: About 4–500 pounds.

I'm confused. Were they on the same trip?

JH: No, this was quite a while ago, maybe eight years ago.

Wow.

LU: Must have been busy that day.

The road map of your injuries. Pretty intense.

JH: Well I wasn't riding, that was the most screwed up thing.

KH: Oh really, someone did that to you?

LU: Was it Dave Mustaine?

JH: Some older dude. I went to save some guy from getting crushed and it whacked me on the head. It was some old dude.

KH: That says a lot for you man.

All right, let's address some direct questions — Bob on bass, people want to know, are you just playing right now?

BR: I'm having fun.

Nobody's going to attach the phrase 'in the band,' nobody wants to?

JH: No.

KH: He's in the pocket all the time.

BR: The thing is, just so everybody knows, when they did the "Mission Impossible" soundtrack song, Lars and I went over to James' to work out the song before going into the studio. We worked it out together, I was on bass, and when we did that we went into the studio. We did that song really quickly, and that was almost a bit of a new thing for everybody. It had just gone really quickly, they threw out all the rules and we just did it at The Site, this studio here, we did it in, like, three days, mixed it, boom, done and everybody really enjoyed it. When Jason left, the thing was not to disturb the whatever was going on, and they said 'why don't you just play bass?' So I've been filling in like we did that day. And I'm not replacing anybody that's been there, we're just continuing so these guys can make music and don't have to stop and go through a whole big thing.

LU: The biggest thing about it to me, is not only do I feel that we and Bob certainly, like Kirk says, have that pocket thing going on, but we know each other very well. It's the idea of not having a foreign outside person in the studio with us that we don't know that well. The intimacy that comes from just us is pretty awesome, and I think that having somebody else would…

KH: There's no room.

BR: At this time anyway for these guys.

LU: Right.

KH: There's no room for anyone else at this point.

JH: It would be hard for them to play catch up no matter who it was.

OK, so in black and white, as of now you'll (Bob) be playing on the record and that's how it will be.

BR: Yeah, but who knows? Who knows where the record's going? There doesn't need to be an answer. Right now we're having lots of fun.

Any thoughts of playing live? I know we just talked about an 'if and when,' but have there been any firm thoughts of playing live? These are the things people want to know.

KH: We've been throwing things around here and there.

Is there a possibility that people might see you play live in the next few months?

LU: Always a possibility. **(As soon as this round-table was finished I was asked if I was going to Kimos for the show that night — In-The-Dark Ed.)**

OK.

BR: You just never know.

LU: It could happen in literally, I mean, I'd say turn around in, like, hours literally.

KH: He says hours, I say minutes. **(Oh dear they really mugged me — clueless, feckless Ed.)**

One thing I've never asked you about James, is the Swizz Beatz song that came about when you were away. Did you like it?

JH: Yeah I did.

Were you surprised to like it? I mean you've never been noted for your love of rap. (Lars laughs)

JH: That's very true. You know, I really wanted to hate it a lot, but it was pretty cool. I was more kind of wrapped up in the 'what they had done without me' part. Then there'd been this '... if the song is great, oh that's cool that they did it' feeling and 'if the song is crap, see you can't do it' feeling. But it was more that something went on (without me), I understand that it had to, I understand they had to keep their hands busy, I understand that part. And to kind of bond together through that thing helped them. And that's worth it completely.

Do you think it would have happened without the situation being what it was? I mean, if you guys had all been recording the album and this Beatz guy had come along and said, 'by the way I'd like this to happen,' do you think you would have been like, 'ahh not really...'

JH: Of course not, it wouldn't have happened the same way.

KH: It wouldn't have been the same.

LU: It wouldn't have been the same.

JH: I'm not saying that it wouldn't have happened, I'm saying it wouldn't have been in the same way.

LU: Again, of course it wouldn't have been the same. But I think that we certainly are at a place where we consider ourselves to be more open to anything. More so than the last time I said it. I'm guilty of saying that every six months or whatever, but it...

Were you guys pleasantly surprised with what came out?

LU: Yeah, I heard it when it was mastered about four to six weeks ago. I think it sounds very strong. It's very unique.

KH: It is unique.

LU: Yes it is. I wish, like I said to you before and like I've said to James, my biggest regret about it was that James wasn't a part of it, simply to share the experience. Because it was a really enriching experience.

Finally, is there any prospective release date for the new Metallica album?

KH: It will come out when it's done.

LU: No, it will come out probably...

JH: After it's done.

KH: After it's done.

BR: Hopefully it won't come out before it's done.

LU: Hopefully it won't come out before it's been done....

Let it be known, dear readers, that the peanut gallery is alive and kicking here.

LU: (indignantly) I think we've been on our best behavior the last hour and half!

JH: (seriously) I'd like it to come out soon because I think it's great and I want to get it done.

OK, so you guys are working fast?

JH: We're working faster than we've ever worked.

KH: But it's just like the whole, the big picture, it's hard. It's hard to get an accurate answer. Things might change. I mean we might take a left turn that brings us to a totally different spot.

BR: The great thing is with the experience of the Presidio and even some of the other stuff, it's a little slower now because we're doing a lot of talking and work and stuff, other kinds of work like the Ramones thing, but the funny thing is, you know, when we get back from our little break (everyone took three weeks in June off – Ed.) that's happening, we could write, these guys could put together like a song, 10 songs and we could just go 'that's it.' So, it's really up in the air. That's what's so great about working this quickly and the way we are.

The thing to note is that it is working well and everyone's happy about how it's working and it's strong. The Ramones song quickly before we switch off.

LU: Which one, there are so many?

I don't know which one you're doing and I don't know what it's for, so...

LU: But, um, when we figure it out we're going to tell Rob Zombie to not keep him waiting.

KH: Should I call him tonight?

So, basically it's Rob Zombie's Ramones tribute record and you guys are...

KH: It's a Ramones tribute album and it's coming out on Rob Zombie's label. That's Rob's other involvement, other than doing a song.

LU: It was a nice kind of 'easing into work again' and, of course, two seconds after we sat down in that room, we just started jamming on the new great riffs and then the Ramones stuff almost became a little bit of a kind of a nuisance. Because from not playing music together for 11 months, or whatever it was, we were just so psyched to get to the Metallica stuff. But it's been fun, the energy, short spurts of Ramones energy.

Do you want to go into what you've recorded? Do you want to go into track titles?

LU: We've jammed on eight songs.

BR: Down to two now.

LU: We've worked on...basically the idea was just to play some stuff and have some fun with it. So, 'We're A Happy Family,' 'Cretin Hop,' 'Now I Wanna Sniff Some Glue...'

KH: 'Today Your Love, Tomorrow The World.'

LU: 'Commando.'

KH: '53rd & 3rd.'

LU: Songs like that. Mostly from the first four records and we've narrowed it down to four, now today we've seemed to have narrowed it down to two. And there you have it.

Great, good. Thank you.

nce we finished this latest round table, I was aware of the day's significance. This had (as mentioned at the beginning) been their first proper photo shoot day for nearly 16 months, this had been their first 'interview' together since James went into rehab, and later on, they were going to play a live show for the first time in approximately two years.

I always felt they'd be fine, that the genuinely good people at the core of matters would find their way through and re-connect. I think what had always been the single greatest surprise for me throughout the past year, had been when I'd see or hear little snippets of the guys' own insecurities and uncertainties; even reading back over some of this discussion, I'm surprised that they felt that vulnerable at times. But what I can say, unequivocally, is this.

The Metallica which is recording as you read this, is a Metallica that is stronger and more impervious than ever before. That isn't to say it cannot get stronger (and I'm sure it will)... it's to say that they have discovered the sort of personal (and family) strength which quite simply allows people and situations to live longer, richer and fuller lives. Between their courage, and your patience, the future looks rather bright in Metalliland.

BAND COMMENTS

The Love is Back!
The # is up to 3!
The vibe is Good!
The other rejected title for the
book you're holding
"Metallica: The Roundtable Interviews"

THIS PARTICULAR PIECE HAS MAJOR RELEVANCE TO ME IN THAT IT WAS A PERIOD OF TIME THAT FELT LIKE WE WERE FINALLY UNITED AND COMING TO BEING A BAND! I FELT A HUGE AMOUNT OF RELIEF + SATISFACTION BEING ABLE TO SIT DOWN WITH MY BROS. AND RECONNECT WITH THEM AND THE MET CLUB AUDIENCE. THIS WAS A BRIGHT MOMENT AFTER SOME VERY DARK TIMES.

3/04

A GREAT TIME IN MY LIFE. TO HAVE WALKED THRU FIRE AND WORKED AT ALL RELATIONSHIPS. REVEALING OURSELVES TO EACH OTHER. FAMILY LIFE AND BAND LIFE JOINING TOGETHER. BALANCING THOSE PASSIONS IS CHALLANGING AND WORTH EVERY MOMENT.

JH   3/04

Raiders Gig

'Tallica/Raiders STOP PRESS shocker!!!

Andy Lars!

IT FELT GOOD—
REAL GOOD!

WHITE
TRAILER
TRASH!!!

That was awesome. Just unbelievable. **Two passions of mine coming together.** I went out on stage and I said, "Look Mom, I'm playing for the Raiders." And it was kind of, "Hey, wait, I am!"... I can imagine what jitters they go through, because we do the same. You play whether you're sick or not. You get psyched up – there are tons of similarities. But playing in that parking lot and wanting to feel a little responsible for the win…there were lots of people who came up afterwards saying, "That was awesome; the parking lot thing was so cool." And we had no idea what it was going to be like. It could have been one dude with a hot dog out there flipping us off. "Hey, you're disrupting my barbecue!" It was just the right amount of people – everything went just right.
JAMES HETFIELD

Sunday, Jan. 19th 2003 NFL AFC Championship Game
Oakland Raiders vs Tennessee Titans

Raiders Smash Titans 41 to 24!!!

LAUNCH PARTY

ON JULY 6TH 2002, METALLICA PLAYED THEIR FIRST LIVE SHOW IN OVER TWO YEARS, AND THEIR FIRST PERFORMANCE TOGETHER SINCE JAMES HETFIELD HAD EMERGED FROM REHAB. THE OCCASION? A PRIVATE PARTY TO CELEBRATE THE LAUNCH OF THE BAND'S NEW WEBSITE AT THEIR NORTHERN CALIFORNIAN HQ. THE AUDIENCE? 120 FAN CLUB MEMBERS WHO HAD WON A COMPETITION. NOT ONLY DID FANS GET TO SEE THE BAND PLAY ONE OF THEIR MOST INTIMATE SHOWS EVER, A SELECT GROUP OF GRAND PRIZE WINNERS WERE TAKEN ON A MINI-BUS TOUR OF OLD METALLIHAUNTS THROUGHOUT THE BAY AREA. THEIR TOUR GUIDES? LARS ULRICH, JAMES HETFIELD AND KIRK HAMMETT! AND TO CAP IT ALL OFF, ATTENDEES SIGNED UP FOR A SPOT AUDITION TO GO AND PLAY BASS WITH THE BAND ON ONE SONG DURING THE SET (BOB ROCK FILLED THE MAIN BASS DUTIES). IT WAS, AS YOU CAN SEE FROM THE FOLLOWING PHOTOS, QUITE AN EVENT. BUT WHY TAKE MY WORD FOR IT WHEN YOU CAN DIGEST THE WIT AND WISDOM OF WINNER, AND FAN CLUB MEMBER, ANNE SMITH'S DIARY… ERR, THAT SOUNDS LIKE A NOVEL DOESN'T IT?!

EDITOR, MARCH 2004

THE METALLICA CLUB MAGAZINE . VOLUME 9 . NUMBER 3 . 2002

ANNE SMITH

The Metallilair: HOLY SHIT!!!!!!!!!! there is a table set for all of us... weird to eat surrounded by cameras (DOCUMENTARY CREW – ED) w/mike in the face of whoever is talking. We said grace and I felt really comfortable w/them, like they are my friends. The guys remind each other to eat lots of carbs b/c they have to play.

The bus OOOOOHHHHHHMMYYYYGGG-GOOOODDDD!!!!!!!!!!!!! We just got on the bus and my knee is fucking touching James Hetfield's knee! Never in my wildest dreams did I ever imagine I would be chilling on a bus bumping knees w/James!

I am amazed – Lars just spilled a little soda and he is cleaning it up himself! They even have impeccable manners, what isn't super wonderful about these guys????

SUPER FUNNY!!!!!!!! Lars was telling us how he was so jealous of James when they lived together b/c he had a real bed, not just a mattress on the floor. Who would ever imagine that at one time in Lars' life he was jealous over a bed???? He thinks this may have been the start of his inferiority complex. How funny!

By far the absolute coolest stop on the tour was of the infamous Metallimansion. I can't believe how ridiculously small it is! How could so many people live here at the same time and write two history-making albums!

The garage is seriously small! I can't believe this guy let us in his house. I'm not sure if he even knows who Metallica is, hee, hee! The garage was locked which sucked. Kirk wants to airlift the garage so they can have it (like w/the Unabomber's house). How fucking cool would that be?

I thanked Kirk for everything and told him how fucking cool the whole day was and he thanked me for coming!!!! Thanked me for coming???? They open their home to us and then thank us for showing up?

Ear plugs????? They offer us fucking ear plugs???? Do they think the room is filled w/a bunch of pussies or w/ a bunch of hard core Metallifans?????

One of my favorite parts of this whole day was crossing the street. Seems gay, huh? But how cool to cross the street w/Metallica. Four lanes of traffic just stop in the middle of nowhere so these guys can cross! What a life!

Meetime!

What? Can't hear you!!!

It's super late and even after a long day entertaining all of us for so long, and playing, and probably being sick of us, the guys are still hanging out bullshitting w/us peons. Unfuckingbelievable how cool these guys are!

After the fact: it was by far the coolest fucking day of my entire fucking life!

a·perfect·circle

In 2002, The Metallica Club and SO WHAT! magazine decided to run a competition for members. The challenge was both simple and daunting; write 150 words explaining why you should be flown out to the band's HQ to interview them about the making of their then-in-progress "St. Anger" album. I studiously read through hundreds of entries, all of which carried tremendous enthusiasm, but one in particular caught my eye within two sentences. Jim Murphy, a 22 year old East Coast student living near Syracuse, appeared to be the winner. More than wanting to meet his heroes and get autographs, Jim expressed some specific angles and directions his interview would take. Done.

A couple of months later, as we drove up to HQ, Jim was very serenely terrified. We discussed the job in hand, his studious preparations and I spent a lot of time reassuring him. By the end of the evening, Lars had made a new friend. In three weeks time, I received a tremendous story. Indeed, everyone liked it so much that the band made sure he came out during the Summer Sanitarium Tour 2003 for his first 'official' assignment. Here, then, is that rare and wonderful thing; a young fan's view in a mature writer's voice. Editor — January 2004

five minutes ago the closest I'd ever been to Metallica was front row at a concert. Now, standing in the kitchen of HQ in San Francisco, the band and I have exchanged greetings and handshakes (not to mention Hawaiian shirts) and Lars Ulrich is inviting me to hear material from the band's first all-original studio effort in almost six years. "Five minutes ago" never seemed so far away.

I eagerly accept Lars' invitation, and he leads me into the control room. We move through quickly, barely long enough for me to observe the cluttered whiteboard and smile at Kirk strumming along to a song playing overhead. I'll end up spending most of the day there, but for now Lars guides me through the control room and into the musical hub at HQ, the A-room. This is the place where the band jams on and creates most music for the album. Drum sets, amplifiers, guitars, microphones, wires, a giant blackboard, and even a piano help to fill the enormous room to almost full capacity. Engulfed in the array of instruments and equipment, and overcome by a tangible energy in the air, I immediately know that some amazing music is played here. QUITE FRANKLY, I STILL CAN'T BELIEVE I'M HERE...

Bob Rock lets me know that James will be recording vocals today. The notion of watching James Hetfield sing only feet from me is extremely overwhelming. I try to soak in the situation and remain calm, and find looking at the infamous whiteboard helps wonderfully. Lars told me earlier that I'd notice the band started on the left side of the board with serious album name possibilities, but as time and the board go on things get out of control. There are some great titles on the left: "Fame is Not A Medica-tion" and "St. Anger." But those are far outnumbered by the fun names: "Light-Speed Math-Metal," "Air & Feces," and my personal (must-be-Lars' idea) favorite "I Mean, Fuck!"

now that I've been given a tour and preview of music it's time for me to sit back and observe. Bob takes his place at the board and I take a seat next to Phil Towle on the couch. I make mention of its comfort and Lars says he now has a renewed appreciation for the furniture, adding "Phil should know better than any of us, all he does is sit on the fucking couch all day." Phil Towle introduces himself to me as Metallica's performance coach. It's a title that quite often gets him a sarcastic comment or two, such as, "did he actually just introduce himself like that and keep a straight face?" The door opens and James enters the room quietly, sitting by his microphone stand. He observes everyone with eyes half closed, and his mouth open just enough to allow in slow, deep breaths of air. A small smile appears on his face as Lars affirms Phil's perpetual sofa-like presence by dryly dubbing him the "performance couch." For the most part, though, James remains removed from all conversation and concentrates on carefully preparing his voice to work. Moments from now, I'll reflect on the strange dichotomy between his peaceful warmups and the terribly aggressive vocals he'll growl into the microphone shortly thereafter.

James stands and locks the door behind him to prevent any interruptions. Today, the band is working on a track loosely named 'Searching for Donuts.' The guys joke that it will be the theme for the next season of "Cops," but the title only exists as a reference to the song's main riff, to which you can perfectly sing along "searching for donuts, searching for donuts." The tentative title may come from a joke, but the subject matter is less jovial, the proposed theme being a search for meaning in life and death. James lets the group know he intends to focus on that central theme and flush it out using metaphors and imagery. The song begins with the "searching for donuts" theme played by a solitary bass, but the rest of the instruments quickly enter and add aggression. One section of the tune occurs a few times, and is a refreshing break from the barrage of pure metal. In it, Lars plays a grooving backbeat on his snare drum with the snares turned off to give a more tom-tom sound. That percussion, coupled with the overlaid plucking of acoustic strings, gives off a dreamy feeling of something going on and on, with no end in sight. Then the 'dream' returns to nightmare as the frantic guitars charge in and build the aggression back up to a head. Throughout the track, the four guys are scribbling right along on their notepads as I am, but instead of taking notes they're writing lyrics inspired by the music they hear. The song ends on the same theme with which it started, further perpetuating the notion of an ongoing search that ends no farther than where it began. I wait to see what turn the song writing process takes next, and that becomes the most intriguing turn of all.

Of all possible situations I considered before coming to Metallica HQ, sitting alone perfectly quiet with the band for fifteen minutes is one I happened to leave out. There is a stark contrast between the bombardment of sound that so recently assaulted our ears and the deep silence that now consoles them. It's also interesting to note that the room presently holds almost a dozen people: film crew, web crew, production crew, the band, and me. Yet still, the only audible noise is the light scratching of pens and flipping of pages. This is the new songwriting approach we have heard about, and apparently the control room's daily crew is more comfortable with it than I am. For a few moments, I shuffle and squirm in my seat waiting for someone to say something, but I eventually calm myself and just observe this interesting phenomenon at work. Although the environment is one of democracy and equality within the quartet, James Hetfield's body carries the instrument of focus today, and so he has an unspoken control over the room. Lars and Bob are seated at the control board, Kirk is on the couch and James is in front of the microphone. The four are merely feet away from each other, but each is engulfed in isolation struggling to bring their ideas out via poetic words.

Lars breaks the silence and asks Kirk about a Buddhist belief, Samsura, they discussed earlier in correlation with this song. The belief is that everything is a cycle of suffering: birth, life, and death. Bob joins them in the discussion and asks James where his ideas are going. James does not even glance up from his page and only answers, "I'm just trying to be quiet." There is a bit of tension in the air and it seems as though only

James can break it, which he does when asking for another playback. We listen again; this time James mouths lyrics from his page making corrections where words don't fit the melody. Lars and Bob have put down their pads and are talking by the control board. At the song's conclusion, the real process of lyric writing and vocal creation begins. Each member of the group has written his own ideas on a notepad and now they take turns first reading off what they've scribbled out and then discussing them with the group. James leads off. Having nicknamed his page Famous Death Talk, he tells us that the song feels like a frantic search for meaning of why we are here. The search is a difficult one as evidenced in James' contradictory lyrics, 'searching to know how not to die, dying to know where to search. You look in your closet for a monster you don't want to find.' Lars and Bob commiserate with James about fears of birth and death.

A talk of faith arises when Bob mentions a search for God, and James completes the thought by noting that faith allows us to not be afraid of the unknown. Kirk, who has been generally quiet the whole time, finally joins the conversation to read his lyrics. While the other guys had lots of ideas, nothing prepared any of us for the page and a half of poetry Kirk had created. His words not only lament death, but also birth: "bright cold light, bookends this life." After each couple of lines we are all floored by Kirk's lyrics. James is especially fond of the line "my lifestyle determines my deathstyle." Now that everyone's ideas are presented, the sheets are given to James and placed on the music stand in front of his microphone. It's time for him to take his and the group's contributions and record some kick ass vocals.

Watching James sing and record vocals instilled a lot of pride in me as a fan. Album after album, I've admired his voice for its power and strength while also appreciating his ability to sing softly and with emotion. In concert James is also incredibly powerful and usually dead on, yet I was never quite sure that what we hear on records is exactly what comes from James... until now. Right there, six feet away from him, there is as much authority and force in his voice as on a record turned up full volume. Nothing is false. That said, I admit that the vocal recording process is a tedious one. Lyrics, melodies, phrasing, tone and more are changed and changed again, over and over until the best versions are found. It takes a few times to get each part right, and the better half of an hour is spent deciding exactly which vocal melody is best to use Kirk's lifestyle/deathstyle line, but the process is an intimate one and I'm incredibly grateful to have witnessed it.

After the grueling process of choosing melodies and takes of them is complete, we hear one final playback of the tune. The vocals lift the song to a higher level, bringing it one step closer to a polished product. The band seems satisfied with their work for the day, and the mood becomes more relaxed in the control room. James is looking at a new frame for the latest model of the ESP Explorer, Kirk is reading again and Bob and Lars are chatting at the board. Steffan enters the room to inform the guys that it's about time for the interview. It's agreed that we'll hold the Q&A at the kitchen table, so Steffan and I make our way out to set things up.

Jim Murphy: Is there a lot of stuff being left behind from The Presidio sessions?

LU: The way I would say it is that there's nothing about any of this that's that black and white. It's not like, 'this is going to work, this is not going to work, this is going forward, this is being left behind.' It's been a really long musical journey that we've been on for a year and a half, and that has taken us over a lot of different places. We seem to have found something in the last month or two that we're really psyched about. It sits in a fairly different place than some of the earlier stuff on that journey. Like Kirk was saying, some of the stuff from the Presidio is being kind of hepped up. Some more of it might be hepped up. Some of it might be left behind. Some of it might be hepped up for another record, for a B-side, for a Fan Can, for eBay, whatever. So, I mean, there are no real absolutes about any of this because what we've tried to do as we've been going forward in this process is to not – in the past there were always all these rules, and there were always all these things, the way it should be. And me and him [points to James] would write a bunch of songs and say 'here are a bunch of songs that are going to get recorded.' It was all these specifics. So what we've been trying to do in this process is to not have specifics. So there's a lot of material sitting around, a lot of different levels of quality, a lot of different levels of intensity. The stuff that we seem to be psyched about putting on our next record seems to be the more aggressive kind of faster, more fucked up shit. And we'll see where that takes us.

KH: It feels good to be in this place, playing more fast, aggressive fucked up shit. Definitely.

JM: Just watching the whole lyric-writing process, everything seemed really democratic in that everybody's ideas were really appreciated, and nothing was really rejected. Is that always the case? Is there ever any conflict as far as what you're all trying to do?

KH: We try to be progressive and forward-moving. So you don't want to shoot anything down before it has a chance to grow. Because the stupidest riff can lead to the most beautiful part. I mean, with the writing process, you don't really know until it's all put into context what anything is going to be like. And so what we do is we try to put down a ton of music and almost over-compensate for the amount of riffs and notes and parts, and then we put it together. And it's a very simple process. If it's not strong enough, it just doesn't make it into the song. And that's something that's very understandable to all of us. It isn't a point of, oh, my riff made it in or my riff didn't or now you changed my riff or whatever. There's none of that thinking.

LU: I think a good way of saying it is that we used to have different areas that we would all protect individually. It was like I would guard something specific, he would guard something specific, James, Jason – everybody had their kind of things that they would be very protective of, and then end up being incredibly defensive about if that was ever challenged. And I think that's the key thing that's evaporated. Nobody has a particular thing that they're guarding like their own crown jewels – do you know what I mean? – with the lyrics and stuff, and it just becomes this thing that sort of hovers in the space in between us. And we're getting better at hearing other people out. We're getting better at not defending our own position to the point of not hearing what the other person is saying, and all this kind of stuff. And it's an ongoing process. And tomorrow we might be better than we are today, but hopefully today we're better than we were yesterday. And that's a lot of the stuff we've been working on with Phil and so on.

JM: This is directed to James: where did the idea come from for everyone to contribute lyrics? Was it difficult to give up the control that you had over that one specific area, the songwriting?

JH: It was easier than I thought to let go of that area that I protected, the lyric writing. It was easy to let go because I put myself in that place with the last three albums – it wasn't as fun as it was, say, the first three or four albums. It was harder and harder to write lyrics on my own. It took – especially with "Load" and "Re-load," where we had 20 or 30 songs that just backlogged – I had to come up with all these lyrics for 20 or 30 songs. It was too much. It was not fun. It became more of a burden than it became a release. So in that mode, mindset, it was easier to let it go, to get some help. And you know, at the end of the day, we all put lyrics out there and we know which ones sound best, and it doesn't matter so much where it's come from, because there's always a spark that can get fanned and put into a fire easily by another person. The spark doesn't do anything if it sits inside. And once it's out there, everyone else can help fan it and turn it into something really, really great. It doesn't have to be a whole sheet of poetry; it only takes one word sometimes. We've discovered each other more by writing lyrics. We can tell how everyone thinks. You know, 'here's a subject' and then everyone goes in their own little cave for a little while, and when they come out, it's like 'ooh, he's gone about it this way, he's gone about it that way,' and Bob as well. And it's really pretty fun for me to kind of gather all the stuff. Some of it might be super wordy and it gets condensed into something better. Or the other way around – it gets added to. So, in a way I have a say on how it ends up only because I have to sing it. And if it has to stay that certain way, sometimes it doesn't sing as well, but I still try to get that meaning across, or make it more potent or more vague or whatever the situation calls for.

JM: Do the expectations of other people or your own expectations of the album play a role in how you think, or what you want to play, for this record?

KH: Absolutely. You've got to expect the very best from yourself. I personally believe your whole approach makes a big difference in the studio.

JM: But as far as what other people think after everything that's gone on?

KH: You know, I don't give a fuck what any people think.

JM: That's what I was asking.

KH: There's maybe a handful of people who I'm concerned with, whose thoughts I'm concerned with, but past those handful of people – and most of them go in and out of this building anyway – other than that – we're doing this to please ourselves. If people like it, cool, if people don't like it, that's cool, too. I mean, it's the same old fucking storyline that we've been spewing since 1983. It really hasn't changed.

JH: That's a really good question, too, because I go back and forth with that. I want to say 'fuck everybody; it doesn't matter,' but I'm tired of saying 'fuck everybody.' I want to be a part of the world. But what I'm finding is that through the confidence in ourselves, we need less and less of that outside acceptance or validation. But also, I enjoy playing it for other people more, getting their response, knowing that it's more interesting to me how they respond to it, and knowing that I'm not going to freak out or overreact on what their reactions are.

JM: Are there any fears about touring because you've been away for so long?

JH: Oh yeah, yeah. Besides all of the regular ones, like the dreams we were talking about today (during the band's regular morning meeting-ED.) where the drumsticks are made of rubber or you can't cut through the air to hit the drum or my guitar cord's not long enough – you know, like these nightmares we have pre-tour. The guitar cord's not long enough for me to get to the mike to sing, or the neck's made of rubber and all that stuff, all of those kind of anxieties and fears of playing –not actually getting up in front of giant crowds. It takes a while to get used to that again. It's not a normal occurrence for humans. And then for me, the road life was pretty destructive, and now, going through rehab and finding out how to really be me and be comfortable with that – and everything I've tried since then is kind of like trying it again for the first time, really. In the fear department, how am I going to handle this? How am I going to respond to this? Am I going to fall off the wagon or end up wanting to go back to something that's so comfortable but not good for me? So there's some of that fear there. But everyone here is kind of clued into that, and I feel pretty safe that people understand that there's some anxiety and fear there. And I want to tour and I want to do it the right way that's best for me. And everyone's kind of been there for me. It's real nice to feel that, because it hasn't been that way before, in my head.

JM: Will those feelings, those fears, affect the way that you tour and how you go on tour?

KH: We won't know until we get there.

JH: Right now we're agreeing that we don't want to go out for two years straight. There's a different feeling about tour. We want to have more fun, we want to involve the other aspects of our lives, like family, and we want to be able to balance that, because family is very involved in Metallica now, and vice-versa. Metallica is in my home life a lot more than it ever has been, so that has to be taken into consideration. And I'd like us to all have fun on the road. And things like "Summer Sanitarium" and shorter stints like that have always been kind of fun for me. You can see the light at the end, and it seems much more comfortable for me.

LU: I think it's important to acknowledge that when you're talking about that, you're really talking about two different things. You're talking, number one, about playing music with a bunch of guys that you know, love and share an experience with, an audience and so on. That's the two hours a day vibe. Then there's the other 22 hours a day which not only have a different energy from those two hours, but a different energy from home life, from everything else that we've been experiencing for the last two years. So there's a lot of – just the idea of being away from home, the idea of traveling, the idea of kids in school, there's all this shit that fucking comes in the wake of it that is – like James is saying – it's sort of like – up until the year 2001–2001 was the first calendar year we didn't play a show. We've played a show every year since 1982 and before. 'So it's been a while,' to quote Aaron Lewis (from Staind – Ed). We know we want to tour, and what's happened in the last couple of months is that most of the things that we're afraid of, by the time we're done re-entering something we've done before, we realize that what we were afraid of, and the level of fear we had, was unsubstantiated. But at the same time, maybe at some point there will be something that we will deal with again where the fear level won't be unsubstantiated and it will be… you know, who knows?

JM: Something all the fans want me to ask is what sort of tour will this be: U.S. or a world tour?

LU: If they've got something between a backyard and a stadium, chances are we'll show up at some point.

JH: We'll play within 500 miles of where they are.

LU: I mean, there's really no – some of the early stuff we've talked about initially certainly covers North America and major populated parts outside of North America.

JM: Do you think you'll maybe do some smaller shows to put yourself back into playing live?

LU: I hope so. Small shows are a lot of fun for us. Little kids, big kids, big shows, small shows–all of it.

JM: Has there been any sort of talk at all about who might replace Jason when you guys go on tour? Will it be someone who becomes part of the band or someone who just tours with you?

JH: There's been a lot of discussion about that recently. It's something we knew had to happen and we just kind of logged it in the back of our 'we'll get to it' brain. If we've got a deadline for recording, we want to play some shows possibly this summer, we're going to need a bass player, and we would like to have a bass player that's in the band. We don't want to have some hired gun out there. We want a fourth member.

KH: We want to be the unit that we've always been, basically.

JH: So we're making a list.

JM: You are thinking of actual names?

KH: It's a very short list. And it isn't going to be someone who doesn't have previous experience. We want someone who's had experience playing in front of x amount of people and knows what it's like going on the road for six months or so, and can deal with a lot of things that–hidden things that only come with experience. We don't want to find someone who we have to teach all over again. I mean that's really important, that the person that we pick has experience.

LU: Yeah, because I think that experience is also going to help us. The first time we walk out on the stage, it's not going to be particularly easy for us. I think the key thing for us in the discussions we've had is we want somebody that's on the same wavelength. Not to say that that couldn't be, like, a young cat, but the wavelength that we're on right now is certainly age-related. So if it's some really young guy, he'd have to have lived a really full life already. So there's a few names, we'll throw them out in the group, and we're going to get to it now, a little sooner than we planned.

JM: I'd like to totally switch gears now. How does it affect you if fans say negative things about you? Is it hard to ignore that sometimes?

KH: You need to balance it out. You can't just read all the good stuff about you. You have to read the bad stuff too and take it all in perspective. For me, I just find it really entertaining reading all the negative stuff. I really get a kick out of that, because I just apply it to my truths and see whether or not I can live with it or not. But I think it's really important to balance it out, to be balanced.

JH: There's a couple of ways that people criticize. One way–when I read something and I can laugh at it, that means it doesn't really fit. And then sometimes with stuff that's like, 'hey, that hurts a little bit, I think there's a little truth to that. Check that out.' And then there's just the flat out people out to hurt you, just to be mean, and that hurts, no matter what. No matter how strong you want to be, it's going to hurt a little bit. So, the more confidence we have in what we're doing, and in ourselves as individuals, how we have each other's back – you know, like all the Napster stuff, you know, residual stuff that Lars had carried for quite a while, there were a lot of shots taken, and that sucked. I feel we've got each other's backs more now, and it feels a lot better. I look back at all the crap that I did to help instigate some of that stuff, kind of cheap talk within the press and the band and just to make myself feel okay, and it's not okay.

LU: I think it's also, I think in the past we've had this very aloof arrogance and, you know, 'fuck you,' and maybe at that time that was how we chose to deal with a lot of those things. There are some things – I don't mind being more vulnerable and I don't mind being more open about my vulnerability. And some shots you take, they do hurt even though you always try and put the best foot forward and just pretend it ricochets right off of you. James was talking a little bit about how you make the decisions about what you want to take shit for, and so on, but it takes a little while sometimes, especially in the age of the Internet. You know, the privacy that it gives you gives people to take the cheapest of shots possible. That takes a little bit of getting used to. The first time you come across some of that stuff it's like, 'whoa,' and you realize a lot of it has to do with the fact that these people feel they can take these exaggerated steps because they are in the privacy of their own little world on their keypads. Some of that stuff is just not so easy to deal with.

With James having to leave, Lars, Kirk and I continued the interview a little while longer.

JM: I'd like to know if there are any slower, mellower songs on this forthcoming album?

KH: It just wasn't there. No one came up with the music to push any of the songs in that direction. Wouldn't you say?

LU: There's not anything particularly ballady. You know what? We sort of kind of figured out, without wanting to sound too cocky, that we're capable of –here's a song that sits in this shape right now. Give us a day and we can turn it into this over here, or give us another day and we can turn it

into this. So a song is a bunch of chord progressions and a bunch of words that sit in one place and you can take that and you can take the crunch out of the guitars and you can play the same chord progressions picking, and James can sing it in a softer voice and I can slow the drums down to quarter time, and then all of a sudden it's a ballad. Some of the things that you've heard today or some of the things that we're doing that are going to be on the record that started out live in a different shape, then we said 'turn it up a little' – hepped it up – on some pretty precious moments on The Presidio.

JM: That must be hard to do, to take a song that was something and try to make it something else.

LU: It's hard that in the historical content because, at least specifically for me, I've had this very, very arrogant relationship with every song we've ever written, which is, 'Hi, we're Metallica, we write songs and every song we write is a fucking 11 on a 9 scale.' Do you know what I mean? 'And you're not going to tell me any different little man, little person.' Do you know what I mean?

So there's been that kind of arrogance associated with – and a month ago there was a pretty key moment where we showed up here–we had about thirty-five songs – everybody came in with a list of eighteen songs, and that day was the first day in the history of Metallica –you probably read about it – where we – we didn't actually sit down and have like you do with like a kid where you say, 'okay, now we're going to send the diapers back to the store.' But we actually had a bunch of songs that did not make it to the next level. Even though we didn't have a kind of a goodbye party, we walked away three hours later and I realized that we had just discarded more or less half of the material that we'd been working on for the last year and a half –at least, maybe not thrown it away but discarded it back into someplace where it was most likely not going to get into the triple A leagues. We

243

sent it back down to the minors and they will probably hover at least until maybe the next record or some film thing comes up or whatever.

JM: Were those unanimous decisions?

KH: Out of 35 songs, we only agreed on four songs –

LU: And those are the four that everyone talked about. We only had four songs. We sat down, and, well these are the only four songs that we all agree on, so now we have four, but those four were the four that were rrrrrrr [makes metal faces and air drums with hands implying heavy/fast songs]. And it was just so weird that we sat there and agreed on 35 songs, and there were so many different things going on, and the only thing we all agreed on was kind of cosmic. And we sat down and said, maybe we truly are wired to just go 'rrrrrr' all the time, instead of running around and pretending that, like I said before, all this other stuff that we keep searching for. But really, maybe we could forfeit every single iota of a search for something that, when we really open up, what's really in there is 'rrrrrr.' Do you know what I mean?

KH: Yeah, I thought that once we had the Presidio songs, I thought that was the album. I thought we would get here, maybe write a few more songs and then polish those up. But now, I mean, in retrospect, looking back a year and a half, I mean, you can even call the Presidio songs demos. I hate to say that. A demo definitely has a negative connotation as not so good, or rough, but there was a time when I actually thought that that was the album. It's only because we were just so persistent and just forging through and creating new material that we kind of just like broke new ground. And then after that wrote four songs that just raised the bar so high that we kind of looked down on these other songs and they were way down there, and these other songs were just so high. What do you do? I mean, you have to shoot for the moon, or else. You can't just shoot for Texas or something, you have to shoot for the moon. And that's what we're doing in this situation.

LU: That's the third time today you invoked the moon as a symbol. Is that something you need to talk to Phil about? The moon represents –

KH: The moon is lunar. Luna is the Greek word for crazy, 'lunatic.' So maybe I'm just turning into a lunatic.

LU: Turning into one?

KH: Sorry. Have been one for a while and just need to seek help. The Presidio sessions were a very, very good thing for us though. It got us back into the swing of things, made us feel like a band again, because we really did not feel like a band before the Presidio, because there was just three of us and Bob. We hadn't played a note together. No one knew what was going to happen with the band. And so the Presidio was very, very cathartic, and therapeutic, as well as being what it was. It was an important step to get to this point. A large, large step.

JM: As far as bringing the songs up to the level of those four, was it difficult to hold yourselves up to a personal standard that you set? Or was it more of a freeing thing, and less restrictive, because you realized these songs aren't good enough so right now so let's just...

KH: For me there is no looking back. It's take those four and run with them and create more that are of the same quality and the standard. That was my attitude. And you know, it felt good knowing where we stood in the overall project. We had more of a perspective of what we needed to do and what we didn't need to do. I mean "Load" and "Re-load" were so unique. I don't know why the fans are tripping that way. You know, we're not one to embrace a sound for more than a few years. We always change. I can see how people would think we would stick with the "Load" and "Re-load" sound,

but we're all into just exploring, and we're still doing it now. We have a very exploratory spirit. We're bound to head in this direction anyway, I think–or a direction that was different from "Load" and "Re-load."

LU: I would say that I've used this – the record's not even done and I'm already getting bored with my own analogies – but I've used this analogy three or four times already, and maybe this won't be one of the last times, but I had the old shoe theory, which is that you have a closet full of shoes, and there's all these new-fangled weird-assed fucking shoes that you can put on every day. And you keep trying all these different shoes on, and all of them are wacky crazy and new and different, and somewhere else. But over in the corner is this old pair of shoes that you used to wear a lot but for some reason you just don't go over there because you don't think they're going to really feel right. And you go through all these other pairs of shoes and one day you're just – there's no other different pairs of shoes to try on and you go back to that old faithful pair of shoes tucked away way in the corner and you put them on and you know what? Those shoes feel way better than any of the other weird, new shoes in the closet. There's a degree of comfort, putting those old shoes on again, and how you're kind of psyched about how well they actually fit. And you know, we haven't played any of that [aggressive/heavy/fast] shit for 12, 13, 14 years, and now it's just pretty amazing how much fun it actually is. And maybe if we had played – that's what I said before – if we had started doing that shit a year and a half ago, if we'd started doing it five years ago, seven years ago, it would probably never feel right, but some way all the planets aligned. In September, October of 2002, it just fucking lined up again. That's my old shoe analogy.

KH: It's true, and I feel it's evident in our music. Wearing old shoes can definitely take you to a new place.

the sun is setting and the workers on the metal factory assembly line are punching out for the weekend. I walk downstairs to pack up my stuff and see Lars in the kitchen making himself a sandwich. I'm a little hungry, so I decide to steal a tuna sub (sandwich thievery... the mark of a good reporter! – Ed) and join him. During much of my last hour at Metallica HQ, Lars and I sit alone eating and chatting like old friends. I mention to Lars that, while the songs I've heard are new and unique in their own right, they definitely remind me of a younger Metallica. Without pause he wholeheartedly agrees that this album is a return to Metallica's aggressive roots. More is said about the album and Metallica in general, but I refrain from grabbing my tape recorder and instead choose to enjoy the moment. The feeling of sitting and talking music with Lars Ulrich is indescribable. Still, what makes my day most unforgettable is that this man, who inspires me musically and personally everyday, seems to be enjoying my company as much as I enjoy his.

6:00 p.m. — Goodbye, HQ

Five hours and five minutes ago, the coolest Metallica story I had to tell happened in Albany at the Pepsi Arena. I was pointing at Lars screaming, "You're the man!!" He looked back, pointed to himself, shook his head "no," then pointed to me and said, "you." My old shoes have taken me to some new places since then and, although I still think Lars is the man, I now have a new Metallica story to tell. ●

245

WHIPLASH

THE BAND ANSWERS FAN QUESTIONS

Lars, I am a second-year medical student interested in the budding field of pediatric gynecology. Since your wife, Skylar, is also a doctor, does she have any advice for attaining this dream?
Moneal S., Dublin, OH

LU: Skylar, do you wanna answer this?
SU: No, because it's a joke question... tell him he needs a therapist... think about it honey...

Lars, please tell me why you say "basically" so much in your interviews.
Jacob J., Stenlose, Denmark

LU: I don't know. I'm sorry. I've asked our esteemed editor to help me with this inherent problem I have. Thank you, Jacob, for pointing out one of my weaknesses. I strive every day to be the best person I can be, and I apologize once again for disappointing you in any way. If you would like a refund on this year's membership, or any previous years' membership, and a free goodie bag, please write directly to me c/o Vickie Strate.

Do you think girl rock drummers can make it, or will be accepted, in the music business?
Tabitha A., Glendale, CA

KH: Due to our culture and socialization about what gender gets to perform what role, people are conditioned to think that girls can't rock, but girls can rock. Ever hear of a band called Girlschool? Well, check them out... everything else is crap! But girls can rock, check out the Plasmatics... first album only.
LU: I got three words... The White Stripes from Detroit.

Hey guys! My question for all of you is, do you prefer to wear boxers or briefs?
Morven O., Dundee, Scotland

KH: That depends Morven... are you a male or female? Probably female otherwise you would know. Boxers are more comfortable, briefs hold it together more. It depends on whether or not you are walking around in front of anyone later with them on.

LU: (as Lars starts to strip in front of me – excited editor) (what the fuck is he talking about? – LU) it's briefs.

What is your favorite home cooked meal?
Nicki M., WA

KH: My wife's spaghetti sauce.
LU: Scrambled eggs, bacon, hash browns and toast or bagels.

James and Kirk, PLEASE tell all your guitar playing fans how to CORRECTLY play the fast palm muted bit in the main riff of 'Blackened,' it's even wrong in the "official" tab book, horribly wrong!
Chris J., Macon, GA

KH: Thanks for saying our riffs are great...
JH: Just play it really fast and it will sound right.
LU: James, what's a muted palm bit?
JH: Where you rest your palm on the bridge, mute the strings and get the chug and join the Capt Krunch club.

How come you've never played 'Dyers Eve,' off the "...Justice" album, live? Just curious because I have never seen it done.
Gabe G., San Antonio, TX

JH: It's too hard.
KH: It's too fast.
JH: It's too heavy.
KH: It's too far out of the range of our capabilities.
LU: It's just too much.

Kirk, is it true you did some cleaning and made French toast for The Ramones? (Because I heard the announcer said you did from The Rock & Roll Hall of Fame on VH1.)
Dorothy C., FL

KH: This is what happened. Johnny Ramone and I are big fans of breakfast, particularly pancakes, waffles, etc and for the r'n'r hall of fame, Johnny and I were discussing how our wives cannot cook breakfast and we have to do it ourselves. And Eddie Vedder was there and he couldn't believe that I could cook. So I told him that I went over

to Johnny's and cooked them breakfast once. Eddie Vedder then said, 'Kirk from Metallica cooks? Wow, that's a level of sensitivity that I didn't know existed,' and he incorporated it into his rock'n'roll hall of fame speech.

Lars, what the hell does '...so I dub thee unforgiven' mean?
Sergio S. Calexico, CA

LU: Fuck knows.

Guyz, what are the worst mistakes you've made on stage?
Simone M., Torino, ITALY

KH: Sometimes walking on stage.
LU: Probably leaving out the second chorus of 'Harvester of Sorrow' in Vienna in Sept 1991.

Kirk, did you ever think that you sucked at guitar?
Angel G., Bridgewater, NJ

KH: About 15 minutes ago.

Have you had any ideas for the design on your next custom guitar?
Anthony H., Brisbane, Qld, Australia

JH: Yes. I just got one, a kustom kulture. An artist friend of mine Dennis Mc Phail just finished one with all kinds of tattoo art.
KH: I always have a guitar design I wanna do in my head, just getting around to it is the problem.

I always wanted to know your opinion of what you guys would think of yourselves if you saw how you were today back in 1983. I've thought about this one damn question day and night, and now I finally have the chance to ask you guys...
Matt H., Springfield, PA

KH: When I was 20 years old, did I see how I would change into being the person that I am now at 39 years old? What I would have to say is that I would never have thought I would

be a goddamn surfer, let alone play jazz and blues on my guitar and dress up funny. I think nowadays I think I look closer to what I looked like back in 1983 because I have long hair and I'm wearing denim again. I'm wearing long hair and denim and leather jackets, so I mean if you compare me from 1983 to today there's not been much change, but if you compare me in 1983 to 1996 there was a lot of change. So my opinion on all of that is that it has been a lot of fun being all these different people and I don't regret any of it because it has been all very entertaining to me.

How did you guys become familiar with bands like Thin Lizzy? Like they were barely even heard of outside Ireland except for the 'Whiskey In The Jar' cover. P.S., that was really cool when you played Dublin in 1998.
Jonathan B., Arklow/Wicklow, Ireland

KH: I heard of Thin Lizzy back in 1976, when they had a hit single in America called 'The Boys Are Back In Town.' It was a song you couldn't get away from that summer on the radio, so I don't know what you're talking about when you say they were barely even heard of outside of Ireland. They were huge everywhere.
LU: Thin Lizzy was the biggest fucking thing in Denmark from '76–'80, and played there literally twice a year.

Since Metallica has covered Motörhead and I know you like them a lot, what is your favorite Motörhead record?
Ricardo T. , Vedras, Portugal

LU: "Overkill."
JH: "Another Perfect Day."
KH: "Ace Of Spades."

If you could be any kind of floatation device, what would it be?
Grant S., Melbourne Australia

LU: ????? Eh? The one that saves as many Metallica friends as possible, how's that?! (very pleasant—Ed)
JH: I'd be a giant, huge stinky whale.
KH: That's a no brainer...surfboard.

Doesn't being rich kind of take the fun out of Christmas... I mean what could someone buy you that you could not buy yourself?
Jason R., Villa Rica, Ga.

LU: Christmas is not the only thing it takes the fun out of, it pretty much goes for the other 364 days as well. No seriously, it's always cool when somebody does something creative and unique present-wise.
KH: It's not about monetary values, it's more about all the parties! And besides it's not about what you

give it's about what you get! Just kidding.
JH: As my good friend Bob Rock would say it's about the spirit of giving, asshole.

Do you ever listen to your own music during your free time? Like at home or in the car, or is that like being at work again?
Jihad R., San Jose, CA

LU: Is it really 'free time,' if I listen to my own music?

JH: When you're rich you have no free time... you're busy buying yourself gifts...
KH: ...and shopping for Xmas presents.

On looking back at your old stuff, are there any songs that you wish, on mixing down/mastering that you'd changed. (i.e. removing a dodgy effect or turning bass up louder?!!)
Vanessa M., Surrey England

LU: My only regret is that '...Sandman' song. That should've gone onto "The Great Filler Album."
JH: No, it is what it is for a reason.
KH: "...AJFA" (Ed asks 'any particular bit?') "...AJFA" (motions "whole thing" with hands).

There is this great Spastic Children picture of Kirk and James that I've seen where they both have their hair braided. (Which looks very cute! Especially on Kirk). What I want to know is first did you braid each other's hair? And second do you miss just going onstage and acting wild and crazy with no direction like Spastic Children did?
Carol F., Bridgewater, NJ

KH: We go onstage like that all the time, and I don't know how to braid.
JH: Y'mean like last tour? And we were too drunk to braid each other's hair. I think my old girlfriend braided mine; I wanted pipe-cleaners in mine like Pippi Longstocking's.

I heard through the grapevine that Flemming Rasmussen gave you guys a hard time when recording "...Justice." I heard that he was short-

tempered and pressured you guys a lot. Can you shed some light on this?
Angel G., Bridgewater, NJ

JH: I don't remember being pressured by him at all...
KH: I don't either, pressure was from ourselves.
LU: No, Flemming didn't give us a hard time. He challenged us and pushed us to be the best we could be at any of those particular points in time (yawn!).

Lars, are there any cartoons that your kids watch that drive you crazy and make you want to change the channel? Thanks for your time.
Jason, Wabash, IN

LU: Barney should be publicly hung, drawn and quartered while sharing a stage with the beheading of the Teletubbies. Other than that, most of it's tolerable and I would even go as far as to say that Blues Clues (with Steve, not the new guy!) is actually enjoyable.

What do you think about System of a Down? Og tak lars, for at være mit idol!
Jan Rúni P, Fuglafjørður, Faroe Islands

LU: Jeg syntes soad er overfede, et af mit favoritbands I ojeblikket. Og du er velkommen! Hej, forhelvede.

Lars, when the band came in France, on July 7th 1999, you said, at the end of the show, that Paris was the place where you most liked playing. Was it true or do you say this in every place you go to?
Richassen, Cannes, France

LU: For some reason Metallica and gigs in Paris have always gotten on very well. When I think back over the years some of the best shows we have ever played have been in Paris. The fans? Our mood? The way the planets aligned that day? Who knows, but it's always been solid and no, I don't say that in every place I go. ●

11

Everyone has a Ripper inside them

ROBERT TRUJILLO

Who better to speak about Metallica's brand new bassist than the man himself? Please welcome Mr. Robert Trujillo!

"I was born in Santa Monica, California – Dog Town. My mom and dad split up when I was five, and Dad was kind of a hippie, listening to a lot of hard rock– Rolling Stones, Led Zeppelin – and Mom was listening to a lot of Motown, R&B. So I grew up around a fair amount of music, because my parents were younger generation parents. My father played flamenco guitar, and the technique involved in flamenco is similar to a bass player's technique, so watching him play got me interested. Originally I wanted to be a drummer but we couldn't afford a drum set, so that didn't happen. I wanted to be a keyboard/synth guy, but we couldn't afford a piano. And then one time I saw one of the Cal Jam shows and I remember that someone from the band Rubicon did a cool, funky bass solo, and I realized this is the instrument that really moves me."

"...I had a cousin who was really, really into James Brown, Parliament and stuff – more kind of the funk, R&B side of things, Stevie Wonder, E.W.F. And as you know, the main instrument in rhythm and blues and soul music is bass, like with reggae and stuff. I was influenced by a lot of those players in the early days, Stanley Clark, Jaco Pastorius. And of course, on the other end of it, my friends' older brothers were all listening to Black Sabbath, The Who, Geezer, Entwistle, Lemmy, so I was getting it all, man – it was the '70s, so even tracks like 'Earache My Ear' by Cheech and Chong, I used to LOVE that song! I also tripped out on some progressive rock, mainly Chris Squire from Yes and Geddy Lee. I loved the heavy stuff and I loved the R&B stuff. So I got into music playing bass when I was about 14 years old. My Dad had a friend, Ted Trujillo (no relation) who had this beat up hollow body bass. It didn't even work and the action was an inch off the fretboard. It was great for training. I started jamming around in high school with the various backyard party bands. And the funny, ironic thing is I was – there was a band I was in called Oblivion when I was in the twelfth grade. We played a lot of Rush, Van Halen, Led Zeppelin and a shitload of Black Sabbath."

FINDING HIS BASS IN LIFE

"I went to high school with Rocky George and they needed a bass player. There I was, I jammed with them and they liked it and so we were off to join Anthrax in Europe. And it was when I joined Suicidal Tendencies (1989) that I really became exposed to the heavier side of music (hands on training). So, I

BASS IN YOUR FACE

mean, obviously growing up listening to Sabbath and playing Sabbath and all that – I started to make the transition when I joined Suicidal. That's when it all really hit me like a ton of bricks. Metallica made more of an impact on me around "Ride..." and "Master..." 1986/1988—more than around the "Kill 'Em All" time. And with Suicidal – I did love the "Institutionalized" album. That came out in 1983 and was a brilliant record. But when I joined Suicidal, that's when I really started getting into medieval shit, whether it was Slayer or, of course, Metallica."

THE NATURE OF TRUJ VIBE...

"You know what? When I go up and play, it's intense for me. But I'm not thinking about anything emotional as far as like family or anything that pissed me off – I'm just having an amazing time! It's like going into a boxing match or if you're going to surf some pumping waves in Hawaii. When I get up there it's like – prior to a tour, I really try to condition myself for performance, and it's very important to me. And there's a zone that you get into when you're on tour, on stage, and it's special because, as a band, you will connect with your unit – you're all in the same groove, which is great. You find that groove, that niche. And also, too, with your instrument you gain comfort and confidence and it just becomes a really, really fun dynamic experience."

COME AND JOIN US!

"I was in Tahiti surfing, I checked my messages back in L.A. and there was a message from the Metallica camp, from Kirk, asking to speak with me about the audition process that's about to occur, so I'm like, 'Wow, hey, alright.' But this is all going to go down within a couple of days. Now it's probably a Thursday. I'm in Tahiti. I'm coming home Friday. Saturday I'm supposed to be in San Francisco for my friend Michael Bordin's 40th birthday party, which means the Metallica guys want to see me and jam with me on Monday. And obviously I don't have a bass in my hand and I'm not really prepared to get up there and do it. But you know what? Once again it's a challenge. So I showed up, met with the guys, hung out, and the next day, Tuesday, actually jammed with them. And I was able to get a couple of songs in I kind of knew from the past, 'Master of Puppets,' 'Battery' and '... Sandman.' Four months later I came prepared with a chunk of music.

"So there we are, four months later, and they said one Wednesday they were going to audition three more guys and they'd let me know soon after what was up. They were going to call me on the Thursday. They actually called me that afternoon on Wednesday and said, 'Can you get up here in the next 24 hours?' So I came up and basically walked in the room and they all got up and clapped and said, 'Have a seat,' and... I was buzzing pretty hard by then. It was kind of an unbelievable thing for me."

A MIGHTY MOTHERPLUCKER...

"This is the deal. I play with my fingers mostly, but in certain situations, I've used picks. I've played with Jerry Cantrell, I did some stuff with him over the last few years, and obviously there were times where I used a pick in that situation. I try to be versatile, you know. But it's good that I've been playing with my fingers most years because that's more difficult. I didn't know what they were going to want. I know Jason played mostly with a pick, so I thought this might be a pick band, you know what I mean? But I just said, you know what, I'm going to play with my fingers because that's where I'm comfortable anyway, and they actually really, really dug that. That's when I was going, 'All right, this could get really exciting.' And I even asked them, 'Do you want me to play this song with my fingers or a pick? I can do it with a pick if you want.' And they were, 'No, no no, fingers, fingers, fingers... y'know, Cliff...!' ●

I walked in the room and they all got up and clapped and said, "Have a seat." I was buzzing pretty hard by then. It was kind of an unbelievable thing for me.

252

WOW, I REMEMBER GETTING the CALL from Lars, James, Kirk (speaker phone) ALRIGHT, it's just Metallica calling to ASK ME IF I WOULD VENTURE UP NORTH to meet WITH THEM THAT morning. I'm wondering if THE meeting is regarding certain concerns, or maybe saying THANKS, but no thanks, THAT'S just HOW I THINK, 'WORST CASE SCENARIO' AND WHAT A SURPRISE To WALK INTO THE HQ (MET. HOMEBASE) TO A standing OVATION, BAND, Producer, AND A Brand NEW GIG

I'm STOKED!

NOW
IT'S
ALL
ABOUT THE
CHALLENGE

04

James Hetfield
The SoWhat! Interview

FEBRUARY 2003

THE ROAD TO REHABILITATION "I knew that I was living two lives. I don't know if that eventually becomes some form of schizophrenia or something—compartmentalizing my life. And drinking contributed a lot to all of that, just getting out of my head with that – medicating with booze. It was probably seven years ago that I got dry for about a year and a half and I wasn't really ready for that. I hadn't hit any kind of bottom. Then it kind of just slowly snuck back in the form of wine with dinner or a couple of beers or something, "Absolutely no hard stuff. Not crossing this line." "Okay, I'll cross that line but not this one." You know, one glass of wine led to a bottle – and then with the Siberian bear hunt trip it went over the edge. Sitting in Siberia in a chicken coop in three feet of snow, and you've already shot your bear, what do you do? There's nothing to do. It ended up to where I was having a shot of vodka in the morning to get warmed up at 5:00 a.m. to go out on the sled. And it became too much. And then, with the booze, came all the other ugly behaviors around that. It was not the real me. I came home and really hit a bottom with my family, that this along with other things had gone too far – and depression and everything.

"So when I went into rehab, I knew it was the right thing. I knew there had to be a major, major change in my life. So going away and checking myself in, becoming humble with other people, saying, "hi, yeah, I am in a band called Metallica, but I'm James Hetfield – I'm not James Hetfield in Metallica. That's not just me." You know, discover the 'me' I never knew, and start to trust myself, understand why I don't love myself. What am I looking for? Where am I going? How do you handle these situations? Why does it take me so long to make decisions? Why do I need people to tell me what's best for me? Stuff like that. And I came out with a different set of instructions that were a lot deeper, a lot more spiritual, a lot more connected to a purpose in life...

CHILDHOOD "I'd say that in every child's life there is some form of abuse, there's some form of traumatic experiences that happen that scar and help form your survival techniques later on in life. It was very isolating as a kid, having two half-brothers that weren't really brothers per se, because they had a different dad and they were a generation away, but not quite father figures. So they were just kind of my brothers that sometimes are home and sometimes they're not. And my dad threw one of them out of the house. And I can just imagine my dad – he marries someone and he's got an 11- and 12-year old, two boys – man, that's gotta be tough. And the (Christian Science) religion was cult-like, in a way. There was no explanation of why 'that' (whatever it was) doesn't work. It was just, "no, this is the way." And kind of going through life trying to believe it, and feeling that I'm faulty, I'm defective, because I can't believe this, and my parents completely do. And being isolated at school, feeling that I'm just different because of this religion. I'm really different.

"Like, "why does Jamie – that's how I was known at school – leave the room every time we get our health books out?" I have to go stand out in the hallway. Pissing down rain or whatever it is, I'm standing outside the classroom while people are inside learning about the body, learning about health, learning about what shell we have for our souls. I couldn't even learn about it. It was either stand in the hall, and other teachers would walk by and give you the dirty eye, because you're in trouble, because you're standing 'outside the classroom.' Or you go sit in the principal's office and wait in there. Any kid who goes into the principal's office, something's the matter. So you get this shameful look. Like you're shamed. And I took all that in.

You know, you don't want to be different when you're a kid at school, like having to go to the football coach with a note saying I can't get a physical because of my religious beliefs. And everyone kind of

joking about their physical selves – "hey, he touched my nuts!" You can't even joke around with the guys because you weren't a part of it. Just looked at as an outsider. And you know, there's good qualities to that that... I've taken on the power of the rebel somehow, but still, it's always been a lone wolf kind of mentality.

CHILDHOOD "...There's abandonment – my Dad left when I was 12 or 13. He just upped and left. He left a note... didn't say good-bye to us kids. And then there were times when I'd come home from school and I'd see in the garage that, "hey, Dad's trophies are gone. Dad's been here and I wasn't here," and how messed up that was in my head.

"And it was all tough on my Mom, having to get a job and support two kids was too much for her. She couldn't deal with it. Mom was not

the strongest woman there was. Very passive. And sweet. You know, I learned love, the caressing and stuff like that – that's what mom does. She doesn't offer really hard advice or good life lessons – but she was there, and comforting. But not the strong woman who could go out and work. Eventually she got sick and denied her illness – and the denial of pain was a major thing, for Christian Science to be able to get better. As soon as you acknowledge the pain you are giving into the negative aspect or the error or the evil or whatever. So, she's withering away in front of us (she died of cancer when James was 16 – Ed), and we can't say anything.

"Lots of big stuff happened at that same time – 16, 17. Girls, insecurities – there are tons of insecurities already. Me wigging out on marijuana, and all this kind of paranoia just all of a sudden hit me. And abandonment issues were huge. When my mom passed on, my first girlfriend left me, I moved. I mean, huge stuff. And there wasn't a whole lot of grieving going on. That was the other very strange thing that I had picked up about Christian Science – there were no funerals, so there was no grieving process. And grieving, I've come to learn, is an extremely healthy way of cleansing feelings. You have to go through that process, and we never did. We just kind of shoved it way down. Way down. So since then I've done lots of grieving work on my Dad, on my Mom, on Cliff (Burton), and also because we certainly didn't get a chance to grieve properly around that time. I actually found out where my mom's plaque is in the wall, where her ashes are. I didn't even care where they were. I got to go back there and say my piece, and get a little angry and also get a little real."

THE BAND'S REACTION "I told them I was going away and they might not hear from me for a month or so. I didn't know it was going to be eleven weeks. I saw them before that but, yeah, it was – 'I'm unplugging from this. Right now just pretend I'm not in Metallica, because I gotta go take care of my personal self.' That sent them into fear. But I knew what I had to do, and no amazing sense of awareness of how they felt about it was going to stop me from doing it. I could have maybe explained it to them a little better and maybe helped them understand that it didn't mean Metallica's done. And, you know, if Metallica doesn't continue, I have to feel OK about that. I had to set priorities at that point."

BACK TOGETHER "Jamming with these guys has never been more fun. As far as I can remember, this feels amazing. We can look at each other in the eye and kind of know what we're thinking, and not do any smarmy face. There's not any resentment stuff going on. It's all for the good of the team. And there's no-one here that thinks he's going to sabotage this mission, or something, because there isn't anyone who wants to do that."

FINDING ROB "Well, there were seven guys. And the first list of four were all very respected people – people we knew, and knew what they could do, and were very hopeful prospects. When Rob first came in, I didn't even think he'd be on the list. I just thought, 'Wow, this is a guy who really hasn't been comfortable in one band; he has to jump around.' And just what had happened with Jason and

some of my fears of someone not being loyal or happy in the position they are – that just seemed like, 'Wow, he might not work out because of all the other commitments he has.' He's playing for two bands, he's got tons of other stuff going on. But I totally remembered him from Suicidal. The way he played his bass was commanding such respect. And he really meant bass business. So when he came in, he plugged in and started playing with his fingers – he was the first guy in – and it was like, 'Wow, it sounds really good, but I can't wait to move on to other people.' So we went through other guys – Twiggy, Pepper and Scott Reeder. And they're all awesome bass players in their own way. They're amazing people. They've all got great qualities that could blossom in Metallica. And Pepper especially… it was difficult for me because him and I have been such good buddies and he's traveled the rough road with me over recovery, too. What a great fit he would be on the road, kind of knowing what's up. But the playing wasn't as good as Rob's. It's as simple as that. Rob took us to an amazing new level."

MOTORCYCLE MAN "I love cars and bikes, building them, showing them in shows, creating a new way to build a motorcycle, or something to clean up a bike, something unique. Coming home with trophies – that could get old, I'm sure. But I won first place at the Oakland Roadster Show. It's amazing, best chopper. And it wasn't because there was just a bunch of money thrown at it, it was because a rule was broken. 'Hey, you can't do that on a motorcycle. You can't have an internal clutch.' You know, it's something that doesn't work perfectly but it's something we attempted. We tried to do something new on a bike. We went for things that were different, and that's why we won the trophy, which is pretty cool. Building cars, building bikes – that could be a blossoming thing for me." ●

IM SO GRATEFUL TO HAVE A WAY TO GET INSANITY OUT OF MY HEAD, ONTO PAPER AND INTO YOUR HEADS.

JH
3/04

St. Anger
VIDEO SHOOT & CONCERT

SAN QUENTIN STATE PENITENTIARY, CA April 30, May 1, 2003

SUCH A UNIQUE, JAW DROPPING,
EYE OPENING EXPERIENCE
THAT JUST MADE ME THANKFUL
THAT I MADE THE RIGHT
CHOICES IN MY LIFE.
PLUS I RAN INTO SOME
INMATE WHO KNEW MY
MOTHER !?!!!

_5/04_

AN EXTREMELY INTENSE EVENT. EMOTIONALLY DRAINING.
ESPECIALLY MY PRE-GIG SPEECH TO THE INMATES RELATING
MY FEELINGS OF ANGER AND MY RESOLUTIONS. I CAME
HOME THAT NIGHT AND HUGGED MY FAMILY LIKE I NEVER
HAD BEFORE. FREEDOM IS NOT TAKEN FOR GRANTED.
_JH 5/04_

AN UNBELIEVABLE
48 HOUR PERIOD!

A VERY INTENSE, INTIMIDATING,
HUMBLING, EYE OPENING, INVIGORATING,
EMOTIONAL EXPERIENCE,

AND RIGHT IN OUR BACK YARD!

MY
#1st GIG
SCARED
STRAIGHT!
METALLICA*
STYLE,
¿ WHAT?
S.Q.
STYLE!

Rob x Toy

Scenes from the band's hometown warm-up gigs at San Francisco's historic Fillmore auditorium

my neck hurts, my knees hurt, my wrist hurts, my voice is shot and I can't hear anything but it was the best time EVER!!!!!!!
Ninette Freitas aka netjamymz, San Jose

the **Fillmore**
May 18, 19, 21, 22, 2003

259

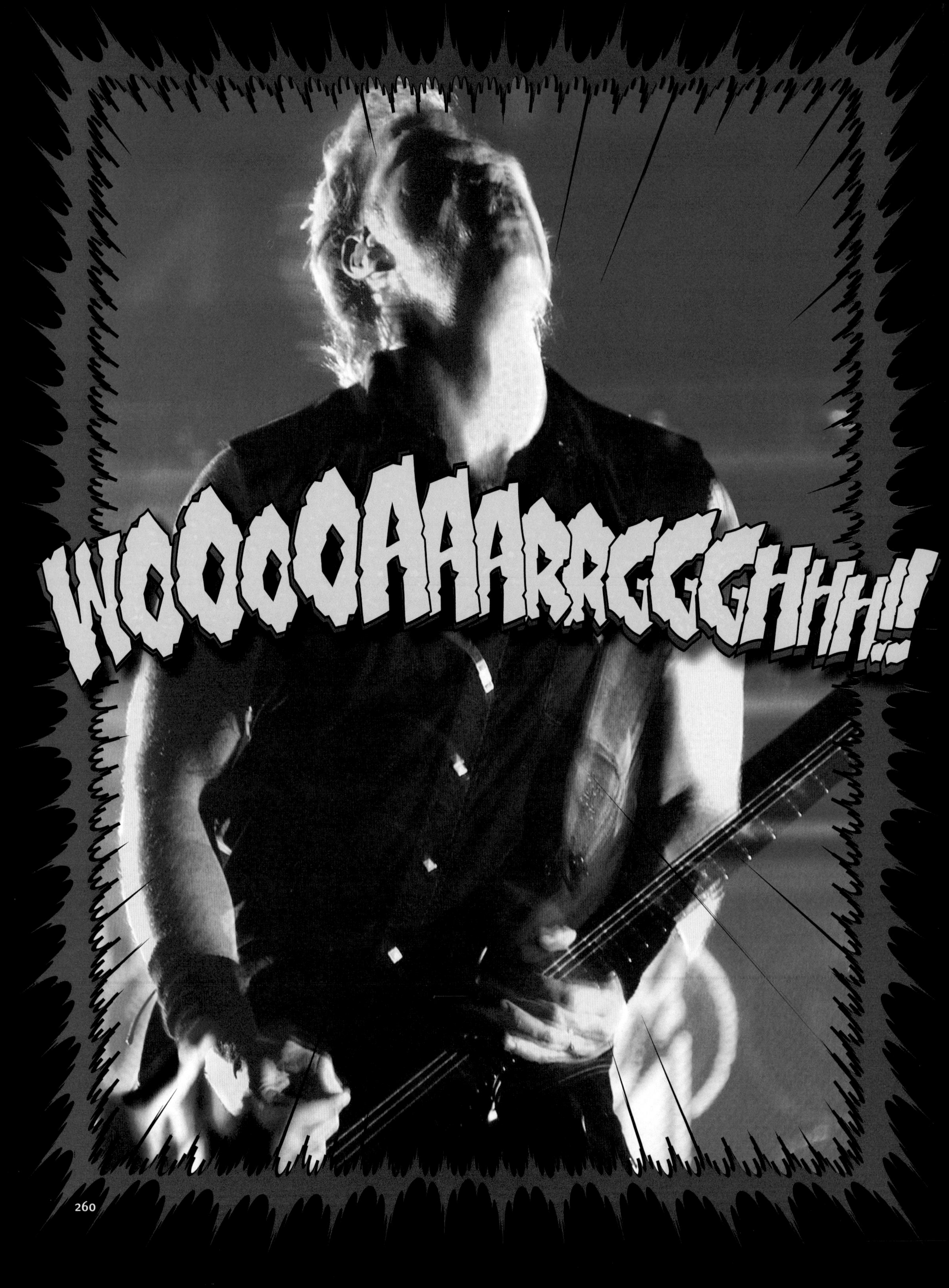
WOOOOOAAARRGGGHHH!!

RAW! LOUD! LIVE! ANGER! BELIEVE IT BABY!

BECAUSE AFTER THEIR TRIALS, TRIBULATIONS, RECOVERIES, REUNIONS AND REACTIVATIONS (NOT TO MENTION A NEW BASS BOY ON THE BLOCK IN ROB TRUJILLO), METALLICA TOOK TO THE ROAD FOR THE FIRST TIME IN THREE YEARS DURING THE SUMMER OF 2003 AND CELEBRATED THE "ST. ANGER" ALBUM IN RAMPANT STYLE. STARTING OFF IN EUROPE WITH SOME TINY GIGS IN 50,000 PLUS STADIUMS (AND THREE PARISIAN CLUBS IN A DAY!), THE BAND DIDN'T TAKE LONG TO FIND THEIR DYNAMIC STAGE SELVES AGAIN, TRUJILLO'S ELASTICITY BOTH AS A BASSIST AND HUMAN BEING MAKING THE RE-ENTRY PROCESS THAT MUCH EASIER. AND HAVING HAD THEIR WAY WITH THE EUROPEANS, THEY ROLLED OVER TO THE U.S. WHERE THE 'SUMMER SANITARIUM 2003' (FEATURING LINKIN PARK, LIMP BIZKIT, DEFTONES AND MUDVAYNE) DREW SIMILAR STADIUM-SIZED CROWDS THROUGHOUT THE COUNTRY. THE FOLLOWING INTERVIEWS TOOK PLACE DURING THOSE EARLY WEEKS IN EUROPE, WHEN ABSOLUTELY TANGIBLE RELIEF AND HAPPINESS WAS STILL TINGED WITH THE ODD SMIDGEN OF TREPIDATION.

RUNNING UP THE BACKSTAGE STAIRS AFTER THEIR 3RD ENCORE...

THE BOYS HAVE ONLY ONE THING, ONE PRECIOUS THING ON THEIR MINDS...

AIR CONDITIONING !!!!

RUUMMMBBLLLLE

THE TRUJILLO FACTOR

KH: The great thing about Rob is that he's just so accessible. He's open to things. I love that about him. And I found that one thing he likes to talk about is music stuff, and I'm totally into that. You know, talking about the gig, talking about music in general, talking about jamming. We're making plans about getting together and jamming. We like to critique the gigs and we like to discuss that sort of thing because we're those types of musicians who like to critique things and see how we can make it better and challenge ourselves. So I think on a musical basis we react to the same things, which is very very cool for me. And you know, we have the whole surfing thing, which is very very cool. And I love surfing with him because he's such a great surfer and he really pushes. He really pushes himself while he's surfing and he charges, and that inspires me to charge waves as well. And I've also found out that Rob is quite cultured. And I didn't know that. I didn't expect that.

I don't know how cultured surfers can get, but he is not your standard surfer. And you know, I like going over to his side of the stage and listening to the fucking sound that's coming out of his amps because it feels good to listen to. It's very smooth sounding, his bass sound. And I can see it in James's eyes and I can also see it in Lars's eyes. it's a great thing. We're together.

JH: It is so much fun jamming with him on stage, and yeah I know the honeymoon part of it, that, okay, it's all glossy, it's all giddy love right now – you know, you're on stage playing together. I don't want to have to come up every time in the same spot and jam, but we're just feeling out the vibe on stage, you know. He definitely plugs right in and, I don't know, just not over-analyzing but looking at our personalities, it's very balanced. Very, very balanced. Rob is so easy-going and really just happy to be there, but he says what he needs...

RT: The Metallica family, in such a short amount of time, it's like I feel like I've known them for years and years and years – actually some of them I have known for years and years and years – but I mean working with them like this. It's amazing. I mean, just yesterday, three shows in one day and our crew was on it, working as hard as us. And that's the whole thing. The togetherness of the team is just an amazing thing about the Metallica camp. Metallica is a combination of different ingredients and spices because their music can be obviously very physical and heavy and relentless, but also there's a certain groove there, a groove that I understand from playing with Suicidal. And then there's even bits and pieces of Sabbath in there. So kind of in all the situations I've been in, there's bits and pieces of that in Metallica. But Metallica's kind of like all of that on steroids. And even like getting up there and performing this stuff, for me there's only one way to perform it and that's extra physical man. You know, it can be like a sporting event.

TOURING IN '03

KH: This is easily the best European tour I've been on as far as mentally, and it has everything to do with the fact that my wife is out here giving me support and just helping me. Because my childhood history is laden with issues, and one of those issues is separation and abandonment, and that's something real deep-seated from when I was a really young child, right? So every time when I've left on tour, and especially when it came to Europe, those issues would always come to the top and I'd always try to medicate my depression by just drinking and doing drugs and what not.

METALLICA HAVE SWAGGERED INTO TOWN WITH THE SORT OF IMPUNITY GENGHIS KAHN EMPLOYED.

But I have a different approach nowadays to my depression. I know the causes of it. And so I try to stay away from things that cause that. And you know, my wife being with me just makes it a lot easier because I have her support, which I totally appreciate her for and I acknowledge.

JH: I'm enjoying that whether it's one hour at the clubs or two hours at the stadiums, I'm enjoying that a lot more. And it's just a combination of everything – the vibe out here, knowing that Lars and I have reached a compromise as far as the set length. And we're packing it full of good stuff. It's not all just fillers, solo-y stuff. You know, the set would be three hours long and we'd have to throw in a solo so I could get a break. Just hit em over the head with two hours, man. But just the vibe overall is a lot more happy. And just the realization that, man, I can be out here and struggle a little with old behaviors, but, hey, it works. I can be out here. I can be in this atmosphere and not just completely fall off the wagon and end up in the gutter – a deeper, deeper gutter.

KH: Now it (touring) feels more like a big long field trip. And now that we're older and a lot different in our approach to thing, it's not so wild which I think is a good thing. The electricity is there but it's a different type of electricity, it's a different type of energy now. But I prefer it a lot more. It's a lot mellower and it's a lot easier to deal with, especially if something goes wrong.

JH: We had Cali's fifth birthday yesterday between three club gigs. It was the craziest day ever, and I loved every minute of it. We had three club shows, a birthday party and then a party afterwards and we made it work. I wasn't freaking out thinking 'oh God, I can't hang the pinata, I've gotta do this and that.' It's just go slow, calm down and it can all work.

LU: I sit there, and it's hour thirteen, and the Italians want another two hundred and fifty autographs at the Italian instore at 12:30 in the morning. I then go back and access the sitting around a year-and-a-half ago thinking how much I would have killed to do what we're doing now and to have a bunch of kids to hang out with at an instore. So I would definitely say that it's been probably the best European promo tour. Sometimes we dreaded the old European promo tour and I would say this time it was definitely fun. The new energy with Rob, talking about this record and also simply because having been through what we've been through the last couple of years, you sort of sit down and you find moments of real deep appreciation for what it is that's going on.

JH: We'll come off (stage) and focus on the great parts of the show. I remember we would always come off and first thing out of any four of our mouths was, 'man, I fucked that thing up,' or something like that. Or, 'how come that tempo's like this?' or 'dude, you screwed the lyrics up.' And now there's not even any talk of that. We'll bring it up like, I laugh about it. Like, 'dude, I knew right when that solo was coming up, I blanked.' We can sit there on stage and laugh at each other about it instead of totally freak out.

LU: It's more enjoyable and there's less stress – the famous 'Phantom Lord' analogy, where two hours before the show I asked Rob if he could play "Phantom Lord" and he said he'd never heard it. So he sat down, grabbed "Kill 'Em All," put the headphones on for ten minutes, learned the basic chord progressions and two hours later we played it… it's just so much more the spirit of what this band is about, has always been about, and to me the spirit of – I mean, you know, to use the stupidest cliché possible, but the spirit of rock and roll. And that kind of thing about those elements of danger and about challenging yourself. Like he says, 'Just step it up, step it up, step it up.' There's less internal pressure, there's less internal pressure and we're all sort of equally out there throwing ourselves in the line of fire. I think in the past part of the old way of doing things was this whole thing of the perfectionism in Metallica. It's like by acknowledging our own weaknesses and making our weaknesses part of something that we're proud of in our human elements, then it sort of also takes a little bit of the pressure off. You sort of sit there and go like, 'all right, I'm going to fuck up tonight,' so now everybody knows that, instead of sitting there trying to defend it afterwards.

THE FAME FACTOR

JH: I'm still sorting all that stuff out because I think being a celebrity doesn't mean your opinion is better than anyone else's. People at interviews ask you 'what are your views on the war?' Well, as a singer in Metallica, I've got nothing to say about it, because this is not a soapbox for me. I really don't like it when someone uses their opinion just because they're popular. And it's not so much them – I know it's the fans of theirs that take it wrongly, too. 'Oh, he's gotta be smarter because he's a celebrity' or something, you know? But for me to get up there and just tell my story, it's not like 'I've been to this place and that place and I've got this much money and here I am and I'm telling you this.' I'm not preaching to them about nothing. I'm just telling them my story. And if they're interested in it because of who I am, that's up to them, but I'm not flying the flag of celebrityism. And that helps me, because I'm up there telling them how human I am, please don't treat me as special, you know? Treat me the same way as you would someone else. Just respect everybody. This self-healing for me – I get up there, and I'm not trying to be a savior of sorts, you know, to tell them the path 'follow me' and all of that, I'm just telling them my story. And if one person out there can identify with it, then cool. If none, then fine.

KH: I try to keep both my feet firmly grounded on the earth, which is really important. You know, the celebrity thing to me, I can take it or I can leave it. I have an 'on again off again' sort of relationship with the whole celebrity thing. Celebrity is not that important to me. What's really important to me is making records and playing shows. It's become its own thing, you know? Making records has become its own thing and playing shows has become its own thing. It's grown to a point where it is what it is. But you just have to accept it for what it is. Sometimes I really appreciate all the acknowledgment and all the attention, but sometimes I can do without the attention. I really, really try to just not forget where I came from, and have a clear picture of where I'm going. I don't want to become something that's difficult for me to maintain. I want to be able to maintain my own lifestyle and just have control of my life without having to rely on other people. I want to still be able to go to the goddamn super-

YEAHH BABEEHHH!

market and buy my own fruit. Even though that becomes more and more difficult, I'm still going to fucking hang onto that. I want to be able to pile my fucking surf boards into a van and drive down to a beach and surf all day and sleep in the van instead of having to bring a fucking entourage of people and security and whatever – hair stylists. I'm not into that.

FINDING SPACE ON THE ROAD

JH: Outside of the hotels, I've noticed the respect that, I'm walking out there, I've got my whole family, we're off to Euro Disney or whatever it is – and obviously having a person along with you telling people in their language that 'hey, he'll do it when he's alone on his time. Don't bother him when it's a day off and his family's out.' And you walk out and they wave and they say 'hi, I'll see you later to sign this thing,' and I say 'yeah.' And there's a respect thing. Before, it would have caused so much friction between me and the family. I'd stop, the family would be waiting, they'd be hot, the kids would start crying and Francesca, my wife, gets irritated at it, and she starts to feel that 'they're more important than us right now' and all of that. I would never have imagined that I could show the more vulnerable parts of me or the parts that get pissed off and just say 'not now, it's got to be later' and they don't turn away and say 'oh fuck Metallica, forget it. We'll go burn all their CDs.'

BY DAY, FRIEND TO ALL...

YES, IT HAS BEEN NICE WEATHER...

BUT SOMETHING STRANGE WAS ABOUT TO HAPPEN...

...SO YOU THINK YOU KNOW ME, HUH...?

"THE RIPPER" TAKES HIS VENGEANCE

MICKEY MOUSE SNUB & HOUSEWIFE'S ELBOW SHOCKER!

JH: Heh Heh, well, my wife bought the kids little Disney autograph books. So we go up to get in line to get some of the autographs. By the time we get the pen out and everything, Mickey's gone. Mickey did a runner. He didn't even get out of the car. He was in a little car and he was all of a sudden gone. So then, yeah, the next thing, we're about to get on a ride and all of a sudden I spotted King Louie from Jungle Book and the Sheriff of Nottingham from Robin Hood. And Mickey Mouse was back. Yeah, I spotted them. I said, "Cali, come here!" So finally we were in the line – the monkey was closest, okay, and I could see he's having trouble signing stuff with his Sharpie because he's got these big monkey-finger gloves. So I'm in line waiting patiently, but the moms are just pushing their way in, you know. It's like, 'wow, now I understand what it's like.' I'm fearful that he's going to leave and we're not going to get an autograph. Anyway, we're getting up there and instantly, when I'm standing there, some lady pushes me out of the way because I'm in the video shot of her kid. She doesn't say anything, just 'move,' and I'm like, 'oh, okay, sorry.' And I'm getting ready to hand him the little book and some lady just wedges in, some pushy English woman, and says, 'If you don't mind, my kid would like a picture.' And the lady's stepping all over my daughter's feet, and I'm saying to her, 'you're stepping on her feet' and she doesn't even care. And then Mickey did ANOTHER runner. We did chase down the Sheriff of Nottingham. He was not nice. He was not having a good day. He was opening people's bags looking for money. That is his gig, but he was taking it a little too far...

THE RIPPER

KH: The Ripper comes out totally on tour when I'm onstage ripping away. And The Ripper also comes out when we're at some beach break and the waves are firing and it's a little bit more challenging than it should be and we should take a little bit more caution. But you know it's all about charging waves, and that's when The Ripper comes out again. Everyone has a Ripper inside of them and no matter how many times you hear that your potential is null or nonexistent, everyone has a Ripper. They just have to learn to connect to The Ripper and fucking execute! Everyone has the potential to be The Ripper. ●

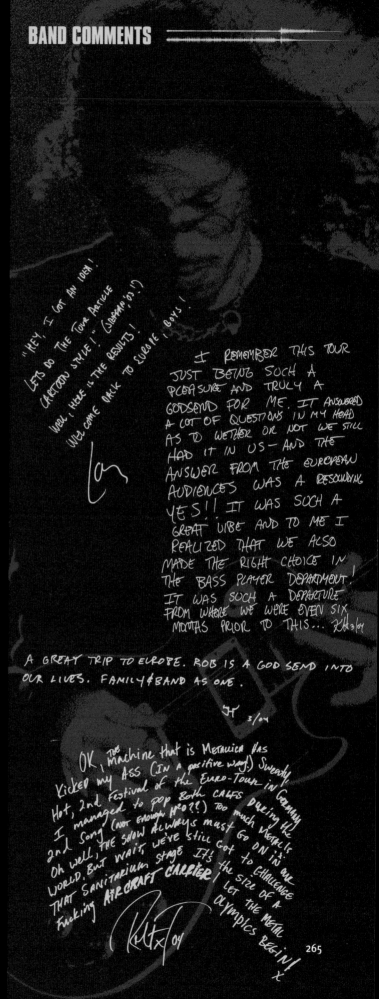

"HEY, I GOT AN IDEA! LETS DO THE TOUR ARTICLE CARTOON STYLE!" (JAPAN '03!) WELL, HERE IS THE RESULTS! WE'LL COME BACK TO EUROPE, BOYS!

I REMEMBER THIS TOUR JUST BEING SUCH A PLEASURE AND TRULY A GODSEND FOR ME. IT ANSWERED A LOT OF QUESTIONS IN MY HEAD AS TO WETHER OR NOT WE STILL HAD IT IN US – AND THE ANSWER FROM THE EUROPEAN AUDIENCES WAS A RESOUNDING YES!! IT WAS SUCH A GREAT VIBE AND TO ME I REALIZED THAT WE ALSO MADE THE RIGHT CHOICE IN THE BASS PLAYER DEPARTMENT! IT WAS SUCH A DEPARTURE FROM WHERE WE WERE EVEN SIX MONTHS PRIOR TO THIS... Rob 3/04

A GREAT TRIP TO EUROPE. ROB IS A GOD SEND INTO OUR LIVES. FAMILY & BAND AS ONE.
JH 3/04

OK, THE machine that is Metallica has kicked my ASS (IN a positive way!) Sweaty, Hot, 2nd Festival of the Euro-Tour in Germany, I managed to pop Both CALFS during the 2nd song (NOT enough H₂O??) Too much Metal is Oh well, THE SHOW ALWAYS must Go ON in our WORLD. BUT WAIT, WE'VE still Got to CHALLENGE THAT SANITARIUM stage It's the size of a Fucking AIRCRAFT CARRIER! LET THE METAL Olympics BEGIN!
Kirk '04
x

265

THE BOYS A

BACK IN TOWN

SO THERE WE WERE, MARCH 14TH '04, backstage in Fresno, California, Lars, James, Kirk, Rob and myself, a pile of waters and juices, a tape recorder and some questions in need of answering. The 'Madly In Anger' tour was in full swing, the schedule slating it to end on November '04... I have to confess, I was surprised that Metallica would ever tour like this again. Of course, when your raw appreciation for the abilities you have get a new lease of life, I'd imagine it'd be hard to stop... hmmm, enough of my pondering, let the guys tell you their current feelings on touring, their relationship and the "St. Anger" album.

Editor — April 2004

ED: Was this level of touring something you expected to be doing? It's a very intense tour.

James Hetfield (JH): I think it's longer than I expected, but it's not that difficult compared to ones before. We're taking care of ourselves. No three-in-a-rows and every two weeks we get three days off at home, that's really good.

Kirk Hammett (KH): For me, it really doesn't feel like the tour has started yet, but then I realize that we've actually been touring for almost 10 months now. But because the schedule is a lot lighter than on previous tours, and there's a lot of breaks and downtime at home, it hasn't really gotten to the intensity that former tours have gotten. At least for me, you know.

JH: I think the word 'intensity' should just be put in a different place. The touring's not intense as in 'difficult' or 'struggle-like.' The intensity is more on the stage now, since we're only doing two-in-a-rows then have a day off. I think we're a lot more intense on stage than we have been on other tours.

KH: I absolutely agree.

There was this expectation that you'd maybe do a month on and then a month off, yet this will see almost the whole of 2004 on the road.

Lars Ulrich (LU): You've got to remember, it's also longer because we have more days off. Three weeks off between legs instead of 10 days.

But surely much like '91–'93 (the legendary 302 date "Black" album tour — Ed), management could call and say, 'well, you know what, in December there's a possibility that we can play another six shows.'

JH: Yes and yes and yes.

KH: It's inevitable.

JH: And we're the boss. We can say yes or no. Our minds, our bodies, will tell us and we'll make a collective decision.

KH: I'm appreciative of the fact we're touring. I'm appreciative of the fact that we're out here and functioning. Because, and I've said this a million times, there was a time when this didn't seem like reality at all, the fact of us being in a position to even tour didn't seem like a reality at all. And I appreciate the fact that all of us have stepped up and been keeping it together.

LU: Look, we're playing 80 indoor U.S. shows. That's the least we've ever done on an indoor tour in America. We sat down nine months ago, or a year ago, and said, 'what encompasses a comprehensive U.S. tour that doesn't take it to the insanity levels of the past?' 80 was the number that Peter and Cliff **(Mensch and Burnstein-managers — Ed)** threw out as kind of like a reasonable, fairly good penetration of the United States without it being five shows in each Dakota. So, 80 shows indoors, which is where it's sitting right now. And I know this thing about the past, about 'here come the phone calls' and all this stuff, and I think the way that we are now, I don't think we're scared of those phone calls anymore because I think we're much more on the same page. And so you sit down and you make the decisions – you know, we got a phone call a couple of weeks ago about an opportunity to play a show up in Iceland, where none of us have been before. It was a really strong opportunity to play in Iceland. And so we just sat down and talked about and how it fit in with everybody's schedule and we found a way. So I don't think there's that kind of old-school fear that there used to be of, 'oh my God – don't answer a call from Peter Mensch after September 1st.'

Do you think for the first six months you were in an 'eggshell' situation given recent history? And was it tough to push through those first six months and rediscover those boundaries and relationships, and so on?

JH: I think it's been the easiest it's ever been because we know that we can talk about those things, and do periodically need to. And if there's a challenge that comes up, we can come to a decision. We don't have to freak out and get defensive and start fighting. We can come to a conclusion. We've gone through some really difficult stuff, and little things we can handle. We do have the tools and – you know, 'were people placing bets on if we're going to make it through the first leg or not?' I don't care about any stuff like that, because I knew inside me that I was going to do my best to have the most fun and be the most accepting and have the best time out there I could. I felt stronger than ever, so for me there was no doubt that we'd keep going.

I just wondered if there was trepidation from management when they first approached you about playing 80 dates in the U.S. in smaller cities?

JH: That's been on the table for a long time. We wanted to get back into the B markets and middle America and all the places that we used to hit. Any place that had an arena that made it financially feasible to get there and do a show without losing our shirts on it. So it was on the table. You know, we were wondering, is that really going to happen? Me thinking that there's no way I'm going to be touring for that long. But Kirk's right when he says it feels like we're just kind of starting – we've gone through different legs of different styles – Europe festivals, indoor stuff and outdoor here and club stuff, and we've already had three or four different stages that we've played on. So it feels like it's a new tour every time we go out.

KH: Yeah, yeah, with a different environment, whether indoors, outdoors. I think what's really great is the fact that we're going to Europe for the fourth time. The schedule looks a bit hectic, but I've had so much fun going to Europe these days. I'm just totally looking forward to it. And I'm seeing that part of the tour as like – almost like the summer vacation part of the tour, where we're going to be in Europe, it's going to be nice...

(To Rob) Are you surprised by how easily it's all working out for you?

Rob Trujillo (RT): For the first time that I jammed with these guys it just felt right. It's just something that – it's like magic, you know – sometimes it's there and sometimes it's not there in other situations, other musicians, but this just feels so right. And that's probably what makes it easier for us to be able to go out and have some fun on stage and take chances and not get all freaked out by it.

On the flip side, let me ask you guys how it is – now you've toured with him for ten months. Talk about that fit.

KH: One thing I have to say is that Rob is so dependable, both on stage and off stage.

RT: Yeah, you know what, man – I show up on time.

KH: He's a rock. I mean, musically, you can depend on him to know the stuff he's supposed to know and play it well. And he plays the stuff like he's always been playing it, which kind of blows me away because he can just naturally slide into it. And it's really seamless.

JH: Yeah, even when we're in the jam room just goofing around with something, he kind of knows where we're going to go. He plays a lot, and he knows what's happening. I haven't heard him ask a lot of questions about, 'how do you play this riff?' Or, 'how does this go?' in certain songs that are just almost impossible to figure out, you know? But also the physicality. I think he's helped at least myself step up to another level. You know, the "Summer Sanitarium II" was like – it was no club stage – it was huge. And covering that thing and still singing as many words as have to be sung. And he's also stepping up singing background vocals. I mean, that's pretty inspirational to me to see someone that saw on our list of what we were looking for in a bass player, and one was singing, and he came right out and said, 'I've never sung before but I'll try it.' And I love it!!!

LU: It feels like we're very much on the same page. I've said this a hundred times, Rob is the most effortless bass player I've ever been around. It's not like standing there for half an hour trying to figure something out. He just kind of gels into it, it's so effortless. It's an awesome feeling. I can't wait to take this to the next step and work on songs and record and all this type of stuff because I think there's going to be a whole different energy also in that process.

RT: The energy right before we go on stage in that room, even if I'm not even playing and I hear Lars and James playing something, it's so exciting. Some of the ideas that are going down in there twenty minutes before a gig are pretty next level. There are times where I don't even want to hit a note man, because I'm just grooving on what they're doing. You know what I mean? I just sit back and listen. It's pretty exciting. The new ideas that have already gone down I think are pretty amazing. And it's going to be an exciting time. We're working on a piece of new material based on what's already been documented.

Do you think that when it comes to eight weeks into a tour and there's a dispute brewing, it's like, 'OK, now I can solve that. I know how to approach this because I know this guy better. I know his family. I knew who he is.' Does getting to know each other deeper as people help those rough spots as a band?

JH: Yeah. I totally believe that. The more you know someone, the more you will respect them and the more you will know their boundaries, the more you'll know some of their defects and accept them. If something's going on, you can tell more if it's their stuff or something that you did. But also, it makes us all aware of each other when we're not congruent too. You know, when something looks out of whack that you're doing at home but not doing out here, or you're doing out here that wouldn't be at home, it tells a tale.

Anyone else want to jump in on that?

KH: We have such a long personal history with each other, and it's good to finally be on the level where, if I have problems at home, I can bring it to these guys and actually discuss it with them and kind of confide in them what I'm going through. There was a time when I couldn't do that. And there was a time in the past when I needed to do that but felt like I couldn't. But now, because of the temperament and awareness that we all have of our home lives, it's a lot easier for me to like open up. I feel very secure about it. And these guys will support me and how I'm feeling. That, to me, is a big step. It's a great level of communication to have that wasn't there previously.

LU: I think the main thing to me is that we just don't bullshit each other anymore. And when once in a while there's a couple bumps in the road or something like that, it's almost like we just jump at the chance to sit down and talk about it because it's so rejuvenating and so--it just feels so awesome to just sit down and talk when something goes a little bit awry. And I really feel that we just learned to not bullshit each other. And it's really pretty cool when you can sit down with a bunch of people and know what's being talked about, know what's being thrown around is 100% the truth and from the heart. And that is an awesome thing to have between a bunch of guys.

Do you feel it's a work in progress still?

KH: Always.
LU: I hope it stays a work in progress. I hope you never reach a point where you stop working at it. But I think we do a pretty good job around here.

ED: How does the post-Towle (referring to Phil Towle, the performance coach initially used during the post-Jason/ "St.Anger" era) Metallica look? Will he be around or potentially used in any future disputes?

LU: I never say never about anything.
JH: I think Phil is a great rock and he's helped us a lot, so we know he's there. And I don't think we need him to hold our hand across the street anymore, which is great. But individually is different from band-wise as well, but as a band I think we're getting along pretty good.

And finally, how do you feel about the public reaction to "St.Anger"?

KH: It's not as accessible as some of our previous albums, for sure. James and I were talking just the other day. I've heard a few journalists say that once they've seen the movie ("Some Kind Of Monster," the Joe Berlinger/Bruce Sinofsky documentary film made during the "St. Anger" era — ED) and they've gone back to the album, all of a sudden it sounds completely different, the lyrics take on a new sense of meaning, and people find themselves getting it. I thought about it when I was talking to a journalist about it, and I thought, well, maybe this album is a concept album of everything we went through. And when I was talking to James about it, he said 'all our albums are concept albums.' It's just that this concept is just so in your face and confrontational and also addressing themes that not a whole lot of people want to address. But somehow or another the film is working in tandem with the album, I'm finding.
JH: How could it not be a concept album if you're honest with your feelings and writing a bunch of songs in a period of time? They're going to address certain issues that you're thinking about in your life at that time. And yeah, that also just tells me that the journalists aren't giving it enough time, or being as open to what it might mean to them, and then when they do see the film, it's like, 'oh, then it makes sense.' And man, you can do that with any record if you want to.
LU: It's what Andrew WK said himself. My favorite quote of last year from the great man who I've never met. He said about "St. Anger," and I quote: 'The reason people don't get it is because it's so ahead of its time.' 10 years from now it will be probably like the "...Justice" album.
RT: I think it's a great launch pad for what this band can do. It's a great starting block for this unit, where we're at now and what's going to happen. For me, even though I didn't play on the album, it feels like a new beginning. ●

NEW BEGINNING

Hey guys well here it goes...
If it was the last time you guys would ever play a show, with what other band would you like to share the stage?
Gladys M., L.A., CA

KH: Spinal Tap for all the obvious reasons.
RT: Zeppelin because I think that as a member of a band like Metallica, there's so much respect given to an juggernaut beast of a band as Zeppelin was and the history of Zeppelin, I think that would be special... but JPJ would have to be in the group. Would be a good idea if they could get John Bonham out there too, somehow someway!
JH: It wouldn't be another band, it'd be just us, we'd play for ever and wouldn't wanna end. Get all previous members, live or dead, in then house somehow.
LU: I agree with James. No fucker else is needed!

During the Napster dispute Fred Durst said some inflammatory things about you guys (i.e. Lars), How does it feel to be touring with him now?
Rich P., Cedar Rapids, IA

KH: It's all water under the bridge, Napster was something that was much bigger than people firing insults at each other and we all know what happened to Napster, so you're free to draw your own conclusions.
RT: For starters Fred Durst has always been completely respectful to me personally and my previous groups, so he's been nothing but a good sweet spirit in my world.
JH: Feels no different. I think Napster was so black and white you were either for it or against it, and time will tell how people really feel about how it affects them and their careers.
LU: Me and Fred kissed and made up about five minutes after that shit and we have been respectful, dare I even say friends, since then. I like limpbizkit and I have respect for Fred and it's all fuckin' good.

During the 'Summer Sanitarium' show at Giants Stadium there was a video of Cliff playing on the big screen while Rob was jamming the intro to

Bells. I thought that was awesome on so many levels. Whose idea was that? Also, was there any hesitance from any members in the band regarding this part of the show?
Brian T., Morris Plains, NJ

KH: I can't remember who's idea that was but I know it kicks ass, I totally love it when that happens myself, and no, there was no resistance to the idea.
RT: That was actually JB, lighting designer, and the majority of the band thought it was a special moment.
JH: Great question, I'm not sure who came up with that particular idea, we were all involved on what came up on the screens, I think JB our lighting designer came up with that. It was difficult at first, wanting Rob to be his own person and moving forward but it's also a prime opportunity to introduce Cliff to some of the people who haven't had the chance to see him.
LU: It was definitely JB, our LD or the stock answer, if you like the idea it was mine, if you don't it was someone else's.

What's your favourite book? Thanx.
Sveta, Moscow, Russia

KH: I couldn't tell you what my favorite book is, but I could tell u what my favorite novel is, and that would have to be "The Shining" because it's one of the best fictional stories ever written.
RT: Many, but "Fear and Loathing in Las Vegas" by Hunter S. Thompson was a wonderful book.
JH: Room service menu!
LU: A scrapbook my Mom put together continuously updating my experiences growing up as a little Danish child.

If you had a choice, would you go back in the past or into the future? What would you see or do?
Dana Hancock, Indy, IN

KH: I don't think in those terms, I try to be completely 'in the now' that this question is irrelevant to me.
RT: I would go back into the past so as I could see Hendrix play, weather report play with Jaco Pastorious and a young Sabbath. I would also

wax my surfboard and go to all the secret spots which are all now over-crowded.
JH: That's an awesome question. I'd like to do both but I also don't want to manipulate how I feel in this moment by doing those. I'd probably go back and ask my parents a few more questions about why maybe they got divorced, more of our family history and ancestry. Just get to know my parents better.
LU: Don't get me started! I'd wanna go back so as I could see my parents fuck me into being in this world so I truly knew where I came from. Would you like me to continue?!...

Be honest with me... OK, I'm not telling you that you should play like this band I'm about to tell you... but would you ever consider having a couple more guitar players in your band? Because Lynard Skynyrd has four guitar players, and the song 'Freebird' kicks ass.
Andrea, Cincinnati, OH

KH: Well Andrea, for starters Lynyrd Skynyrd only has three guitar players, and two guitar players in this band is more than enough to cover whatever we need to do musically.
RT: Another guitar player? No. Maybe harmonica...
JH: Well if we ever consider 'Freebird' in this live set we'll ask a few friends up...
LU: We did for 14 years with Jason, we're happy now with a more traditional set-up.

Are we all just recycled dust??
Peter R., Melbourne, Australia

KH: We are clearly a virus with shoes!... Recycled dust? Let me ask you this. Are we mass with consciousness or are we consciousness with mass?
RT: Yes.
JH: I guess I'd like to ask Peter who he was recycled from?
LU: You are.

Do any of you know Buckethead?
Taber H., Greenwood Village, CO

KH: I've met Buckethead once before in a pizza place, and he didn't have the bucket on so I didn't recognize him, but he's a killer nunchucks expert.
RT: I have not yet met Buckethead but I did have the pleasure of meeting his bucket.
JH: No but I've hung out with Pail Ass.
LU: No, but I've been to Buckhead, Georgia

I am going to your August 7th show in Seattle this summer, and I have never been to a concert before. For a first time concert attendee, do you have suggestions or recommendations?
Wendell F., Idaho Falls, ID

KH: Make sure you wear pants and shoes.
RT: Bring your battle armour depending on where you are standing and bring your ear plugs for the pyro.
JH: Save your money for the official t-shirts, and if you have any physical ailments or heart conditions stay away from the mosh pits, otherwise lose your voice. It'll come back.
LU: Enjoy.

How long does it take to complete one song?
Saadullah Bakir, Singapore

RT: It depends, with Infectious Grooves we could write a song in 30 minutes and record it in an hour, but different bands mean different situations and times. With Ozzy it could take a couple of years, with Metallica? We'll see!
LU: In the case of 'Enter Sandman,' minutes, in the case of (song with 'forgive me father' 3rd or 4th from end of "Load," what the fuck is that one called?)... still not finished.
JH: On the new album 8.5 minutes, which is much too long.
KH: Anywhere from a couple of hours to a coupla months, there's no real rule.

Have you ever considered doing a pan pipes moods version of a Metallica album/greatest hits? Or perhaps bagpipes?
Phyllida S., Sydney, Australia

RT: No, but I have considered utilizing Latin percussion and a horn section.
LU: Fuck you!
JH: Too young to smoke a pipe. It's hard to top Zam Fir, master of the pan flute.
KH: When is this person going to wake up from her horrible nightmare?

Regarding Eminem, what are your thoughts and feelings?
Sara S., San Luis Obispo, CA

LU: the fukker stole my haircut
KH: I only eat brown m&ms
JH: I like the new color.
LU: Top that Rob!
RT: Wow that was barrage!

Do you eat with your mouth open, and what is your shoe size?
Mickey N, Redlands, CA

LU: How are you supposed to get the food in?
KH: I'm not going to put my foot in my mouth.
JH: Are these questions screened? Luv james.
RT: Only on a date do I eat with my mouth open.

For the upcoming Australian tour, how do you or whoever go about selecting the support acts besides for the first support i.e. Godsmack (European tour)?
Dennis, Melbourne, Australia

RT: I should decide. They need to surf.
LU: Whoever you don't want, we bring.
JH: We start thinking of bands we like and see who's available and when everyone says 'no' we start thinking of bands we kinda like.
KH: We just pick whoever we think is the fuckin' coolest and who will get there and shake their behinds and bang their heads.

Is there anything special you wanna do before you move to the grave?
Johan Y., Lund, Sweden

RT: Be able to defeat Roy Jones Jr. in a boxing match. Phwoosh, I wish!
LU: Yeah. Reclaim Sweden.
JH: Wind Denmark up into frenzy so as they'll go to war with Sweden and tell Lars to reclaim it. (answered at a different time to LU – Ed)

KH: No.

Do you like eating noodles boiled in beer and bacardi?
Frederik M., Lyngby, Denmark

RT: Sounds kinky, yes. What's yer phone number?!!!
LU: Forhelvede!
JH: Negative.
KH: I don't know.

What is your take on this John Doe character, who filed suit against recording or media industry saying he has the constitutional right to file share any copyright material he wishes?
Tonya, Shreveport, LA

RT: Hoodrat!
LU: I don't give a fuck about no fucker, man.
JH: Would you name your kid John Doe? It's got to be his real name, right? With a real name like that he couldn't feel guilty.
KH: It's the first I've heard of it.

Could you give a sentence each about Rob, welcoming him?
Fred Butler, Collingsworth, CA

LU: Welcome Rob
KH: Rob, I hope you're feeling welcome
RT: I am, you guys are wonderful.
JH: I'm glad you appeared for us and help us kick ass.

Hey hey, I have a weird question. I'm traveling to Dublin to see u guys (from Surrey England!), then flyin' to Leeds to see u again, but I have no way of getting back down to Reading to see u for a third time! Could u give me a lift down, or summit?? I know its stupid askin' but I really have no other way of getting down to Reading! My number is...
Cheers, Lee C., Surrey, England

LU: Do you have a thumb?
JH: Do you have a Mom?
KH: Do you have legs?
RT: I've got a skateboard you can borrow.

I find myself listening to 'The Unnamed Feeling' over & over but I can't comprehend why I relate to it. Can you guys give your insight on this song?
Andres M., Reading, CA

LU: Take this 'unnamed obscenity' and stick up your 'unnamed orifice.'
RT: Y'know? I need the same thing. Can you help me?!!!
JH: I wrote the song about anxiety... I can't say anymore I'm too anxious!
KH: It's an unnamable answer... the reason is truly unnamable. ●

CREDITS

DESIGN & PRODUCTION

Creative Director: Steffan Chirazi • Art Director: Mark Abramson • Design: Mark Abramson, Rose de Heer, Aleksandra Jelic, Lesley Crawford • Production: Miriam Lewis, Suzanne Howard, Aleksandra Jelic, Lesley Crawford.

PRINCIPAL PHOTOGRAPHY

Mark Leialoha: front inside endpaper photo, pages 18–29, 34–35, 40–56, 59–70, 100–107, 113–118, 122–125, 160–172, 178–181, 186–193, 216–232, 239, 243–245, 250–257, 259–260 • James R. Minchin III: pages 132–149, 151–155, 266–271 • Niclas Swanlund: pages 119, 150, 182, 234–237, 240–245, 258, 265 • Harald Oiman aka Harald 'O': pages 4–9 • Anton Corbijn: page 121 • Michael Agel, back inside endpaper photo • Steffan Chirazi: pages 127, 144, 261–265 • Steven Wiig: pages 183–185 • Tony Smith: page 57 • Jodi Hilderbrand: pages 100–103.

CHAPTER COLLAGE PHOTOGRAPHY

Mark Leialoha, Niclas Swanlund, James R. Minchin III, Anton Corbijn, Marc Paschke, Michael Agel.

MISCELLANEOUS PHOTOGRAPHY

Mark Leialoha, James R. Minchin III, Niclas Swanlund, Harald Oiman aka Harald 'O', Brian Lew, Metal Mike, Steffan Chirazi, Michael Agel, Danny Clinch, Jodi Hilderbrand, Tony Smith, Annamaria DiSanto, Anton Corbijn, Marc Paschke, Steven Wiig, and also various anonymous family members, friends and club members who have contributed over the years.

Every reasonable effort has been made to accurately identify all photography. If you feel your work might have been used without credit, please do not hestitate to contact us via info@metclub.com.

ILLUSTRATIONS

James Hetfield: jacket, book cover, pages 174, 177, 276.

FEATURES

All band interviews and stories written by/conducted with Steffan Chirazi for So What! magazine other than: "Cliff Burton," pages 6–8, quotes from interviews conducted by Greg Mainer • "The Truth, The Whole Truth," pages 18–29 by Lars Ulrich • "A Day In The Life Of Bob Rock," pages 34–35 by Lars Ulrich • "Perspectives," pages 104–107, interviews conducted by Steven Wiig • "Kirk Hammett, The Sanity Remains," pages 178–181, interview conducted by Marc Paschke • "Shit Sandwich," pages 183–185 by Lars Ulrich • "Launch Party," pages 235–237, quotes by Anne Smith • "A Perfect Circle," pages 238–245 by Jim Murphy.

ACKNOWLEDGMENTS

SPECIAL THANKS TO EVERYONE WHO HELPED MAKE THIS BOOK POSSIBLE: The design & production team – Mark Abramson, Aleksandra Jelic, Rose de Heer, Leslie Crawford, Miriam Lewis, Suzanne Howard, Lydia Wills at the Writers & Artists Agency, Adam Kornfeld & Alison Weinflash at Writers & Artists Group International, Charlie Conrad, Alison Presley, Kim Cacho and all at Broadway Books, The Metallica Club Crew – Vickie Strate, Niclas Swanlund, Jeff Yeager, Toby Stapleton, Danna McCallum, Kimberly Vosti, Samantha McNally, plus Jean Reichart and Elisia Chestang, everyone who worked at the club during the Knoxville days especially Jodi Hillderbrand, Q Prime – Cliff Burnstein, Peter Mensch, Marc Reiter, Sue Tropio, Tony DiCioccio, Mike Calderella, Christine Zebrowski, Warren Christensen, Randi Seplow, Michelle Munz, Erica Collins, Peter Paterno, Howard King, Debra MacCulloch and KHPB, Joni Soekotjo, Wendy Hoffhine, Fred Duffin and Provident Financial Services, Richard & Meg Joseph, Bob Rock, Rex King, Gio Gasparetti, Steven Wiig, Thomas Robb, Don Oyao, Dan Braun, Lee Rosenblatt, Wendy Overs, Jerry Gilleland, Alan Doyle, Stuart Ross, Zach Harmon, Flemming Larsen, Justin Crew, Chad Zaemisch, Mike Gillies, Matt Olyphant, Chip Walker, Todd Sarner, Frank Munoz, Phil Towle, 'Big' Mick Hughes, Mike Wozniak, Butch Allen, Paul Owen, John 'JB' Broderick, Janine Doyle, Heather Kjollesdal and all members of the mighty Metallica crew past and present, Mark Leialoha, James R. Minchin III, Harald Oiman aka Harald 'O', Brian Lew, Marc Paschke, Metal Mike, Michael Agel, Anton Corbijn and Danny Clinch. Special thanks to Tony Smith for founding SO WHAT! and being its editor for 7 years.